East Street, Sittingbourne
A Historical Insight

by Helen Allinson
with contributions from
Michael H. Peters
John Mount
Allen Whitnell

Sittingbourne Heritage Museum

East Street, Sittingbourne
A Historical Insight

SHM017
ISBN 978-1-911662-17-4

Copyright © Sittingbourne Heritage Museum

Published by Sittingbourne Heritage Museum, 2019
Registered charity number 1070698

Also published by Sittingbourne Heritage Museum:

The Story of Gore Court House and Estate, Tunstall
Family Businesses of Sittingbourne
More Family Businesses of Sittingbourne
The Inns, Taverns, and Public Houses of Sittingbourne and District
Sittingbourne High Street Volume 1
Sittingbourne High Street Volume 2
Historic Buildings and Grand Houses of Sittingbourne
A History of the Sittingbourne Co-operative Society
The Spicer Homes
A Look at Key Street's Past
The Rise and Fall of the Beat Groups in Sittingbourne
Wartime Heroes of Borden Grammar School Remembered
Sittingbourne in the Second World War
A Sittingbourne Miscellany
A Walk Through Sittingbourne in Days Gone By
The Story of the Convent of the Nativity School

Printed in the United Kingdom by Biddles Books Ltd, Kings Lynn

www.sittingbourne-museum.co.uk

Table of Contents

Cover picture: a painting by museum member the late Eric Goldsmith

Foreword
Helen Allinson

During the writing of the second High Street volume it struck us that we could not leave East Street and West Street undocumented as they are extensions of our long High Street and indeed prior to 1876 had been known as High Street East and High Street West.

The system which we employed for the project was that each volume had a lead writer with background research being contributed by the museum's history group and also some sections being written by other members of the team.

We gradually assembled directories, census returns, electoral registers, maps and photographs and delved into old volumes of the East Kent Gazette. We made an outline 'skeleton' of information for each building in the street and it did not always become apparent whether one house should be written about together with another one until everything was to hand. The online resources of Ancestry and freebmd.co.uk have been invaluable in discovering more about the residents of the street.

Amongst the members of the museum are some whose families had run shops in the street for generations and who had lived there themselves. So gathering up their memories has given us another rich seam of information to add to the book.

This has been a large undertaking as there are or were 179 houses (many of which were also shops and had workshops behind them), a couple of churches, a doctor's surgery and a number of inns and pubs.

One of the interesting discoveries we made in the course of our research was how common the cycle of a building being a home then a shop and a home and then just a home again has been. The usage of buildings changed regularly with the turning tide of the local economy. Those who had shops often opened another in West Street too.

Another fact which struck us forcibly was the number of families who moved from house to house within the street or from one side of the road to the other, often spending their whole lives in the street. Such small distance moves by tenants were often dictated by a change in the size of the family or an ambition to extend a shop or retire from running one. This was a close community and many residents had relatives in the street.

East Street was always busy, horses trotted by, mail coaches sped past, loaded wagons lurched close to the pedestrians on the muddy pavements. The sheds and workshops behind the houses echoed to hammering and buzzed with talk for here coaches were built, horses shod, baskets woven and leather cut for boots. Orchards still grew up to the roadside, cows were milked and pigs slaughtered just yards behind the houses. The gasworks stood nearby for many years adding its own smell to the air.

Today cars and lorries make most of the sounds of the street. No orchards remain, nothing but food is made here and there are fewer shops as the road has become more residential with many old buildings replaced.

We have done our best to ensure that details mentioned are correct, and have tried to state sources and references, indicated in brackets at the end of a sentence. Inevitably there will be some inaccuracies and there is always the possibility that there are errors in some of the source material. Errors from transcription and interpretation can creep in and there are difficulties arising from renumbering of premises which has taken place from time to time. However we believe that we have been successful and hope that you will enjoy discovering some of the stories that we have laid out here.

Helen Allinson, 2019

Introduction:
Shopping in Sittingbourne
New Trends and Developments Continuing
Through the Centuries

As has been remarked in almost every book about Sittingbourne's history, it is obvious and certain that the town's origins lay at the point where the Roman road – the main thoroughfare between the capital, Canterbury and the coast – passed close by the ancient creek-side town of Milton.

Here, beside the section of the main road, that became our High Street, there sprang up, gradually over the centuries, a series of hostelries – hotels and inns, together with related establishments all devoted to, and thriving upon, the passing trade.

Hence the centre of our town, unlike many, is longitudinal – long and narrow.

Readers of the Museum's two volumes covering our town's High Street, are reminded, more than once, that the original heart of our long commercial street was where the Roman road crossed the Bourne – the meeting point for East Street, the High Street, Bell Road (formerly East Lane, the approach road for some of our farmers from the south) and what we now call Crown Quay Lane (frequented by the folk of the creek, the Swale and the open sea beyond). This road, flanking the course of the Bourne down to the creek at Crown Quay, used to be known as Water Lane.

The East End of the town, looking west up the High Street c.1900

This neighbourhood, known as the East End, near the ancient parish church – was an address which, in centuries past, was regarded as 'special', but from the mid-19th century, after the railway arrived here, the commercial nucleus of our town was gradually drawn westward away from the historic heart – the railway station was new and exciting – a major magnet.

At the other end of the town, about a mile to the west, another rather soggy location acquired a similar name – Water Lane Head – marking the point where the main road passed the end of Ufton Lane (formerly Tunstall Lane, another approach road for our farmers). At that point, across the street, forming another cross-road, was another Water Lane leading alongside another watercourse heading for the creek. After terraces of houses were built alongside it, this western Water Lane was renamed Cockleshell Walk – to distinguish it from the other Water Lane at Crown Quay.

We shall have more to say about that in our volume on West Street and its vicinity.

Between these two Water Lanes, the main road crosses a plateau which became our town's West End – the new smart, town centre. Soon after the railway station opened, it was decided to establish, in that vicinity, a new purpose-built Corn Exchange. Capitalising on that opportunity, and overcoming opposition from a rival entrepreneur, in whose premises the district corn market was functioning at that time, a local notable, named Samuel Dean offered from among his several properties, a site that turned out to be highly suitable. The entrepreneurial genes evident in the Dean family became even more obvious in the next generation when Sam's son George became one of our town's leading men of business.(HSI,HSII)

The High Street looking east from the Corn Exchange
A painting by G Thomson 1906/7

On its prominent site at the West End, the Corn Exchange building with its tall clock-tower, stood for more than century; though, for most of its life, it served, not just farmers, but the community at large – it became our Town Hall.

Now, over 150 years after the Corn Exchange was put here (and half a century after it was torn down) this vicinity remains the commercial centre-point of our town – hence this central spot was chosen for our town's one and only public statue – the barge captain and his dog.

Here, in local terms, the properties have a 'premium' commercial value, a higher level than those down the hills at each of the town – as the road rises at one end of the town and falls at the other, so, in general terms, do the values of the buildings beside it.

The plaque that was over the entrance of the Corn Exchange – until 1969

This book is about East Street, known before 1876 as High Street East. With one exception, East Street has never embraced any of our town's larger shops – neither those run by local business men, nor others managed from head offices elsewhere. Incomers, like Daniel Easton from Ashford, chose to establish their 'emporia' at the West End, rather than the old-established east. Likewise the 'multiples' – shops with branches in other districts – have congregated at the West End of the High Street. The only exception to this tendency was Sittingbourne Co-operative Society whose history has been recounted, with her customary, thoroughgoing skill, by Helen Allinson.(75) But then, even the Co-op, after the better part of a century, ensconced comfortably at the eastern extremity of the town, followed the trend and moved to a new prominent, purpose-built structure at the west end.

Making this move, the Co-op were following a natural trend which in the mid-20th century, almost precisely 100 years after the railway arrived here, was given added energy by a new policy initiated, promulgated and _enforced_ by the local council; in 1960, the leaders of our community decided to re-shape our town's commercial heart – making it shorter and wider. Thereupon, the council's planners, began to favour residential use of East Street's premises rather than commercial. Naturally, at first, this drive was unpopular amongst many established east-end traders and other townsfolk who regarded the proposal as dictatorial use of the powers which had been vested in the local authority barely a dozen years previously by the Town and Country Planning Act 1947. Now, a couple of generations later, the continuing trend is perhaps accepted as natural and inevitable. As more shops close, the level of business elsewhere along the street tends to decline.

Around 1970, a decade or so after the Council's new policy was initiated, this trend was boosted by two new developments – two commercial prosthetics – two new shopping centres tacked onto the flanks of the High Street – The Forum and Roman Square.

By choosing those names, the developers and the collaborating local elders – the town council – were paying tribute to the Romans, who had laid the foundations of the High Street, but, by their very existence, those extra shopping centres, like every other one throughout the land, were bound to challenge the dominance of the historic High Street – a process which is continuing today.

The next phase in the retail history of our town began when another extension to our town's shopping area was laid out on an expanse of 'brown' land, between the railway and the creek. This site had been owned in the 19th century by the Simpsons – a family from Canterbury – property-owning entrepreneurs – long-gone.(HSII)

Following the post-war clearance of the small houses and shops that had been put here in the 19th century, this area had been left empty for a generation and more. Here was constructed 'Sittingbourne Retail Park' – a **park** for cars, surrounded by **retail** outlets – where the motor vehicles of **retailers** and their customers could be **parked** free of charge – and free from worries about being disciplined by the traffic wardens, who are paid by the council to hover around the High Street and the neighbouring car parks.

Not long afterwards, Sittingbourne's paper mill, one of our dwindling stock of local ikons, was acquired by developers from elsewhere and quickly demolished. A new supermarket now stands on part of the site. The remainder is to be covered with residential streets, most of which, we are sad to note, will bear names without any local significance or meaning.

The latest elements of this policy are the current redevelopment schemes, both sides of the railway station, connected by our town's historic bottle-neck *'under the arch'* as it is known. Here, on more land that the Simpsons used to own, there was more 'slum clearance' half a century ago, creating an empty space beside Princes Street, where the Council put its depot. Now the depot has been swept away and they are 'plugging the gap' between the High Street and the 'Retail Park'. Here on the old depot site and across the railway, on the major car park beside the Forum, the plan is to create even more shops and a cinema.

This latest development, continuing a trend that began nearly two centuries ago, will provide yet more competition for the old High Street and for the other cinema, erected 80 years ago at the historic crossroads – the ancient heart of our town – where this resumé began.

Michael H Peters

The North Side (odd numbers)

1 – The Alms Houses

The Alms houses   3   5   7   9   11

Hasted listed the charities of the parish of Sittingbourne and one of them concerned the alms houses: *'John Allen, of Sittingbourne, by his will in 1615, gave 40 shillings per annum for repairing the alms-houses in Crown-key-Lane, and firing for the poor in them, to be paid out of Glovers, now Mrs Bannister's. The original donor of the charity is unknown as is the date at which they were first built'.*

The Allens were a large family, prominent in our district for many years. For more information on Glovers see HSII.

This is nevertheless useful to us as it tells us that the alms houses were already in need of repair by 1615 and we feel it is likely that the original donor died before the Reformation – the 16th century revolution in Western Christianity.

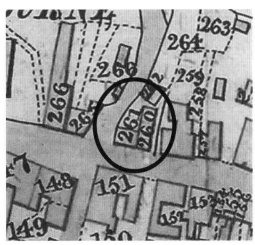

The tithe map of 1840 showing plot 261 on the corner

The alms houses stood on the corner of East Street at its junction with Crown Quay Lane and their address was later number 1 East Street where Swale House is now. They consisted of a room each for eight poor widows and had been rebuilt in 1804 by public subscription. On the tithe schedule (1840) the alms houses are on plot 261 recorded as belonging to the churchwardens of Sittingbourne and they were certainly conveniently close to the church for the churchwardens to keep an eye on matters there. An addition had been made by 1851 when there were ten rooms.(6)

Council minutes record that the alms houses had been demolished by 1928 and in fact this had happened by 1918 as our next photograph shows. Percy Hubbard writing much later (in 1961) said: '*The old Alms Houses standing at the entrance of Crown Quay Lane have been pulled down, making a much better entrance to the road'.*(70) Perhaps in their later years they had become something of an eyesore.

In this 1861 drawing of St Michael's parish church the chimneys of the row of alms houses can be seen in the distance.

Census returns give us the names of the women who lived here:

Jane Brown	65	labourer	Milton
Sarah Robinson	82	labourer	Lynsted
Frances Bunyan	78	Gunsmith	Rodmersham
Mary Mungeam	73	Victualler	Rochester
Elizabeth Fisher	60	labourer	Tong
Mary Pretty	83	Waterman	Milton
Mary Crittenden	73	Victualler	Surrey
Sarah Stone	82	Blacksmith	Kent
Sarah Blake	11	Visitor	Sittingbourne
Mary Coleman	68	Publican	Godmersham

In 1851 there were nine widows and one visitor. Their places of birth and the occupations of their late husbands were given. Some of the ladies will not have been pleased at having to declare their ages too, but such revelations had become compulsory in the census ten years earlier.

By the time of the 1861 census just three of these ladies remained in their rooms – Mary Mungeam, Jane Brown and Elizabeth Fisher, the others had been carried to their graves in the churchyard.

Jane Brown had been a resident for over 20 years when the 1871 census was taken and was well into her eighties. There were nine women living there that year all but one born in Kent; the odd one out was Mary Kite who had been born in Ireland. Each room would have had a fireplace for heat and cooking and brewing tea. What long chats and what sustained disputes must have gone on between the women over the years – deep friendships and bitter feuds sustained by living so close together.

The 1891 census enumerator found six residents, one of whom was a spinster, showing that the rule as to being a widow had been relaxed, and ten years later there were eight women living there.

In 1910 The East Kent Gazette reported that Mr W. R. Baum, the relieving officer of The Milton Union, experienced a surprise.

> 'He had occasion to see to the removal to the infirmary of an elderly spinster who had lived at the Sittingbourne Alms Houses for some years and who being ill and unable to look after herself was taken to the workhouse Infirmary where she would be well looked after.
>
> Before leaving the old lady handed Mr Baum a purse and a small packet and remarked now that she was going to the infirmary it was only right that she should give the Guardians what little money she possessed. Mr Baum accepted the packet and thought no more about it, until he opened it expecting to find a few shillings at the most, what was he's surprise to find that the packet contained money to the amount of £20/15/-. Which included eleven sovereigns'.

That £20 would today be worth £2,000, so no wonder Mr Baum was amazed. The old lady was Miss Mary Ann Weller who was the only single woman living in the alms houses when the 1908 directory was published – all her six neighbours were widows. She died in 1915 aged 84. Mary Ann had grown up in Bell Road (or Lane as it was then known) the daughter of a farm labourer and stayed with her parents into her forties. She had then moved round the corner and lived alone at 35 East Street in her fifties. She had entered the alms house by the age of 59 when the 1891 census taken and there as we know she remained until being admitted to the workhouse in 1910. Clearly she was a thrifty woman not tempted by the idea of getting a jug filled at Three Kings or The Ship across the road and with a strong sense of what was right. There were only five widows in residence in 1911 when the census was taken in one room each. So it is likely that by then each woman had double the space from the earlier days when ten women filled the ten rooms. All five women were receiving out-relief and their ages ranged from 64 to 82.

In 1928 G. Bowes & Sons of number 13 applied to the council for permission to erect a bill-posting hoarding on the old alms house site (in extension of the gable of number 3 which they already used) It was allowed on payment of £5 a year to the council. Mr Valentine Tyler objected to the proposed hoarding on the grounds of interference with light to his premises at number 5. It was erected to be no more than 12 feet high.

The 1918 photograph below shows the bills posted by the Bowes on the gable end of number 3 and the space where the alms houses stood so giving us proof that they had been demolished by 1918.

1918 photograph of road works at the junction of East Street and Bell Road
The Three Kings pub is on the right of the picture. The alms houses had already gone.

The site where numbers 1 to 15 had once stood remained undeveloped and used by
Roland & Hales for car sales until construction began on the new office block in 1974
(EKG)

Numbers 3 and 5 and the two homes behind them

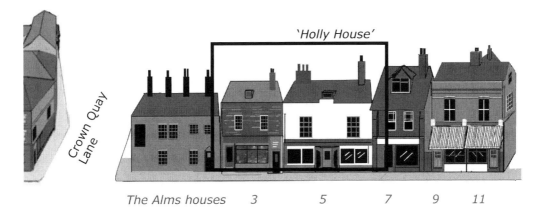

The Alms houses 3 5 7 9 11

We know from directories that the ancient houses which were numbered 3 and 5 were demolished between 1964 and 1968. Being so close to the junction of the High Street and Bell Road, at the very heart of the town, this site would have been cleared and built-on repeatedly in the centuries since the Romans first laid the street. The site lies now beneath Swale House.

Number 3 was a house on parcel 260 of the tithe schedule close up against the alms houses. An alleyway separated it from the much larger building in parcel 259, later known as number 5.

Both buildings were owned in 1840 by 'the heirs of John Wilson.' Parcel 262 was a workshop behind the house which was also owned by the same people. This, it seems, was later adapted to be a home accessed by what was called 'Burley's Passage' in the 1891 census return and is recorded in several of the census returns as being 'behind number 5.' Ascertaining occupancy from the 1841 and 1851 census returns is complicated by the fact that there were not only people living in the building behind number 5 but also (in the first half of the 19th century) in a building behind number 3.

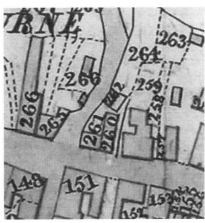

Parcels 260 and 259 in the centre of the map were numbers 3 and 5. The workshop parcel 262 can be seen behind and to the left

The 1911 census gives the information that number 3 had four rooms one of which was in use as a shop. Number 5 was larger with seven rooms.

Number 3 East Street
Thomas Stedolph, grocer

In 1841 Thomas Stedolph a Kentish man in his forties lived here with his wife Alice and four children and ran a grocery shop. He had moved away by 1851 when the grocer here was Lewis Sillis.

Lewis Sillis, grocer

Lewis was born in 1819 in Chatham. He married Caroline Dennis in 1848 and it was probably then that he established himself at number 3. Poor Caroline died a year later aged only 26, just months after giving birth to their son John. Lewis soon married again to Sarah Bates Barnard. Lewis and Sarah were not blessed with children so their household was a small one. In 1861 it comprised themselves, Lewis's son John and two live-in shop assistants. In later life electoral registers show that Sillis had purchased the house, but during the year before he died, 1877, when perhaps he was already ill, he had sold it to Benjamin Burley.(115)

Lewis Sillis died in 1878 aged 59. The executors of his will were William Hartridge the Milton cornfactor and William Hyde a Milton gentleman.(111) Widowed Sarah moved up to number 114 where she lived quietly with a companion.(9)

Thomas Arthur Burley, grocer and pork butcher

Young Thomas Arthur Burley, the nephew of Benjamin Burley who had bought the house took on the business and remained until at least 1891 selling groceries and fruit and vegetables. Tom Burley was the son of old Thomas Burley the tailor next door but one at number 7 and had learned his trade with his Uncle Benjamin who had a grocery in Milton.(7) Benjamin himself lived in Park Road.(115) The 1891 census recorded young Tom living at number 3 with a resident housekeeper and shop assistant. He was then 34 and his brother Edward was running the family tailoring business at number 7.

In January 1887 Tom, was one of the long list of local shop-keepers who announced in the East Kent Gazette that they would participate in a new ground breaking practice – they would close their shops early on Wednesdays. The new closure time was not to be at lunchtime, as became the custom later on, but at 4pm. We can imagine the discussions that preceded this decision and the recriminations against those traders who did not join in.

Wednesday early-closing continues in our town-centre to this day but most shop-keepers now ignore the custom, treating Wednesdays like any other weekday.

By 1901 Tom had sufficient funds to retire at the early age of 44 to Albany Road with his wife Florence and two young children. It may be that funds did not last as long as predicted or perhaps Florence and Tom liked the idea of living in London, at any rate they later moved to Paddington where Tom worked at one of the museums as an 'exhibition attendant.'

George Offen

Meanwhile another grocer had moved in to number 3. This was George Offen who came from Bethersden. He and his wife Laura did not stay long before moving to Gillingham.(12)

J. Wood
It appears that a Mr J. Wood was the next occupant of number 3 but the only reference we have to him is a notice in the 1907 East Kent Gazette: *'Auction of household goods of Mr J. Wood who is leaving for America includes a good pianoforte.'*

Charles Attwood, fishmonger
Grocery had come to an end at number 3 by 1908 when the directory listed Charles Henry Attwood fishmonger at number 3.

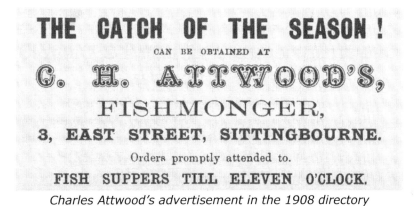

Charles Attwood's advertisement in the 1908 directory

William Sawyer, fishmonger
The next fishmonger here was William Sawyer from Clapham who had moved in with his wife Kate and two children by 1911, but this too was a very brief stay for a notice appeared in the local paper in 1912: *'To be let with possession Fried Fish Shop 3 East Street. Low inclusive rent'.*

Harry Colwell
One Harry Colwell ran a dining room here in 1915.(47)

Ernest James Louch, boot repairer
By 1922 Ernest Louch a boot repairer was living in the little house and he was the first to remain there for a period of many years until his death in 1952 aged 73. He was a local man, born in Cowper Road Sittingbourne in 1880. He grew up in Pond Cottages Tunstall and his father was an insurance agent.

Working life for Ernest began with an apprenticeship at a local cycle factory. (9) In his thirties he still lived with his widowed mother Susanna at Pond Cottages, working as a domestic gardener. It was after Susanna's death in 1920 that Ernest moved to East Street where he would spend the rest of his life. Never married, his effects at death in 1952 were worth over £4,000.

Ernest was not quite the last person to live at number 3 for after his death the owner, Mr Bowes, was required to make improvements to the building. Council minutes for 1955 record that the unsafe front of the building was rebuilt and a new shop front fitted.

One Forty

The final business at number 3 before demolition was 'One Forty' a dry cleaner's, whose name we cannot explain. The tenants living over the shop in 1960 and probably running it too were David and Wendy Gray. In 1963 J. M. Barns lived there. In 1965 the living accommodation was vacant.

*One Forty Cleaners Ltd, corner of Crown Quay Lane and East Street
probably early 1960s (EKG)*

*This 1961 photograph shows numbers 3 and 5 and in the foreground number 7. Behind
the brick façade of number 5 the roof line revealed a timber framed house. It can be
seen that number 5 was twice as wide as number 3. Number 1, the alms-houses, had
been demolished many years before the photograph was taken.*

Number 5 East Street (Holly House)
George Lake and Mary Wilson

In 1841 a young painter named George Lake lived in part of number 5 with his wife and baby whilst the person who then owned the building, Mary Wilson, in her fifties and of independent means lived in the other part attended by a servant.

Ten years later Sittingbourne bred Mary Wilson was still living here but in the other half of the house dwelt Amos Buley who had taken on George Lake's painting business and added plumbing to it.(N01)

Amos Buley

Amos Buley was then in his thirties with a wife and children. The Buleys moved the short distance to 34 High Street around 1860 where Amos's business flourished for he was not only a plumber but a sign-writer, painter and glazier. (for more on the Buleys, see HSII)

Harriet Tilley

In 1861 this was the home of widowed Harriet Tilley, her daughter Mary Ann, their lodger and a servant. Other members of the Tilley family owned property in East Street. Harriet died in 1870.

Charles Bates

Brickmaker Charles Bates was listed here in 1866 but we have not been able to discover anything about him.

Ann Croxford's Holly House School

A small school for young ladies had been opened at number 5 by 1870. Mrs Ann Croxford ran it. It may have been Mrs Croxford who named number 5 Holly House presumably because of a large holly tree in the back garden. She had previously lived in Thrapston, Northants with her husband Charles who was a veterinary surgeon. She herself then worked as a day school mistress. Ann's niece Alice West worked with her aunt as a teacher and lived with the Croxfords.

However in 1871 when Ann was a widowed governess, Alice was recorded as her daughter and in fact she was illegitimate – in the quaint language of the law, this means that she was born before her mother was married – an event that is now normal, but in those days it was, shall we say, frowned upon.

In 1864 Alice married Francis Bourquin, a Swiss national who taught languages, and they had three young children who were listed as Ann's grandchildren in the 1871 census return. Francis Bourquin was much older than Alice and by 1871 they lived apart, he resided in Clerkenwell and as far as we can tell never lived in Sittingbourne.

Holly House School closed between 1879 and 1881 by which time old Ann was to be found at 1 West Street with her daughter and three grandchildren. Both women described themselves as governesses. However they had merely moved in order to acquire better premises for their school which then opened in Park Road and was listed in the directory by 1882.

In 1891 the two women still lived together, by then at 12 Park Road. Ann had retired but Alice was working at their school as was her daughter also named Alice. Old Anne died in 1893; her effects were only worth £22 and her daughter

Alice Bourquin (listed as the wife of Francis Henry Bourquin) was her executor along with Tom Witham a miller.

James George Wilson – dentist

From 1876 to 1888 dentist James George Wilson rented rooms at number 5 where he advertised that he could be 'consulted daily 9am to 8pm all diseases of the mouth, painless operations by nitrous oxide, full set of teeth on vulcanite for £4 4s to £8 8s.'

Mr Wilson also pulled teeth at the other end of town at 34 West Street on different days of the week. This was helpful to those clutching their jaws in agony.

William Cook Gardener and Mrs Roberts

With the dentist no doubt upstairs, young William Cook Gardener from Dorset opened a drapery at number 5 during the 1880s. He and his wife Kate were still here in 1891 when the census was taken. During the early 1890s he moved his business across the road to number 4 where more can be read about him. However, although Gardener moved his business across the road he and his wife remained living at number 5 whilst Mrs Priscilla Roberts opened her second-hand clothes shop downstairs.(N01,10) This was clearly no threat to Mr Gardener's sales for he sold new goods. The arrangement had begun during the 1880s when Gardener must have found he had retail room to spare and could do with some rental income.

Mrs Roberts lived with her husband Adam, a labourer, at 19 High Street.(10) By September 1894 when Mrs Roberts put this advertisement in the paper, Gardener's shop was across the road.

'Mrs. Roberts will commence her annual sale of autumn and winter clothing this Saturday for 21 days only. A capital chance for people to spend their Hopping Money.'

The following year Mrs Roberts was preparing for her final sale before retiring to that favourite haunt of Sittingbourne ex-shopkeepers; Park Road:

'Last Great Sale, note the address, 5 East Street. Mrs. Roberts wishes to thank the inhabitants of Sittingbourne, Milton and District for their great support during the last 21 years, and begs to inform them that, owing to failing health and outrun of lease, she will be removing from the above address to Priscilla Villa, Park Road, at Michaelmas, and that she is now offering to the public, for the last time, the whole of her enormous and valuable stock, at greatly reduced prices. A very large stock of ladies dresses, mantles, cloaks and jackets. A large quantity of new dress materials at less than cost price. Sealskin jackets, tea gowns etc. A number of children's costumes, frocks etc. A quantity of baby linen, robes and cloaks, white and coloured. A large number of gentlemen's and boys' suits, trousers, coats, overcoats, shirts (white and coloured). New and second-hand. A large stock of curtains, sheets and table cloths. Feather beds, bolsters and pillows. A lot of furniture, carpets and hearth rugs. Feathers and flowers. A large quantity of ladies, gentlemen's and children's boots and shoes. Sale to commence on Saturday 3rd August,'

After that an auction of the remainder of the stock was held and the notice advertising it described Mrs Roberts as '*a wardrobe dealer*' which meant her goods were secondhand.

By the start of 1896 the double-fronted shop with plate glass windows and the seven roomed, house yard and garden were up for rental at £30 per annum.

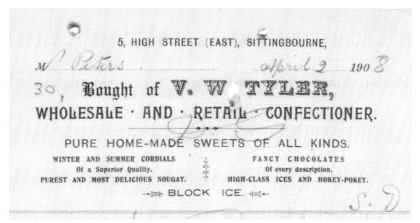

An invoice from V W Tyler in 1908, 5 High Street (East)
Purest and most delicious nougat. High class ices and 'Hokey-Pokey' (honeycomb)

Valentine William Tyler

Valentine William Tyler was the next occupant of number 5 and the shop must have smelt sweet for he was a confectioner. Born in Sittingbourne in 1862 the son of a labourer, he had started work as a mariner but in 1881 was to be found in the Milton Workhouse having fallen on hard times. However life improved for young Valentine, he found work again and in 1884 he married. He and Jane lived across the road at 30/32 where in 1891 he was described as a bargee 'hoveller' or inshore boatman. They opened up shop at number 5 in 1896. Mrs Tyler was kept busy for they eventually had a family of seven. The Tylers remained many years and added a restaurant to their sweet shop. Jane died in 1929 then Valentine died in 1932 leaving an estate worth £1,550. Whether any of their children continued the shop for a few years is not known but we do know that sadly their fourth son Eric Valentine Tyler died in 1933 aged 27. He had trained as a bootmaker but had to give up work a year before his death due to ill health. The newspaper recorded that he was '*an old Bordenian, like his father keenly interested in cricket and football and respected by all who knew him.*' His funeral was at the Baptist Church.

Mrs Doreen Thomas, 'The Work Box' and 'Tommy's'

By 1938 Mrs Doreen Thomas ran the double-fronted shop as two separate enterprises – a confectioner's and tobacconist named Tommy's on one side and, on the other, beside number 7, The Work Box selling wools and embroidery silks. Logically, Tommy's should have been identified as 5a, but confusingly, in some records, it was called 7a. However the arrangement whereby number 5 was run as two shops continued for the remainder of the life of the building.

In 1939 it was reported in the Chatham News that Doreen Thomas appeared at Canterbury bankruptcy court (the court was Canterbury because she had moved to Whitstable).

Mr and Mrs Alec Alexander had the shops in the 1950s and the name the Work Box continued into the 1960s. In 1965 E C Desmet lived there.

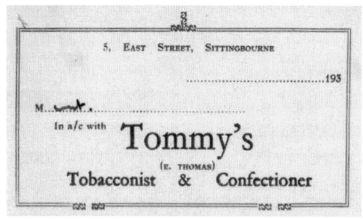

5, EAST STREET, SITTINGBOURNE

....193

M..

In a/c with

Tommy's

(E. THOMAS)

Tobacconist & Confectioner

Letterhead from "Tommy's" prop. E Thomas, 1930s

The house behind number 3

Perhaps this had been an outbuilding originally and then adapted to be a simple home. In 1841 John Alp a young post-boy his wife and baby were the tenants. Then in 1851 another labourer William Covis and his wife lived here. We hear no more of a house behind number 3 so perhaps it was demolished in the 1850s.

The house behind number 5

In a home behind number 5 in 1840 lived an elderly labourer William Gebbe, his wife and two lodgers one of whom was old William Harnden the shoemaker whose son had the shop at number 16.

By 1851 coach-building was in decline and Stephen Masters the elderly coach maker who had previously lived at number 9 moved in to this building with his wife, son Stephen junior who was also a coach maker, daughter and granddaughter. This was beside the Masters' yard. Old Stephen's brother and nephew had given up the trade and moved along the street.

For a while the Masters rented the building out to Mary Ann Strutton a widow who lived alone, but by 1871 when the building was described as 'near number 5' old Mary Masters widow of Stephen senior was back here with her son Stephen who still built carriages. Mary died in 1875 aged 88.

The building was listed as uninhabited in 1891 and not listed at all in 1901. In 1910 a small advertisement in the local paper noted houses to let in The Square (Terry's Square) at 4/- and at the rear of 5 East Street at 2/-per week. Such a low rent indicates a very poor property indeed.

Listed after number 3 on the 1911 census return is '5 Burley's Yard' which we take to be the same property and there William Croucher, a single labourer, occupied the four rooms.

Perhaps the old, disused building mentioned in the following council report of 1919 is this home:

> 'With regard to number 5 East Street the light and ventilation of a room which was reported by the Medical Officer at the last meeting to be obstructed by an old disused building. The surveyor reported that he

had inspected the place. The room deficient of light and ventilation was formally an outhouse, now used as a kitchen. The building objected to was not such as could be described as dangerous, and the kitchen of number 5 might be extended into the building concerned. On the motion of Councillor Filmer seconded by Councillor Millen, the surveyor was instructed to approach the owner with a view to carrying out his (the surveyor's) suggestion.(N01)

In 1922 a Mr Henry Beesley lived at the rear of number 5. Probably the building was demolished soon afterwards.

Number 7 East Street – **The Lamb**

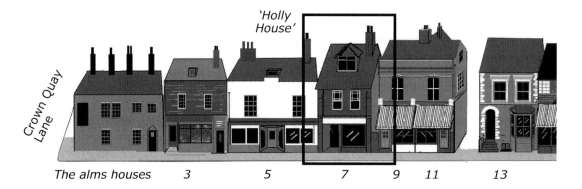

It is thanks to Canon Scott Robertson that we know that the building which stood on the site later known as number 7 was an inn called The Lamb.(63) In 1562 it belonged to one Thomas Weldish, and before him to a John Prior. How long it had stood before that we cannot say although the origin of the inn name 'The Lamb' is a religious one – referring to the Lamb of God and such inns were usually medieval i.e. dating from before the Reformation, when England's established religion became a Protestant version of Christianity.

Thomas Wise ran the inn after Weldish and was followed by a distiller named Mr Cain. In the 18th century Sittingbourne brewer James Tong junior owned the old building and he was followed by Thomas Goldsmith the final owner of the old Lamb. (for more information on the Tong family, see HSI & HSII)

Scott Robertson reported that in 1752 William House 'was the owner of the new erected tenement called the Lamb.' So the old building had been demolished and replaced with something more up to date and brick-built, with seven rooms.(10) However in spite of having new premises the new Lamb did not last long as a licensed premises (perhaps it lacked the atmosphere of the old one) and soon the building became the home, workshop and shop of the Burley family. Land Tax returns show Thomas Tong the Sittingbourne brewer owned the premises when the Burleys arrived.(HSI,HSII)

Number 7 is in the forefront of this 1960s photograph

Generations of tailors – the Burleys

The final generation of the Burley family to live here had been told that the firm had been established in 1780, so there had been an unbroken line of tailors from the same family dating back some 250 years. The particular Burley who founded the firm, was master tailor Joseph Burley of Lynsted. Joseph Burley's eldest son Thomas Burley, a master tailor himself, married Ann Watts in Nettlestead near Maidstone in 1794. All nine of their children were born in Sittingbourne no doubt at number 7. Land tax records for the parish reveal the year that Thomas Burley began to rent number 7. It was 1798. There were no Burleys in Sittingbourne before that date.

Sadly Thomas died aged only 39 in 1809 but Ann continued the business with the help of her father in law Joseph. The Burley headstone in St Michael's churchyard reads: *'In memory of Thomas Burley of this parish who departed this life the 3rd December 1809 aged 39 years "The Child of Affliction" Also one son and two daughters of the above. William died 20th August 1807 aged eight months, Elizabeth died 5th July 1809 aged ten years, Fanny died 12th of July 1818 aged 17 years also Ann wife of the above Thomas Burley who departed this life 22nd January 1828.'*

So 1809 was a tragic year for Ann with her daughter dying in July and Thomas in December. "The Child of Affliction" phrase on the memorial perhaps implies that Thomas had a life of perpetual ill-health and ill-fortune.

A major upset for widowed Mrs Burley occurred in 1810 when Sarah Bancroft who had managed the drapery side of the business for Ann was arrested charged with theft from her mistress. She was sent to the Assizes at Maidstone accused of taking a gown, ten pieces of muslin and four handkerchiefs worth over £2. She was found guilty but in view of the fact that she had a young child was only sent to prison for a year. This was a much lighter sentence than might have been expected.

However Ann Burley was declared bankrupt in 1813. Nonetheless the tailoring business somehow survived in the hands of Ann's eldest son Thomas (born 1796) who must have been assisted by his grandfather Joseph until he was able to take charge himself.

This Thomas married in 1823 and he and his wife Frances had at least seven children the eldest of whom, another Thomas, (born 1828), was to continue the business at number 7. A snapshot of the household at number 7 in 1861 is given by the census return. There was Thomas Burley aged 64, Frances, and their son Charles; a shipwright, for not every Burley became a tailor. Sharing the house were young Thomas the tailor his wife Eliza and their three infant children.

Ten years later the old couple remained but young Thomas's wife had died and he and his son Edward Felton Burley were the only two of the family living with old Thomas and Frances. Old Thomas died the following year aged 77.

Thomas and Edward continued to live and work at number 7 throughout the 1880s and by 1874 electoral registers show that Thomas was able to purchase the property. This must have been very reassuring at times when trade was poor. By 1891 it was Edward and his wife and young family who inhabited the house, although the firm was known as 'Thomas Burley & Son'.

Business did not thrive under Edward Burley and Percy Hubbard in his memories of the town written at the start of the 1960s recalling the 1890s tells us why: *'Now we come to a tailor's named Burley. They used to employ quite a few skilled tailors, who sat cross-legged on the bench making clothes for the gents of the town. The then proprietor, notwithstanding his good qualities as a cutter and tailor and also as a very pleasant personality, had a loving taste for his beer and this resulted in his eventual poverty. A son, returning from the Wars, took on the competition of merchant mass tailors and is today trying to carry on, so a Burley is still there'.*(70)

Hubbard was correct for in 1902 a bankruptcy sale was held of the household furniture.(N01) However Edward carried on the business somehow as directories record. By 1911 he had trained his second and third sons as tailors and they took the business on after the First World War when the name of the firm became 'T. Burley & Sons.' A 1924 advertisement boasted of the firm's age:

'T Burley & Sons, Established 1780 Ladies and Gents Tailors. Latest London & Paris styles. All work cut and made on the premises. (practical tailors).'

Edward lived on until 1942 when he died in his eighties.

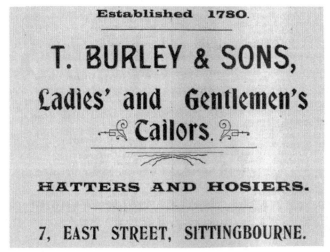

1927 advertisement which mentions the ladies department

In 1963 Burley & Sons closed down, described in the local paper at the time as 'Sittingbourne's oldest family business'. Brothers Wilfred and Alfred had run it for the last 30 years and lived over the shop all of their lives.

The Burley Brothers

Their customers had dwindled to a loyal band of elderly men whose first suits had been made by the Burleys. Wilfred was an expert on orchids; a longstanding member of the British Amateur Orchid society he had collected orchids since he was ten.

Soon after the Burleys closed up shop for the last time the building was demolished along with its neighbours on each side. Today the site is covered by Swale House.

Numbers 9-11 and the market in the passageway

'Holly House'

3   5   7   9   11   13   13a   15

When first we come across this building in 1840 (later known as numbers 9 and 11) it was partitioned in two like so many others in the street and so it remained for most of the rest of its life. The photograph of the building was taken in the 1960s before demolition and shows it was taller than neighbouring number 7. It was centuries old and had been modernised in Victorian times with a new frontage. Number 7 was close up against the building but 9 and 11 were separated from number 13 by a passageway which would have formed the entrance-way to the yard and workshop when the Masters family were building coaches there.

It was demolished along with those on either side of it at a date between 1964 and 1968.(58,59) The site then stood empty for a few years before the office block was built in 1974. This was later taken on by the council and named Swale House.

John, Stephen and John Masters, coach builders

The 1841 census return reveals a family business of two Sittingbourne brothers John and Stephen Masters, both coach-makers, then in their fifties, living next door to each other with their wives and families. In addition John Masters junior lived next door but one, also building carriages with his father and uncle. The Masters brothers had spent all their adult lives working together in this spot on East Street.(14)

John senior's wife Elizabeth née Houghton was his second wife and 20 years younger than he. They had three young children and a servant. Stephen's wife was Mary, who was near to him in age but they still had six children at home.

A study of the tithe schedule shows Stephen and John at parcels 257 and 256 on the schedule. They jointly owned and occupied 256 and 257. Parcel 257 was the house later numbered 9 and 11. Stephen is listed at 257 which had buildings behind it which no doubt were the workshops.

As the trade in coach-building declined John senior retired and moved along the street with Elizabeth and one of their sons to West Lane where, according to the 1851 census return, he worked as a fruiterer. He died in 1863 aged 81 and has a headstone in St Michael's Churchyard.

Brother Stephen was still working at the business in his late sixties with his son Stephen junior assisting but seem to have moved into the building behind number 5.(see number 5)

Stephen senior and Mary eventually also moved a few doors along the street leaving their son, Stephen junior still using the workshop. Stephen senior died in 1864 aged 80 and by 1871 old widowed Mary was back to her old home living 'near number 5' which we take to mean behind number 5 with Stephen junior who still worked as a carriage painter. Sadly by 1901 Stephen junior, who had never married, was in the Milton Union Workhouse described as a retired carriage painter.

Number 9 East Street
George Mungeam, coal dealer

In 1861 it was George Mungeam, a labourer born in Doddington, who lived at number 9 with his wife. By 1870 George had ventured into business as a coal dealer doubtless using some of the Masters old buildings out the back for storage. By 1878 the Mungeams had moved a few doors along to number 17.

Number 11 East Street

In 1871 number 11 was the home of carpenter, William Norris and his wife. By 1881 widowed Mary Ann Hollands, a charwoman, was the tenant with her two sons.

Numbers 9 and 11 in joint use
Rosetta Pearcy, butcher

Rosetta and Thomas Pearcy had not long moved to Sittingbourne from Gravesend and purchased both parts of the building – 9 and 11, when Thomas Pearcy died aged 54 in 1883. We know from a deed in the museum's care that the Pearcys owned the building.

Thomas was a butcher and left Rosetta with their twin sons, both also butchers, to take on the shop with her. A year later Rosetta's name appeared in the local paper: '*Mrs Rosetta Pearcy butcher of East Street was fined 8/- by the local inspector of weights and measures. Her scales were an ounce out. A very small amount and he asked her to close the door in case the scales were affected by the draft.*'

Rosetta had an eye for a good display and Christmas was the time when this could fully be expressed in the shop. Her 1886 festive array was described by the Gazette:

'*Mrs Pearcy fully sustained the reputation for artistic decoration which has been a characteristic of exhibitions here on previous occasions. Amongst the rows of huge joints of beef and mutton gaily decked in rosettes, could be seen four fine beasts, two Devons...and two polled Scots. The sheep comprised half a score of prime Southdowns fed by E. & H. Maxted of Key Street, while a dozen choice porkers completed a very formidable bill of fare. The head of one of the Devons, specially adorned with rosettes and other attractions looked very conspicuous in the centre of the shop, while holly and the motto "A Merry Christmas" significantly placed over the counting house were the finishing touches to an attractive show.*'

The 1891 census shows us something of Rosetta's circumstances then. She had been born in Southwark, and by 1891 was in her fifties. John and William, the twin sons were approaching 30, still single and lived with her as did daughter Ada, a milliner, and youngest son Ernest who was apprenticed to a builder. By 1893 Rosetta had stepped back from the business and the twins advertised as 'Pearcy Brothers family butchers and poulterers of 9 & 11 East Street. It is quite unnecessary to buy foreign meat. We offer prime home-killed English beef and mutton at low prices.'

Butchery was a competitive business; there were others nearby in East Street and more still in the High Street. The Pearcys began to struggle and this led to the necessity of letting out number 11 from 1894 whilst continuing at number 9.

So they placed an announcement in the paper:

'Pearcy Brothers having let that part of their premises which has been used for carrying out the pork and poultry department of their business, will still supply pork and poultry of the very best quality at 9 East Street in conjunction with their butcher's business.'

However two years later the time had come for Rosetta, William and John Pearcy to let out number 9 too. Both twins had married and were to pursue their butchering in different towns; William in Worthing and John in Chiswick. So in 1896 the Pearcys leased number 9 to Ernest Millen, a butcher who lived in Albany Road, who was to keep it going as a butcher's shop, keep it in good repair and pay them £26 a year.

It was Alfred Millen, Ernest's father, who was listed in directories as having the shop at number 9. He already had a thriving butcher's shop at 87/89 High Street and saw an opportunity for extra trade at number 9. The Millens did not need the living accommodation as they resided over the shop at 87/89 High Street. They kept the shop here until at least 1908.

As for Rosetta she remained in Sittingbourne living in retirement in a house on the London Road with her two younger children.(11)

Perhaps Rosetta and Thomas were related to E. C. Pearcy, the surveyor and architect, about whom we wrote in our High Street volumes. We shall leave that for genealogists to research.

Horace William Wiles, fishmonger

Horace Wiles, a Milton man had a fishmonger's shop at 112 High Street from the 1870s and sold it in 1901.(HSII) By 1911 his son Horace junior, then in his forties and also a fishmonger, was at number 9 with his wife and two sons, having moved from Newington where he previously had a shop. His father lived on until 1915 and no doubt gave him plenty of advice.

The Manuell family, cooked-meat sellers

It is interesting to find in the 1918 directory that David Manuell had an 'art needlework depot' here. This was not the trade that David Manuell was associated with as he was a sausage-maker with a cooked meat shop already established at 48 West Street, where he lived. Needlework at number 9 would have been run by one of his younger daughters. The eldest, Alice, was already fully occupied by her café at 24 West Street. Needlework did not last long here before the Manuells reverted to their expertise in cooked meats. So by 1926 this was another Manuell cooked meat shop.

David Manuell himself died in 1925 leaving effects worth just over £2,000 which must have included number 9 East Street. He had appointed his eldest daughter, Alice as executor along with his friend and neighbour Harry Carpenter of 67 West Street. David and his wife Mary Anne had been blessed with a large family (see 24 West Street) many of whom assisted in the business.

Sadly Alice, at the time a principal in the business, was killed, aged 62, in an air raid when a bomb destroyed her home and shop at 48 West Street in September 1940.

MANUELS 9 East Street

Cooked Meats a Speciality

All kinds of Groceries in Stock

Mis-spelt advertisement for Manuell's

David's son Victor Ernest inherited number 9. He did not live over the shop but in Park Drive. The shop was very popular with many loyal customers. Victor Ernest Manuell ran number 9 for many years. After the war his son Victor John joined him in the business but had to wait until meat came off rationing to do so otherwise the income would not have been enough to support them both. Number 9 was demolished along with the neighbouring buildings in the mid 1960s. Carol Mantle née Manuell recalls that her father (Victor John), grandfather (Victor Ernest) and great-grandfather (David) owned the shop and did all the cooking themselves. *'The shop had a wonderful aroma of all the cooked meats. They also made pork and beef sausages and my husband's favourite, lamb and tomato sausage.'*

11 after the Pearcys

The living accommodation of number 11 was to let in 1890: *'The house, not the shop, with side entrance,'* for the Pearcys were using the shop, but living in number 9. Then as we have seen they let the shop at number 11 too.

In 1894 one J. Ingram put an announcement in the paper to say that he had just taken the shop 'which had been William Wise's' to sell fruit and vegetables and milk and eggs. So it appears that one of the women of the Wise family, coach-builders of 38/40 East Street had taken the shop at number 11 for a while and then Ingram took it on. This did not work out for in 1896 appeared the notice: *'To let well fitted shop East Street suitable for almost any trade and now in occupation of Mr J. Ingram.'*

The next two occupants of the shop were also here for only brief periods. They were Caleb White, a watchmaker, and the appealingly named Topsy Hayden.

It was Topsy who altered the type of stock that number 11 carried and although she was there only for a couple of years it was to be a change that stuck for number 11. When Topsy arrived in 1901 she was 40 a widow from London and a tobacconist who also did some baking. She and her son had moved on by 1903 and were to be found running a toy and fancy goods shop in Kingston upon Thames.

Tobacco and sweets at number 11– The Cigar Box

Alfred Milner took on the shop after Topsy left and he was soon followed by widowed Mrs Ann Smart a Kentish woman who was also a tobacconist and confectioner. She however did remain much longer. Her son Walter a commercial traveller in confectionery, daughter in law Lily who managed the shop, and their daughter lived with Ann in the six rooms. Ann died in 1920 aged 73.

Sometimes Walter and Lily took lodgers as in 1921-22 when the Tanner family lived with them, probably renting the upstairs from the Smarts who needed the extra income. Alice and William Tanner were on the electoral register for 1922 at number 11.

Early in 1926 Walter Smart, was declared bankrupt and the Smarts then left number 11. As well as running the shop they had let out stalls in the market arcade between their house and number 13 as we shall see.

William and Emily Godden moved in to number 11 when the Smarts left and continued the tobacconist's shop. They were still there in 1935 and were followed by Anita and Laurence Porter who remained until 1949. The Porters added an attraction to the shop for they made their own ice cream to sell.(105) Perhaps it was they who first named the shop 'The Cigar Box', a name which continued under the following tenants. Jim and Joyce Johnson were the next couple to move into number 11 and ran the shop through the 1950s. Next came a Mr and Mrs Monty Whittle who again retained the name The Cigar Box They were living here in 1963 but, a couple of years later, the Sutton family lived upstairs.

Number 11 when it housed the Cigar Box is in the foreground with number 9 being the other half of the building with the shop canopy out in this 1960s photograph. (EKG)

The market in the passageway which became 'The Arcade'

This was in the passageway between numbers 11 and 13. It was open to the elements until 1926 when it was taken on by Mr Berry and the council approved plans to put a glass roof on it and add a toilet.

The Smart family of number 11 ran the market whilst they lived there; we know this as it was advertised as 'Smart's Market'.(N01)

The stalls were numbered and in 1924 the directory listed them as:

    4 and 5 – Charles Thomas Cooper, butcher
    6 and 7 – W. R. May & Co fancy draper
    9 and 12 – Frank Hawkins, lamp and oil dealer
    14 and 15 – Marsden and English, greengrocer
    1 and 16 – John Samuel Connell, hardware dealer
    18 and 19 – Charles Ballard and Son, leather merchants
    20 – Mark Frederick Davis, cycle accessories

We can all imagine what a lively place that market must have been – how dull our 21st century High Street market would seem in comparison.

When the Smarts left, Harry Berry took the little market on, which became 'Berry's Market', letting out stalls and being granted permission by the council for an extra stall. Harry Berry was the licensee of the Fountain Hotel by the station and this was to be a way of adding to his income.(105) Harry must have had plentiful energy - and resilience - managing that market must have been quite a challenge – not easy for someone who, at the same time, was running a busy public house.

The stall holders changed rapidly as people tried their hand at this way of making a living.

In 1927 they included:

  Beatrix Cox's 'refreshment's room'
  William Bridges fancy goods
  Ed Drury a greengrocer
  Smith & Moor a grocer
  and John Hemmings a 'retail confectioner' who also had a shop at 21
  Canterbury Road where he made sweets.

By 1938, we learn from council minutes that Mrs Florence Berry of Rhode House still owned the market arcade. She was the widow of Harry Berry of The Fountain.

Evidently, by now, the stress of running a multi-occupancy market had been abandoned: the market was now one man's emporium – known to everyone as Smith's Arcade. Here until his death in 1960 Charlie Clement Smith sold household hardware and second-hand items. Charlie had been born in 1876 in Sussex and married in Sittingbourne in 1901. We see from his advertisement below that Charlie had worked at Dan Easton's in the High Street before deciding to go it alone. His mention of Mr Easton in the advertisement tells us something about the local community in those days: few of us, in our commercial advertisements, would mention a previous employer – moreover a competitor. Clearly, Charlie reckoned that, by mentioning his former employer, he embellished his own image!

Charlie's granddaughter recalls that Charlie, known to all as 'Big Dad', kept a little notebook in which he pencilled in payments for those customers who paid in instalments. The bicycles and prams were kept at the front of the long arcade with cutlery and china at the far end. Charlie hired out cutlery and china for events and the Convent was one of his clients for this. At lunch times he would pop across to the Ship for a quick pint and his cats would sit in a row seeming to guard the entrance to the Arcade until his return. Not that anybody went in when he wasn't there.

The entire site was cleared long ago to make way for the office block which eventually became Swale House.

Charles Smith's advertisement

The arcade can be seen in its last days before demolition (JC)

Numbers 13, 13a and 15 East Street

Although we are able to see what they looked like from old photographs, no trace of numbers 13 and 13a/15 remains today (Swale House stands on the site). Number 13a/15 may have been medieval; it was timber framed and weather-boarded. Number 13 was built in the 19th century and was brick with stone facings. It was erected in part of the wide gap which formed the entrance to the yard between numbers 11 and 13a/15.

The old building 13a/15 was often in joint occupation; with both parts described as 'semi-detached' in sales particulars. When street numbers were applied in 1870, this building, being in single occupation, was given one number – 15. When, later on, it was divided, the western part was numbered 13a – number 13 having been allocated to the house next door.

Number 13a/15 was demolished by 1938 whereas the more modern 13 continued to stand until the mid-1960s.

On the eastern side of 15 was a footpath. In 1974 the ground on which 13 had stood was covered by the eastern end of the new council offices which were built for British Anzani and only taken on by the council in 1983. The site of 15 still remains as an empty space between the council offices and number 17.

On the front left of this photograph c.1900 we see number 13 with its single bay window and, beside it, the weather-boarded 13a (the former Star Inn) with the canopy out. Number 15 is beyond that. Next comes an alley to a yard and fields at the back. Beyond that can be seen the familiar outline of number 17 – still there today 'Forster's', though the two-storey bay windows have gone.

Behind 13a/15 was a large yard with stabling and outbuildings. This proved important in the usage of the property. At times there were tenants of the dwellings and separate tenants of the yard and stabling where work of various kinds was carried on.

A section of the tithe map showing the building later numbered as 13a/15 which, on the tithe map, was parcel 256. It belonged to John Masters the coach-builder in 1840 and he lived next door (see 9/11)

The Star at the old number 13

For a few years the old number 13 was a public house known as The Star, to which we have only found reference in the 1858 directory and 1861 census return. Samuel Beeching an Ashford man, presided there with his wife Audrey. In 1861 they had eight children at home, a servant, two visitors who were labouring men and an additional two labourers who boarded with them. The house must have bulged at the seams. We know Mr Beeching had obtained a licence during the 1850s because the family already lived in the same house in 1851 but Sam had then been a dealer. He had tried to support his family in a variety of ways for in 1852 he was licensed to let horses, making use of the stables behind the building. By 1862 The Star had closed and the directory lists Sam as a pork butcher. He died in 1866. Number 13's brief period as The Star was recalled in 1884 when the shop there was named the 'Star Oil Store' run by a Mr J. Chapman – see below.(N01)

James Hammon wheelwright at 15

Young James Hammon from Norton lived at number 15 with his wife Frances and young daughter in 1851 making good use of the out-buildings for his work as a wheelwright. Sadly Frances died in 1853; James remarried to Matilda Roper in 1855, and, by 1861, had changed jobs and crossed the road to become licensee of The Plough.

William Thorner and John Peters at the old number 13 and 15

In 1871, when the census return was taken, the only resident here was William Thorner the chimney sweep (about whom we learn a good deal at his later address, number 25) He lived at number 15 then, with his wife, Caroline, and a boarder.

In 1873 John Peters the auctioneer of 15 and 19 High Street rented rooms next door to hold periodic sales by auction. We met Mr Peters in High Street volume I and we meet him again at 74 East Street. At that time, John Peters was running his business in ancient premises, shared with his neighbour W. J. Parrett. Both families were living there, and the accommodation offered no space for auction sales. Here in East Street were stables and outbuildings ideally suited for the purpose. However John Peters was not here for long; about this time he and Mr Parrett were exchanging accommodation in the old building in the High Street. In 1877, John acquired from his neighbour Mr Filmer, the freehold of the adjoining premises, number 15 High Street, which became his business headquarters. Four years later, John constructed a new building on that site with plenty of retail and office accommodation on three floors, and storage above.

In 1880 the electoral register records that a Daniel Sharp of Rochester owned 13 and 15 East Street.

Reverend John Doubleday at the new 13

In 1881 Reverend John Doubleday a young Baptist minister from Lincolnshire was living at the new number 13 with his sister Martha who kept house for him and two boarders who were labourers. The new number 13, was a smart 'villa' with a bay window for the parlour, complete with venetian blind and lace curtains. Though a smart new house, it was in a poor situation near the gas works and a couple of coal yards.

At that time, the Manse of the Baptist church stood beside the church facing Denmark Road at the smart new end of town. Robert Makin, the first pastor, *(makin' a new congregation)* was living at the Manse in 1871. He was followed by two short-term incumbents. In April 1881 the Doubledays had only just arrived in Sittingbourne. They may well have been put into 13 East Street as a temporary lodging whilst the Manse was "done-up" for them. Perhaps the Doubledays were here in East Street only for a few weeks. We learn more of Reverend Doubleday in our West Street volume.

Stephen Kemsley was the tenant of 13a from 1882-1890. This may well have been the Stephen Kemsley, farm labourer who was living and working at Bayford Farm in 1881.

Thomas Williams, jobmaster at 15 and then 13 /13a too

Thomas Arthur Williams was an energetic and enterprising man. He had moved into number 15 by 1881 with his wife, Annette, and their three children; young Thomas Reginald (who sadly died aged seven in 1887) Olive, Ada and a maid. Thomas, who had been born in Canterbury, was then in his early thirties. Before his marriage Thomas had lived with his parents at Goodnestone Road Sittingbourne and worked as a warehouse-man. When he first moved to number

15 he was employed as the town carter but had clearly seen all the space at the back of 13 and 15 as offering an opportunity to start his own business and, when he did, it flourished. Initially he only rented number 15 but soon the placard on the front of the building read: '*T. Williams contractor & job-master 13 and 15 East Street Sittingbourne furniture removed to all parts of England with or without risk. Pleasure parties catered for either small or large at the shortest notice.*'

On the steps of number 13 stand three of Thomas and Annette Williams children; Arthur, Connie and Gertrude.

Thomas in his heyday (FC)

Throughout the 1890s he carried on this business although the 1891 and 1895 directories simply list him as a carter.

By 1891 Thomas and Annette's family had grown and they had two more children. They were listed as living at 15 whilst 13 and 13a were in use for the business. Ten years later the census return records that the family lived at number 13 which must surely have been more comfortable.

Thomas was the grandfather of our museum member Flo Court and she has told us that he delivered groceries for the High Street shops and did deliveries for Lloyd's paper mills. He took people on party outings in a charabanc.

Thomas's two sons Harry and Arthur worked for him. All the family were musical; the daughters were keen singers and cyclists too. By 1906 Thomas had retired; the coming of cars which were so much faster and more convenient than horses and carts closed his business. He was then at an age when he felt too old to start a new enterprise and the expense would have been too much. The Williams family moved the short distance to number 103 East Street which was a smaller house. Thomas again worked as the town carter with the help of his son Arthur who still lived at home.(12)

Thomas Williams, Contractor and Job Master, and hired out charabancs for outings such as this one for the regulars of the Globe and Engine in Berry Street (HSI,77) (FC)

The premises at East Street were then advertised to let: '*double fronted shop with warehouse over shop & store & yard.*'(N01) The yard was slow to find a taker and in early 1908 was still being advertised: '*To be let large yard, stabling situated at rear of numbers 13 & 15 East Street suitable for job-master or contractor low rental.*'

Family descendants tell us that Arthur and Harry Williams changed their lives and then made a living by teaching the piano. The younger daughters, Constance and Gertrude, were often invited to parties because one could play the piano and the other had a lovely voice.

By 1908 Alfred Reynolds was using 13a for auction sales; his headquarters premises were nearby, at number 5 High Street.(43) As mentioned above, just over 30 years earlier, these same premises had been used for the same purpose by an ex-employee of the Reynolds family – John Peters, who had set up in competition almost next-door to the Reynolds shop, opposite the church.

Henry and William Read wheelwright and cycle-builder in the yard

Henry Read lived with his wife and son at number 71 but rented part of the yard and outbuildings of 11/13 for his coachbuilding business in the 1890s. When Henry retired in 1897 his son William announced in the local paper that he was going into partnership with Robert Alexander to continue the business which had adapted to add cycle building to carriage building. William's advertisement in the directory two years later: '*carriage builder and cycle maker and agent, old machine and carriages taken in exchange*' makes no mention of Robert Alexander. At any rate William Read continued the business until at least

1903 and also had a '*cycles & motor works*' in Edward Street Sheerness where he lived with his wife Ada and children.(11)

Edwin Ledger Robinson, photographer at 13

Edwin Ledger Robinson is listed in the 1908 directory as a photographer. In the 1903 directory he was at 103, East Street. Edwin had been born in Kent at Otham in 1867. In 1881, aged 16, he had boarded in East Street at number 85 with Robinson relatives. He married Mary Ann Barrett in 1885 and by 1891 was working as a sewing machine salesman in Folkestone.

In 1901 he and Mary Ann and their family of six children were lodging in four rooms in Shortlands Road and Edwin was trying to establish himself as a photographer.(11)

The Robinson family's stay at number 13 East Street was a brief one, for late in 1910 they left Sittingbourne in hopes of a brighter future in Canada. Edwin was 44. Some of the children accompanied them to Ontario including Edwin junior, who was an adult and a baker, younger son Arthur and daughter Lily.

Even during 1910 Edward had been trying to establish himself as a photographer. The National Archives have a document which records that he filled in a form to receive copyright on a postcard of Teynham to be sold by Alf Shrubsall at 24 High Street in September 1910.

An advertisement for number 13 was placed in the paper: '*13 East Street Semi-detached dwelling house. Two Sitting rooms, three bedrooms, kitchen, scullery, cellar, yard, back entrance from East Street. Gas and water laid on.*'

Francis Sanderson, journalist at 13

Francis Sanderson and his wife Alice then moved into 13 with its six rooms as the 1911 census records. He had been born in Ireland and was employed as a journalist on the Kentish Express and Ashford Times. The Sandersons soon left and the following year a notice appeared in the local paper: '*To let no. 13 East St. Office & Dwelling house 3 beds, sitting room, kitchen & scullery.*'

The Chapman family – blacksmiths in the yard behind 15

From 1882 to at least 1895 William Chapman a blacksmith worked in the outbuildings at 15; there was plenty of room for more than one business out the back and so his time overlapped with that of the Williams. Although Chapman advertised in local directories as being at 15 East Street we know he did not live in the house. For example in 1891 he and his wife Ellen were recorded on the census return living at number 34 across the road whilst the Williams family still lived at number 15. Before living at 34 the Chapmans had lived at 66. Working in the yard at 15 William Chapman was in direct competition with the main East Street smithy, at 26/28 across the road, run by the Burtons followed by Alf Buggs, but, on that main road from London, there was still plenty of work to be had. William Chapman died at Milton in 1900 aged 73. From then on the Chapman family <u>did</u> live at number 15 for, in 1901, his widow Ellen was listed there in the census with a daughter, a nephew and a son Thomas, who worked 'on his own account' in the yard, as a blacksmith. Ellen died in 1907 and the Chapmans left the house which was empty in 1908. Thomas and his brother Edward had moved to Mackies Yard just up the road into the High Street, where they described themselves as 'blacksmiths working in barge building'.(12)

Frederick Moore at 15

The next tenant of number 15's five rooms was Frederick Moore listed here in the 1911 census return with his wife Fenella and their enormous brood of ten children. Fred hailed from Portsmouth and worked as 'manager to a dealer in iron'; his employer seems to have been Willis Simons at number 41. Upon Mr Simons's death in 1913 the Moores moved to number 41 where a full account of Fred's enterprises can be read.

The last tenants of number 15

The last tenants of number 15 were Florence and George Puxty who lived there through the 1920s. By 1930 the house was up for sale described as: *'freehold semi-detached house suitable for conversion to business premises.'*

It appears the Forster's the outfitters next door at number 17 briefly expanded into number 15 in 1937 and then it was demolished. After demolition of the old building on the street frontage, the address 15 East Street applied to the yard behind where the house had stood.

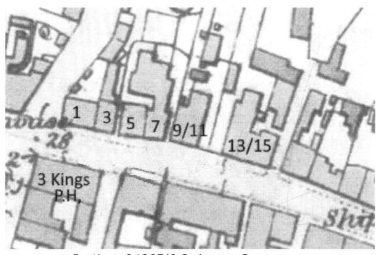

Section of 1865/6 Ordnance Survey map

Section of 1909 Ordnance Survey map

The 1909 map at the bottom shows a change since the above 1865/6 map. Number 15 has been partitioned into 13a and 15 and the new number 13 has been built in part of the space between number 11 and 13/15.

Leonard and Lawrence Bowes, bill posters at number 13

After the Sandersons' brief period at number 13, the next owners and residents were Harriet Bowes and her two sons, Lawrence Fred and Leonard George Bowes. They moved in in 1913 just after the death of their father George who had died far away in Wales on tour no doubt as he had been in 1911 when he was found by the census enumerator boarding in Consett, Durham describing himself as a theatrical manager. On that night his wife and two sons had been listed at home in Glovers House in Sittingbourne enjoying the 12 rooms of the mansion.

George had owned and run Bowes Park on the corner of Bell Road and Highsted Road where he had laid on many and various events for the townsfolk of Sittingbourne.

We say much more about Glovers and Bowes Park in HSII.

Probate records show that George left Harriet the tidy sum of £3,669.

For reasons not obviously apparent now, Glovers House and some of the land beside it, was then sold; Mrs Bowes and her sons took a big step down in the world – moving to number 13.

We can only speculate as to the reason, but perhaps, in due course, it became apparent that George's estate owed large debts, which were undeclared at the time of his death.

Leonard and Lawrence earned their living as bill posters which had been part of their father's business.(12) Harriet died in 1921 aged 81. The Bowes brothers continued to live at 13 until the late 1920s, when they moved out and sold the premises to George Dutnall resident of Elmcroft, Borden School Road (later renamed College Road) Sittingbourne. We meet Mr Dutnall more than once in this book, as owner of several properties in East Street.

Rebounding, geographically and financially: having retained some of the site beside Glovers House, "Larry" Bowes (as he was known) built there number 1 Highsted Road, where he lived for the rest of his life. The adjoining land was also sold for building.

The last years of the house

In 1928 council minutes record that the house was changed to add a shop front. George Dutnall, the new owner (who lived in College Road), realised that the house had commercial potential.

A couple of years later, we find George William Denham here, running a confectionery. By 1933 he had been replaced by Frank and Lilian M. Kennard. Frank was an insurance agent whilst Lilian ran the shop selling everything you might need to do needlework and embroidery. Her shop was described as an 'art needlework depository'.(56,57)

By 1945 number 13 was empty and (doubtless to the dismay of Mr Dutnall) was requisitioned by the council for the purpose of rehousing an overcrowded family with five children from Shortlands Road. A month later a tenancy was granted to William and Mary Witt, who may have been the final tenants of the property.(105) William died aged only 40 in 1951.

Between 1963 and 1968 13/13a was demolished and the open space behind it was used for car sales.

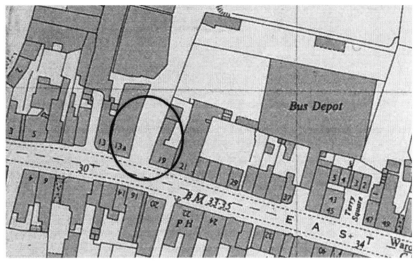

On this 1960 map the space where 15 had stood can be seen – in use as one of the entrances to the bus depot.

G. Hales and Sons in the yard and outbuildings

Mr G. Hales was George Hales who lived in William Street in 1911, a painter and coachbuilder then in his twenties with a wife Frances and two young children. He had been born in Stockbury in 1883 and began his working life as a wheelwright. He had workshops behind number 13 and 13a by 1915. George Hales was a man ready to adapt to the modern age and leave coachbuilding behind in favour of taking on the motor car. Initially his advertisements were for wheelwrights such as this one of 1916: *'Wanted wheelwright (ineligible for army) Apply G. Hales East Street.'*

By 1924 he advertised as a *'motor-body, van & cart builder & painter specialising in motor bodies.'* From 1926 onward he called the business the 'Motor Body Works'. George was a devout Methodist and supervised the Sunday School at the East Street Chapel, and remained active in that congregation until the late 1950s.

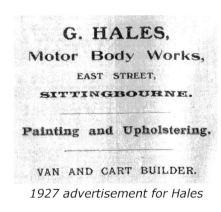

1927 advertisement for Hales

In 1931 the council approved his plans for a new workshop behind 13a. By this time George's son Leonard was working with him and the business was called 'G. Hales & Son'.

Sharing the Premises
J. T. Bruce at 13a
Perhaps at the instigation of young Len, from the mid 1930s to at least 1950, the Hales family shared part of the premises (and the phone number 74!) with a stone-mason, J. T. Bruce & Son. Mr Bruce lived in Park Road.

J. T. Bruce at 13 East Street in 1950

By 1946 Hales was able to take over the dwindling business of G. Barry (the blacksmith at 26/28) who, unlike Hales, had not adapted to the age of the car. This transfer of business notice appeared in the paper: '*G. Hales & Son, East Street, have acquired the old established business of G.E. Barry & Son, welders & general smiths, added to their own modern facilities for oxyacetylene & electric welding. We will maintain same high standards of workmanship*'. (see 26/28)

In 1950 the council gave Hales permission to put a petrol pump and underground tank into the garage. By 1959 Len was advertising in the local paper as 'Hales & Son Agricultural & Motor Engineers.'

Roland Car Sales in the yard with Hales
By 1960 Len, who lived at 61 Bell Road, had allocated part of his site to Roland Car Sales, whose business was named Roland after a son of the Friday family who was killed in the Second World War. (It is not to be confused with the later car-sales firm Rowlands which was based in St Michaels Road and was a separate company.)

Len kept his own business functioning independently on the site. In the 1963 directory, number 15 is '*G. Hales & Sons coach builders and horticultural machinery.*'

The 1964 advertisement put the emphasis on car repairs: 'G. Hales and Son, East Street, "*You Bend Them We Mend Them*" Car repairs.'

By 1968 Hales had amalgamated with Roland to become Roland & Hales selling cars and agricultural machinery. This was the whole site covering numbers 1 to 15.

The adjoining site was occupied by the Maidstone and District Bus Company depot, to which the vehicle entrance was between Hales at number 15 and Forster's at 17. The pedestrian entrance was beside the bus company office at number 39.

Leonard George Hales died in 1969. Then, by 1971, there was a change of ownership and it was Peter Newman cars and agricultural machinery. All this came to an end when the site was sold to developers who built the new office block here which was opened in 1975. (see 1-15 Swale House).

The new building on the site of 1 to 15 East Street – Swale House

The British Anzani building at the junction of East Street and Crown Quay Lane in 1979 where buildings numbered 1 to 15 (Odd) had previously stood. It later became Swale House. (EKG)

Here, at the historic heart of our town, stands the office block known as Swale House – seat of our local authority known as Swale Borough Council. This site, where used to stand numbers 1-15 East Street, was cleared in the late 1960s and then stood almost empty for some years.

In 1974 work began on a new office building by construction firm Laing for British Anzani. The hope was that commercial tenants would be found for the building or its various parts. Eventually the office block was completed and opened in 1975 – at a time of economic turmoil around the world, triggered by a steep rise in the price of crude oil and the building stood empty for a number of years, much to the embarassment of the planners and developers.

At about this time the local authorities for Sittingbourne and Milton, Faversham and Sheppey and the surrounding areas were merged to form Swale District Council (later renamed Swale Borough Council). The new conglomerate then had to restructure and relocate the network of its various offices, dotted in and around the four conurbations of the new council district – overall, an area of about 144 square miles. In our town alone, as recounted in our volumes about the High Street, the offices of the former Urban District Council had been scattered around the town in various buildings – converted houses and rooms over shops.

After struggling with this inefficient separation, Swale Council decided to centralise here, taking on the huge empty space on the busy corner of East Street. Doubtless this decision brought immense relief to the owners of this building – and their bankers – it was a long time for a newly-completed building to stand empty.

So the eight year old building was converted for use by the local council in 1983 and was named 'Swale House'.

From a historian's perspective, there was logic in centralising the government of Sittingbourne here at the ancient heart of our town, but, as with all major changes, the move to Swale House did not take place without opposition. The historic boroughs of Faversham and Queenborough resented the new prominence given to the parvenu Sittingbourne.

There were problems too, with the building itself: the Council Chamber of our former Urban District Council in Central Avenue – then just over ten years old – was a purpose-built structure. The floor area now allocated for the new Council Chamber here at Swale House was beset with pillars, interfering with views of the proceedings.

To the satisfaction of Sittingbourne's local partisans, it was soon decorated with large oil paintings of historic worthies such as Henry Payne and, of course, George Smeed both of whom, long ago, featured prominently in the life of our town.

The corner plot, shortly before construction began, 1974 (EKG)

The construction site in 1974

An aerial view of what was to become Swale House from the north in 1980
St Michael's Road is at the bottom of the picture, with Crown Quay Lane running up
between the office block and the cinema

Swale House in 2008 with entrance steps reconfigured for its use as a council building
with public access (CA)

Numbers 17, 19, 21, 23, 25, 27, 29 East Street

13a   15   17/19   21   23 25 27 29   31 33 35

Nowadays Forster's the school outfitters at numbers 17 and 19 is the first building in East Street after Swale House, from which it is separated by the entrance to the council's car park. Forster's building is one double-fronted shop with an oriel bay window on each side of the upper floor at the front. The building was severely damaged by fire in 1912 but not to the point where demolition took place. The rebuilding would have been internally and at the back. The bays on the first floor front were added then. The brickwork on the front and west flank and the main roof structure are Georgian.

Beside Forster's on the other side stands the distinctive number 21. This was for so long Webb's ironmongery but now arguably it has come down in the world, it is emblazoned with the bold words 'Bargain Booze'. Number 21 was built in 1912 replacing an earlier building on the site. It abuts a terrace of small early 19th century dwellings; numbers 23, 25, 27 and 29.

When the 1901 census return was taken each of the properties had just four rooms. Numbers 17, 19 and 21 were often in joint occupation and so their story is told together. Number 23 was for a period used as one shop with number 21.

Forster's at 17/19 in 2017 (BA)

Numbers 17 and 19 East Street

We believe that this house may be about 300 years old. Canon Scott Robertson recorded that it was, in the early years of the 18th century, *"the property first of Wm Bingham and then of John Bunce."* The Bunce family were well-established hereabouts – their name crops up at Bunce's Farm an ancient timber-framed hall-house at Tonge, which now survives, in a rather exposed position, on a platform surrounded by low land from where brick-earth was extracted, long ago, by Smeed-Dean. Further away, over at Throwley, the Bunce charity still dispenses funds to good causes. Scott Robertson continues: *"Bunce's niece and heiress borne* (sic) *the delightful name of Pleasant Sweetlove. Thomas Banister, of Glovers* (see Rose Inn, HSII) *married her, and obtained this and other house property with her as dowry."* The Canon then lists several generations of the Banister family, from the last of whom, this house was passed *"to Thomas Wilson, and to his daughters, Mrs Divers and Mrs Blackader"* (their names crop up more than once in this series see 100–108 and 110–118 East Street and HSI & HSII.) Occupiers of the house during this period, according to Canon Scott Robertson, included Messrs Stronghill, Chapman and Beeching, but he doesn't say when.

The house had been partitioned in two by the time we can first be specific about its occupants. It is shown as parcels 254 and 253 on the tithe schedule, both parts described as 'part of a house and yard' and these two parts were later numbered 17 and 19 East Street. In 1840 when the tithe map was drawn, this house was owned by Thomas Bishop, the blacksmith and James Blackader, (these men also owned a small property in Berry Street – and James was very likely related to the lady of the same name mentioned above).(HSII) Their tenants in East Street were Charles Hadaway at 19 (253) and William Sellen at 17 (254).

However, a few months later, when the census was taken, it appears that Mr Hadaway had rented the whole building. Hadaway was a currier and leather seller who was back to renting only number 17 by 1851. He and his wife Louisa came from Chatham. He must have carried on his unpleasant-smelling trade in an outbuilding and the yard at the back. He remained at number 17 until at least 1866.

Young cabinet-maker George Beckley, who had been born in Sevenoaks in 1824, worked and lived at number 19 in 1851. He was only 26 but employed two apprentices and had his sister Sarah to keep house for him. He would have shared the yard and out-buildings with Charles Hadaway. By 1861 he had left the town and as we cannot find him anywhere else in England in the 1861 census return he was probably the George Beckley who died in Sevenoaks in 1858.

John Furner, whitesmith at number 17

A whitesmith named John Furner was living at number 17 with his family when the 1871 census was taken. He was a Sittingbourne man then approaching his sixties, assisted in his work by his son Alfred who still lived at home. Daughter Ellen was 29, also unmarried and at home working as a charwoman, but perhaps the two grandchildren listed as living in the house were her children. Ellen's younger sister, a dressmaker, completed the household. We come across several whitesmiths in East Street and their work involved working with tin and making household utensils. The Furner family had only lived in the street for a few years having moved from Railway Terrace.(30) By 1881 they had left again for Station Place where John and Alfred continued making tin goods. John lived on until 1895 when he died aged 84.

Charles Fairbeard at number 19

Number 19 was a private dwelling in 1871 and was occupied by a labourer, Charles Fairbeard who had been born in Doddington, his wife Elizabeth and their three children.

George Mungeam coal dealer at 17

The next tenants of number 17 were the Mungeams. George, a coal dealer and his wife Mary Ann had previously lived a few doors away at number 9 but, by 1878, had moved to number 17 where they remained with George delivering coal until he died in 1887 aged 74. His wife Mary Ann had died two years earlier. (8,33)

George's mother, old Mary Mungeam, was an inmate of the alms-houses at number 1 along the street during the 1850s and 1860s.(6,7)

All change at 17, 19, and 21

Surprisingly the 1891 census lists numbers 17, 19, and 21 all in the occupation of the ironmonger George Panteny of whom we write more below.

By 1901 the three buildings had reverted to separate occupancy with the Pantenys retaining only number 21.

Number 17 a private house again

For a few years number 17 was again a private house; the home in 1901 of Albert Parker, a labourer in the paper mills who lived in the four-roomed house with his wife Alma.

By 1908 the Parkers had moved on and James Hollands had opened a greengrocery here. This did not flourish and so he and his wife moved along the street and crossed the road to rent number 42 where James reverted to market gardening whilst his wife Lydia ran a confectionery shop.(12) (see number 42)

The house and shop at number 17 were advertised to let when the Hollands left in 1910: 'With possession, dwelling house and shop. Good position & suitable for almost any trade.'

The new tenant was Samuel Cohen, a photographer who did not live on the premises.(N01)

The old number 21

Parcel 252 on the tithe map was what was later known as number 21 East Street, a house and yard owned by John Arndell Barnard (see 87/89 High Street) in 1840 and occupied by Edward Smith from Wye. Smith was a butcher who had a wife, Harriet, and seven children to support. He remained there in 1861, in his sixties. Scott Robertson tells us that the "house had formerly behind it a field called Ship Meadow." – convenient for a butcher who needed somewhere, nearby, for grazing animals before slaughter.

In earlier years, "the owners of the dwelling were, successively John Sell, Thomas Fleet, Mary Birch (who married John Reeve), and R. Wyles"

The Pantenys at 17, 19, 21 and 23

By the time the 1881 census was taken young George Panteny, the ironmonger from Whitstable, had moved his wife Annie and young family into number 19. His shop was already well established at number 21. He was doing well and the shop had expanded from number 21 to number 23. At this point George was able to employ two men and three boys.

Ten years earlier the 1871 census, taken when George was 23, shows that he and his wife Annie (née Goldfinch) had begun married life round the corner in Shortlands Road and George had been trained as a ship's block-builder which was a less skilled craft than that of a shipwright, for the block-builder made the wooden blocks on which the ship stood whilst it was constructed.

George was a young man with an entrepreneurial spirit and plenty of energy and by 1874 had set up shop at number 21 as an oil and colour man. Number 21 had previously been the home and shop of John Westgate an elderly, widowed general dealer. Mr Westgate's married daughter, Ann Bennett, lived with him, as no doubt did her husband William when he was not away. John Westgate died during 1871.

The 1891 census reveals that at that time the Pantenys were renting numbers 17, 19, and 21 rather than 19, 21 and 23. The family still lived at number 17.

All this success could not prevent tragedy striking the Pantenys in 1896 when their younger daughter Nellie, died aged 19, followed within weeks by George himself aged 47.(N01) The national probate index reveals that George's effects, left to Annie, were worth a goodly £1,226.

Herbert, the only son, continued the business with his mother. He married Jane Gullick in 1900 and set up home more comfortably in Albany Road with Jane (who liked to be called Maude as we can see from the 1901 census return), his mother and a servant.

With the Pantenys having moved house and requiring only number 21 for the shop, numbers 17, 19 and 21 reverted to separate occupancy.

At this point the four rooms which made up number 19 were rented by a coachman, Charlie Pearce.(11) By 1908 number 19 had a shop front and the tenant was a jeweller and watchmaker John Seaping Benton. He and his wife lived in the three rooms using the fourth as a shop and were still there in 1912. (12)

Matthews writing of the town of his youth recalled number 21 under Herbert Panteny: 'What are now Webb's ironmongery stores were then the business premises of Mr. H. Panteny, oil and colourman. This was a large and extensive business in those days, when the usual domestic illumination was by means of the paraffin or benzine lamp'.(69)

Herbert Panteny ran the business until 1910 when he and his wife Maude and daughter Nellie emigrated to Canada. They left from Bristol on the 'Royal George'. Herbert's mother Annie was still alive but had no desire to leave England. She was living with her daughter Flora who had long been married and lived in Scarborough.(12) Annie later returned to Sittingbourne and lived on until 1929.

The fire, 1912

On a Monday evening in September 1912 a disastrous fire destroyed number 17 and spread rapidly to number 19. The old number 21 was separated from number 19 only by a party wall. Number 17 was then the photographic studio of young Sam Cohen. Born in Russia he had only moved here from Bethnal Green the year before.(12) The building had been locked up for the night and was empty. Flames were spotted by Miss Roberts who lived opposite. It was nine at night and the captain of the fire brigade, Hedley Peters, was fortunately just up the road at the Liberal Club. He dashed home for his helmet and tunic and then ran to the fire station where the men assembled and arrived rapidly in East Street.

The fire was intense. There was some highly inflammable material at the photographer's shop where the windows melted and flames leapt right across the roadway licking the houses opposite. By this time number 19, the home of the Bentons was alight. Ellen Benton had been lying ill in bed whilst her husband and her brother played cards downstairs. She was taken from the house along with just a few items across the road to The Ship. She was overcome with shock and both she and her husband were naturally in a distressed state whilst all they possessed in the world was destroyed. William Webb and his brother quickly arrived at the scene and quantities of oil and methylated spirits which had been were stored at the back of their premises were removed whilst the firemen endeavoured to prevent the flames from catching hold of number 21 and policemen held back the interested crowd. Dr Ind paced to and fro smoking a cigarette ready to treat any injured firemen.

The men managed to bring the fire to halt in the centre of the building. It had been thought that a party-wall separated number 21 from 23 but it turned out to be only matchboard under the roof and so if the fire had not been stopped it would have destroyed the terrace from 23 to 29. As it was, the furniture of elderly Mrs Bootle of number 23 was removed for safety during the blaze. At midnight, with the crowd gone home and the buildings made safe, the exhausted firemen sat down to hot coffee at number 5, the shop of Valentine Tyler. The next morning numbers 17 and 19 were boarded up. What caused the fire was unknown and it was fortunate that all three of the businesses were insured.

Forster, Webb's, Home Crafts and A. Cooper in 1967 (EKG)

We've come a long way since our business was established in 1910

OUR SHOP AS IT WAS IN 1910

But we still continue the traditions of personal service and expert advice to all our customers on all matters concerning ironmongery and hardware, both domestic and agricultural

WEBBS Agricultural and Domestic Ironmongers

EAST STREET, SITTINGBOURNE

Telephone Sittingbourne 24141

1960s advertisement

We have seen that Pantenys ran a flourishing ironmongery here until Herbert and Maud emigrated in 1910. They had sold the business on to young William Webb who wasted no time in calling in a sign-writer to cover the outside walls of the old building with information about what could be purchased inside. As we can see in the photograph above this included shovels, forks, stoves, ranges, locks and keys. Every morning buckets and ladders were arranged and hung outside to tempt the customer in.

The 1911 census return reveals that William Webb had seized the opportunity to buy number 21 and was lodging comfortably in Albany Road whilst he got the business going. He was 25, single and had been born in Southsea, Hampshire.

He grew up in Hastings where his father, Charles Webb, ran an ironmongery for 30 years. William was bright and hardworking; the youngest Master Ironmonger of his time. The Webb family have told us that after his first day of opening the shop he was to be seen sitting at the edge of the road outside, head in hands saying "No one wants to buy my kettles!" Having invested all his money in this new venture panic started to set in because he had not made his fortune overnight. His mantra was always "Do it now, not later."

The report of the terrible fire reveals that William's parents and brother had moved to Sittingbourne to support him in his new venture and were living with him at the charming Aspley House (near the Billet, public house) on the London Road. Number 21 was empty and locked up for the night when the fire spread along the roof from number 19 and took an instant hold.

After the fire William placed an advertisement in the local paper: '*12th October: Due to Fire. Great salvage sale at 21 East Street All stock must go, regardless of cost, previous to premises being pulled down. Bargains for everybody.'*

The re-constructed number 21

Reconstruction of number 21 for William Webb began promptly. The ground floor was to have a central door with a shop window on each side just as the old building had, but unusually, above the door, a semi-circular, large window was inserted which survives today and gives distinction to the building. The shop was rebuilt as one very large shell with a galleried landing only. The vast stockroom that exists upstairs now was put in later. So although the shop would have appeared dimly lit, daylight would have been allowed in through the tall, arched top window. There was a very long mahogany-topped counter with the weighing scales down one end. Here stood the assistants. Behind the counter were drawers housing all manner of everyday items required for living in the

Edwardian era. The range of one particular item of stock could be phenomenal, for example there were not just two particular types of garden spade or forks, but page upon page of different ones available from big catalogues. The same could be said for handsaws too. Nails and screws and all items of ironmongery were sold loose with a vast array of choice. William also sold building and plumbing goods, sanitaryware, paraffin lamps, stoves and spares, hollowware, kitchenware and lawn mowers. Repairs were carried out on site. As qualified locksmiths they would have stocked a huge range of locks.

William married Ethel Victoria Ridley in St Michael's Church in the High Street in 1913 and they had two sons Ron (born 1914) and Eric (born 1916).

William and Ethel Webb

The shop flourished and William was able to purchase a shop in Tenterden in 1921. After marriage the Webbs moved to a bungalow in Woodstock Road until 1935 when they moved to Tenterden. There William built his own home, now The Little Silver Hotel beside the Ashford Road at St Michael's.

Both of William's boys learned the trade in the Sittingbourne shop under the careful eye of the manager Arthur Mount. Arthur was not tall; his stature, his spectacles and his quiet genial nature, was said to resemble another of that name: 'Big-hearted' Arthur Askey, a popular comedian of those days.

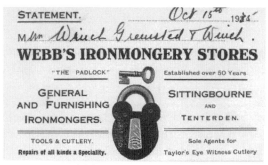

Webb's stationery in 1935

Mr Mount's popular and capable deputy was Harry Day of Borden Lane. Michael Peters can remember that, when buying a water-barrow from Webbs, Harry Day told him that the previous time he had sold a water-barrow, the buyer was the Archbishop of Canterbury.

Ron and Eric were called up during the Second World War leaving the two shops to be manned by William and just a few staff.

William died in 1958 leaving the shops to be run by Ron and Eric.

William Webb

Ron and Eric Webb

Ron had no children but Eric had three sons: Nigel (born 1957), Graham (born 1960) and Charles (born 1969). The front of the Sittingbourne shop was modernised in 1961 and Arthur Mount was succeeded as manager by Frank Smith. Ron and Eric continued the business and opened a further shop in Tenterden in 1963 (now the Cookshop). Eric died in 1998 and Ron in 2002. Nigel and Graham continue to run the two Tenterden businesses with another Webb's shop which opened in 2002 in Battle and a partnership in a Cookshop in West Malling which opened in 2009. Charles has his own Cookshop in Cranbrook which opened in 1997.

Ian Weeks-Pearson was the final manager of the Sittingbourne shop. Ian's father was a senior officer in the local fire brigade – responsible for Fire-Safety Regulations in this district; he might have been particularly interested in the history of this building, for which his son was responsible. It was Ian who closed the doors for the final time in 2008 after 99 years in business. This was a great loss to the town for this was a magical cave of a shop where the staff knew exactly where everything was and would dispense helpful advice about what was required in order for the customer to successfully complete any job they were doing. From then on, the folk of our town had to go elsewhere to buy their "fork 'andles".

After a long pause, the building reopened as Costcutter Convenience followed by Bargain Booze.

Number 21 in 2017 (BA)

Numbers 17 and 19 East Street after the fire

Mrs T. Goodhew was the owner of 17 and 19 when they were so badly damaged by fire and when she had the property renovated it was as one shop right across the front two rooms, a stable at the back and four bedrooms.(105)

The Bentons who had been so distressed by the fire moved to number 3, High Street where John continued his watchmaking business.

The Clark family rented the house during the First World War. Frank Gray Clark (born 1891 in Faversham) was serving in the Navy as a Leading Stoker on 'H.M.S.Osprey.' He had enlisted in 1909, survived the war and lived on until 1957.

George and Alice Goodsell, greengrocers at 17/19

In 1911 George Goodsell, a Tenterden man, aged 54, was to be found running a greengrocery at number 4 High Street. The name of his wife Alice is crossed out on the census return form, along with the information that she was aged 51. Instead, on the next line George wrote the name of Alice Parker, the lodger, single, aged 24, a butcher. Ten years previously George had been a cement labourer in Murston with a wife named Fanny. Fanny died in 1903 and in 1907 George had married an Alice but not Alice Parker, Alice Clark. Quite a mystery!

By 1921 George and Alice Goodsell were living in the attractive new building 17/19 running a greengrocery and confectionery shop. The Goodsells remained here until at least 1933.

Forsters School Outfitters at 17/19 since 1931

The amply named Stanley Frederick James Forster trained as a tailor and opened his outfitter's shop for men and boys in 1931. He had been born in Sittingbourne in 1904 and grew up round the corner in Shortlands Road. His father worked on the brickfields. It was in 1933, not long after setting up shop that Stanley travelled to Oxfordshire to marry his sweetheart, Ivy Dingle. They ran the business together and it flourished. They had two children named Doreen and Alan.

1933 Stanley Forster letterhead

At Forster's you could order a suit or an overcoat to be made to measure. The Forsters worked hard through the depression of the 1930s and the business thrived. At the outbreak of war Stanley served at Sheerness Dockyard in the naval police. Mrs Forster continued to run the shop with part time help.

Stanley was a public-spirited man and in 1946 he was elected a town councillor as an independent, and served as chairman during 1958-59.

Stanley Forster in his regalia
as Chairman of the Sittingbourne and Milton Urban District Council

Stanley was a magistrate and a school governor. For many years he was also on the committee of Sittingbourne Football Club. Sadly in 1964 he was killed in a car crash aged 59. Stanley and Ivy's daughter Doreen Williams carried on the shop with her husband Fred and son Paul. They acquired franchises as school uniform stockists.

In 1980 they were able to open a new branch in Faversham followed by one in Sheppey in 1985 and Maidstone in 1988. They still have the branch at 16 High Street, Sheerness.

1981 Advert for Forsters

Numbers 23, 25, 27, 29 East Street

Numbers 23 to 29 in 2019 (AJW)

Now we move on to the terrace of early 19th century two-up two-down cottages, later numbered as 23, 25, 27, 29 East Street. In 1840 they were numbered together as parcel 251 and described as *'cottages owned and occupied by Mary Tilley'*. Evidently this lady, whom we met at 20 High Street, used some of the cottages to house her servants and/or short-term tenants.

The previous building on the site, whose history Scott Robertson recounts, had been *"divided into three tenements, which the overseers of the poor rented."* Our readers will note that the ancient building across the street (now numbered 10-14) was also divided into three. Such a fate often happens to large buildings, whose environment has deteriorated.

Sometime after 1811, the overseers surrendered the old tenemented house, which was then pulled down.

We date the present terrace to about 1830. Perhaps the cottages were built by Mary Tilley, who owned them in 1840. Or perhaps they were built for (or by) her predecessor here, Michael Oakeshott.

Scott Robertson recounts an outline of the site's history. He suggests that *"this was the probably the site of a house occupied by John Byxe, whose will was made in 1480."* He goes on to list successive owners as William Bix, Richard Tillard, Jonas Smoothing, Elizabeth Fowell (one half) and then, as recounted above, John Bunce and the Banisters who sold the place to Michael Oakeshott before 1819.

	1841	1851	1861
23	Henry Knott, labourer+6	Richard Fever, labourer+2	John Weller, shoemaker+1
25	William Hatch, labourer+7	George Sidders, labourer+2	Willis Simons, shoemaker+4
27	Thomas Lucas, labourer+1	William Higgins, labourer+1	Henry Houghton labourer+3
29	Thomas Brockwell, horsekeeper+3	William Payne+4	Sarah Ann Hodges dressmaker+3

Known residents of numbers 23 to 29

Number 23 East Street

Number 23 was only briefly adapted to use the front room as a shop during the 1880s when as we have seen George Panteny expanded his business into it.

1871	Edwin Chapman+family	agricultural labourer
1881	Shop for Panteny	
1887	Thomas Hunt	chimney sweep
1891	James Bacon	brickfield labourer
1901	Fred Calkin+2	shipwright
1919	H. Couchman+wife	
1922	Elizabeth and Harry Weller	
1926	Harry Weller	

Residents of number 23 East Street

In 1931 the council approved alterations to number 23 for George Dutnall, the then owner. He had a new shop front installed and here Joyce and Ray Mitchell sold books for a time.(56,105) They were followed by Joseph William Gregory who opened a grocery here in the years leading up to the war.(N01) From approximately 1947 to 1952 the shop housed a greengrocery business run by Mrs Gwendoline Branch.(87)

Homecrafts at 23, 25 and 27

By 1963 J. and J. Burton had opened their shop called Homecrafts at number 23. They stocked everything from plywood and hardboard, to wrought iron gates, mirrors and lamps.

There were just two rooms upstairs at 23 and the following tenants Mr and Mrs Lacey lived there for about a year and kept the same name for the shop which Mrs Lacey ran.

Then, by 1965 Bernard J. and Mary Harris took it on and remained until 1986 using the upstairs rooms for storage and an office. Bernard Harris recalls:

"*Our business was DIY, curtain rails and timber, which we cut to size in a workroom at the rear. It was the days before the large DIY multiples when it was possible to buy single screws. We originally had the lease for number 23, and later extended into 25/27 when Cooper's hairdressers moved above the jewellers in the High Street. Again with 25/27 we just used the upstairs for storage. It was already one large space having been altered for the salon. After a few years we reverted back to just number 23.*

The shop at number 23 when it was selling giftware etc.

1981 Advert

"We traded in East Street for around 24 years, gradually reducing the DIY element of the business (the opening of Redways, followed by Payless in the High Street was the beginning of the end for the smaller DIY business) and moving into giftware until the old Co-op building further along East Street was redeveloped into a shopping Mall with the Regis Suite over the top. We took on one of the adjoining units to sell giftware, and traded there for a couple of years before giving up the business." (Bernard Harris)

HOME-CRAFTS
Personal Service
(B. J. HARRIS)
FOR TIMBER, HARDBOARD, CHIPBOARDS, PLYWOOD, HUNDREDS OF D.I.Y. ITEMS IN STOCK
Curtain Rails our Speciality
SWISH, DRAPE, LUXAFLEX, DECORAIL FROM 3' to 14' LENGTHS
VENETIAN & ROLLER BLINDS

23 EAST STREET, SITTINGBOURNE
Telephone: Sittingbourne 3655

1972 advertisement

In 1986 the shop was taken on by Anthony Swain trading as Periwinkle Press booksellers and picture-framers. The firm had been founded in 1968 by Anthony's parents, Eric Swain and his wife Audrey in Old Mill Cottage at Periwinkle Mill, Chequers Hill, Doddington in 1968. Anthony had taken over in 1977 when his parents retired.

By 2000 all the shops were empty and then the terrace was converted back to four private homes with sash windows.

Number 25 East Street

Number 25 was the home of Mary Hatch an unmarried woman in her thirties with two children and a lodger in 1871.

William Thorner, chimney sweep

By 1874 William Thorner and his wife Caroline had moved into number 25 from their previous home at number 15.(8,32) Thorner was a chimney sweep and in spite of his advancing years he continued to ply his trade until his death in 1882 aged 76.(33) Although he hailed from Ticehurst in Sussex and had lived in Maidstone into the 1860s, he was described as 'a genuine townsman' of Sittingbourne. We are fortunate that a recollection of Thorner was published in the local paper in 1929, long after his death:

> 'He was the leading chimney sweep in the town, and although he seldom if ever shook hand with anyone, he was nevertheless warm-hearted, had a smile on many occasions – despite those trade-mark facial smudges, without which a sweep could scarcely hope to obtain employment. William Thorner was a natural sweep, he looked it and he lived it very thoroughly…Outside his home in East Street was exhibited in a most conspicuous position a sweep's brush. It was not a dainty, perfect and unused brush, but one which had seen much service, turned many awkward chimney flue corners and cleaned off many bushels of soot. There it was, a sign of a very necessary calling and a very honourable one too, exhibited as a token of thoroughness and wear and tear and as a sure and certain guide to the right door knocker should the sweep's services be required.
>
> As a child, certainly not ten years of age, one was sent to Wlliam Thorner's house with this message – "Please Mr Thorner, mother wants her chimneys swept, and please when can you come, so that she can be ready?"
>
> The answer came, sharp and staccato like, "Tomorrow morning, me little boy; at five o'clock, tell yer mother I'll be there". And so it came to pass, and well enough one remembers this first visit to the sweep's house and the early morning watching for the sight of the brush out of the chimney top, and the bag of soot that was taken away. The skill of a chimney sweep is accepted if he leaves no marks behind, finger prints or worse, and in this respect Mr Thorner generally succeeded.
>
> If there was little soot and difficult to clear, as sometimes happened, when much of the firing had been wood and not coal, then a higher charge was made, and if there was a plentiful supply of soot it was less than the average fee, for soot was a not inconsiderable source of income.'

Caroline Thorner died in 1888.

Mrs Charlotte Hubbard

Mrs Charlotte Hubbard was the next tenant of number 25 where she opened a little shop to supplement her income for she was also a 'monthly nurse' which meant she looked after women in the month after childbirth. Charlotte was a widow in her thirties with four children to bring up and had moved across the road from running The Plough, which, without her husband, proved too large a task. At number 25 she was assisted by her father in law who lived with the family and worked as a labourer.(10,36) By 1900 Charlotte and her family had left.

The Rice family

James and Jane Rice were living at number 25 by 1900 which was the year that James died aged 51 leaving Jane who was ten years younger with five children to care for in the four rooms. However Harriet, the eldest, was 18 and earning a living, if a poorly paid one, making collars at home.

Walter and Lily Scales

By 1908 Walter Ernest Scales a porter at the railway station had moved to number 25 with his wife Lily and three children. They were both local people in their thirties. The Scales lived here until Lily died in 1935 in her fifties. Walter had moved out by 1938 and the Gallones had moved in.

Amcot and Emilio Gallone

We have been able to find out very little about the Gallones who we assume were born in Italy. In 1939 Amcot Gallone, who had been born in 1914, Emilio Gallone and three children lived here. They made and sold ice cream which required a licence for the council to make sure it was hygienically done. They stopped for a while during the war but in 1946 Amedeo and Giuseppe Gallone (born 1919) were re-licensed and they continued to make and sell ice cream until the late 1950s.(105) Local people called the Gallone's shop 'Joe's'.(87)

Number 25 came into joint occupation with number 27 when the Gallones left.

Number 27 East Street

In 1871 Jonathan Freeman a mariner in his thirties from Essex rented number 27 and moved in with his wife, his own son, four stepsons, and mother in law. The house with its four rooms must have bulged at the seams.

Some other occupants are listed in this table:

1881	Charlotte Colegate	widow
1891	James Westaway+2	Shoemaker
1894	John Mabbs	
1901	Charles Saunders	shipwright
1908	Edward Southgate	
1911	Edward Brown+4	labourer

The Slade family

By 1915 this was the home of William Louis Slade and his wife Edith. William served during the First World War as a private in the 20th Hussars. He came from Bedford and Edith was a Kentish girl. They had married in 1905 and were still in their twenties when they moved to the four rooms of number 27 from two rooms in Shortlands Road.(12) After the war William Slade returned to his previous work as a farm labourer. William and Edith lived at number 27 until at least 1933.

George Dutnall owned both entire terraces number 23 to 29 and 31 to 37 Since the 1920s he had lived in College Road and the council required him to make good defects so that the toilet flushed as it was *'prejudicial to health'*.

By 1947 Dennis and Sylvia Huxted were the tenants of number 27.(115) Two years later Mr Dutnall applied to have a shop front put on number 27 but did not go ahead with the plan until 1958. In the meantime we have been told that number 27 became the Labour Party branch HQ in the 1950s.

25 is combined with 27

It may have been as soon as the Gallones left that numbers 25 and 27 were combined to make a good sized ladies hairdressing salon for Mrs A. Cooper. Certainly the salon was running by 1961.

Home Crafts at number 23 and
A. Cooper hairdressers at number 25-27 in
1967

1961 advertisement for the salon

Mrs Cooper was the wife of A. W. R. Cooper, known as Roy, who came to Sittingbourne from Norfolk in 1954 as a jewellery shop manager and later opened his own shop at 27 High Street then moved to number 45 High Street. (HSI)

The salon continued here until 1976 when it moved to the High Street, upstairs above Mr Cooper's jewellery shop. At that point 25/27 became part of Homecrafts. When Homecrafts returned to being only at number 23, Videomart was the new tenant at 25/27 (definitely 1982-84 Goad) where videos could be rented. From 1985 25/27 was vacant and still empty in 1995.

Number 29 East Street

Some of the inhabitants of number 29:

1871	Henry Houting+6	brickfield labourer
1881	Mary Ann Harlow	widow
1891	Edward Houghton+1	labourer

It was Henry Pittock, who already ran a successful butcher's shop in the High Street at numbers 95-97 who opened a branch in this modest building.(HSI) He very soon realized it was not going to prosper and announcements in the local paper in March 1894 record that Herbert Carter bought the business lately carried on by Mr. H. Pittock, and *'will continue to supply the best New Zealand beef and mutton and the lowest possible prices for cash'*. Years later Henry Pittock opened up shop at 151 East Street, a far larger building where business flourished.

By December 1894 it was another member of the Carter family, Edgar, who *'thanked his numerous customers for their kind support in the past and hoped in the future to receive a larger share of their patronage'*. Edgar had been running a grocery in Epps Road when the 1891 census was taken and was in his thirties.

By 1899 the shop had been taken over by a chain of butcheries – the 'Colonial Meat Store'. Nobody lived in the house for a while. However, even this chain of shops could not make a go of it in this little building and by 1908 number 29 had come full circle and become once more a private dwelling, the home of Alfred Boorman a widowed jobbing gardener, his daughter Maud and three grandchildren. Members of the Boorman family continued to live here into the early 1960s as recorded by the electoral register.

Number 29 was then briefly used as the premises of the Thanet Driving School who left in 1970.(121)

A takeaway shop

By 1975 this was 'Barbecue Takeaway' and this was soon followed by many years of the 'Golden House Chinese Takeaway' through the 1980s and then 'Lee's Takeaway' which was also Chinese.(121)

Home Crafts at number 23, Videomart at 25/27 and Golden House at 29, in 1985

A private home again

Number 29 was converted, along with the rest of the terrace, back to a private home by 2005.

BAYFORD SOUTH FIELD
On the north side of East Street
Michael H Peters

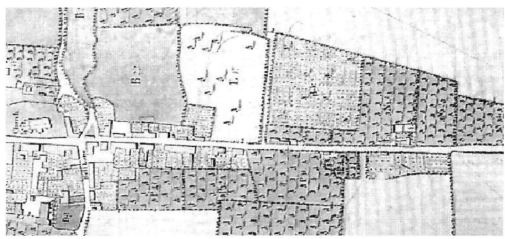

1791 map by Thomas Yeakell

In the 1870s Canon Scott Robertson, writing about our town, mentioned Bayford South Field, some of which appears on this map which was produced in 1791 by Thomas Yeakell *'Surveyor to His Majesty'*.

The Canon was referring to a map of Bayford Manor, dated 1590. At the time of his writing the map was owned by George Smeed, to whom surely no reader of this series (or indeed anyone who takes an interest in our town's local history) needs any introduction.

The above extract of the 1791 map shows the main road, eastwards from St Michael's church – clearly identified at the left edge.

Eastwards from the principal crossroads of the town the main road, since the Canon's time, has been known as East Street. Beyond that, logically, the main thoroughfare bears the name Canterbury Road.

This extract does not show the entirety of Bayford South Field, but it gives an idea of the layout of the southern portion, a couple of centuries after Mr Smeed's old map was produced. This part of the field was still within the Bayford estate owned in 1791 by William Drake. Very likely William was a forbear of John Drake whom we encountered at Brenchley House and the former George Inn.(HSI, street numbers 37 and 75)

Pointing northwards from the middle of this extract is what the Canon calls West's Lane, though in his day it had been renamed Orchard Lane – known now to us as West Lane – confusingly because it is at the east end of the old town centre. Helpfully, the Canon records that, in 1574, John West had a house there.

We regret that the Canon was unable to tell us more about the three holdings of *Robert Blak, John Calett* and *Mr Farrel,* on whose land the five houses on the 1590 map were built.

It is by chance that the map above produced 200 years later, also shows six houses, but they are not those noted by the Canon on the 1590 map, because, in that stretch of the street – there is no gap for the *'long row of palings'* which he mentions.

At the left of the extract, beside the winding lane (Crown Quay Lane) is the carrot-shaped Long Meadow. Beside that is the roughly square Ship Meadow (just over four acres) with a chunk taken out of the bottom left corner on which the almshouses were built maybe about two centuries before this map came out.

Incidentally, by 1909, the Ordnance Survey plan tells us, Long Meadow and the Ship Meadow had become brickworks. The site was connected by tramways to the Wills and Packham brickyard at Crown Quay and, by another line following the route of our present-day Princes Street, the track was connected to the goods yard beside the main railway and ran on towards the creek at Milton.

Shown on the 1791 plan, eastwards of Ship Meadow, is another parcel of similar size, dotted with trees, identified, rather vaguely in 1791, as 'Field by Ship Meadow' and owned at that time by a certain Mr John Friend. The Canon tells us that, in 1590, this field was called Stalkes Garden and otherwise as the Hart Garden. He adds *'the origin of the name is unknown'.* In his note, quoted below, the Canon lists successive owners of these four acres or so – a long list, spanning the 18th century and some of the 19th:

Edward Filmer
John Berry of Borden (who married John Thurbon's widow)
1728 Elizabeth Burgess (née Bradd)
Waller
Burgess
Upton Heneage Morton
(we are far from sure whether that was one person!)
Anty
Jennings
Reverend Henry Friend
Thomas Gascoyne (probably the Bapchild landowner who was church warden
1800-14)
Zachariah Blaxland and his sons Thomas and John
John Hinde (of the acquisitive family of solicitors and money-lenders
based at what used to be known as Hinde House, Milton – now bearing the
name of later owners – Burley's Flats)

In 1751, the Canon tells us it was a hop-garden and in 1835, part hops, part arable. It had been a cherry orchard too. In the middle of the 19th century, the East Street frontage was built up with numbers 61 to 79. Between the two world wars the frontage to West Lane was filled with houses and, 30 years later, most of the remainder was covered by the development known as Lime Grove.

At the bottom left-hand corner of Stalkes Garden we can see a smaller plot, mottled green, a small rectangle with one corner cut away. This parcel of land was long known as Plough Orchard, named after the inn, almost opposite, across the street. In 1840, this was rented by the job-master Ben Peters to graze his horses. We say more about old Ben in our section dealing with the buildings on the Plough Orchard site. The frontage is now occupied by numbers 51-59 East Street and much of the remainder by Victoria Mews – standing on the large yard which, for many years, occupied the space behind number 59.

Canon William A Scott Robinson

Scott Robertson's account of the various sites and premises standing along the old streets of Sittingbourne's heart in the 1870s is informative – uniquely valuable for our purpose – but not as carefully tabulated as we might wish or require. It is evident that a major source of information for the Canon must have been various old deeds, many of which seem to have been in the hands of George Smeed or his son-in-law George Hambrook Dean or perhaps Smeed's step-son Harry Greensted, the solicitor.(HSI,HSII)

It is a blessing that Scott Robertson's light duties as Rector of the thinly-populated parish of Elmley on the Isle of Sheppey, left him with sufficient spare time to indulge his interest in local history, as a result of which, for a spell of nearly 20 years, he served as Hon. Secretary of the Kent Archaeological Society and Editor of its learned annual publication Archaeologia Cantiana.

We regret that the outline history of our town that the Canon construed from those old deeds, was not filled out with more facts – more flesh on the skeletal accounts that he provides. We, who, more than a century later, have to struggle with his work, would have been helped had Scott Robertson made use of the street numbers which had been applied to all our streets around 1870; evidently he preferred instead to refer to the buildings by the names of the occupiers or the trade or profession practised there. No publication of his beloved Kent Archaeological Society these days would pass muster with so few references, but since he was extracting information from private deeds, perhaps he was being deliberately discreet.

We do appreciate too that the information given in ancient deeds was often vague – sufficient for the parties at the time to understand and recognise but rather a challenge – a puzzle – for historians hundreds of years later.

Consequently, just as the Canon had to construe, sometimes, which properties were referred to in the old deeds, we have to do the same in our examination of his writings. Sometimes this is a challenge, sometimes a hopeless task. Not every occupier to whom he refers appears anywhere else in the public record – or in those few private ones of the period to which we have access.

Nevertheless, setting aside our gripes, we are grateful to Canon Scott Robertson for all his diligence – without him the various accounts setting out our town's earlier history, prior to the tabulation of the public record in the 19th century, would, of necessity, be even more short of information – far more general and vague.

The worthy Canon wrote separately about the south side of the street; so do we.

Numbers 31-45, Terry's Square, and 47-57 East Street

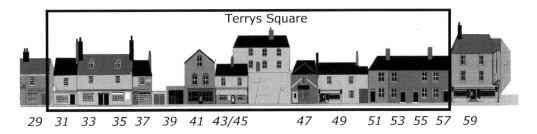

These properties on several adjoining sites are grouped together here because, some of them were in joint ownership or occupation at one time or another.

In 1840, the four small parcels of land occupied by the premises which, years later, were numbered 31, 33, 35 and 37 then belonged to one Thomas Gilbert. There were a surprisingly large number of men named Thomas Gilbert living in Kent in 1841 but none lived in Sittingbourne and so we cannot say more about our Mr Gilbert.

Scott Robertson tells us that, before 1760, the property was owned by George Savin. His French name suggests that perhaps Mr Savin was a Huguenot refugee or of that descent. He was followed by Edward Swiffinton and then 'Widow Budds' before Mr Gilbert acquired it.

Significantly the tithe schedule describes each of these four properties as *'part of house and yard'*. This indicates that, at some time previously, the four had been a single dwelling – perhaps Widow Budds and her predecessors lived there. Numbers 33 and 35 seem to be about 300 years old and appear to have been one house, to which the structures on each side – on parcels 250 and 247 – would have been, at one time, merely attachments.

Number 31 no longer exists. In its final form, it was a modest single-storey structure which had been built in the late 1940s to replace an earlier cottage shown as parcel 250 on the tithe map of 1840. The site has been cleared to widen the alley leading to the back of the adjacent terrace, numbered 23-29. Most of this back land has now been developed as Olivia's Mews, approached by the widened alley, which is now bridged by the new dwelling now identified as 33a East Street.

The ground floor of 33 is Barclay's Café. The other half of the ancient building is a private dwelling divided into 35 and 35A. Attached to number 35 is number 37 – a modern three-storey house, quite narrow, built of brick in traditional style.

On the east side of that, parcel 246, was owned in 1840 by the unusually-named Edward Betts Hopper. At that time, only one house stood there – later identified as number 41. Number 39 was built later.

Edward Betts Hopper also owned a house up at the West End, in the High Street, where he had lived. His will records that, having lived in Sittingbourne, he moved, at the end of his life, to Dover.

The houses beside number 37 were demolished in recent times and the site, including the land at the back where numbers 4 and 5 Terry's Square used to be, remains a stretch of uneven open ground, part of which is used by a van company, whose premises in St Michael's Road are adjacent – or as lawyers might put it: 'contiguous'.

On the site eastwards from that, on Parcel 245 of the 1840 schedule, were two dwellings 'house, cottage and garden'. The tithe map shows one building on the frontage of the site and a larger one at the back.

In 1840 according to the tithe schedule, Mr Terry was the owner and also the occupier here. Perhaps, at this point, we might remind our readers that those listed in the tithe schedule as occupiers included landlords of short-term tenants and those on service-tenancies. In 1841, according to the census, Mr Terry, a brewer, was living at 25 High Street, beside the entrance to the yard of the brewery owned by the Vallance family. They, doubtless, were his employers. Hence, we think it quite likely that Mr Terry, in 1840, had let these two dwellings, perhaps planning to use the rental income to provide his pension – in 1841 he was 60 years of age.

The photograph in the following section, covering number 47 East Street, shows buildings on part of this site – numbers 2 and 3 Terry's Square, as they were known in the early 20th century. Their style is that of the mid-19th century, making clear that they post-date the tithe schedule. They appear on the 1865/6 Ordnance Survey plan, telling us that the big single building at the back of the site, recorded here in 1840, had been demolished before that.

To complete our preliminary overview of Terry's Square, we should add that the property adjoining on the east side, parcel 244 (Plough Orchard) was owned by Betsy Milner. Her holding included numbers 47 and 49 East Street, attached to which, in the corner at the back, was a cottage known later as number 1 Terry's Square.

The new number 37 in 2019 and area of car park where Terry's Square once stood between numbers 45 and 47 (MHP)

Judging from the outline of the buildings on the tithe plan from 1840 and the Ordnance Survey plans from the 1860s to the 1960s, we believe that the ancient buildings (later numbered 43/45 and 47/9 East Street) fronting Terry's Square, survived until recent years when the site was cleared.

Part of this site is now a car park reserved for Swale Borough Council.

Hence the whole site once occupied by Terry's Square and the properties on both sides, is now used simply for parking vehicles – some from East Street and some from St Michael's Road.

We have noted, also, that the bushes and scrub on this site provide suitable accommodation for sparrows.

At the end of this section, we come to the remaining portion of the frontage of Betsy Milner's Plough Orchard, upon which now we find the terrace of four Victorian cottages numbers 51 to 57.

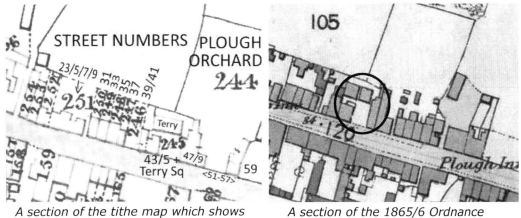

A section of the tithe map which shows Terry's Square

A section of the 1865/6 Ordnance Survey map which shows Terry's Square

Number 31 East Street

In 1871 this was the cottage home of George Ward. He was a brickfield labourer in his thirties and with him lived three people described in the census return as 'boarders.' But since one was an unmarried woman and her two children, there may have been a closer relationship to George. By 1881 widowed Mary Ann Weller lived here alone. Then for a while the house became the offices of Pepper & Ratcliff, accountants. John Edwin Ratcliff was a young accountant from Medway and soon returned there and worked as an auctioneer. (10)

Henry Herbert Hall, hairdresser

Now we come to the longest occupation of number 31 by one tenant. This was Henry Herbert Hall who had moved his hairdressing establishment for men across the road from number 18 by 1899 when he was 26. Here he remained until at least 1947.(115) Henry was born in Queenborough. For quite some years he and his wife Alice had no children and made a little extra money by taking in a boarder, this in effect left them two rooms to live in. Eventually they had a daughter Gladys, but while she was small they let a room to a nephew. Henry was still cutting hair in 1938 and still lived here until his death in 1949. (115,110) Alice had died in her sixties in 1938.

After the death of Henry Hall the cottage must have been demolished. In the photograph below, you can see the outline of its roof on the adjacent wall of number 33. The single-storey shop was erected in its place.

This 1966 image shows clearly Barrow's single storey shop, number 31, beside Barclays Café. (NMR)

Barrow the baker

The next occupant whom we know of at number 31 was the baker from the High Street, A.E. Barrow & Son, who had a branch here by 1961. We have Sheila Hepburn's memories of working at the shop during the early 1960s:

"I worked for Barrows from 1961 as a Saturday girl, and also during school holidays. I worked in both the High Street shop and the East Street shop depending on where I was needed. The East Street shop was managed by one full time permanent member of staff and a Saturday girl. When I started in 1961 my wage for a Saturday was 10s 6d with an increase every year.

In those days we were working in old money, including halfpennies. To make it easier to calculate the cost of cakes at various prices we used to take every cake at three old pence, and then add or deduct the odd halfpennies or pennies. This all had to be done in our head. In those days people would come in, and ask for a box of cakes in varying numbers, and this was an easy way of calculating the cost.

We had a break in the morning and afternoon. We were allowed to choose one fancy cake and one plain cake to eat at each break. The one 'no no' was that we were not allowed to choose a fresh cream cake.

At lunchtime we had a small electric heater which had the element on the top, and we used to boil a saucepan of potatoes on it for our lunch. There was no health and safety then.

If you worked in the High Street shop you were allowed to choose a meal from the restaurant menu. We had to wash all the removable shelves and trays in the kitchen at the back of the shop.

The advantage of working on a Saturday was that at the end of the day the doughnuts, dough buns, Chelsea buns and sultana slices, together with the rolls filled with cheese or ham, which had not been sold were given to the staff to take home as these could not be kept over the weekend."

The shop was open until at least 1997. By the millennium number 31 stood empty and so it remained until demolition in 2002 or 2003 when the rest of the terrace was converted to private housing.

The entrance to Olivia's Mews beside number 33 (BA)

Numbers 33 and 35
Eliza Allen

When first we encounter the inhabitants of number 33 the house was being rented with number 35 as a home, a shop and a bakery. Mrs Eliza Allen (née Luck) lived here renting both houses in 1871 with her three young daughters and a live-in 'servant' who in fact was a young Herbert Page, a baker from Westerham who baked the bread which Mrs Allen sold in the shop. Eliza was a Sittingbourne woman, already a widow at only 36 years old. She had advertised herself as a baker in 1870 and did so again in 1878. Nevertheless when she described herself for the 1871 census; it was rather over-optimistically, as a 'cornfactor' (ie someone who dealt in corn).

Eliza had been married to William Allen a labourer from Essex. When the 1861 census was taken he had been visiting Eliza and her brother in Sittingbourne and married Eliza later that year. They must have prospered during the short years of their marriage and somehow William acquired the money to try his hand at selling corn. However he was listed as a baker in the directories of 1862 and 1867. Sadly he died in 1868 aged just 34. By 1874 Eliza employed a man to run what had become a grocery shop for her and then by 1878 it was Stephen Terry Tong who worked for her and lived at number 35 with his wife and six children in 1881. Eliza remained at number 33 with her daughters in 1881 by then describing herself as a grocer.

The Higgins, Wall and Broads at 33 and 35 – all one family

Eliza Allen left East Street during 1882 and numbers 33 and 35 were once more occupied by one family.(N01) John Thomas Higgins a general labourer in his fifties from Eastling lived at number 33 with his wife Olive and three children whilst at 35 lived their eldest son George a labourer with his wife and baby. The women of the family ran the shop. John and Olive Higgins had formerly been in charge of The Rendezvous public house in the High Street.(HSII,77) John died in 1900 and Olive continued the shop at number 35 whilst living with her two daughters and son Albert, a house-painter, at 33.(12) Olive's shop was a sweet shop and she ran it until her death in 1924, aged 81. Her obituary notice in the local paper read:

> '1924 Death: November 17th At 33 East Street. Olive Higgins in her 82nd year Widow of John Thomas Higgins, had confectionery business in East Street for the last 43 years. She leaves two daughters; Mrs Smith of 100, East Street and Mrs Wall, and one son T. J. Higgins of London'.

Olive's daughter Annie Wall, (whose first name was actually Olive too) had lived with her mother and continued the tenancy of number 33.(N01) Annie Wall had a daughter herself, Vera who married Alec Broad in 1936, and Vera continued to run the sweet shop as her mother and grandmother had before her.(110) Vera and Alec Broad lived with Annie until she died in 1957 aged 73. Mrs Wall is remembered by Jack Brett, whose teenage years were spent across the street at the Brett family home and shop, numbers 26 and 28. Mrs Wall told Jack that she remembered when number 26 was a blacksmith's forge. During the First World War she saw many a line of pack-horse mules lined up along the street, awaiting attention to their hooves, en route to the western front in Flanders and France.

We know from council minutes of 1954 that George Dutnall of College Road then owned number 33, for, in that year, he was served with a notice to improve the building. The Broads were still here in 1963 but, by 1968, William and Sheila Irwin had moved in.(59,84,105) Here the Irwins established Barclays Café; word on the street (supposedly emanating from Mr Irwin) suggested that they chose that name for the café because Barclays bank provided the funds.

In 1974 the café was taken on by James William Price and his wife Maureen Ivy from Poplar in London. Jim, as he was known, did the cooking, Maureen was 'front of house'.(N01) Soon the café run by the folk from Poplar became popular with a large customer-base. In 1982 the advertisement for the café in the local paper read: 'OAP dinner with sweet and cup of tea £2.50. Open 7am to 3pm six days a week'. In 1986, after Mrs Price fell seriously ill, her role was taken by Shelley, the Prices' daughter who continued to work happily with her father for many years. After Jim died in 1992, Shelley, emulating the success of her parents, continue to run the café until her retirement in 2017. Following that, she let the premises to tenants who continue to run the business today.

Barclays Café in 2011 (CA)

Number 35 East Street

The Higgins did not retain number 35 along with number 33 into the 20th century. By 1895 it was Stephen Mount who fried fish here, four years later 1899 number 35 was where John Edwin Saxby had his fish and chip shop although he didn't live above it but nearby in Harold Road. Saxby continued some years longer at number 35 but by 1908 it was Stephen James Jacobs who was frying fish. Unlike Mr Saxby, Stephen Jacobs, a local man then in his fifties, moved into the four rooms of number 35 with his wife Elizabeth and daughter Mildred. Members of the Jacobs family continued to live at number 35 and run the fish shop until at least 1935.

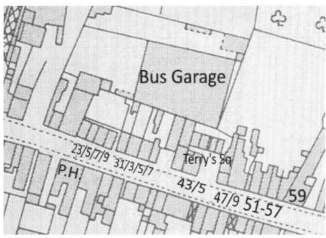
Part of the 1938 Ordnance Survey map

In 1937 the Freegard Press moved to number 35 from Banks Yard and remained until after the war when they moved to better premises in Crescent Street. Edwin Harold Freegard had set up the press and, when his three children were old enough they all worked with him. The Freegards did not live in the house but in Bell Road. The photographs of the move to East Street were taken by Harold's elder daughter Agnes, known as Bubbles. There is a full account of this business in our publication 'Sittingbourne Family Businesses.'

The Freegard Press moving to number 35 in 1937. Next door on the right is number 37.

The Freegard Press at number 35

Charles and Florence Butcher were the tenants at 35 in 1947 and may have reopened the fish shop. Iris and Leslie Goldacre who married in 1948 lived here by 1951.(121) Iris Goldacre ran the local dancing school under her maiden name of Iris Thomas. Classes were held at the Masonic Hall in Albany Street/ Road. (That section of Albany Road used to be Albany Street)

William and Florence Mount already had a florist's shop next door at number 37 and, for a few years in the 1960s, they also lived at number 35.(121)

By 1968 number 35 was vacant and then L. & M. Scott who carried out watch and clock repairs moved in as tenants, followed in 1976 by Kent Aerials.(121) Mistakenly Tunstall parish magazines for 1976 also carry an advertisement for W. Mantle Ltd gentleman's hairdresser at 35 – but he was at number 37. The Mantles also had a shop at 33 William Street. Perhaps the Scott's part of the premises was upstairs.

In 1982 number 35 was empty and then in 1984 Royale Furniture was tenanting 35 and expanded into 37 the following year. This was followed in the early 1990s by Technic Microwave Service. By 1995 number 35 was vacant before it took on new life as The Cavern tattoo shop.

By 2005 number 35 it had been converted back to a private house as it remains today.

Numbers 37 and 39 East Street
The Barnes family at 37

By 1851 the Barnes family were established on this site when it was a two-up two-down cottage; Robert Barnes ran a butcher's shop here with his wife Mary Ann and son Daniel whom he had trained in the trade. Robert was then 57, a Sittingbourne man born and bred who previously had his home and shop at the other end of town – Valenciennes, West Street. By 1861 son Daniel had improved the range of the shop and described himself as grocer and pork butcher whilst still working with his father. The house was a hive of activity for daughters Susan and Agnes had their own dressmaking business at home too. Robert Barnes died in 1869 aged 75 but had retired from the business sometime before his death. Directory entries from 1862 until 1870 list Daniel selling groceries, accompanied in 1866 and 1867 by Agnes with her dressmaking. In 1870 Agnes married and moved away leaving Daniel, who had married in 1863, living and working at the family home with his wife Sarah and their child. Daniel died young in 1871 aged 40; it seems that his widow and child then went elsewhere.

The rebuilt number 37 with the open ground beside it in 2018 (CB)

The Barretts at 39

The Barrett family were already established at number 39 in 1841 when William Barrett, a local man, was recorded in the census return as a 50 year old labourer with his wife Mary and three children. William died in 1856 and Mary then supported herself by keeping a few cows and selling the milk. This we know from the 1861 census return where she described herself as a cow-keeper, which meant she had a few cows and sold their milk at the door. The backyards of the terrace adjoined a field (tithe parcel 255) where perhaps the Barrett's cows could graze, though there was also a little space for a cow-shed beside and behind the house, in which case, provender could be brought in. Mary Barrett was then 69, a country woman from Marden, who had the help of her son, Walter, a labourer, and her granddaughter. To add to the household income there were two lodgers and indeed Mary had taken lodgers before her husband died.(6) The household changed considerably over the following decade; although Mary still kept cows Walter was married and his wife Fanny and five children made up the household. Old Mary lived on until 1875 and, after her death, Walter continued to keep the cows and made extra money by being a carter too. He described himself in directories as a dairyman.(39,43)

Walter Barrett, dairyman, 39 East Street

After Mrs Barnes vacated number 37, the Barretts took on those premises and, for many years, held both. Perhaps, at this time, the buildings were reconstructed or altered. In the census returns of 1881 and 1891 number 39 East Street does not appear, but the census tended to record dwellings rather than commercial premises where nobody lived. In 1901 and 1911 it was listed as the Barretts' shop.

In the following section, covering number 41, we have a photograph showing the front of number 39 – as it was in the First World War – a single-storey building, alongside number 37 which, at that time, had two storeys.

By 1901 Walter Barrett, then 60, was delivering milk and so he continued for many more years, still having an entry in the 1927 directory as a dairyman. In the following year he died, aged 90.

Not long after Walter's death, number 39 was demolished. The bus company acquired the premises and number 41 next door. The bus garage was built at the back with its entrance over the site of number 39. (see number 41)

It seems the shop at number 37 continued as a dairy although all that we know of this phase of its history is that in 1933 Harry Godden and Annie Richardson lived there and then by 1938 William and Mary Polhill kept the shop. By 1945 George and Margaret Hann were the tenants and George Hann delivered milk from number 37 until at least 1953.

It was around this time that we believe number 37 was demolished and rebuilt as a single-storey lock-up shop.

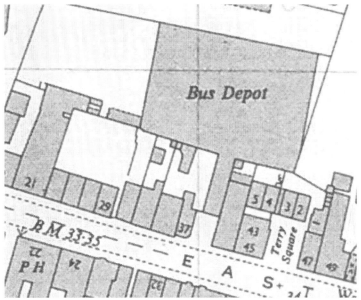

A section of the 1960 Ordnance Survey map

The Mounts at number 37

From the 1950s to at least 1983 number 37 was a florist's shop run by Norman and Pam Mount. During the 1960s the Mounts also had a shop at 49 West Street. Eventually they relocated their business to the Bell Centre in Bell Road which was later demolished.

This photograph shows number 37 when the original house had gone and the lock-up shop had been built. Here the Mounts had their florists shop. The roofline of the previous building can be seen on the adjacent wall of number 35

In 1991 number 37 was vacant but, by 2000, was in use as Thatch, a ladies hairdresser.

The record of occupancy and the fact that number 37 has been recently built suggests it was demolished in 2003 or 2004 and the new house was built by 2005 when Goad lists it as a dwelling.

A new building at 37 East Street in 2019 and the area up to where 39 to 45 and Terry's Square once stood

Numbers 39 and 41 East Street
Edward Betts Hopper

We recorded at the start of this section that in 1840 the site of numbers 39 and 41 belonged to a well-off gentleman named Edward Betts Hopper who had left for lodgings in Dover probably in the hope of improving his health but there he died in 1841 still owning his two Sittingbourne properties.

Mr Hopper was widowed and his sister Abigail Farley inherited his High Street house and the income from an investment of £1,000. The child of a friend was left a similar amount of money. This house in East Street was bequeathed to Thomas Pilcher of London, the husband of Hopper's niece Harriet; he rented it out.

Willis Simons, shoemaker

In our research into Sittingbourne shops the unusually named Willis Simons, a shoemaker, has popped up all over the place – in the High Street, in East Street and in West Street. This can partly be explained by the fact that there were two Willis Simons, father and son with the same trade. If you search the 1871 census for all of England on Ancestry you discover just one other Willis Simons. He too made boots but does not come into our story. This was poor old Willis then in his seventies, languishing in the Orsett Union Workhouse in Essex. He was the father of our Willis senior and probably never came to Sittingbourne.

Our Willis Simons senior who had been brought up in Essex arrived in Sittingbourne from Crayford and took up residence and opened shop in East

Street in 1861 when he was 35, (we can tell when the family arrived from the birth places of his children given in the 1861 census return). Soon he and the family were living at number 41. He must have been a good shoemaker and a good business man for by 1866 he had another shop at 86 High Street which he retained into the 1870s.(HSII)

Willis Simons directory entry of 1867 shows that he was also selling marine stores alongside his boots and shoes. The household then consisted of Willis, his wife Sarah, eldest son Willis junior in his twenties (a bootmaker who still lived with his parents in East Street in 1871 working with his father), two younger children and one live-in worker.

Ten years on the household had changed – the two younger sons, Alfred and Walter, were working from home as general dealers, whilst their sister Annie was a dressmaker. Their mother Sarah continued the shop and Willis senior continued to make and mend shoes and boots. Willis junior was living at 86 High Street and running the shop there with his wife Elizabeth. They had two sons of whom the eldest by family tradition was, of course, named Willis. By 1901 Willis junior and his family had moved home and shoemaking business to West Street. (see West Street 60-62)

At number 41, East Street the household remained the same in 1901 and Willis senior was still making boots at the age of 77. By the time the 1903 directory was printed Willis had given up on the boots and joined in the dealing in second-hand furniture with his two younger sons Alfred and Walter, who had never left home.

W.G Matthews in his account of Sittingbourne during his childhood gives us the interesting information that Willis Simons was a Mormon or member of the Church of Latter Day Saints.(69) In fact he was the leader of the local branch as the 1908 Directory shows:

'A few members of this sect reside in the district, and worship at the Oddfellows Meeting room, Pembury Street, Sunday Services 2.30 pm and 6.30 pm. Elder, Mr Willis Simons of 41 East Street.'

Hubbard also recalls number 41 for us:

"The old property where an aged, bearded man named Simons carried on a marine store and business for many years is now the office of the Maidstone and District Bus Company'.(70)

In 1910 a sale notice for number 41 was placed in the local paper but without giving the name of the owner, nor is there a notice telling whether it sold. The census the following year tells us that number 41 had seven rooms. Willis lived on at number 41 until 1913 when he died aged 89.

Fred Moore, a man with a finger in many pies

The family who moved into number 41 when the Simons left were the Moores. It seems that during the old age of Willis Simons Fred Moore had managed his business. A look at the 1911 census return (when the Simons were still at number 41) reveals that Fred Moore described himself as a 'manager to a dealer'. His two eldest sons Fred junior and Norman also worked in the marine stores business with him. Fred and his wife Fenella had seven sons and three daughters and it must have been a relief to move out of the five-roomed 15 East Street into the large number 41.(see number 15) Moore was a Portsmouth man, born in 1869, who would have known all about marine stores and all the children except the youngest, then two years old, had been born in Portsmouth too.

Fred was a man of drive and ability and was able to take on the Simons business and add enormously to it. He added buying and selling waste products such as rags and bones to the marine store business. By 1919 he was also running a successful motor-haulage business. Over the years he placed numerous advertisements in the local paper. During the First World War he emphasised the wide range of what he was willing to collect – *'F. Moore will collect scrap iron, tailor's cuttings, bones, metal, jars, paper, bags etc'.*

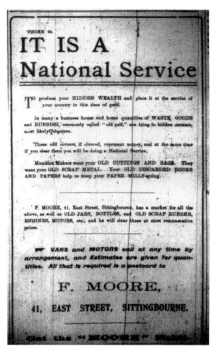

1917 advertisement

Moore employed a clerk, who because of the war, had to be a female:

'1916 Wanted Lady Clerk knowledge of type-writing preferred F. Moore, Marine Stores, East Street.'

A new maid was frequently required by his wife who may have been a difficult employer: *'Respectable maid must be strong and willing, 41 East Street'.* After the war the family could afford to employ a cook too.(N01)

Then there were rabbit skins to be bought and sold:

'Messrs F. Moore & Sons 41 East Street. Sell your rabbit skins direct to F. Moore & Sons. Prices paid for skins. Tame Rabbits 6d. 1/- per skin Wild Rabbits 4d 8d. Note our lorries will visit all streets of Sittingbourne and Milton Regis on Boxing Day.'

In 1919 the advertisement was:

'Remember the war is over. In a comparatively short time prices for all sorts of "old pelf" will drop considerably. Therefore turn out your odd corners at once. Don't wait for spring cleaning. Best prices paid F. Moore & Sons 41, East Street.'

Fred Moore clearly had excellent wheeling and dealing abilities and he thrived during the war as well as after it when he had a good line in government surplus stock. One of his 1921 advertisements offered *'Bargains for farmers & others. Messrs Moore & Sons offering waterproof covers, for ricks, wagons, lodges in all sizes about ¼ ordinary price. These wonderful bargains can be seen at 41, East Street'.*

Fred Moore's premises at 39/41 East Street. We believe that this photograph was taken during the First World War when Fred employed girls to collect and then sort the scrap materials which he was dealing in. It shows number 39 as a single-storey building and, at the left-hand edge, number 37 which at that time was still two-storeyed.

By then he had at least three lorries and was generous in using them to help others less fortunate than himself: *'F. Moore wishes to thank all the friends who so kindly helped at the Fete at Wormshill treat to children. Old folks outing by F. Moore and Son'*

Soon Fred was the proud owner of both a large and a small *'Motor Char-a-Banc'*. The large one carried over 30 passengers. The council approved new buildings at the rear of number 41 to house the vehicles.

It was in 1921 that the council approved plans for the building of a new store of up to the minute design for Mr Moore and his sons on the other side of the road at 18-20 East Street. For reasons which are now unclear, the family only used the new store for three years and then rented it out. It seems that the new shop was where their new butchery department opened although the advertisements do not make clear where different items were on sale.

> *'New departure at Moore's Market – This week end the special feature at Moore's Market will be the opening of a butchers department where English and colonial meat will be sold at greatly below existing town prices Before purchasing elsewhere Visit Moore's Market.'*

By now motor cycles and second-hand furniture were on offer at Moore's and it seems that the new shop was named 'Moore's Market.'

The electoral register for 1922 records five of the family Clarence, Fenella, Frederick, Lynn and Roland Moore living at 41.

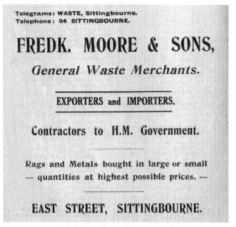

1927 advertisement

Fred died young in 1928 in his fifties and the business did not long survive his demise. Fred junior advertised the marine store and waste collection in the 1930 directory, but a year later the many Moores had left East Street for pastures new.

We can see what the substantially sized number 41 looked like when Maidstone and District Bus Company used it for their offices around the 1950s. The alley between numbers 37 and 39 survived: the buses drove over the site of number 39.

Maidstone and District Bus Company at 39/41

In 1931 the Moores moved out of number 39/41 and were replaced by the Maidstone and District Bus Company who applied straight away to the council for permission to put up a new shop front. Downstairs was to be used as their offices and behind there was plenty of space for the buses to be garaged and serviced. The company let the upstairs of number 41 as residential accommodation into the 1950s as the electoral register records.

In addition to their regular services the company ran frequent excursions and holidays which they advertised in the local paper.

The Home Guard Unit formed by employees at the Sittingbourne Bus Depot during the Second World War

Chairman, Directors and Snt Management at bi-annual inspection of the Sittingbourne bus depot in the mid 1950s. The building in the background was L. Hales coachbuilding and car maintenance workshops – he had a showroom that fronted on East Street

Aerial view from the north showing the large bus garage and parking area in the centre of the photograph in 1980. East Street runs left to right along the top of the image and there is access from St Michael's Road which can be seen at the bottom

In 1958 council minutes record that an application for a new access and exit to the bus garage and new offices were being considered. This therefore is the likely date of demolition of number 39. The bus garage was actually rebuilt in 1960 and remained here until 1990.

Confectionery and photography at 43

David William Williams lived here by 1870. Born in Plymouth he described himself as a 'hard confectioner'. Presumably this implied he made hard sweets such as boiled ones rather than fudge! He possessed other skills too; when the 1861 census was taken Williams was living in Dover where he earned his living as a photographer and ten years later, at the age of 59, he had got his studio set up at number 43 East Street whilst his wife no doubt kept the sweet shop going. There were six children to support. The eldest son, Arthur, was 17 when the 1871 census was taken but had no job, having been in trouble with the law a few months earlier:

> 'At the police court Arthur Williams a lad of 16 whose parents keep a shop in East Street was charged with breaking into a shop near the railway station at stealing 1s 6d in farthings, 15 old penny pieces, two loaves, a Dutch cheese, two bottles of sweets, five bottles of pickles, 2lbs of tea, and 1lb of tobacco, valued £2 the property of George Mallett on the 22nd December. The evidence was not considered sufficiently conclusive to go to a jury but the lad was committed for three months hard labour, for being found in the shop for an unlawful purpose.' (N03)

It was a collection of random objects which had come to hand to steal. David Williams lived on until 1881 but does not seem to have prospered as a photographer for in the year that he died he again described himself as a 'hard confectioner.'

Confectionery continued to be sold at number 43 by Williams successor James Dean, a much younger man who hailed from Halstow.(9)

Number 45
Charles and Charlotte Harris, greengrocers at 45

By 1870 Charles Harris had opened a greengrocery at number 45. The following year he described himself in the census as a market gardener. He was in his thirties with a wife and four children and had been born at Lynsted. In 1876 Charles died aged 40 leaving his wife Charlotte to continue the shop which she did until 1879 when she married John Masters who lived at number 65. She moved in with him taking her children.

Numbers 43 and 45 are combined again

By 1890 one **Henry Hills** rented both 43 and 45 to sell grocery and fruit and vegetables. He and his wife Eliza were locals and, having the extra space of number 45, took in a couple of boarders to help make the books balance. Henry died in 1907 aged 65 and Eliza moved out. After his death the East Kent Gazette advertised number 45 *'For sale small general business 45 East Street stock & fixtures & effects at low inclusive price'* it added the interesting information that this was a double fronted shop. However it was not sold quickly. One Edward Bennett moved in briefly but in 1909 the shop was advertised as to let again. A single woman in her fifties from Sussex, Phoebe Fermor, took on the sweet shop and the living accommodation of 43 and 45 and briefly enjoyed the freedom of roaming six rooms on her own. But within the year she too had left and at last a couple moved in who were to live here for some years. This was Ashton Sidney Goodhew and his wife Eliza. They changed the shop from sweets to greengrocery and made a go of it were still here in 1924. Ashton Goodhew lived on until 1972 when he died aged 90 and is buried in Sittingbourne Cemetery.

Ashton Goodhew's memorial

By 1926 Victor A. Winn, a Sittingbourne man born in 1897 and brought up in Bayford Road, ran a tobacconist and confectionery shop at 45.(12) Throughout the 1930s Harry and Sarah Wickenden lived here continuing with confectionery and they were still here in 1951. As we can see from their advertisement below they also had a shop at number 4 High Street.

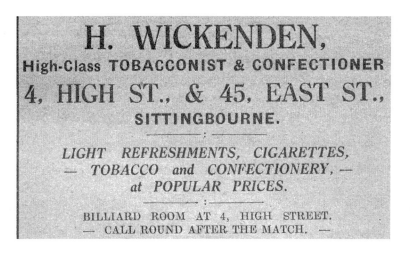

H. WICKENDEN,

High-Class TOBACCONIST & CONFECTIONER

4, HIGH ST., & 45, EAST ST.,

SITTINGBOURNE.

LIGHT REFRESHMENTS, CIGARETTES,
— TOBACCO and CONFECTIONERY, —
at POPULAR PRICES.

BILLIARD ROOM AT 4, HIGH STREET.
— CALL ROUND AFTER THE MATCH. —

The Wickendens had moved away by 1958.

Launderette at 43 and 45

That year council minutes record that a change of use of numbers 43 and 45 from confectioner to launderette was approved. The facilities of this up to the minute establishment were considered worthy of a detailed description in the town guide of 1964:

> 'Customers bring their laundry to the launderette where there are 12
> washing machines, two spin driers and two hot air tumble driers. The
> charge is 2s 10d for wash, soap and spin dry (9lb load) and 6d extra for

the use of the tumble drier giving an iron-dry finish. Each customer's wash is done individually in 26 gallons of soft water. Customers unable to spare the time can leave their laundry to be done by the courteous and helpful staff. (6d extra)

We realise that parking is a problem but motorists can pull up and drop their wash in and collect later, Blankets can be washed for the modest charge of 1s 9d, a beautiful, soft, fluffy finish being obtained. Open daily 8.45 to 5.30pm. Early closing Wednesday.'

We believe that a Mr Middleton ran the launderette in the 1960s. His wife worked for the East Kent Gazette and they lived in Whitehall Road. Later the business was run by the Parker brothers who had other similar businesses.

1965 advertisement

The final businesses to be run at 43 and 45 are given in this table. The dates do not imply that this is the only year or years that the business was there.

1972	Sheila's Ladies Fashions
1973-1982	Disco Carpet Specialist
1984	The Floor Shop
1985	The Way to Good Health

Perhaps the last occupier was Howfield the craftsmen-locksmiths from Canterbury – who also had a branch in Maidstone. By 1995 the property was vacant and, by 2000, it was demolished.

Terry's Square

This early 20th century image shows, on the right, the side door to number 47, with flanking windows. What where those long poles doing? Clearly they held each end of the washing line. One of them is long enough to have been used by a knocker-up. In some towns, in the 19th century, men were employed, by major employers, to tour the streets, early in the morning, tapping on bedroom windows to wake up those who ought to be getting ready for work. We do not know if such a service was provided in Sittingbourne or Milton. Tucked away at the back was number 1 Terry's Square. The more modern 2 and 3 Terry's Square are towards the left. The Ordnance Survey plans show a tunnel between numbers 3 and 4, in which, perhaps were their respective entrance doors. That to number 2 was probably at the side, facing number 1. Number 5 was built hard against the side boundary so, unlike the others, its entrance may have been on the front. (TG)

The five cottages which made up the housing of Terry's Square were never good homes. They were basic two-up two-down for the poor to rent.

Though Mr Terry owned part of the site in 1840, Terry's Square did not acquire its name officially until much later – perhaps when the old structure at the back was replaced by four cottages, which, for some reason, were left out when street numbers were applied to East Street.

As late as 1881 the cottages were still un-numbered so we cannot say who lived in which one.

The much older cottage, tucked away in the back corner, on the east boundary, eventually became number 1. It was attached to the frontage building later known as 47/9. In 1840, as we have pointed out already, both of these properties were owned, not by Mr Terry, but by Betsy Milner. In later years, they were in the same ownership as the rest of Terry's Square, but we have (not yet) found out when this happened.

There were instances of overcrowding in the square. At number 1 in 1901 Frank Hunt, his wife and niece lived in three rooms with a lodger with a wife and two children in the fourth room. At number 2 in 1911 Alfred Hills, a brickfield labourer, from Rodmersham, lived with his five children, his sister and her child.

The cottages seem to have been badly built – or neglected – or both. Certainly, by the 1920s, council minutes record the concern of the sanitary inspector and medical officer of health that the dwellings had become unfit for human habitation. Notice was served on the owner that numbers 1, 2 and 3 were to have damp walls made sound within three weeks. In addition, during those three weeks, number 2 must have the roof, the scullery and the ceilings repaired and the toilet made efficient.

Matters did not improve much and, in 1933, the sanitary inspector recommended that the cottages should be demolished. None were in good repair either inside or out and the communal backyard was in a bad state. Windows at the back were too small. The ceilings were low and the floors needed work. The council served notice on the owner's agent, Laurence Smeed of Crescent Street, requiring demolition. However this did not happen. Smeed sold the dwellings, presumably for next to nothing, to Montague Easton (who owned John Peters and Sons in the High Street). Easton had plans to hold off demolition by improvements. So council minutes of 1934 record that he proposed making number 1 part of the adjoining 47 East Street, combining 4 and 5 Terry's Square into one house and improving numbers 2 and 3.

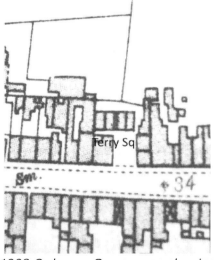

1908 Ordnance Survey map showing Terry's Square

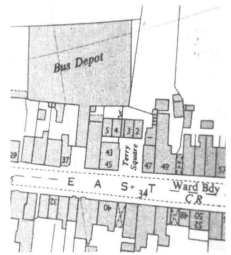

1960 Ordnance Survey plan showing Terry's Square and the changes at 37 and 39 caused by the bus depot.

The table shows heads of household at various dates

	Number 1	Number 2	Number 3	Number 4	Number 5
1891	Frank Hunt	James Newman	Philip Heathfield	empty	empty
1901	Frank Hunt	Albert Hart	William Cox		empty
1908-11	Mary Ann Hunt	Alfred Hills	Thomas Wilson	Hannah Bills	
1922	Harry Godden	Alfred Hills	Sidney Dutnall	Norman Moore	
1926	Harry Godden	George Parker	Sidney Dutnall		
1933	Harry Burlton	Alfred Hills	Sidney Dutnall	Eric Read	Matthew Powell
1938	Peter Mockler	Walter Ralph	Sidney Dutnall		Alfred Burleton
1945		John Goldsmith	William Spickett		Harry Burlton
1953	Elsie Mockler		James Mackie		
1960-75				Mary Fletcher	Mary Fletcher

The cottages were demolished in the 1960s and the eastern part of the site was taken over by the council in the 1970s when they moved into Swale House.

Numbers 47 and 49

Forming the last part of Terry's square, enclosing it on the east side and fronting the street, was the building later numbered 47 and 49. It appears in the earlier photograph, which shows the back part butted onto number 1 Terry's Square.

In the 1865/6 map, number 49 can be seen abutting number 47. The building was large, extending a long way to the rear – to the back boundary of the adjacent Terry's Square.

As mentioned already, the Ordnance Survey plans from 1860s to 1960s suggest to us that this structure, outlined on the 1840 tithe plan, survived until not very long ago. In 1840, it marked the south-west corner of Betsy Milner's tithe parcel 244. In those days, there were no other dwellings on the frontage – numbers 51-57 were built later. The open frontage provided access to the Plough Orchard – which extended to about half an acre (about a quarter of a hectare). Evidently that name derived from the inn across the street. Doubtless, at one time, a publican at the Plough had the use of this site – perhaps to graze post-horses.

The tithe plan shows another building – at the east end of that frontage. Since the tithe schedule lists just one house and garden here in 1840, and armed with the preceding photograph – showing windows and doors in the side wall of number 47, we must suppose that this other structure was an outbuilding – perhaps a coach-house and stable and/or shelter for animals grazed in the orchard – and provender for them.

So far, we know nothing more of the freeholder Betsy Milner but we know quite a lot about her tenant, Benjamin Peters. He was a great-great-great-uncle of Michael Peters, one of our contributors.

Knowing that, in 1841, Ben was living, in some comfort, with his family at Hillside/Hill House (known later as 74 London Road and now as Beaumont Guest House) we may assume that the occupier of number 49 was a short-term tenant of Ben's – perhaps an employee on a service tenancy. As a Van Proprietor, Ben would have employed staff to drive and look after his vans and horses. We might thus deduce that the occupier of what became 47/49 East Street had responsibility for the horses grazed at the back and probably, if male, he was a van-driver. For more about this, see also 74 East Street.

In later years, Ben, clearly an energetic entrepreneur, became perhaps the first licensee of the Fountain and Railway Hotel in Station Place – now known as the Fountain of Ale.(77)

The preceding photograph gives us an indication that number 47 was old by 1851 when young Mrs Matilda Hadlow whose husband was a waterman (away on his barge that census night) lived there with her two young children and her mother. A Sittingbourne labourer Henry Broadbridge was the tenant in 1861 with his wife and four children.

Sarah Spillett

The first time we hear of a shop at 47 is in 1871 when the census gives us the name of the tenant, Sarah Spillett, then 65, who was a general dealer. We can imagine her buying and selling second-hand goods in the little shop.

Mrs Mary Fairbrass

By 1874 Mrs Mary Fairbrass was the shopkeeper at 47 she is listed in the 1878 directory as 'shopkeeper'. She perhaps continued old Sarah's dealing. Three years earlier, already widowed, she had sold toys from her Canterbury home to support herself and her young son. Mary was still living here in 1881.

A third widow, Emma Petley is the next tenant we know of and she had three adult children with her living in the three rooms of number 47 in 1891. They were not running a shop.

We know the Bone family lived here in 1895 for an announcement appeared in the local paper in 1895: 'Death, Bone, 5th August, at 47 East Street, Sarah Ann, wife of William Bone, aged 57'. Bill Bone was a farm labourer and the couple had previously lived in Frederick Street.(10)

The 1901 census lists Margaret Baker a married woman from Sheffield living in just two of the rooms. It also lists James William Heap who actually lived in Rock Road with his wife and three young children. But in fact Mrs Baker and Mr Heap would have met every day for James had his modest tailoring business in the other two rooms of the building.(40) The census confirms that he worked for himself and not for another tailor. He was a Yorkshireman from Holmfirth and his wife came from Suffolk. Their stay in Sittingbourne does not seem to have been long or successful for by 1908 the directory records number 47 as 'East Street Bazaar' run by Misses Fryer and Beeching. We have not been able to discover anything about them and, by 1911, the building was empty.

Absalom and Florence Beaney had moved in by 1922. Absalom had grown up in Murston the son of a general dealer. Manuel Beaney and his wife Mary then took on the tenancy. Manuel was a horse dealer and his wife Mary dealt in second hand clothes. They remained throughout the 1920s.

Monty Bunting

Briefly in the 1930s there was a butcher's shop at 47 which was that of Montague Arthur Bunting. Monty had been born in the town in 1888.

Elsie Mockler

Elsie Mockler lived here from the 1940s; whether she had a shop we have not discovered. By 1951 she was gone.(105)

Mr Hall

Mr B. Hall was the final person to have a grocery shop here, which opened in 1954 and which, council minutes record, was licensed to sell milk. The business closed down in the early 1960s.(58)

This 1965 photograph shows number 47 when Mr Hall's business had closed down. By this time, the premises had been empty for some two years (EKG)

The building was demolished by 1968 when Goad records a gap here.

49 East St

Number 49 no longer stands; its site, adjoining number 51, forms a part of the Swale Council car park.

A home and a bakery
The Cooper family

The numerous Cooper family was established at number 49 by 1851. Head of the household was John, a baker born in Milstead. Then there were his wife

Mary Ann, son Henry who ran the grocery side of the business, daughters Mary Ann and Maria, younger sons William and Fred and baby Harriet. Next door at number 51 were son John and his wife. There was plenty of the room behind the house for a large outbuilding to bake in.

It appears that it was the Coopers who started the bakery at number 49. They had moved in when the house was new, during the 1840s from further along the street at number 111. Surprisingly, before this move John senior was a gardener.(5) He saw an opportunity for himself and at least one of his sons in the expanding town and must have learned to bake well.

The 1861 census return shows the bakery flourished and could employ three Cooper sons; William, Frederick and John junior. Unmarried daughter Maria no doubt helped in the business too.

The family prospered and during the 1860s John Cooper senior and his wife moved to Goodnestone Road leaving the bakery and number 49 in the hands of their second son Fred.

It is the probate index of 1868 which gives us the Goodnestone Road address for that is the year old John died aged 66. The executors of his will were his eldest son John and George Payne the Sittingbourne brewer. Old John's effects were valued at over £700. His widow then moved into one of the new houses the family had purchased which was 183 East Street (later renumbered as Canterbury Road.)(8)

Numbers 47 and the bakery at number 49 probably around 1910

Eldest son John gave up baking and traded as a fruiterer whilst living at 179 East Street another of the houses the family had bought which was later part of Canterbury Road. Brother William had married and had his own bakery business in Chatham by this time.

So brother Fred lived at 49 with his wife two little daughters a nursemaid and an assistant for the bakery.(8,31) The electoral register for 1880 records that

Fred still resided here but had acquired ownership of the family's houses at numbers 179,181 and 183 East Street.

By 1881 Fred and his wife Elizabeth had six children. That year Fred sold the house and business to Thomas Baldock possibly in order to travel to America – his brother Henry had emigrated and remained in Massachusetts for the rest of his life. But if Fred and his family did go they were homesick and came back for the 1891 census return lists Fred, already retired at the age of 46 living comfortably in Albany Road. He died in 1904.

Thomas F. Baldock

So in 1882 Thomas Frederick Baldock a baker, confectioner and grocer in his thirties took on the shop and moved in to 49 with his wife Clara, three children, brother William who worked as his assistant, another assistant who boarded with the family and a servant. Tom Baldock had been born in Stoke on the Hoo Peninsula and his first shop locally had been 61 High Street Milton where he ran a grocery which he kept on until 1893 in addition to the East Street premises.

Baldock advertised regularly in the local paper his usual line being: '*Baldock's bread and cakes are not to be beaten.*' He was a Freemason, initiated into St Michaels Lodge in Sittingbourne in 1897.(111)

By 1901 the Baldocks had moved to 1/3 High Street above their shop there where they had run a business since 1893.(HSI) And so in 1901 it was the baker employed by Baldock, George Longfield who lived at 49 with his family.

Thomas Badock ploughed his profits back into the business and invested in the latest technology so that by 1906 he could advertise: '*Sittingbourne model steam bakery*' at 49. In the 1908 directory he added the information that he was a pastry cook.

William Hartridge was the baker who lived at 49 in 1908 and worked for Baldock. (see number 9 in the West Street book) By 1911 Hartridge had left and George Longfield from Teynham, and his family had moved into the six rooms which constituted number 49.

Thomas Baldock lived a very long life dying in 1946 aged 92 at Bridge. He had sold up the bakery by 1926. The last man to knead dough at 49 was Frederick Rofe who probably worked for Baldock.

Fish and chips

In 1926 John Brewster of 12 West Street sought council permission to refit the shop at 49 in order to sell fish and chips which he already did in West Street. Matters prospered for the Brewsters in East Street rather than West Street and so in 1930 Brewster announced in the local paper: '*A. J. Brewster fish wet & dried & fried has disposed of his West Street shop and will concentrate on East Street.*'

By 1933 Horace Shortland and his wife Adeline had taken on the fish frying and continued certainly until 1939. Later fryers of fish included Helena and Lesley Chatfield and Edward Kaye and his wife during the 1950s. It was they who were here until the shop closed down prior to demolition. At that time the shop was called 'Shooter's Fish café'.

Evidence from electoral registers and Goad data shows that 47/49 were demolished in 1966 or 1967.

Numbers 51 to 57 East Street

These four plain and modest houses form a terrace which still stands today. At the western end of the terrace, beside number 51, where once 49 stood, is the small car park used by Swale Council.

In 1840, before the houses were built, Plough Orchard features in the tithe schedule and plan. We offered some information about that in our coverage of numbers 47 to 49

We can deduce that numbers 51 and 53 were built by 1860 – in the census for Spring 1861 we find Ann Keeler at number 53 (where she was in 1871) Next door, at what became number 51, was Jane Spice.

This terrace appears on the 1865/6 Ordnance Survey map and it can be seen that three of the four houses already had additions at the back.

Beyond Betsy Milner's east boundary, the taller number 59 was built structurally separate from 57 but abutted to it. Approached by an alley beside 59, there is a large yard at the back of these five houses, which we describe separately.

Numbers 51-55 East Street in 2013 – at the east end of Betsy Milner's Plough Orchard (DW)

Behind them, occupying some of the land once known as Plough Orchard, stands Victoria Mews, a modern block development of dwellings.

In 1871 the census records the occupants of the terrace as Charles Wickens a corn dealer's clerk with his family at number 51. At 53, as we have said, was Ann Keeler and her husband John who worked as an ironmonger's foreman. At 55 lived William Daniel a grocer's assistant who had been born in Devon and his family. The end house was home to Fred Sollett a shipbuilder from Yorkshire his wife and four children.

The Packer family take over the terrace

For a number of years the Packer family dominated the terrace. They were basket-makers whose workshop was round the corner in Bell Road. We have written a good deal about the family at number 10 East Street.

It was during the 1870s that Charles Packer moved into number 55 with his wife Margaret and family and there they were recorded on the 1881 census return. Charles was in business with his unmarried sister Frances who still lived across the road at number 10.

Charlie and Margaret's youngest son Herbert was still at school when they moved in to number 55 from number 101. The other four offspring were old enough to work. Charles junior and Frank were in the basket making business following generations of family tradition, whilst Kate and Emily had their own dressmaking business.

Number 55 proved comfortable and was only a five minute walk from work in Bell Road and so by 1891 the terrace was packed with Packers for they lived at 51 and 53 as well as 55 only leaving 57 as a relative-free house. Those who had joined Charlie and Margaret in the terrace were actually their sons Charles junior and Frank who were by then married with their own families and still working at basket making.

The Packers were clearly a close family in every way, able to work together and live cheek by jowl too. During the 1890s they also took on number 57. Old Charlie and Margaret moved there so that their son Herbert and his wife could live at number 55. The death of Charlie Packer senior in 1896 was recorded in the local paper:

'The death of Mr. Charles Arthur Packer, of 57 East Street, on Tuesday evening. Mr. Packer, who was 66 years of age, has, in partnership with his sister, Miss F. Packer, carried on the business of a basket maker for many years. Mr Packer was a native of Sittingbourne, and he belonged to an old and well known family. He leaves a widow and three sons and three daughters.'

The three Packer brothers and their families still filled the whole terrace in 1901 with their widowed mother Margaret and unmarried sister Kate at number 57. Kate ran her dressmaking business at the house and every now and then throughout the 1890s advertised for apprentices in the local paper as in this one of 1894: *'57 East Street, Miss Packer, dressmaking apprentices wanted.'*

Old Margaret Packer died at home in 1908 aged 77.(N01) Matters had changed a good deal in the terrace by 1911 for there remained only one Packer household here – that of Herbert who still worked at basket making and his wife Amelia. Herbert's brothers Charles junior and Frank had moved to larger homes in Park Road. After his brothers retired Herbert was helped in the business by his son George. Herbert died in 1943 and George carried the business on but times had changed and in spite of diversifying the trade was coming to an end.

Further information on the Packers and their basket making can be found in *More Family Businesses* – Helen Allinson.(80)

After the Packers
Herbert and Amy Atkinson at 51

Herbert Alderman Atkinson and his wife Amy were living at number 51 by 1908. They had probably moved in when they got married in 1907. Herbert had grown up in East Street at number 143, the son of Josiah Atkinson the ginger-beer maker.(see 143) Herbert worked for a baker as delivery man. He and Amy settled in and number 51 was home for the rest of their lives. For Herbert however the First World War intervened and meant he was away for a prolonged period. In 1916 he left his job as a tally clerk and enlisted in spite of being 40 years old. He signed on at the Buffs Depot in Canterbury but was directed to serve in the Durham Light Infantry.(111) Military papers reveal those endearing human characteristics which of course we lack with most residents of the street. So we know that Herbert was slightly knock-kneed, had dentures and stood five foot eight inches tall in his socks. He served in Salonika and was demobbed to return to Amy and their daughter Gladys in 1919. Herbert lived on until 1956 when he died aged 80.

Some later residents of number 51

After 1960 these are the residents we know of. The dates are just when we are certain they lived there:

1960-63	Eliza Hanley
1980	Angela Gidley
1985	Henry and Joyce Boreham
1990	Glenda Anderson, Jonathan Neville

Number 53

After the Packers moved out of number 53 there were three residents who did not stay for many years – Alfred Smith, Charles Pamplin and Ernest Hawkins. Then in the early 1920s Arthur and Mabel Dennett moved in and stayed for the rest of their lives. Arthur had been born in 1873 in Sedlescombe He married Mabel Lukehurst in 1907 when he was 34 and she was 22 and they lived initially at 169 East Street with Mabel's widowed mother and two boarders. (12) Arthur served as a Gunner for the whole duration of the First World War. (see number 169) He worked in the paper mill. Arthur died in 1949 and Mabel continued to live here until her death in 1973.

In her later years Mabel had a lodger Miss Josephine Jopson (b1912). Josephine was sole tenant after Mabel's death and remained at 53 until her own death in 1991.

Number 55

The occupants of number 55 that we know of after the Packers are shown on this table:

1922-39	Frederick and Mary Harris
1947-60	Florence and Wilfred Cook
1975	David and Sheila Hall
1980-90	Arthur and Marjorie Wheeler
1995	Louise and Robert Langley

Number 57

After the Packers moved out of number 57 Albert Joseph Mace (born 1867) a farmer and dairyman moved in with his wife Kate.(12) Before his marriage Albert lived with his parents at 82 East Street and worked at the dairying business with them. He continued to work at the family business after marriage

103

so number 57 was Albert and Kate's home and they crossed over the road to work with the older Maces in the dairy.

In 1921 Albert was summonsed for selling new milk that was deficient in fat to the extent of at least ten percent.(N01) It was reported that he and his father had been in business for 30 years and this was the first case he had against him. Albert was fined £2 with two guineas costs.

Old Mr Mace had died in 1916 and his widow in 1918. It was not long before Albert and Kate moved over to number 82 and left the terrace.

Allan Rueben Hedges who had been born in Oxfordshire in 1884 and his wife May were the following tenants Allan Hedges died in 1942.

Arthur and Catherine Cassell were the next couple to live at 57. Arthur had been born in Sittingbourne in 1899 and in 1934 married Catherine Mahony on Sheppey.

One of their sons, the late Gerry Cassell, in some reminiscences provided for us a few years ago, recalled that "In those days my father made the sweets in our 'factory', which was more or less a shed at the back of 57 East Street. There were no robust health and safety regulations at that time – the factory was actually adjacent to the outside toilet!"

Another son, Will, ran 'Eileen's' sweet shop at number 10 in the 1960s. The Cassell family remained at number 57 into the 1970s although old Arthur had died in 1967.

During the 1980s and 1990s residents of 57 included Ruth Daye and Alan and Gillian Gray.

Before leaving this section we should turn back to the writings of Canon W. A. Scott Robertson who goes into some detail about previous ownership hereabouts. As usual, because he does not provide street numbers (although many had been applied at the time when he was writing) it is necessary to examine carefully what he has written, in order to deduce or clarify the exact whereabouts of the property whose history he is recounting.

East of Plough Orchard, he tells us that there were two tenements, whose whose successive owners he proceeds to list. From what he has written, it is not clear whether these were the two buildings at the south-east corner of Plough Orchard or whether they were within the curtilage of the adjoining site known then as West Lane Orchard.

Whichever it was, the property was owned before 1731 by Anne Essex, then, successively, by John Banks, John Ellen, W. Willinor, and George Smeed.

Since the tithe plan of 1840 shows no buildings on the frontage of West Lane Orchard, it could be that Scott Robertson here was addressing the buildings at the south-east corner of Plough Orchard, owned by Betsy Milner.

However we have noticed that, in the yard approached by the alley between numbers 59 and 61, there appears on the Ordnance Survey plans from the 1860s until the 1960s, a couple of buildings, one of which, by the early 20th century, had fallen into ruin. On balance, we think it is more likely that these are the tenements about which Scott Robertson was writing at this point.

Number 59 East Street

51 53 55 57 59   61 63 65 67 69

We come now to the first property which we have encountered within the borders of what, in 1840, was known as West Lane Orchard, owned, at that time, by William Gascoyne and let to Jesse Thomas. Identified on the tithe map as parcel 243, that site of just over four acres (about 1.7 hectares) is covered in some detail at 73 East Street, Using material provided by our old friend Canon Scott Robertson.

This is a large house compared to many others in the street. It still stands; double fronted, three storeyed, extending far out at the back and with the shop front recently removed. It was erected right up against number 57 but it is separated from number 61 by a wide passageway, Leading to a development of housing named Victoria Mews.

We believe number 59 was built between 1861 and 1866 for it does not appear on the 1861 census return but is there on the 1865/6 map.

A butcher's shop and home
Samuel Attaway

Number 59 seems to have begun life as both home and shop. Samuel Attaway may have been the first resident for he was here by 1870.(31) He was a young butcher from Faversham, with a wife and four children. Before his marriage Samuel had worked as a butcher's assistant in a shop in Milton High Street.(7,8) By 1878 the Attaways had left to establish themselves at the butcher's shop in the middle of Borden.(9,33) Later they returned the short distance to Sittingbourne but this time settled at 70 West Street.

Edward Goldfinch

The next butcher to take on number 59 was Edward Goldfinch whom directories record here in 1878. He was a young man from Whitstable, married with two young children and as the 1881 census shows, could afford a live-in domestic servant.

However Mr Goldfinch suffered a financial loss in 1885 when an outbreak of swine-fever was discovered amongst 26 live pigs he had purchased at Dargate. Three died of the fever and all the rest had to be slaughtered and disposed of and out-buildings specially cleaned.(N03)

In December 1886 Mr Goldfinch's fine Christmas display of meat was described in the local paper. The stars of his beef section were the carcases of two Hereford heifers, whilst the plenteous mutton consisted of portions of five Southdown sheep.

The directory reveals Edward was still at number 59 in 1887 but soon afterwards the Goldfinchs resettled in Penge in another home-cum-butcher's shop. The family had grown to five children during their time in Sittingbourne.

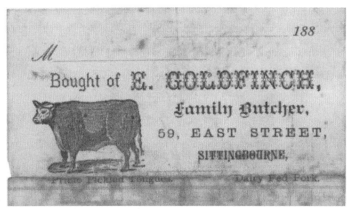

An 1880s receipt form for Goldfinch

Albert William Harris

Albert William Harris from Rodmersham was next to take up the knives as butcher here.(10) Albert was a married man with children and a servant just like his predecessor. In 1881 he had still been living with his mother at the Fruiterers Arms in Rodmersham which she ran whilst he worked from the inn as a general dealer.

Matters did not go well for Albert in East Street and so in 1891 the Harris family left number 59 which was then advertised as to let with its 'newly erected slaughter-house and out-buildings.'(N03) The East Kent Gazette announced an auction *'on premises: a mare, a light spring fruit van, butcher's spring cart, ten pigs, utensils of trade including two sausage machines, scalding tubs, weights, pulleys, and household furniture and effects.'*

Sadly it seems that the auction and moving house may well have been due to Albert being too ill to work for he died aged just 35 in 1893 leaving his widow Esther with the children to bring up. She supported them by sewing shirts at their home in Dover Street.(12)

Thomas James Redhead

Another hapless butcher came to number 59 after Albert Harris. This was Thomas Redhead, a rather different character. He was accused of not being a proper butcher and certainly he could have been found living at 64 High Street working as an agent of the Singer Sewing Machine Company in 1891 just before the move to 59 East Street. He had only been in the High Street for a year.

Trouble arrived fairly quickly at number 59 in the form of bankruptcy at the start of 1894 and the charge of *'falsely trading as a butcher'*.(N01) This was not correct as we shall see. Perhaps an irate debtor had stated that Mr Redhead knew more about sewing machines than slicing mutton.

Nevertheless at the end of the same year Tom was back butchering at 59:

'Notice to farmers, dealers, butchers and others. T. J. Redhead and Son are prepared to make arrangements for the slaughter of all kind of cattle for market or otherwise as they have every convenience for the same.'

In spite of these efforts Tom was bankrupt again in 1895: 'Failure of a local butcher. Thomas James Redhead appeared at Rochester Bankruptcy Court. Gross liabilities of £401 6s. 0d.' The paper further reported the future sale of 'Furniture of Mr. Redhead, together with pony cart, light trade van, harness and the tackle and utensils of a butcher'.

Tom Redhead had been born at Haddenham in Bucks in 1850 the son of a wheelwright. By 1871 he was working for a butcher in Brixton and was still in the trade, but on his own account, in Hammersmith ten years later, by which time he was married with four children.

After the 1895 bankruptcy the Redheads moved on from East Street to Bray in Berkshire where in 1901 Tom, working as a butcher but in much reduced circumstances, was living with his wife Sarah and two of the children in just three rooms.

In spite of his financially unsuccessful life Tom lived to be 87.

British and Colonial Meat Company

When the Redheads moved out the butcher's business was taken on by the British and Colonial Meal Company. They advertised the sale of 'prime New Zealand mutton and lamb, and also finest quality American beef, at competitive prices'.(N01) By 1899 the Company had taken smaller premises at number 29.

Robert Adams and William H. Kemsley

Robert Adams, a London butcher who boarded in William Street took on the shop then whilst the living accommodation was rented by George Parker and his family.(11,39) Adams' stay here was brief.

Mr Parker, a local, was probably the first man to live at 59 who was not a butcher. He earned his living as a pickle salesman and merchant. The Parkers remained in the house when Adams left the shop.

Number 59 was cleared of meat and the outbuildings emptied of animals and carcasses in 1901 for William Henry Kemsley who sold fruit, vegetables and game was taking on the shop. There were plenty of Kemsleys in Sittingbourne but this William seems to have been a market gardener who lived in Goodnestone Road.(11)

Mrs Minnie Budgen confectioner

The 1908 directory lists Mrs Minnie Budgen, confectioner, at 59. Minnie had previously had a general shop in Tonbridge where she and her husband George, a bricklayer had lived with their family.(11)

By 1911 George Budgen had died and Minnie had left Sittingbourne. It was George Fowle, a carter from Hollingbourne, who had moved in upstairs with him were his wife Annie and their daughter Frances and her husband Jesse Goodhew. Jesse described himself as a pruner and grafter so he worked in the orchards. Jesse and Frances had a baby and the rest of the house was filled by three boarders two of whom were carters who worked with George. Whether there was a shop downstairs during these years is unclear.

P. A. Turvey in the outbuildings

For a while during the 1920s the stables at the rear were used by an engineering business called firstly *'Turvey & Sons Agricultural, Electrical, General engineers & Haulage Contractor'* who were listed in directories.

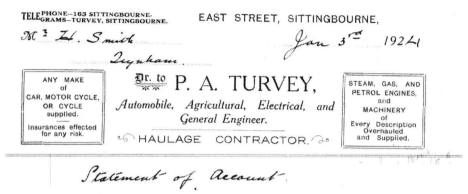

P. A. Turvey was using the buildings at the rear of number 59 in 1924

Butchery returns to number – 59 Samuel Bennett

In 1924 the shop reverted to selling meat under the hand of Samuel Bennett and this proved to be a long-standing business as it then passed to his daughter Iris who had been born in 1918.(51)

To begin with Samuel rented number 59 and it belonged to Mr C. J. Howard of Chatham, a substantial owner of property of whom we hear more than once in East Street and HSI. In a sign of the times Mr Howard applied to the council in 1930 for conversion of the stables behind number 59 to four garages.(105)

Mr Howard had further ideas for renting out parts of the property which had never been rented out before. Two years later the sanitary inspector reported to the council that premises at the rear formerly used as workshops were being used as a dwelling which was not suitable for human habitation Mr Howard was requested to make it suitable for a dwelling.(105)

Instead he sold number 59 to Samuel Bennett and we hear no more of people living in workshops in the yard.(105) There was a pie-maker, George Crooks, listed in the 1938 directory who must have rented one of the workshops for a while to roll out his pastry. Mr Howard retained ownership of the yard, and after the Second World War, he erected blocks of individual garages which were let out to short-term tenants.

Even though Samuel now owned the building all was not plain-sailing for him for he had never lived over the shop and there were the sitting tenants Jesse and Frances Goodhew and their children who had been there since at least 1911.(115) The war came and the Goodhews remained until in 1944 Iris Ledger née Bennett applied on behalf of Samuel her father, to Sittingbourne magistrates to have the Goodhews evicted. Iris stated that she managed the butcher's shop whilst her husband was on active service. (She had married John Ledger in 1941.) The business had been her own since 1939 and she needed the accommodation that the Goodhews had. She carried her case and the Ledgers later moved in to number 59.(115)

Samuel Bennett died in 1950 but Iris and John retained the Bennett name for the butcher's shop. Iris died in 1979 and John in 1984 but as early as 1981 the shop was being run by their son Alan who also had a butcher's shop at Leysdown.(N01) The living accommodation was divided into two flats and rented out.

During the 1990s Alan Ledger let the shop to the florist from number 73 who moved 'FlowerWorld' here and then by 2009 it was in use as a hairdressing salon named 'Blow'. The Ledger family sold number 59 in 2011.

1981 Advert for the butchers at number 59

Number 59 East Street with striped sun shade in 1985

'Blow' at number 59 in 2008, with the entrance to Victoria Mews to the right (CA)

Businesses Behind 59

For some years in the 1980s and into the 2000s an engineering firm named Kirk-Morgan Ltd used some of the buildings behind number 59 as their premises. Nowadays they are still in Sittingbourne and based in Castle Road.

Number 59 in the centre of this 2016 photograph. The ground-floor was being converted to residential use at the time. (BA)

Numbers 61 and 63 East Street

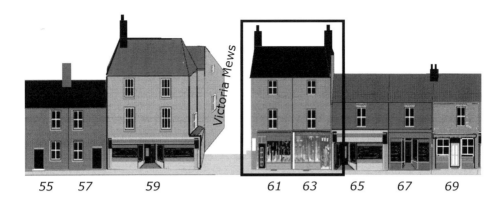

55   57   59   61   63   65   67   69

Here, on the other side of the alley leading to Victoria Mews, we are well within the borders of West Lane Orchard, where numbers 61 and 63 would later be built. As recounted already at number 59, this big orchard was let at the time to young Jesse Thomas the fruiterer of Rodmersham Green and owned by William Gascoyne the farmer of Bapchild Court.

Because Sittingbourne was growing, a site so close to the centre of the town with frontage to the London to Dover road was ripe for building by the 1860s. We believe numbers 61 and 63 date from the early 1860s for they had been built by the time the 1865/6 map was drawn but had yet to be erected when the 1861 census return was taken.

Looking at the facade of 61 and 63 they appear to have been built as one spacious three-storeyed house with cellars. Nevertheless when we first know who inhabited the building the two halves were not occupied as one and for the rest of its history the two parts of the building have had different tenants.

There were ample grounds at the back accessed by a large alleyway big enough to take a horse and cart on the western side.

From the mid-20th century onwards, as noted at number 59, the back yard was filled with individual garages let to short-term tenants. The owner for some years was Charlie Howard, a property owner from the Medway towns. We have encountered him more than once in this series. In recent years, a small housing estate, named Victoria Mews, has been built in the yard behind 59, 61 and 63 actually stretching behind numbers 51 to the edge of 73 East Street, but using this alleyway as access.

Number 61
Henry Hoile and the first café at 61

Even on its own number 61 constituted a capacious house which lent itself to having a ground floor working man's café or 'eating house' as well as giving more than enough room for the family to live and to take in lodgers The first occupant we know of is from a listing in the 1870 directory. It was Henry Hoile who set up as a fruiterer and also opened a 'coffee house' though it was already described as the more ordinary 'eating house' in the census a year later.

Victorian eating houses generally served a roast or two every day with vegetables. There might be a choice of roast mutton or boiled beef.

Henry Hoile, a labourer, and his wife Elizabeth had previously lived round the corner in West Lane. He had been born in Sandwich in 1829 and Elizabeth came from Wormshill. The household was completed by their two sons, a niece, Richard Saywell who was Elizabeth's father, and two lodgers.

Henry and Elizabeth (for she would doubtless have done the cooking) failed to make a success of the business and all too soon left for Buckland near Dover where Henry was employed as a brickfield foreman.(9)

Thomas Baker

We know from the local paper that the suitably-named Thomas Baker was running the eating house from 1872 to 1877: *'Thomas Baker has succeeded Mr Hoile at this address. Tea & coffee always ready, as well as hot joints daily between 12-1.'*

Unfortunately we cannot say anything of Tom Baker for there were several men of that name in census returns who might have been him.

In every case of a man moving to 61 and named as running the café I suspect that it was actually the wife who was the most important person in determining the success of the enterprise. Was Mrs Baker a good cook as her name suggests? Could she serve up a tasty roast at a cheap price? Did she yearn for a life away from a hot stove?

Joseph Cooper Brittenden

The 1878 directory lists Joseph Brittenden in charge of the 'Refreshment Rooms'. Joseph was born at Stockbury in 1846 and still lived there in 1871 when he was working as a labourer. In 1876 he married Elizabeth Coe in Milton and she must have felt ready and able to take on the café when they moved to number 61 but by 1881 the Brittendens had moved to Danaway and Joseph was working as a builder. There they remained.

George James Reeve

So the next couple to move into number 61 were the Reeves; George and Harriet. Here they were ensconced by 1881. George who had been born at Pluckley described himself for the census as a 'house painter and eating house keeper'. Harriet would have had her hands full with six children and the café to run but run it she did until at least 1887 or 1888.(35)

It must have been a relief to Harriet that George's painting and decorating business flourished and the family were able to move to number 131 and give up the café. (see 131)

Robert James Rogers

After the Reeves moved up the road Kelly's Directory of 1889 gives us the information that Robert James Rogers (born 1835 in Faversham) was the next 'Refreshment Room Keeper.' This was a brief foray indeed into the café business for in less than a year the Rogers were living up at Keycol Hill where Mr Rogers was employed at the waterworks as an engineer and his wife Agnes was able to take life more easily with her six children.

After so many people had tried it must have appeared then that a good profit could not be made with a café at number 61 but at any rate the next family to move in did not try.

Thomas Fuller – who did not run a café

The 1890 directory lists Thomas Fuller at number 61. Surprisingly he was a market gardener (born in Folkestone in 1859). With him were his wife Emily, three children who had all been born in Folkestone and baby Alfred who was born when the family arrived in Sittingbourne in 1891.(10) They had a general servant and one boarder William Kemsley a fruit dealer from Borden. The Fullers moved on after less than three years and in 1901 could be found keeping a public house in Croydon.(11)

We presume their foray into market gardening took place behind the house in the erstwhile orchard.

Henry Cox

In 1893 Henry Cox moved into 61 with his wife Fanny to live and to re-open the Refreshment Room business.(115) He was then in his forties and had previously worked as a farm labourer and sexton in Teynham.(9,10) The Coxs remained here perhaps until 1899 when we know Robert Rogers again had the business. The Coxs then moved on to Chatham where Henry was employed as a labourer again.(11)

Robert James Rogers again

What are we to make of the fact that Robert Rogers returned to number 61 in 1899? His time here had been brief as we have seen and he was a civil engineer. Could it be that Agnes Rogers had in fact really enjoyed it all? The directory of that year has him listed again at number 61 as 'refreshment room keeper.' However the Rogers did not actually move back into number 61 for in 1901 they were living at 28 Dover Street.(11) Agnes was presumably working at 61. Robert Rogers died aged 66 in December 1901 and the eating house had already been under the management of two women for most of that year.

Ann Wood and Emma Arnold – women in charge

Mother and daughter Ann Wood and Emma Arnold lived at number 61 in 1901. Both women were described in the census as 'eating house keepers'. Ann Wood was a widow, born in Lenham 60 years previously. Emma Arnold was her married daughter and it seems likely her husband was a mariner like many of his neighbours. Certainly he was not present on census night. The other residents in the house that night were little William Arnold aged six and two young female servants. There was one final resident; a boarder Herbert Rogers. He was a young, unmarried 'play actor' from London. Probably he was just passing through, perhaps on his way to Canterbury.

The two women were still here in 1903 when they had decided in their directory entry to call themselves 'Coffee house keepers' and yet, like so many others before them they did not stay long and had left by 1904.(N01)

The McCartney Family at 61

The following residents of number 61 stayed a lot longer and their name remained attached to the for many years. They were Thomas and Sarah McCartney. Thomas was a Sittingbourne man, born in 1844 he grew up in Murston Road and his father worked on the brickfields. Thomas too laboured on the brickfields and moved about locally for work. He lived for a while in

Teynham and for a while in Newington.(8,9) By 1891 he and Sarah lived in Shortlands Road where they remained until the move to number 61 in 1904.

It is interesting to note that the 1908 directory named number 61 as 'Eastry House' a name we have not found before or since in all the records we have seen. In 1911 the McCartney household comprised Thomas and Sarah who by then were in their sixties, one of their daughters, a granddaughter who at 14 was old enough to be useful, and three boarders.

There was considerable noise and disruption at number 61 when war broke out in 1914 for the army took over a wooden shed behind the house to use as a cook house for 100 men who were fed in the yard (some of the cooking was done outside when possible) and a slaughter house also at the rear of 61 was used as a meat store for the 8th Battalion Northants Regiment.

What a lot of tramping about and shouting there must have been for the McCartneys to put up with.

A glad day of celebration for the family came in October 1917 which lifted the wartime gloom. The local paper carried a full report of the golden wedding celebration of Thomas and Sarah McCartney:

'An interesting event in the history of Mr and Mrs McCartney of 61 East Street Sittingbourne, occurred on Friday in last week for it was their Jubilee Wedding Day. Fifty years ago they were married by the vicar at Teynham Church, and after that long period of married life they were able to commemorate the happy day surrounded by a large gathering of relatives and old friends.

Mr Thomas McCartney who is 74 years old and a native of Sittingbourne comes from a long-lived race. His Grandmother, Mrs Mary Ann Rose was the celebrated local centenarian who lived to be 102 years and six months, whose death took place several years ago. Mr McCartney's father and mother who died a few years ago both reached the advanced age of 89 years.

Mrs Sarah Ann McCartney is 69 and a native of Greenstreet. She is the daughter of the late Mr Thomas Trigg who died within a few hours of his wife and husband and wife were buried together

Mr Thomas McCartney made the first brick at Lomas for the late Mr George Smeed the king of the Kent stock brick industry at Sittingbourne. As a boy Mr McCartney can just recollect coming out of The Butts school Sittingbourne (at the time Mr Beddesworth was schoolmaster) and going over to Lomas to see his father make bricks. Mr McCartney is an old brickmaker himself, for he has made bricks at Teynham, Faversham, Newington and Hoo. He can recall interesting experiences of development of the brick making industry in this part of Kent.

But the family gathering of Friday brings us to the present day, and in spite of the war and all its worry and anxiety a happy party assembled at 61 East Street. Mr and Mrs McCartney have had an eating house business for the last 12 years.

Outside was all darkness and mud, inside about 70 people young and old for gathered in honour of the occasion. Out of a family of 12 children (all of whom have been christened at Teynham Church) six are living Viz: Mrs George Chapman who is in Toronto. Mrs Emily Mills, Who with her husband and three children are home from Toronto and they will remain in England until after the war. Mr Mills who belongs to Sittingbourne is an Assistant Master in one of the Canadian Regiments, Mrs Fanny Kemp of East Street, Mr Albert Mc Cartney of Cowper Road, Mrs Irving Swan of Bredgar and Alfred McCartney who is serving with The Buffs at Salonica.

Mrs McCartney's three sisters were there too. All the husbands, wives and children helped to make up a happy party, and photographs were taken of the worthy couple and their descendants. Hearty congratulations and handsome and useful presents were received.

Mr McCartney gave his wife a jubilee wedding ring. Mrs Mills and Mrs Swan gave their mother a keeper ring. Other members of the family including Mrs Barry gave Mr McCartney a gold signet ring. Mr and Mrs Putney gave the jubilee bride a gold broach. Mrs McCartney received a dressing gown from all the children and grandchildren . Mrs McCartney gave her husband a cheque.

Mr and Mrs McCartney were wished many more years of health and happiness and the memorable family gathering was prolonged till a late hour. It was a bright family anniversary in the dark days of war.'.

After the war the McCartneys' son Albert took on the café with his wife Audrey and daughter, also named Audrey; they moved into 61 where they continued to take in lodgers and used the top floor as a dormitory for working men.(115,53) Albert McCartney had worked as a brickfield labourer like his father. Early in 1927 Thomas died aged 82, Sarah had died the previous summer.

By 1933 Edward and Eliza Mount were running the café and living at 61. Edward too had been a brickmaker. He may well have been related to the McCartneys for the café continued to be called McCartneys and during 1938 the business was taken on by George and Audrey Ranson. Audrey was Albert McCartney's daughter so it was still known as McCartney's. They remained there in 1947.

Ted Epps

Ted and Constance Epps lived at 61 in 1953 and may have taken over sooner. The café in the 1950s and 1960s, still known as McCartney's, is remembered as a typical working man's café serving breakfast and midday meals and still offering lodgings upstairs for lorry drivers and others – simple, basic accommodation with several beds to a room. By this time, in the evening and weekends, it was popular with bikers.

Ted was assisted in the running of the establishment by his wife and daughter. Because the yard at the back was occupied by Charlie Howard's garages, the café used the Plough Yard across the street as a car park for the patrons. It was still in business in 1968.(121)

McCartney's café in about 1953. Customers Daniel Ralph and Ron Mannouch with Ted's daughter Marjory and grandchild

D&A Fashions

Between 1969 and 1971 an enormous change took place at number 61. It no longer housed a café. Instead Doris and Arthur Haffenden had opened a ladies fashion shop known as 'D&A Fashions.' The Haffenden family, who lived for some time at 61, went on to open other shops in the town such as D&A sports and D&A Toys.(HSI) This shop continued until 1980.

D&A Fashions at number 61 and Allen Tool Hire at 63 in 1980 (EKG)

R&S Ralph TV and Kebabs

The next shop to open at 61 was 'R&S Ralph, Televisions and Electrical'. Their electrical shops had begun at 161 East Street and then they added number 135.

They also had a shop at Rainham. Sometime between 1987 and 1991 the Ralphs vacated number 61 and the smell of cooking once again emanated from the front door: North Kent Kebabs takeaway had moved in.

There have been slight changes of name for the kebab takeaway – 'North Kent Charcoal Grill'; and now 'Kent Charcoal Grill' but it remains a kebab shop.

Kent Charcoal Grill at 61 in 2019 (AJW)

Number 63
Walter Kimmins

Walter Kimmins was Henry Hoile's next door neighbour in 1871 when he and his wife Emily née Thomas, three daughters and a servant lived at number 63 and Walter was working as a hay salesman.(8) So number 63 was a private house. Walter who had been born in 1839 hailed from nearby Greenstreet where he had started his working life as a baker in the family business. That was not the only job he had had for during the 1860s he worked as an agent for the Kent Coal Company.

An 1865 advertisement gives us evidence that the Kimmins had already moved in to number 63 by then: *'Coal, Coal, Coal. Sittingbourne & Teynham Railway Stations. W. Kimmins agent to Kent Coal Company. Particulars can be obtained at Mr W. Kimmins Opposite The Plough East End'.*

By 1871 Walter was dealing in hay and corn but in 1877 he went bankrupt. The Whitstable Herald reported that his creditors had accepted four shillings in the pound. Walter must have accumulated debts. The family's possessions had to be sold – a piano, oil paintings, a safe, a seven foot mahogany bagatelle board were advertised in the East Kent Gazette a few months later. All the household furniture was auctioned in March that year for Kimmins was leaving the neighbourhood to make a fresh start. There was some good furniture; carpets, a telescope, bookcases, clock and even damask curtains. Everything was on offer even the kitchen items.

1878 auction sale 'Mr W. Kimmins is leaving the neighbourhood' (EKG)

Walter and the family were to be found in Camberwell in 1881 where he was employed as a hay salesman. Having a steady income being able to employ a servant, and not risking being bankrupt again must have been a relief. In 1891 the Kimmins were in Deptford where Walter still worked as a hay salesman. He turned to fruit growing in old age back in Rainham and died there in 1919.(12)

Fordwich Gorely

The next inhabitants of number 63 were the Gorelys. We cannot doubt that Fordwich Gorely's most unusual Christian name came from the ancient little town of Fordwich for although he always stated on census returns that he had been born in Canterbury, Fordwich is only two miles from the city so we suspect it was there that he was born in 1831. Fordwich's working life began as a grocer's assistant in Dartford.(6) He married Sittingbourne girl Eliza Shutton here in 1861 so forging a lasting bond with the town. The couple lived in Ramsgate in the 1870s where Fordwich had a grocery.

By 1881 they had moved into number 63 with their five children and taken on two boarders. It is likely that the purpose of the move to Sittingbourne was actually to establish son Frank's grocery at 19 High Street. At this point Frank was an 18 year old grocer's assistant in Chatham and would have needed his father's money and expertise as well as the support of his Sittingbourne relatives to get going. It does not appear that Fordwich opened a grocery at number 63.

The Gorely family's stay in East Street was not a long one for, by 1891, they were nicely established at 6 Park Road with the other children apprenticed to various trades.

In fact they must have left number 63 by 1887 when the property was auctioned described as: '*all that desirable messuage or tenement situate and belonging to no 63 East Street. Containing sitting room, dining room, three bedrooms, scullery & cellar and has a convenient work shop & out buildings at rear. The property stands on land 100ft deep and width 16ft 6inches or there about and is of the estimated rental of £18/4/0 and is held for the unexpired term of 500 years from 16/10/1738 free of rent'.*

We do not know if the property sold quickly but in 1891 it was empty.(10)

Fordwich's son Frank's grocery did well at 19 High Street and in 1889 he announced in the local paper that he was moving his business to the larger 42 High Street.(HSII)

Eliza, Fordwich's wife, died in 1904. Their daughter Eliza had married Sittingbourne builder Henry Tidy. After old Eliza died widowed Fordwich moved in with his daughter and son in law at 80 Park Road where he died in 1917.(12)

Scale makers

A scale maker named Frederick A. Ingram is listed in the 1895 directory as living at number 63. Frederick came from Rochester and had plied his craft in Tunbridge Wells before moving to Sittingbourne in his forties with wife and family perhaps in 1892. Scale makers made scales and weights for shop-keepers; a skilled trade. Being unable to discover where the Ingrams had moved to by 1901, search was made of the Ancestry probate index in case Frederick had died before 1901. Sadly he died at the end of 1895 aged 45. His effects which his widow Sarah received were only worth £120.

No doubt it was one of the Ingram sons who placed this notice in the Gazette early in 1896: *'Gooseberry bushes for sale 1,2000 Lancashire Lads. Would change for good potatoes. J. Ingram 63 East Street.'*

Young Ingram must have been making good use of the land behind the house where Fuller had grown his vegetables.

Scale making continued at number 63 under new hands; those of Fairburn Brothers.(39) The brothers did not live in Sittingbourne but employed young Jesse Fry from Maidstone as their scale maker.(11) The 1901 census reveals a William Fairburn, scale maker and employer living in Maidstone so he was one half of Fairburn Brothers. The other has proved elusive.

By 1905 the Fairburns had abandoned this branch of their business and the premises were to let again described this time as a large shop with bold front, house, workshop, yard, low rent and side entrance.

Thomas Kirk Biddle – art photographer

The next enterprise at 63 was that of Thomas Kirk Biddle who had moved in from Dartford by 1908. He and the family only lived here a couple of years probably finding too much competition from the well-established photographers in the High Street. By 1911 the Biddles had returned to Dartford which was nearer home territory because Thomas came from Welling. Whilst at number 63 he advertised himself as an art photographer and picture framer.

T. KIRK BIDDLE,

Art Photographer,

(Over 25 Years' Experience),

63, EAST STREET, SITTINGBOURNE.

20 Years at 73, High Street, Dartford.

PICTURE FRAMING.

Advertisement in the 1908 directory

Whilst they were at 63 Biddle was in his forties and his son Samuel was living at home trying to get work as a piano tuner.

David Mannering's hardware shop

A different kind of shop and one which endured much longer was that of David Mannering who was the next inhabitant of number 63. David was an ironmonger from Rye with a wife and two children.(12) David and Ella Mannering lived here and ran the shop for many years, with the assistance of their son Leslie as soon as he was old enough. When his parents retired Leslie continued the business.

D. Mannering hardware shop at 63 East Street, 1930s

An article in the East Kent Gazette during 1992 had Wilfred Ambrose looking back to 1920s when he worked at 63. He recalled David Mannering had been trained at Webb's just along the street. Mannering was cheerful with a sharp business sense and a fair employer. The shop had excellent stock. They had closed by 1980.

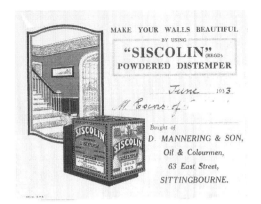

Letterhead from the Mannerings, 'Oil and Colourmen' at number 63 in 1933

Allen Tool Hire, AML Books and Parker Tool Hire

The photographs on an earlier page, taken in 1980, shows 'Allen Tool Hire' at number 63 but by 1982, 'AML Books' which sold both new and second-hand volumes opened here.(N01) It was owned by Marie Lane and was a short-lived venture for according to Goad maps Parker Tool Hire had number 63 between 1982 and 1984. Parkerhire moved along the road to number 73 and by 1987 the premises were vacant.

Quality Discount

We have not discovered any information about Quality Discount who had the shop in 1991.

Creating Cakes

In 1995 this became the Cake Decorating Centre, a family business, run by David Honeysett. In 1997 he was replaced by D. P. Bruton who, with a slight change of name to 'Creating Cakes' continues the business of cake decoration here today.

Creating Cakes at number 63 in 2008 (CA)

Numbers 61 and 63 in 2019 – Kent Charcoal Grill and 'Creating Cakes' (MHP)

Numbers 65, 67, 69, 71 East Street

Here, we are still within the boundaries of West Lane Orchard as it was in 1840.

This unremarkable terrace of four modestly-sized, plain, Victorian houses with cellars and attics, all had their front rooms converted to shops during the late 19th century. They are of particular interest to us for they include our museum at number 67.

In 1871 these were recently built (for they do not appear on the 1865/6 map) Originally, they were private homes let to working families with a skilled head of household. The rentals would have been too expensive for unskilled workers on their lower wages.

The Masters family at numbers 65 and 71

The Masters family lived in two of these dwellings in 1871. At number 65 lived John Masters a shipwright from Aylesford, in his fifties who built barges in one of the yards on the Creek, his wife Amelia and son John junior (a block maker) and their servant. The couple had lived many years in Sittingbourne and had moved here from number 103.(6,7)

John junior the block maker would have worked with his father for block makers were an important part of the wooden ship-building process. They made blocks for the cradles which held the ships under construction. The household would have had two good wage packets coming in hence they could afford a live -in skivvy. John senior's older son Charles, then in his twenties, lived at number 71 with his wife and two small children. Like his father, Charles was a shipwright.

We know that John Masters junior flourished, for council plans of 1880 record that permission was given for a cottage to be built in East Street for John Masters junior with cellar, three bedrooms two living rooms and a wash-house. No street number was given, however John junior and his family were living at 17 Canterbury Road when the 1881 census was taken and Canterbury Road was sometimes called East Street then so that was almost certainly the house he had built. A second house was built for him in 1892, again the plans survive in the archives of the council and again it was described as being in East Street.

Amelia Masters died in 1875 still in her fifties and John senior remarried four years later to Charlotte Harris (whom we have met at number 45), a younger widow with six children aged from 18 to two years old who all came with her to live at number 65. In 1891 John's entry in Kelly's Directory states 'fruiterer and barge builder at Adelaide Dock.'

When the 1901 census was taken John still described himself as a shipwright although perhaps the extent of his activities by then were helping his wife in the greengrocery shop which they had started in the front room of the house. Charlotte had previously run the greengrocery at number 45. In 1895 a fire started:

> 'A fire broke out at 1.30 a.m. on Thursday morning at a disused cottage, which had been converted into a store, at the back of the house and premises in East Street occupied by Mr Masters, greengrocer. An alarm was raised and the Sittingbourne Fire Brigade, with reel and hose, were summoned.
>
> The fire was confined to the cottage which together with its contents, were destroyed. The damage is roughly estimated at £50.'

Evidently the cottage just about survived. It can be seen on the Ordnance Survey plans of 1865/6 and 1909, adjoining the back boundary of the site at 65 with access from the back lane.

Old John Masters had purchased the house and was to remain living in it for the rest of his long life which came to an end in 1903 when he was 87.(115)

The first person in the Masters family to take up the selling of fruit and vegetables for a living had been Charles Masters at number 71. As we have seen he was a young shipwright in 1871, but by 1874 directories reveal that he had become a fruiterer so it seems that number 71 had its shop front fitted at this point. Perhaps Charles had suffered an injury and so could no longer use all his skills. However by 1881 he was once again employed as a shipwright and had moved with his family to Dover Street.

After old John Masters died in 1903 his widow Charlotte fell foul of the law. She turns out to have been quite a risk-taker for she purchased 1½ cwt of stolen lead at the back door for 13 shillings. She was charged with receiving stolen goods.(N02)

Nevertheless the greengrocery continued as we can see from directories and the 1911 census. Charlotte died in 1915 but fruit and vegetables were sold at number 65 for many a year after that.

After Charlotte's death Stephen and Fanny Kemp moved into the house and continued to run the greengrocery.(N01,49) This was taken over in 1926 by Albert and Ethel Grimsdale who remained until at least 1939.(N01,53)

By 1947 Phyllis and Tommy Hughes were the greengrocers here and are thought to have remained until 1983.(115,87) However the electoral register for 1960 records Peter and Shirley Cowles as occupants, so it appears that by then the Hughes just came in to run the shop and sublet the living accommodation to Cowles. When the Hughes closed up the shop it remained empty for a while but in 1985 Windsor Kitchens opened.(121) This was a brief venture and was followed by Grosvenor Studio Photography. Then came Bassant financial services which later moved to West Street.

In 2005 it was vacant but by 2009 the shop had been converted to a launderette named Bubbles and so it continues today.

Number 65 'Bubbles Launderette' in 2008 (CA)

This photograph was taken around 1950.
Thomasson newsagents on the right at number 79

Number 67 East Street
Edwin Carman, sailmaker

Number 67 has been the home of our museum since its inauguration in 1998. The first occupier of the house was Edwin Carman who had previously lived at number 57. A Maidstone man then in his thirties and recently widowed, his mother in law lived with him to look after his son John and baby daughter. Edwin was a sailmaker and we know he worked for George Smeed the self-made owner of brickworks and builder of barges. In 1841 Edwin, newly out if his apprenticeship, was engaged as Smeed's first sail maker.(111) This was to be Carman's life's work. The 1870 directory states that he was 'foreman of Mr Smeed's sailmakers'. Smeed had become the employer of the largest number of men in Kent during the 30 years which had passed since Carman started to work for him.

The 1861 census reveals more about Edwin Carman for it was taken on a night when he had gone to visit his father and brother in Maidstone. Edwin's father Robert was a waterman on the Medway, by then in his late seventies and living with his oldest son, also named Robert, who was a sailmaker too.

Edwin had remarried in 1852 and when we catch another glimpse of his life in the records of the 1871 census we find him with his second wife Ann Sellen, Edwin's eldest son John, and two of the three children from his second marriage as well as a lodger.

Edwin owned the leasehold of number 67 and so was entitled to vote as we learnt from the electoral roll of 1873. In 1890 Ann died and Edwin left East Street at last to live with his married daughter Elizabeth in Gillingham where he died in 1895.

The Shrubsalls

When Edwin Carman moved away, a middle-aged couple, Edward and Susannah Shrubsall, moved into number 67 along with Susannah's brother. At this time the house was still a private home with no shop front. Nautical connections continued because Edward Shrubsall, a local man, was a mariner. (10) The directory of 1899 shows that Shrubsall had left the water by then and become a greengrocer. Bearing in mind that we know the Masters next door at 65 were running a greengrocery Shrubsall must have worked for them for a while. But two years later Edward described himself as a fisherman and his wife had added selling confectionery to greengrocery in the shop.(11) At a guess number 67 did not have a shop front until around 1900 when Mrs Shrubsall began to sell sweets.

Edward died aged 66 in 1906. Susannah continued running the sweet shop. How long she stayed at number 67 is uncertain but she was still here in 1922 and we know that by 1926 Frank and Mary Ann Skinner had moved in and taken on the shop.(115) Susannah lived on to the age of 85 and died in 1929.

Incidentally the spelling of Shrubsall varied between that and Shrubshall in the records but both Edward and Susannah's deaths were registered as Shrubsall so that is what we have used here.

Chocolate continued to be sold at number 67

Frank Alfred Skinner had been a brickfield labourer in Murston but it was his wife Mary Ann who was listed in the directory as the confectioner and who gave the shop the name 'The Chocolate Box'.(12)

Some years ago Maureen Smith née Mills wrote to the museum with the information that she had been born at number 67 in 1933. '*My parents moved to the Chocolate Box, 67, East Street, early in 1933 remaining less than two years. My father was Jack R. Mills and my mother was Ivy, I was born there in May 1933 and we left in September 1934. I think my grandmother, Rose Mary Tendall owned the shop*'. We have no confirmation that Mrs Tendall owned the premises but have found from directories that she was a shopkeeper at Maidstone and then Gillingham during the 1930s.

Mrs E. M. Middleton had the Chocolate Box in 1935 as the advertisement shows but, by 1938, she had been followed by Reginald Roach, who did not stay long.

In 1939 May and Stanley London were living here; May ran the sweet shop for Stanley suffered ill health.

Council minutes record that in 1947 Miss J. Beaney who then owned the house, was given planning permission to add a bathroom to it. Janette Beaney and her sister Mrs Cecilia Lee were wardrobe dealers which means they dealt in second-hand clothes. As well as running the shop, we know from the family that they had a stall every Tuesday in Maidstone Market.

The final confectioners whom we have recorded here were the Cassell family (see also numbers 10, 46 and 57 East Street and the NatWest bank building number 87 High Street – HSI)

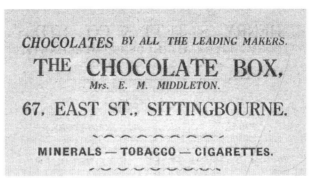

1935 advertisement for The Chocolate Box

The Work Box at number 67

By 1966 the sweets had all gone and wools of every hue were on display to tempt local knitters. Mrs E. C. Dennett advertised her wares in Tunstall parish magazine and the shop was named The Work Box. She was followed in 1970 by Ray and Sheila Spicer, their son Ian and their daughter Vanessa. The Spicers remained for ten years retaining the name The Work Box. The shop was then converted to a salon where you could become bronzed before arrival on holiday in Spain. This was Tan & Tone and Mr and Mrs Burr lived upstairs during the early 1980s. When the 1980s drew to a close number 67 fell empty.

An empty building and then Sittingbourne Heritage Museum

Noel Frewin, who ran a successful family optician's business at number 114 High Street, (now run by his son John) purchased number 67 with a view to opening a branch in the building. However the timing was not good for this venture and so the branch never opened.

The building did not prove easy to let. It stood empty in the early 1990s and fell into disrepair.(121)

In 1997 John Frewin agreed with Peter Morgan that, if his band of volunteers could put number 67 into good order, it could become the premises of the fledgling Sittingbourne Heritage Museum. Squatters were living in the building, graffiti defaced the walls, floorboards and wiring needed replacing. Under the leadership of Peter Morgan, a band of volunteers renovated it and prepared to open the museum. They dug out the cellar a further two feet to make two more useful rooms. Mr Frewin has kindly allowed the museum to be here for over 20 years.

The Museum opening in 1998 with left to right: Terry Fallon (Chairman), Cllr Gerry Lewin (Mayor of Swale), Christine Rayner (Editor of the East Kent Gazette), Peter Morgan (Secretary)

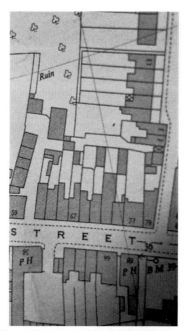

This section of East Street on the 1960 Ordnance Survey map

Number 69 East Street

In 1871 James Busler, his wife Mary and children lived at number 69. James worked as a gardener. In 1874 number 69 became the first shop of the Sittingbourne Cooperative Society which had been founded that year. Shop windows were installed and the society expanded so rapidly that they had to build new premises at 123 East Street which opened in 1877.

THE STORES, 50 YEARS AGO.
The shop in East Street, a short distance from the present Stores, where the Society first started trading.
This view is reproduced from a sketch by Mr. Marshall Harvey, architect, Sittingbourne.

Number 69 with the shop-front put in for the first Co-op shop in the town.

They no longer required number 69 and so it came into use as the home and business of S. Ockenden, a watchmaker. Mr Ockenden did not stay here long but was followed by the Thomsetts who remained for many years.

The Thomsett family

Alfred James Thomsett, a fisherman, was born in Milton in 1841. By 1881 he and his wife Lavinia had a family of eight children to squeeze into number 69. The Thomsetts turned the shop into a fish shop which Lavinia and the older children could run whilst Alfred was out fishing and his catch could supply the shop. Alfred fished with his son Alfred junior and courtesy of the Thomsett family we include a photograph of their boat.

The 'Lydia' owned by the Thomsett family.
Alfred James Thomsett's oldest daughter was named Lydia.

The family have been told that Alfred junior's business thrived and he had several fishing boats.

Lavinia Thomsett died in 1907 aged 62, and in that year Alfred placed this announcement in the local paper:

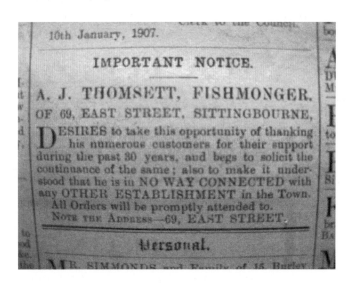

Amos had opened up shop as fishmonger in competition with his father at 112 High Street where he lived over the shop with his wife.

Alfred lived on until 1914 when he died aged 71. The East Street business had by then been run for some time by Harry, another of Alfred and Lavinia's sons.

In 1916, during Harry and Mary Jane Thomsett's time at number 69, the property was purchased by Albert Jesse Thomas, a Rodmersham fruit grower.

The house changed hands again in 1927 (*Fermor family papers shown to us*) when Albert Thomas conveyed the property to Ernest A. S. Passby of Rochester. Harry Thomsett was still selling fish here then.

Harry died in 1941 in his sixties but had moved away from number 69 by 1933 when Daisy and George Spice moved in with Daisy running the shop at least until 1939.(N01)

The ownership and tenancy of number 69 then changed on several occasions and so this is most clearly shown in the table below:

Date	Owner	Occupier
1947	Ernest Passby	Fred and Gladys Leeks
1951	Ann Passby	Adolph and Hilda Pries
1954	Ann Passby	A. G. Bateson
1955	Miskin and Ann Passby	
1963	M. D. Fermor	M. D. Fermor

The Fermors

From 1972 the Fermors owned and ran number 71 as well as number 69 which they already ran as a greengrocery. They leased 69 and 71 out together until 1982 when they were leased separately. Malcolm Fermor was tall, hard-working, and a leading member of Round Table club – married to Barbara. They bought a house in Dane Close Hartlip.

For a while in the late 1970s Stephen and Margaret Smith ran the shops at 69 and 71 and lived there and they were followed by Edward and Jean Davenport, who ran a Pet Food and Garden Centre in the 1980s.

The Fermors had alterations carried out in the 1980s to amalgamate the upstairs of both properties into one flat to be rented out.

Fermor's shop at 69 and 71 in 1972 (EKG)

Number 71 East Street

We have seen that Charles Masters lived at number 71 in the 1870s and he was followed as tenant by Henry Read, a master wheelwright who hailed from Dorset and was able to employ one man. His workshop was behind number 13/15 just down the street.(N01) Percy Hubbard remembered that Henry Read *"carried on a carriage and cart making business"* in *"a part brick and part weather-boarded building"* towards the west end of East Street on the north side of the road.(70) Meanwhile Henry's wife Harriet ran a toy shop; she had only one child at home, and a boarder to look after. The boarder was a coachbuilder who worked with her husband.(9) We know the Reads were here by 1880 for the local paper carried advertisements for his carts for sale and also showed that he had additional premises in Shortlands Road.(N01) They were still there in the early 1890s by which time Henry's son William was able to work with him. In 1897 Harriet died in her early sixties, Henry soon decided to retire and move to live with his elder son, a shopkeeper in Sussex.(11)

A period of rapidly changing newsagents followed for number 71. A certain Henry Stedman was followed by Arthur Gaskin, then Jabez Homewood all before the appealingly named pair of ladies Amelia Eke and Ada Ost who were there in 1911 running the shop as a sweet shop and filling the four rooms of the house with three boarders to add to their income. How long Amelia and Ada remained is not known but by 1922 the sweets were being sold by Eliza Thomas and William Dunham (known as Bill) who remained until at least 1933.(115)

Number 71 had been fitted out as a hairdressing salon with the unlikely name of 'Maison Leslie' by 1938. A mention in the local paper in 1940 gave us 'Leslie's' name and the fact that he lived on the premises: *'William Cheal proprietor of "Maison Leslie" of 71 East Street summonsed for not paying two employees national insurance stamps and fined £1 on each count.'* William Cheal was not actually a hairdresser but employed two people as we see. The 1939 register records that he worked as a salesman and motor driver and lived alone at number 71.

We have not discovered how long Maison Leslie lasted but by 1944 Christina and Robert Shufflebotham were living at number 71 and were still there in 1951.(115)

The ownership of number 71 had changed in 1927 when Albert Thomas sold it to Mr William Thomas Denham of Orsett House, Rodmersham who in his turn bequeathed it to Ann Denham on his death *(source: family papers)*. In 1935 Ann Denham sold it to Percy Henry Willis tailor of Pelham Villas, on the other side of East Street and Albert James Hollis. They sold it on that same year to Roger Alfred Wanstall. In 1955 Dr Frank Miller Mallinson of Hales House Tunstall and R. A. H. Wanstall bought the property.

It seems that number 71 had reverted to being a private house during the 1940s for in 1954 the owner, Roger Wanstall, applied to change the use of number 71 from home to shop and this was agreed by the council.

In 1963 Roger Wanstall sold the property to John and Miss Rebecca Richmond. By 1963 the shop was known as 'Joy's Farm Shop',

The Goad map of 1968 shows number 71 as The Pin House – presumably a haberdashery shop – and this continued until 1972.

In 1972 the property was sold to Malcolm and Barbara Fermor who ran number 69 as a greengrocery and 71 as a garden and pet shop as the photograph from 1972 shows.

In 1979 the Fermors leased the shops to tenants who continued in the same trade. Later number 71 was used as a branch of Seekers estate agency which had 70 branches nationwide and they remained until at least 1994.

1994 Advert for Seekers

By 2005 'Alive' beauty salon were at 69 and by 2002 The Cavern tattoo parlour were at 71 and they both remain trading there today.(121)

In 2014 Malcolm Fermor died and in 2016 his widow had the property auctioned along with number 69. Both were purchased by the local Holliday brothers who continue to let the shops to the present tenants.

'Alive' Beauty Salon at number 69 in   *The Cavern at number 71, 2008 (CA)*

65-71 in 2018 (CB)

Numbers 73-79 East Street

67   69   71   73   75   77   79   81

In our notes on the South field of the Bayford Estate – among the opening pieces towards the start of this book (qv) we have referred to the writings of Canon Scott Robertson, who identifies the land beside this section of the street as part of the Stalkes garden; he lists some of its early owners.

In the 1870s when Robertson was writing, the contemporary records such as the census and street directories, came into play. From 1871, the census had listed street numbers and the directories followed suit, though retaining for a while, the archaic name 'High Street East'.

Just before the street numbers were first applied, these four houses plus the six houses on their west flank, numbers 61-71, were built along the East Street frontage. They do not appear on the Ordnance survey map published in 1865/6, but, sometimes, these maps were published a long time after the surveyors had examined the sites. It seems that William Thomas opened his shop at number 79 in the mid-1860s.

Behind the terrace a lot of agricultural land was left 'undeveloped' – i.e. without buildings. As recently as 1960, most of the site at the back, according to the Ordnance Survey, was still orchard – it is now occupied by the cul-de-sac called Lime Grove, though it is unlikely that the orchard had any lime trees. As historians, we do wish that the names chosen for the new roads of our town always bore some link with the land on which they stand.

Very few, if any, of our readers will be devouring the contents of this book cover to cover. We authors suppose that this series on the High Street and its extensions will be treated as a source of reference rather than bedtime reading! Hence quite often we repeat ourselves. It therefore seems appropriate to set out again some facts about the vicinity in which these properties stand.

The 1840 tithe map shows that a large orchard (just over four acres) named West Lane Orchard (parcel 243 on the map on the adjacent page) covered the site, which then belonged to William Gascoyne, the Bapchild farmer, and was worked by Jesse Thomas of Rodmersham. It was bounded to the south by East Street and to the east by West Lane, which, in those days, was called Orchard Lane. By the way, as mentioned elsewhere in this book, West Lane was re-named after a Mr West who had a house there in 1574. Were he to revisit today Mr West would doubtless mourned the loss of his orchard, but many a farmer would agree with the words of one of our more substantial local farmers in the 20th century *the best crop of all is houses'*. Many a farmer might agree with that, but not necessarily the population at large.

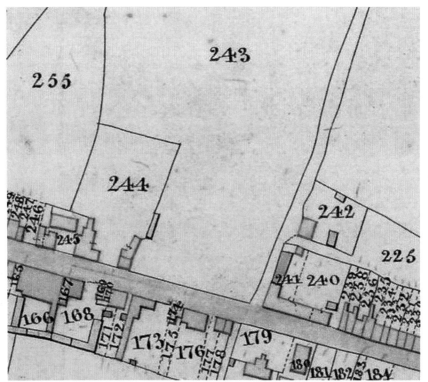

The tithe map 1840 showing parcel 243 – Mr Gascoyne's orchard on which these properties were built

In their early years, perhaps for a full decade, each of these premises had separate occupiers – as they do now. Today this Victorian terrace houses R and A Chinese Takeaway at number 73, Dill's Express Convenience Store at 75, Co-op Funeral Care in the double-width number 77 and Premier Express Convenience Store on the corner with West Lane at number 79. All are believed still to have living accommodation in use upstairs.

Number 73 East Street
Following construction in the 1860s, this property, for its first half-century, was occupied by cornfactors.

Numbers 73 and 75 in joint use
George Gibbons
In 1870 the directory indicates that George Gibbens, a young cornfactor aged 30 from Barham, east of Canterbury, had moved into the new building with his wife Jane (from Littlebourne) and three children. He was sharing numbers 73/75 with George Feakins a local farm labourer and his family who may have been Gibbons's sub-tenants. (As we see below, his successor, James Harris, suggested, years later, that Mr Gibbens's arrived here in 1867).

During the 1870s George Gibbons decided, at that time of expanding population and house building, that there was money to be made from brick making than dealing in corn. Within a mere three years Mr Gibbens had moved to another new building – in Park Road. The Gibbons family then moved to

Rhode House on the London Road at the other end of town where George employed 12 men and six boys to work his brickfield.

After Gibbons left, number 75 was occupied separately by Alfred Baker, a watchmaker, who, by 1878 had gone to Milton Road – perhaps urged by Mr Parton to move on – see below.(32,33)

William Robert Parton

These premises were then combined again – in the hands of William Robert Parton, of 88 High Street, the cornfactor, who had taken over the business of George Gibbens.

Parton did not stay here long: in 1878 he announced in the East Kent Gazette that he was selling his seed and corn business here and at 88 High Street, where he had lived. The buyer was Walter Prentis.(HSII) Mr Parton, then only in his twenties, had been born in Horsmonden.(9) Soon after leaving here, he went on to farm over 100 acres near Dartford.

James Thomas Harris – a man of many parts

At about this time, James Harris appears here, as Mr Parton's manager. By 1881, Jim (as he was known) had taken over the business.

Born in Boughton-under-Blean in 1855, Jim had been brought to Sittingbourne during his first years by his parents Henry Harris and Anne (née Maple, of Littlebourne). With Jim's elder brother and sister, they made their home at Railway Terrace, off the High Street.

Like many country folk in those days, Henry Harris had migrated from the countryside to our town for employment – in Henry's case as a sawyer in the yard of Smeed Dean. We tell more about the family in HSII.

The family home at Railway Terrace was just round the corner from Parton's corn and seed warehouse at 88 High Street, where, very probably Jim had his first job. We know that Jim's younger brother Ted started work with Mr Parton, and very likely, when Mr Parton took over Gibbens's business in East Street, Jim was deployed down there – and maybe Ted too.

By 1881 the census tells us that Jim (aged 26) was well-ensconced here in East Street with his wife Alice and two children, James and Gertrude. Alice, a local girl, was a member of the prominent Millen family, who appear more than once in this series. We have not studied the genealogy, but the Millens who were at this time in business as butchers at numbers 83/85 East Street, may well have been Alice's cousins. James Harris describes himself as a Cornfactor's Manager and a Local Methodist Preacher – an interesting combination – doubtless he particularly enjoyed telling and re-telling the parable of the sower (Gospel according to St Matthew Chapter XIII verse 18).

In his day there were four Methodist/Wesleyan places of worship in our town:
    the church/chapel at 32 High Street
    the chapel at 127 East Street
    the chapel at 19 Shakespeare Road
    the chapel at Snipes Hill.

We do not know which of these Jim and his family frequented, nor at which of them he preached.

The Harris family were living at number 75. The 1881 census does not mention 73, suggesting that it was uninhabited at the time – perhaps it was used for storage only. At the back of the premises there are large two-storey stores.

Of the four cornfactors who were here in succession, Jim's tenure was longest by far. Even so, we suppose that these warehouses were built by Mr Parton, who was obviously a substantial man of business. It is of course possible that Jim made some changes; maybe, for example, he built the smaller store which adjoins the back alley. During his 40 years in business here, Jim diversified into several different occupations, though, throughout that long time, he never abandoned his original occupation of cornfactor-cum-seed-merchant – until he surrendered the premises at the end of the First World War.

Though long-lasting, the business did not always run smoothly – in April 1887 Jim was advertising an exhibition of flowers at number 75, but by June 1890, he was in financial difficulty: to set against unsecured liabilities of £1,937 0s. 3d. he had assets of only £392 14s 6d. Hence he entered into a deed of arrangement with his creditors, presumably avoiding, by a whisker, the disgrace of bankruptcy.(61)

At about this time, Jim's brother Ted left Sittingbourne to establish himself in business at Kingston-upon-Thames. We might speculate as to why he decided to break away: was he concerned about the stability of Jim's business, or its capacity – too small to support both brothers. Maybe Ted, quite simply, was craving independence or, noting the considerable distance between Sittingbourne and Kingston-upon-Thames, perhaps he simply wanted to get far away!

Ted Harris 1864-1948 and his wife Isabella neé Brown 1864-1936

It is surely significant that, in 1890, Ted married the girl next door – Isabella Brown who lived with her family at 77-79 East Street. Ted whisked Isabella away to Kingston-upon-Thames, where his cornfactor's business was established and, it was not long before they produced a daughter and a son.

In 1891 Jim was still a cornfactor whilst, from 1893, he was listed as a seedsman who could offer a *'large variety of vegetable and flower seeds'* – a side of the business, that, naturally, ran alongside the cornfactor's.

Harris advertised his wares in the local paper in 1894:*'J. T. Harris, seedsman. A fine selection of peas, beans and all kinds of vegetable seeds, flower seeds and seed potatoes.'* In the following year he was offering: *'Tested seeds. J. T. Harris, 75 East Street, has for present sowing a large selection of vegetable and flower seeds, with all leading kinds in cultivation. Seed potatoes in great variety, and true to name. Catalogues free on application*.'

Throughout the 1890s Jim continued to advertise himself here in East Street as a seedsman offering *'a fine selection of peas, beans and all kinds of vegetable seeds, flower seeds and seed potatoes.'* In May 1895 he offered *'For present sowing, a large selection of vegetable and flower seeds, with all leading kinds in cultivation. Seed potatoes in great variety, and true to name. Catalogues free on application.'*

About then, this branch of the Harris family moved from the simple rooms above and behind the shops at 73 and 75. Their new home was much more grand – Bekesbourne House, a substantial, detached, double-fronted house, with five bedrooms and three reception rooms, facing the park landscape of the Recreation Ground at the top of Albany Road.

Their large walled garden (big enough for four more houses) extended to the corner of Valenciennes Road.

Jim and Alice (Millen) Harris (seated left) at the wedding of their daughter Flo
Bekesbourne House, Albany Road, Milton – June 1906 (MHP)

A few years later, Jim's parents moved from Railway Terrace to Valenciennes Road and younger brother Ted had moved from East Street to a new house nearby in Park Road.

In 1899, evidently still in expansive mood, the irrepressible Jim took on the shop next-door – number 71, where, diversifying, he entered (for a short while) the book selling trade.(61) This odd, perhaps unique, combination in the directories *'bookseller and cornfactor'* lasted only four or five years.(61)

For a brief while Jim was a sewing-machine agent too...... corn, seeds, books and sewing-machines? Then, guess what! By 1908, he decided that selling pickles was the way forward and, in the local directory, described himself as 'cornfactor and pickle merchant'. Given the ups and downs of his business, local wags might have pointed out that Jim was often in a financial pickle.

It will be noted that the word pickle does not appear in this advertisement in Parrett's directory published in that same year.

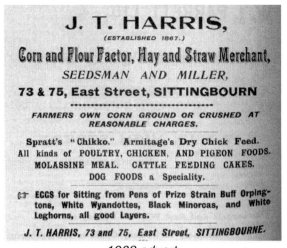

J. T. HARRIS,
(ESTABLISHED 1867.)
Corn and Flour Factor, Hay and Straw Merchant,
SEEDSMAN AND MILLER,
73 & 75, East Street, SITTINGBOURN

FARMERS OWN CORN GROUND OR CRUSHED AT REASONABLE CHARGES.

Spratt's "Chikko." Armitage's Dry Chick Feed.
All kinds of POULTRY, CHICKEN, AND PIGEON FOODS.
MOLASSINE MEAL. CATTLE FEEDING CAKES.
DOG FOODS a Speciality.

☞ EGGS for Sitting from Pens of Prize Strain Buff Orpingtons, White Wyandottes, Black Minorcas, and White Leghorns, all good Layers.

J. T. HARRIS, 73 and 75, East Street, SITTINGBOURNE.

1908 advert

Incidentally, we note that, in 1908, after running the business on his own account for a quarter of a century, Jim is claiming in this advertisement that the business had been established in 1867 – when Jim himself was aged just 12. This suggests that Mr Gibbens, who had established the cornfactor's here, had opened for business in that year.

Four decades later, around 1912, Jim and his family were going through a fateful time; Jim made some heart-breaking decisions. Bekesbourne House, the fine home in Albany Road, where he and his family had lived for about 20 years was sold at auction.

Jim T. Harris   *Alice Harris (neé Millen)*

From the local historian's point of view, an interesting snippet emerges from the particulars of sale prepared by the auctioner, Hedley Peters: fronting Valenciennes Road was a 'motor house' – in other words a garage for a motor car. Timber-built, with galvanised roof, three windows and double doors, it was surely purpose-built for a motor-car – not accommodation for a horse and carriage.

The description in the particulars of sale is our only evidence that Jim Harris had ventured into the realm of motoring – in those days, a pastime restricted to the most affluent, but given Jim's 'adventurous' attitude to cash, it may well have happened. We do know for certain about a horse-less carriage owned by another local resident at that time: the auctioneer's wealthy brother-in-law Ernest Packham (of Wills and Packham, brickmakers and barge owners) living on Hollybank Hill.

As it happens, both Ernest Packham and Jim Harris were great-uncles of one of our contributors – Michael Peters, who is still the proud owner of Ernest's galvanised 'motor house'.

Back in East Street, the Harris shop-premises were split: the cornfactor's business was restricted to number 73 and rebranded Harris and Co – suggesting, perhaps, that Jim had taken on a partner – who may have brought in some outside finance. The premises at number 75 were reserved for a brand-new business as a 'cycle dealer' – rather a come-down if he had indeed been a motorist.

Jim Harris was clearly an optimist, who felt there was always a better way to make a living and that he had just discovered it – or maybe he was simply casting around, fishing in new pools in sheer desperation.

After leaving their treasured home in Albany Road, the Harris family returned to East Street – this time, to number 114, which Jim rented – for a yearly rent of less than £20. Though semi-detached and far smaller than Bekesbourne, it was what estate agents might call 'commodious'. Part of an old house that had been divided into two, number 114 had been extended to the side and, according to the advertisement, contained *four bedrooms, two reception, bath, kitchen, scullery etc. pleasant garden overlooking cherry orchard.'* There some of the family lived, including son Bertram, who, a couple of years later, married Marion Kemsley and brought her to join the household at number 114 – perhaps Bert (as he was known) was not able to afford a separate home – or maybe Marion played a vital role helping her mother-in-law to run the household. Bert seems to have been sickly, unable to join the forces in the Great War, which broke out in the same year as his marriage. We don't know how active a part he played in his father's roller-coaster business, but his work, helping in the family shops, is unlikely to have been regarded as a reserve occupation, allowing Bert to avoid the call-up.

The effect of all this turmoil upon the Harris family can only be imagined. In all, Alice and Jim had produced nine children. Two of the daughters, Ethel and Florence, had married and moved away, but Jim and Alice, like many families in those days, had lost several of their children: their eldest son, young Jim, a missionary, died in his twenties, barely three months after his marriage and just one week before his young wife, baby Sidney lived just 15 days and, most tragically of all, Nellie, aged just 14 months, died of burns. In 1917, five years after leaving Bekesbourne House, Alice died, aged 61. At this time, the family moved house again: to the run-down, formerly swanky, residence in the High Street – number 29 – which, until the 1890s, had housed some of the richest and most prominent of our townsfolk, the bankers and brewers Vallance and Payne. There, despite their ups and downs, perhaps the Harrises were 'tickled' to think that they were living where the wealthy Vallances had once lived in some style – complete with footman (HS1) For the Harrises there was no let-up in the sadness – in 1921, Jim's married daughter Florence died and, in the following year, Jim died too. In 1923, they were followed to the grave by Gertrude, another daughter. The youngest son, Hedley, having married Ella Measday (of another established local family) emigrated to Kenya, where his youngest sister Dorothy (Dorrie) soon joined him. Of that large family, only Bert and his wife (and their daughter Joan) were still here; maybe it was Bert who, showing solidarity with his siblings in East Africa, gave to their family home in East Street the name 'Nairobi'.

Bertram Harris, son of Jim and Alice
1888-1925 (MHP)

Meanwhile, at East Street, after half a century in these premises (since the 1860s) there was virtually no cornfactor's business left and hence no buyer. The premises were vacated, when Bert and Marion withdrew the cycle business to 29 High Street. Tragically, only three years after Jim's death, Bert died too; it seems that he was never in good health. Heroically his widow Marion (née Kemsley) continued with the cycle business and, like her father-in-law, began to diversify – she started selling gramophones.(HS1) *'Whatever next?'* the townsfolk must have wondered. Marion answered that question in West Street, where she established a new business selling clothes and equipment for babies and very young children. She appears in our companion volume telling the West Street story.

Back here at East Street, there now came a big change: the new occupier of number 73 East Street was Ernest Witten who opened a drapery-cum-tailoring shop. In this context we have explained the nuances of the language in regard to drapery for ladies' clothing (see HSI number 43)

Number 73
Ernest William Witten – tailor

Ernest Witten had been born in 1887 at Chislehurst and grew up there, where his father ran a cycle and sewing-machine shop. Given this family background and his own intentions, Ernest might have been drawn to these premises when he caught wind of what Jim Harris had done here.(10)

During the First World War, Ernest had served in the Royal Flying Corps (later the Royal Air Force) He married Constance Martin at Milton in 1916. When he was 'demobbed' he opened this shop and was advertising in 1919 that he sold suits, raincoats and overcoats. In 1921 Mr Witten paid for a large advertisement in the East Kent Gazette, but he seems to have missed the deadline for 'copy' – perhaps because it slipped his mind, being too concerned with family matters – in February of that year, his wife gave birth to a daughter whom they named Peggy.

In 1924 his advertisement drew attention to the fact that he could cater for ladies too: *'Lady and Gentlemen's Tailor. 73 East Street and 4 Railway Terrace.'* He also advertised for staff – *'good all round competent tailors to take charge if necessary'*.

Noting that 4 Railway Terrace appears in the advertisement, we wonder whether the Wittens were living there; we raise this question because it has been noted that, in 1924, a certain W. Brewer was advertising for sale at the property a 'Tortoise' slow-combustion stove for sale at 73 East Street. As yet we have not ascertained on what basis Mr Brewer was on the premises; perhaps he was Mr Witten's lodger or a tenant.

The Wittens were here at least until 1927, but soon afterwards, moved to take charge of The Fruiterers Arms at Rodmersham.(54) Ernest lived until 1965 when he died aged 65.

William Hanley upholsterer at 73 and 75

By the time of Jim Harris's death in 1922, number 75 seems to have stood empty for a while before William Hanley *'Practical upholsterer of Station Street'* moved his business here. In Station Street Mr Hanley had been trading as Allberry and Hanley. He had been born in 1878 in far-away Limerick where his father was an upholsterer. It was actually William's father who had brought the family to England, no doubt in search for more work. William did not get married until he was 48 when, in the Baptist Church in Sittingbourne, he married Elizabeth Matthews, a Murston woman. By 1933 Eliza and William Hanley were living at number 73, into which, presumably, they had expanded whilst still having the shop at 75.

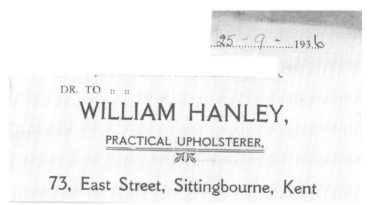

The Hanleys using number 73 as an address in 1936

The Hanleys seem to have moved, more than once, between the two addresses in 1926, Parrett tells us that they were at number 75, but, in the early 1930s, the directories and the electoral roll say that they were here at number 73. In 1938, the Hanley business is listed again at number 75, where William and Eliza remained until the 1950s.(115)

It seems that nobody has lived at number 73 since the second war. In 1946 Sittingbourne Food Office had moved here from the Town Hall. We presume that, in some way, this office was involved with rationing and the supply of food to the populace.

Brickies, Kent Ltd at 73

Brickies ran a chain of butchers' shops in Kent; by 1963 they had here a branch which remained open until at least 1975. They were gone by 1977 when number 73 stood empty.(121)

Sittingbourne Pottery at 73

A short-lived pottery was in business at 73 from 1980-1983. It was followed by two double-glazing companies, each of whom were only here for about a year. These were Apex Double Glazing and then Pinnace Windows.

Apex Double Glazing (Windows) at number 73 in 1984 (Number 75 is empty). (EKG)

By 1987 number 73 is a tool hire company (EKG)

By 1987 Parkerhire were the tenants of the shop and Goad data shows them still there in 1991. Number 73 then stood empty for some years as the century drew to a close. In 2002/3 the shop was in the hands of Duncan Holliday.

R and A Chinese Takeaway at 73

From 2003 onwards, a new direction for the premises was the serving of takeaway food; R. and A. Yeung established the business of R & A Chinese. In 2006 they were succeeded by S. Chai Ng, who in 2017 passed the business and premises to Mrs F. Zhen; she remains here in 2019.

R & A Chinese at number 73 in 2011 (CA)

Number 75

In the early 1920s, following the death of Jim Harris, we have traced no record of occupancy here.

In 1926 Parrett recorded Mr Hanley the upholsterer here, but, soon afterwards, between 1930 and 1933, we find here at 75, a grocery in the hands of John Thomas Taylor.(52) He stayed for a few years, but during some of that time, in 1933, Ethel and Percy Bourne were living here perhaps Mr Taylor was employing them.(115)

By 1938, the Hanleys had returned from next-door, staying put until the 1950s – see above. They seem to have been the last residents.

Co-op Laundry and dry cleaning

By 1963 the Co-operative Laundry and Dry-cleaning service had set up at number 75 and traded here until the mid-1980s.(55-59)

Fashion, Flowers, Flooring and Food

There followed two very brief fashion enterprises: Elli's bridal gowns and Denise Bridge ladies' wear; neither of whom appears to have been open for more than two years.

Then, for most of the 1990s until 1998, the florist Flowerworld (run by Mrs LeMasonry) traded here.

For nearly five years the premises were vacant again. The next occupier was K. Downes, trading as All Floors until 2007 after which, for a couple of years, the premises stood empty once more. In 2007 the premises opened again as Dill's Express, a grocery and convenience store, run by Mr E. Deniz. He was succeeded in 2011 by Sittingbourne Foodstore Ltd trading as International Food Store which was run for a single year until 2015 by Miss D. Rudzika. Since 2015 the premises, owned by the Co-op Group, has, yet again remained unoccupied.

Dill's Express at number 75, in 2008 having kept Flowerworld's awning (CA)

The rear view of numbers 73 and 75 showing the substantial buildings at the back of number 73 with scaffolding. Pictured in 2017 (MHP)

Numbers 77 and 79 East Street

Although the two houses at the east end of the terrace maintained separate living accommodation over the years, their shop space was combined in 1880.

Before 1880
Number 77

Here, the first resident whom we can name was young Stephen Masters a bootmaker from Teynham who, by 1870 until at least 1874, lived here with his wife Ann, a local girl, and their infant son, whom the census enumerator failed to name. After a few years Stephen managed to improve his prospects by becoming a sewing-machine agent and was able to move to 64 High Street.(9)

Sometime between 1874 and 1878, the premises were taken over by James Brown and his wife Sarah Jane, and merged with the premises next door.

Number 79
William Thomas – grocer and provision dealer

Number 79 began its existence as a home and shop for its first occupant William Thomas a grocer and provision merchant, born in Rodmersham in 1827 who, with his wife Mary Ann, had five young children by 1871.

We know the Thomas family arrived here in 1865 for, that March, William placed this notice in the local paper:

'W. Thomas.Grocer and Provision Dealer. East End Sittingbourne. Late of the High Street Milton. In returning thanks for support received during the period he carried on business at Milton begs to inform his friends and the public generally that he has opened a new shop at the corner of West Lane Sittingbourne, where he hopes by careful attention and by supplying good articles at moderate prices to merit a continuance of their patronage.'

We have noted that Mr Thomas appeared in the 1862 directory as a grocer and provision merchant in Milton High Street. He was part of the large Thomas clan from Rodmersham and had relatives in East Street. He was still here in 1874, although not listed in the 1878 directory. It is possible that he expanded the business into number 77 before leaving. However, by 1881, this Thomas family had moved to Islington where Mr Thomas described himself for the census return as a 'retired grocer.' He was then only 53 – we may surmise that ill-health had enforced the big change.

After 1880 – 77 and 79 combined
James and Sarah Jane Brown

By 1878 Mr Thomas's business and the premises (here and next-door at number 77) were taken over by James Brown and his wife Sarah Jane, beginning a period of occupation by them and their family lasting nearly 40 years.

Mr and Mrs Brown were not of shopkeeping stock; nor were they natives of our town. Born in 1823 at Lower Halstow, where his father had made bricks, James began his working life humbly enough as a brickfield labourer and spent some of his early years at Bapchild.(6) After his father died, the family moved to Faversham where James's mother Harriet established a dame-school – a primary school for young children run usually by a lone woman in her own home. There in Faversham, in 1848, at the parish church, young James married Sarah Jane Barton, daughter of a Folkestone wheelwright. They had 12 children over 17 years, though three died in infancy.

The Browns' first home in Sittingbourne seems to have been the building on the corner of Murston Road and Shortlands Road, where, by 1861 James was in business as a grocer and draper. They ran two adjoining shops, trading as bakers and drapers (as mentioned earlier, a delicate Victorian euphemism for a ladies' outfitter) a his and hers business; James ran one, Sarah ran the other. At first (according to the directory) these premises were known as 17 and 18

Murston Row and (in the census) 17 and 18 Murston Lane, then 17 and 18 Murston Road and now 106 Murston Road.

James and Sarah Jane seem to have been the first occupiers of that building; for a while, to distinguish the bakery from the drapery, they called part of the premises 128 Shortlands Road.

In the mid-1870s, with a growing family, the Browns branched out – presumably to create commercial opportunities for their two young boys Stephen James and Henry. At the top of Snipeshill, fronting the Canterbury Road, beside the public house on the corner (the Prince of Wales, now known as Flame Grill) was a terrace known as Malcomb Place. A block of modern yellow-brick dwellings now occupies the site, designed by Robert Banister of Gillingham for Sittingbourne and Milton Urban District Council (HSII, number 14). The archway in this block marks the site of George Street, where the Browns opened their second corner-shop – grocer's and bakery – of which, in due course, their two sons took charge, first the elder son Stephen James (bearing the names of his grandfather and father) and then Henry.

In the 1870s, James and Sarah Brown, in the prime of life, were certainly in expansion mode. Forsaking their premises at Murston Road, they moved into the town centre transferring their grocer's business to William Thomas's grocery at 79 and installing their drapery and millinery next door in the double-fronted shop number 77.

In 1880 James placed an advertisement in the local paper drawing attention to a sale that he was holding, before improvements to the premises took place.

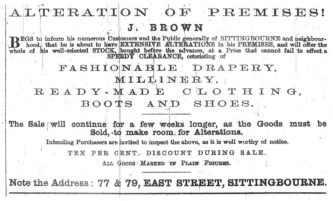

James Brown's advertisement of 1880

The records suggest that the grocery here did not last long. Perhaps the competition from the Co-operative Society, a few doors away along the street, became too strong – that at any rate is the tale that has been passed down the family (Sarah and James were great-grandparents of Michael Peters, one of our contributors). The shops at Murston and Snipeshill remained as grocers but, in the double-shop unit here, the drapery took over.

James Brown 1821-97 (MHP)

By 1881 the Brown household consisted of Sarah and James, two unmarried daughters – Sarah Jane and Isabella (known as Bell) and Sarah (Sally) Knott, their 40-year-old servant.(9)

Ten years later in 1891, when James had reached the age of 68, he and Sarah still had the help of their unmarried daughter, Sarah Jane, in the shop as well as Frank Saunders, their live-in shop-assistant.

Frank Saunders (MHP)

Frank might have been related to one or other of the families of that name who were living in the town at that time. In 1915, Kate Saunders, who, not long before had been living at 120 East Street, married the son of Ted Harris (see earlier picture).

Two granddaughters of school age were here – members of the Weaver family – daughters of Lizzie (Brown) Weaver – elder sister of Isabella (Brown) Harris. Also living here was sister-in-law Mary Ann Savage (who supported herself with her own income). Completing the household, was a servant Sarah Ann Knott, known as Sally – a colourful character, about whom some fruity tales are still recounted in the family. Within the accommodation provided by their two premises there would have been ample space for so many people.

It was a terrible blow to the old couple when their daughter Sarah Jane, who lived with them, died aged 34 in 1893. In the family she was known as Aunt

Sevinus – referring, it was said, to Sarah's strong religious feelings, though the precise significance of this nickname is now lost. An active and enthusiastic member of the Salvation Army, Sarah, on parades, sometimes carried the banner and at other times crashed the cymbals. Evidently a strong personality, she enjoyed collecting tea-towels bearing words such as 'hell-fire' and other inspiring phrases.

It was said that, after her death, James's health never quite recovered. The result was a major restructuring of the family household.

From our account of numbers 73-5 East Street, our readers may recall that Jim Harris's brother, Ted, had married Isabella Brown and they moved to Kingston-upon-Thames where Ted was running his own business as a cornfactor. They were not there long. Following the death of Isabella's sister Sarah Jane, they came back home with their two children (Louie and Harry) and moved in to number 77 next-door.

Sarah Jane (Barton) Brown 1826-1904 (MHP)

Isabella was able to fill the gap left by her late sister – helping in the shop and caring for her parents – though not in the realm of religion! No member of the family aspired to follow young Sarah down that road. Isabella's husband Ted, instinctively family-minded, was once again, fulfilling his role as a mainstay – a strong bridge between the neighbouring households, guiding and supporting everyone and their respective businesses, not least the turbulent business affairs of his elder brother Jim, where Ted's more steady approach to life and business was always acknowledged as beneficial and wise. During those years, to the surprise of nobody who knew the background circumstances, Ted went to work for a competitor – Mr Filmer at 23 High Street.(HSI)

The Browns, meanwhile, continued their business and, in September 1894, the East Kent Gazette tells us that James took action in the local county court by suing William Bingham Hoare, a commission agent, of 99 William Street, for the sum of £21 3s 1d – moneys *'had and received by defendant as collector for Plaintiff'*.

By then, James was ailing – his deterioration was putting extra weight on the shoulders of his family, but he was averse to seeking medical advice.

In the winter of 1897 he died of bronchitis and lung congestion, aged 74.

These are the headstones of the Browns in Sittingbourne cemetery reading: *'In loving memory of James Brown who passed away suddenly January 27th 1897 aged 74 years leaving a wife three sons and two daughters to lament their loss also Sarah Jane wife of the above who fell asleep August 23rd 1904 aged 78 years – Peace perfect peace – In loving memory of Sarah Jane Brown second daughter of James and Sarah Brown died September 28th 1893 aged 34 years. Resting in Jesus. Also William James aged three months, James Perkins aged four years eight months and James aged three years, all brothers of the above'.(MHP)*

James Brown's death was registered by his son-in-law Ted Harris, who was still living at number 77 with his wife Isabella and their two children.

In 1900 Isabella gave birth to her third child Winifred May, mother of Michael Peters one of the team producing this book – now you know why there is so much written here about these families!

In 1903 Isabella and Ted moved from East Street to their new home, which they had built at 216 Park Road – a much smaller place than Jim's.

Widowed Sarah Jane, still at number 79, continued to run the business, as draper and clothier, until her death in 1904. In the family, it was said that Sarah, rather than James, was the 'brains' behind their business. Her obituary in the East Kent Gazette wrote that she was '*a lady of remarkable business ability, and was endowed with great powers of endurance and perseverance. She was admired...for her many good qualities and consistent life*'.

In 1905, the year after Sarah Jane died, her executors instructed Jackson and Sons to sell by auction the contents of the household – most, if not all, the furniture including the 'Chippendale' card tables and 'Sheraton' dining-room chairs, 250 books, a harp and a rosewood 'cottage' piano by Moore and Moore. However this mass clearance did not bring an end to the Brown family connexion: Bell Harris's elder sister, Lizzie Weaver, aged 46, returned to her family home with her husband, Thomas, aged 56, from Pluckley, to take over the business and occupy, with two children and an assistant, the living accommodation in the combined building – six rooms, kitchen and bathroom.

*Lizzie (Brown) Weaver with her husband Tom standing behind her
and flanked by their family – three sons, three daughters.
This is a classic example of the solemn expressions adopted when people had their
photograph taken in those days. Doubtless they wanted the picture to be taken, but they
all appear to wish that they were somewhere else. (MHP)*

Even so, it is clear that Thomas was not settled here. Helen Allinson's research in the records of the Co-operative Society has revealed that, after just two years, in 1907, he offered the freehold to the Co-op – his competitors a few doors away who, for years, had been challenging this family's business.(75)

In 1908 we have a further insight as to the long-term uncertainty; according to Parrett's directory, number 77 and 79 stood empty.(43) Yet a couple of years later, in 1910, the business had re-opened – with a new name, the East Street Drapery and Millinery Company, though we find in the local paper that, in addition to the drapery, part of the combined premises was, once again, a grocery. In that same year, 1910, Tom Weaver was again offering the business there for sale – this time on the open market: declaring to the world that the grocery had been in *'Same hands many years'*. In that same year one Henry Stace was charged on remand with having stolen from a Mr Weaver, a pair of breeches value 9s 11d. The prisoner pleaded guilty and was sentenced to 14 days hard labour – a rather tougher sentence than he might expect nowadays. Mysteriously to us, the claimant was Ernest Weaver, whom we cannot identify. Tom's sons were called Jack, Richard and Bertie, but perhaps one of them had Ernest as his first name.

In 1911, the census records that the Weavers were still here, but, in 1912, the East Street Drapery Millinery and Clothing Company closed down – nearly 40 years after the Browns had arrived.

Then, in 1912 'opposite The Picture Hall' Hedley Peters (of 93 High Street) advertised, in the East Kent Gazette, that he had opened an auction hall here (N01). We can imagine the conversation: Hedley, having become aware that the premises had fallen vacant, or maybe instructed by the owners to find a tenant or buyer, saw an opportunity for himself. His office premises at 93 High Street, which was also his family home, did not have sufficient available floor space for an auction hall. Here, on the West Lane frontage, was warehousing, some of which has been rebuilt recently as a brand-new dwelling named the 'old' Coach House.

In conducting auctions here, in East Street far away from his main office premises, where there was less available floor space, Hedley was following the lead of his father, John, who, in similar circumstances, almost 40 years earlier, had opened, for a short while, an auction hall at numbers 13 to 15 East Street. In later years, Hedley (and his son and grandson, in succession) rather than renting premises full-time, simply hired, on a weekly basis, the main building in the cattle market behind the Bull Hotel, where, at regular intervals, they conducted auction sales of chattels. Auction sales of real estate property, buildings, land etc, were conducted, normally, in the more comfortable accommodation offered by the Bull Hotel in the High Street.

Hedley Peters was not here for long; numbers 77 and 79 – after being combined for over 30 years - were split again into separate occupation – as they had been originally and as they remain today.

This 1953 image shows Thomasson's shop in the forefront on the right – where James and Sarah Brown used to be for so many years.

Number 77
George W. Crane fruiterer and confectioner

The next occupants, of whom we know at number 77 was George Crane who, in 1915 ran a fruit and confectionery business here.(47) In 1918 George met and married Eremada (known as Ada).

In 1919 Mr Crane was offering for sale here a good half cart – a term, whose meaning we have not been able to trace.....scope there for some rather weak jokes, but we shall resist the temptation.(N01) Mr Crane assured readers of the East Kent Gazette that this vehicle *'would suit cob 13 hands'* – which we would interpret as just over four feet high.

Shirley Mannouch, one of our team, has contributed these notes: This picture, outside number 77, was taken in 1921. It shows, standing on the right, my mother-in-law Mrs Iris Mannouch, beside her employer Mrs Ada Crane. The shop was double-fronted with sweets on the left and fruit and vegetables on the right

As well as working in the shop, Shirley's mother-in-law (Miss Iris Madeleine Knight) lodged with the Cranes in Home View Murston. She too was a Salvationist. In the 1911 census at Portsmouth young Iris was recorded as a typist. Possibly she moved here after the war – her sister married a Sittingbourne man in 1920.

In 1921, Mr Crane, ever versatile, was trying to sell '*two one-ton vans, also flat trolley, all in good condition'.*(N01) In 1924 the Cranes left the area, having transferred the business to a member of the Gulvin family – a name that was widespread in this district.(N01)

Henry Thomas Gulvin, fruiterer and confectioner

The shop continued to sell fruit and sweets for another few years under the hands of one Henry Thomas Gulvin. We have not discovered any information about Mr Gulvin but perhaps he obtained some of his stock from John Gulvin a fruit grower at Hartlip or from Fred Gulvin who ran Parsonage Farm at Newnham or from Mrs Gulvin at Bunces farm, Tonge. Henry left here in the late 1920s and then there was a change of direction for number 77.

Allan Gray's cycle shop

Allan and Lily Gray had moved in by 1930, having transferred their businesss from Milton Road. In that year, their daughter June Goodhew was born in the flat over the shop. Allan Gray sold motor bikes and pedal cycles and repaired both in his workshop. He and Lily were blessed with ten children who were gradually squeezed into the three bedrooms of number 77. As well as the kitchen and sitting room downstairs there was the shop and workshop and a large yard out the back. In 1933, the electoral roll tells us that this place was still rather crowded: living here at that time were five members of the Biggs family – Arthur, Mary, Alice, George and Lily as well as Allan and Lily Gray. Though this building is twice the size of others in the row, there must, at certain times, have been keen competition for the bathroom.

Though, by 1934, the business was trading as L Gray and Son, we know that Allan and Lily were still here in 1951; they had left by 1953 when the Sittingbourne Co-operative funeral service had moved in.(115)

Co-operative Funeral service

Since 1953 number 77 has been home to the Co-operative Funeral Service as it still is today. The name has changed slightly for it is now 'The Cooperative Funeralcare'.

Funeralcare at number 77 in 2008 (CA)

In 1960 the residential occupiers were Aerona and Thornly Rogers and by 1980, according to the electoral register, the occupiers were Leslie and Margaret Alice, followed in 1985-1990 by Jennifer and Stephen Jerome. By 1998 the living accommodation at 77 was occupied by Ian and Lisa Mactaggert.

Number 79

Following the separation from number 77 during the war, we know only that, in 1922, George Harris was living here, with his wife Annie, trading as 'Funland' but what exactly that entailed we simply do not know.(47,115) Nor do we know whether George was related to the others of that name who were living here and nearby for so long.

By 1924, Edwin Jones had established a business here.

Edwin Jones – hairdresser and tobacconist

In 1924 he was advertising in the East Kent Gazette:

Corner West Lane.
Hairdressing and Tobacconist
Childrens Hair carefully attended to.
Bobbing a speciality,
Razors ground and set.
Gillett blades, Shaving soap, Shampoo powders always in stock.
Workmanship guaranteed

We assume that, in his mention of Bobbing, Mr Jones was not referring to the parish on the western outskirts of our town.

By 1930 the versatile Mr Jones had opened a newsagency; that business, with the tobacconist's, is still going at these premises today – over 90 years later.

A. Hewitt – newsagent and tobacconist

In 1933, for a brief while, Arthur and Ivy Hewitt were on the electoral register here and running the business.(55) Within the year the business reverted to Mr Jones, who sold it to Albert Thomasson and his wife Evelyn, from London.

J. Thomasson Ltd – newsagent and tobacconist

Trading as J. Thomasson Ltd, their business thrived for over 50 years in the hands of three successive generations of early-risers.(N01, 115)

Albert had been training to be a solicitor but the family had been rocked by the bankruptcy of his father James. Albert's grandson Michael has provided the following account:

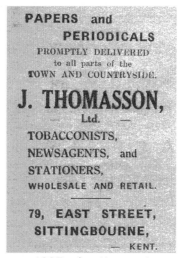

PAPERS and
PERIODICALS
PROMPTLY DELIVERED
to all parts of the
TOWN AND COUNTRYSIDE.

J. THOMASSON,
— Ltd. —

TOBACCONISTS,
NEWSAGENTS, and
STATIONERS,
WHOLESALE AND RETAIL.

79, EAST STREET,
SITTINGBOURNE,
— KENT.

1935 advertisement

To restore the family's name and fortune, Albert realised he had to take over his father's failing shop; borrowing £25, he paid off the outstanding debts and began to rebuild the business. This was done quite quickly and the family prospered. Unfortunately Joan, their daughter, developed severe chest problems; they were advised to leave London and move to the country. They chose Sittingbourne because of the security provided by the paper mills and the brickmaking industry. They purchased Mr Jones's business around 1933/34. Mr Jones retained ownership of the premises but he died quite young and his widow married a Mr Cardew.

Albert Thomasson and his son Ken ran the business together with Ken's wife Doris until 1939 when Ken, aged 24, was called up for the army. Serving in North Africa, Ken contracted tuberculosis of the bone. Invalided out of the army, he was transferred to the Royal Sea-Bathing Hospital at Margate, where he was cured by a stern regime of fresh air and plaster beds (specialist treatment for patients with tuberculosis). Coupled with his own cheerful approach to life, this treatment scheme eventually brought Ken back to moderately good health.

Meanwhile, over the years various members of the Thomasson family were living at 79 and helping each other to run the shop. During the war, in 1944 Gordon C. Martin married Ken's younger sister Mabel and they lived upstairs here for some years. Gordon worked at Lloyds paper mill; he was never part of the business. Back home after that dreadful episode in his life, Ken was never physically strong enough to enjoy sport, so he concentrated on the business. In 1947, he and Doris purchased a house in Eastwood Road and they later moved to Bell Road.

By 1960, tenants were living upstairs here, whilst the Thomasson family continued to run the shop. In the mid-sixties the tenant was D. Hammond and, in 1970, Patricia Norris was on the electoral roll.

Albert died in 1965. Four years later, Ken and Doris separated; Ken moved to Cornwall, leaving the business here to be run very successfully by Doris and her son Michael.

One of Michael's favourite tales of those years concerned the Funeral Directors next door: one morning sorting the papers, first-thing, Michael had a call from his neighbour, the manager of the Co-op Funeral Service, who, on arrival at the premises, had found that coffins in the basement were afloat. Apparently the drains were blocked at the Co-op premises across West Lane, causing some 'inconvenience' in the neighbourhood.

After two decades in charge, Michael sold the business in 1986, but he continued for another five years in his newsagents in Canterbury Road, which he then sold.

East Street, junction with West Lane. 1985 (EKG)
J. Thomasson Newsagent (79), Co-op Funeral Services (77), the dress shop (75), Apex
Double Glazing (73), Davenports (69-71)

Amin – newsagent

After the Thomassons withdrew, number 79 continued to sell sweets and newspapers but now it was run by the Amin family (Bharti and Rajanikani Amin) who remained until 2011.

Amin's General Store at number 79 on the corner of West Lane in 2008 (CA)

From 2013 to the present it is has been in use as the Premier Express Convenience Store.

Numbers 81, 83, 85, 87, 89, 91, 93, 95, 97, 97a, 99 East Street

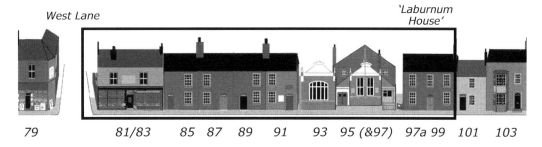

Of all the 19th century buildings that used to stand on this site, only the hall and numbers 97a and 99 remain today. The hall occupies the sites of 93, 95 and 97.

On the corner of West Lane, where numbers 81, 83, 85 and 87 have been demolished for road widening, there is now plenty of empty space, occupied only by a small tree or two and a public bench and a small memorial to a little girl, Emily, aged four, who died in the Herald of Free Enterprise disaster in March 1987.

Looking north down West Lane from East Street towards St Michael's Road and the railway line. The small memorial garden is on the right. A sign, further down on the right still indicates a former entrance to the 'The Regis Suite' which existed for about a decade from 1984 (see the Co-op at 121) (AJW)

The Well Pharmacy now covers the ground where numbers 89 and 91 used to stand – they were demolished around 1970.

An article appeared in the East Kent Gazette in 1926 on the subject of the history of East Street. It stated that, 200 years ago, there were only two houses beyond West Lane on this side of the road. One was number 151 (now on the corner of Shakespeare Road). The other old house stood where the hall is now.

According to Scott Robertson, in previous centuries, from here to the corner, there was *"a solitary house with garden or orchard land beside and behind it....distinguished by its age.... This was a messuage and garden in Bayford Manor, which had belonged to Mrs Wright but passed to John Tappenden, whose son John inherited it before 1731. The quit-rent paid for it was 8d, per annum."*

A quit-rent was a rental payment for use and occupation of land or property. It was a monetary substitute for the service required of a tenant in feudal times when tenants-in-chief were entitled to require their sub-tenants to perform various kinds of service (sometimes military service) - or perhaps to offer a share of their livestock or crops grown on the land. The word 'quit' in this context, does not mean leave – quite the opposite.

Scott Robertson also tells us that the *"ancient house* [was] *cut up into tenements."* In 1870 these were numbered 95 and 97. He went on: *"This house occupied the site of the Drill Hall, and was pulled down when the Sittingbourne Foresters built the hall some years ago."*

Scott Robertson tells us that, apart from this old house, the site *"remained void of dwelling houses until 1835."*

The tithe plan gives us some idea of the scale and layout of this corner site as it was in 1840, comprising then four parcels: numbers 238, 239, 240 and 241. On the West Lane frontage, the plan shows an outbuilding, described in the schedule as malt house and yard.

"In course of time" wrote the Canon, *"a ware-house was added....."* He was writing in the 1870s. As recounted below, within ten years of the compilation of the tithe schedule, the building had ceased to be a malthouse.

The Canon adds that, at some time in the five years *"Before 1841, several tenements had been erected and George Monk Tracey, the owner of the land, had sold it in seven or eight parcels to various persons."*

According to the tithe schedule, this entire block of land, from the corner of West Lane to number 99, was owned, in 1840, by John Clifford, who seems to have lived here. The malthouse was worked by Mr Clifford's son-in-law, William Bate, originally from Chatham; he lived here too – in what was known as Malthouse cottage.

John Clifford died in the year when the tithe map was made; he was buried in St Michael's Churchyard. He left six married daughters and two sons. He requested that his properties in Sittingbourne and Milton (including the Blacksmith's forge at number 26-28 East Street) be sold by his executors so that all his daughters might inherit something.(111) Evidently one of the buyers was the above-mentioned George Monk Tracey.

The present Hall was built in two stages; the outline of the original building is shown on the Ordnance Survey plan of 1909 occupying the site of numbers 95 and 97. In the following year, Council minutes reveal it was extended, necessitating the demolition of number 93.

Beside the hall, numbers 97a and 99 form a pair of semi-detached 19th century cottages, now housing shops as well as living accommodation upstairs.

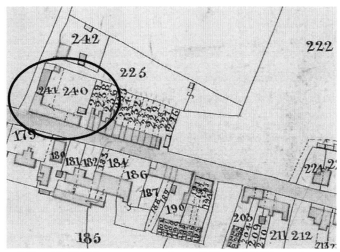

On this section of the 1840 tithe map numbers 241 and 240 can be seen beside West Lane.

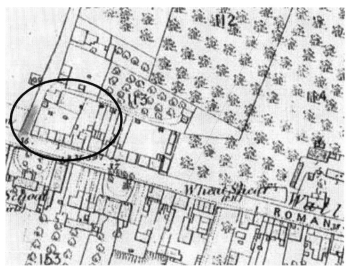

In the 1865/6 Ordnance Survey map the malthouse has gone – and probably the cottage too, so that new homes could be erected.

In 1851, evidently the Malthouse was no longer used for its original purpose. Clifford's son-in-law, William Bate, having vacated Malthouse cottage, he had been succeeded by John Masters a young shipwright from Aylesford, who lived there with his wife and children. (later the Masters family moved to number 65)

Fifteen years later, the 1865/6 map (above) shows that the malthouse has gone. The so-called Malthouse cottage was still there – apparently part of the large old house. Four new homes have been erected on the site. These feature in the census of 1861; the tenants of all four were labourers with families. Looking at the street numbers set out on the map published in 1960, it is clear that the new number 83 was joined to, but <u>behind,</u> number 81 so that it was actually one building partitioned as two small cottages, with numbers 85 and 87 alongside. This is also borne out by the fact that, after 1871, numbers 81 and 83 were always in joint occupation.

Numbers 81 and 83 in joint occupation

In 1861 labourers Edwin Warren and Edward Keeler were the tenants of numbers 81 and 83.

Percy Terry Greensted butcher

By 1870 young Percy Greensted from Faversham inhabited both 81 and 83 and ran a butcher's shop there. Like his brother Walter, the grocer at number 173, he had no doubt been set up in business by his father Thomas Greensted a retired miller who lived with Walter at 173. After some years Percy moved to Margate with his wife and young family and established his shop there.(9)

John Vincent Millen butcher

It was then that John Vincent Millen moved in with his wife Ellen and a clutch of children and took on the butchery.(9,10) He was one of the sons of John Millen the butcher of 87 High Street.(HSI) In January 1887 Mr Millen was one of the long list of local shop-keepers who announced in the East Kent Gazette that they would close early on Wednesdays – not at lunchtime as became the custom later on but at 4pm.

John Millen junior was still running the shop in 1901 but, by 1908, although the Millens remained, the shop was closed.

Sheerness District Sanitary Steam Laundry

John Millen took on an easier task as he grew older; he became branch manager of the Sheerness District Sanitary Steam Laundry which opened in the necessarily spotless refitted premises.(N01,12) Millen retired and lived on until 1926 when he died aged 76.

Sittingbourne Co-operative Chemist

In 1924 Sittingbourne Co-operative Society opened their new pharmacy at numbers 81 and 83 under the management of Mr Newman Hulme. At some point around 1970 the old building was demolished and the present one erected on the site of 89 and 91.

The Co-op Chemist in 2008 (CA)

The chemist and the 'Net Church' next door, in 2019, together occupying land where numbers 89 to 95 previously stood (MHP)

The shop was still known as the Co-operative pharmacy until 2015 when all their pharmacies across the country were re-branded as 'Well.' They are the largest pharmacy company in Britain. Sometime between 2000 and 2005 a sub-post office was housed in the pharmacy too, but it did not remain for long. In fact it was shut down in 2008 in spite of being one of the busiest sub-post offices in town.

Number 85 East Street
A private house

Number 85 was a four-roomed private house. The residents we know of are listed in this table and we can see it was often overcrowded. The properties are not listed on Goad maps after the early 1970s and nor do they appear in the electoral register so this is an indication that they could have been demolished during the 1970s.

1861	William Savage+2	labourer
1871	William Richards+6	brickfield labourer
1881	Luke Robinson+7	general labourer
1891	George Mitchell+1	carpenter
1901	John Bottle+7	general labourer
1911-1933	Arthur Bottle+7	general labourer
1947	Ernest Bottle+1	
1963	Lily Bottle	

It seems odd for a small cottage but in 1968 these were the premises of Allwood, a builders' merchant and then by 1971 for a few years it was where Co-op sheds could be purchased.

Previously this business had been conducted across the street at numbers 78 to 82 – part of the premises known as the French Houses. The builders' merchant and the sheds were housed here on open ground where the cottages had stood.

Number 87 East Street

Number 87 was also a four-roomed cottage which was a private residence.

1861-1871	James Bedelle+3	labourer
1881-1891	Harriet Bedelle+4	charwoman
1901	Emily Dean+3	
1908	Harry Waller	
1911	Ellen Smith +4	
1914-1926	William Jarrett	
1933	Edith Batty	
1939	Frank and Lydia Wakelen	
1947	Frank Barney +1	
1951-1963	Filmer Wellard	

One of James and Harriet Bedelle's sons – Alfred – later ran the newsagent's shop at 30 West Street.

William James Jarrett spent one month as Red Cross volunteer working as Hospital Orderly Duty and Convoy work before he joined the RAMC.

In this image from around 1911 the cottages of numbers 87, 89, and 91 are in the foreground with the Drill Hall set back and tucked away – its gable can be seen above the cottage roof. Number 93 has already been demolished and the Drill Hall extension built.

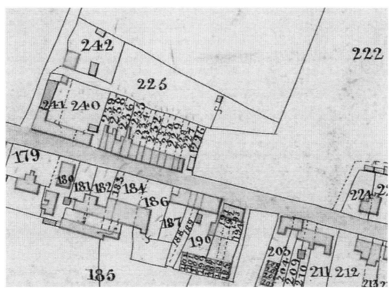

On this section of the tithe map Clifford's plots 241, 240, 239 and 238 can be seen.
In later years, numbers 81-97 East Street were built along the frontage of that site.
Houses also stood along the rest of the row from plot 237 to plot 226 but only those on
plots 239, 238 and 236 survive – now numbered as 97a, 99 and 101
Sharp-eyed readers will note that parcel 237 does not appear here.
For some reason, that number was given to part of Chilton Farm on the south side of the
road - extending to more than six acres it was known as Chilton Orchard. Its narrow
frontage to East Street was a tongue of land, between parcels 194 and 203 – the point
where, nowadays, South Avenue meets the main road.

Number 89 East Street

Number 89 was a four roomed cottage like its neighbours.
These are the residents we know of:

1851	Edward Simmons+4	shoemaker
1861	John Mirams+2	labourer
1871	William England+2	labourer
1881	William Stone+5	mariner
1891	Charles Tevelein	shoeing smith
1894	James Brown	
1901	Henry Wraight	
1908	Mrs Celia Willis	
1911-26	Mrs Emma Medhurst	
1933	Katherine and Leslie Mears	
1947	Charlie and Jessie Gould	
1951-63	Jessie Gould	

Number 91 East Street

Although number 91 also had only four rooms there were several times over the years when it housed a shop in the front room. In 1851 it was the home of Edward Johncock a labourer from Faversham, his wife Mary and four children. The Johncock family were widespread in this district. In Milton, until the mass clearance of the 20th century, there was, leading from Church Street, a pathway called Johncocks Alley. Another labourer, William Edmonds and his family were the next tenants and lived in the house for at least ten years.

A section of the 1865/6 Ordnance Survey map showing these properties

Stephen Robinson, dealer and greengrocer

It was Stephen Robinson who opened the first shop we know of in the house. He was a dealer and greengrocer from Bearsted, with a wife Sarah Jane and six children. Ten years earlier Stephen had been a labourer at the cement mill and the family lived on the other side of the road at number 72. Having the shop was an attempt at a better life.

By 1891 young Fred and Sarah Maynard lived at number 91. Fred was a general labourer and there was no shop. Minnie Norton and then William Sutton followed as tenants at number 91 whilst it remained residential.

Harriet Ingram's shop

Somewhere between 1901 and 1908 widowed Harriet Ingram opened a little sweet shop and tobacconist's in the front room. She also sold mineral water and was trying to support her two children who were then aged ten and four. Harriet continued to live here until she died in 1933. In 1927 Harriet's daughter Ellen had married Alfred Richardson and the couple moved in with Harriet.

These are the later tenants we know of:

1939	Mabel and Jack Hyland
1944	Mrs G. Lockyer
1947-1951	George and Rosetta Eaglestone
1953	Eric and Violet Hughes
1963	G. W. Gibson

Number 93 East Street

Number 93 was never anything but residential. These are the tenants we know of:

1851	Emily Wilson+1	husband is waterman
1861	Stanley Bates+5	mail man
1871	Thomas Brisselden+1	labourer
1881	George Mannering+2	carman
1891	Charles Wright+3	hawker
1901	John Wildish+2	wood-chopper
1908	John Goodwin	

This house was demolished in 1910 to make way for the extension of the Drill Hall.

Number 95 East Street

Number 95 was a private dwelling and only in 1861 did the number of occupants give an indication that it was 'a large house split into tenements'. David Hodges and his wife had five children, a grandchild and three lodgers in the house.

These are the other occupants we know of:

1841	Thomas Elfick+5	labourer
1851	Mary Elfick+3	needlewoman
1861	David Hodges+10	labourer
1871	uninhabited	
1881	not listed	
1891	John Thorogood+7	shoemaker

The house was demolished in 1892 to make way for the hall.

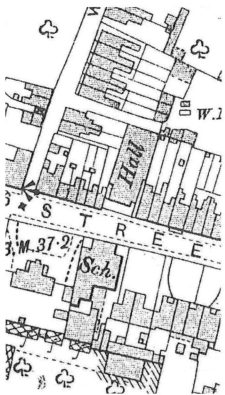

1909 Ordnance Survey map showing the hall before it was extended

The Foresters Hall/Drill Hall

In 1892 number 95 was demolished and the large Foresters Hall erected which, within a few years, became known as the Drill Hall. It could seat as many as 700 people for it was 70 feet long and 36 feet wide.(N01) Designed by local architect Leonard Grant who designed many other local buildings including the Baptist Church, the hall was opened by the vicar of Sittingbourne in May 1892 with a large evening gathering of men who belonged to the town branch of Ancient Order of Foresters and many others from neighbouring branches. The front of the building was admired for its classic design and dressing of cement and artificial stone. The builder was Henry Tidy of Bell Road and the total cost was £1,300. A week later wives and friends were invited to join the members for a tea and a musical entertainment. The hall had been furnished with an excellent piano.

The Ancient Order of Foresters was a friendly society formed in 1834 with branches all over the country. Friendly Societies aimed to help working men through times of financial difficulty such as ill health or old age. The idea was that if a group of people contributed to a mutual fund, then they could receive benefits when they required them. The meetings were held as a social gathering when the subscriptions would be paid. Belonging to a Friendly Society staved off the fear of having to enter the workhouse. Foresters meetings were called 'courts' and the Sittingbourne branch was court 3570 which had been founded in the town in 1861 and, by 1908, had a membership of over 500.

From the start the Foresters hired out their hall to other users for they had no use for it on a daily basis.

In the museum archive is a letter written in 1906 by Lt Col J F Honeyball, Commandant of the Company of the 1st Volunteer Battalion of the Buffs - the East Kent Regiment. Writing from his family home at Newgardens, Teynham, Honeyball says:

"I am looking out for a site for a Drill Hall and Headquarters for the Sittingbourne Volunteers and I notice that the nursery adjoining Messrs Knight & Co's premises is unoccupied. I should be glad to know if the freehold of this could be acquired and if so the price asked together with particulars as to any charges - tithe, land tax, quit rent etc - upon the property. Yours truly J T Honeyball"

The nursery to which he referred was known as Station Nursery, located where the Forum is now. The term quit rent is explained in our section about 81 East Street. For further information about this see HSI – number 119 and HSII – Crescent Street.

Captain Honeyball's search evidently ended when the Foresters Hall became the local headquarters and recruiting office of E Company 1st Volunteer Battalion of The Buffs.

The name of the Foresters Hall was changed and in 1908, the directory described it as the Drill Hall (late Foresters). It seems the friendly society had sold the building but still met there once a month.

In 1909 the local paper noted that the army recruited in the town under the auspices of the local East Kent Regiment, The Buffs. They required smart young men with a minimum height of 5'2". They could join up at the Drill Hall where Captain Arthur Atkinson had the headquarters of E Company which was the Territorial Battalion of the Buffs and had over 100 members who met for training every week often attracting young men to join the regular army.

In 1910 council minutes record that the hall was extended. On the photographs it can be seen that the main hall with its high roof is behind two lower parts which project to the street. The projection to the west is at the side of the main hall whereas that to the east is directly in front of the main hall. The projection to the west was the 1910 extension which would have necessitated the demolition of number 93.

Smoking concerts and lectures continued to be held in the hall as the first war approached. Because this was the local headquarters of the Buffs it was where the townsmen volunteered to serve when war broke out in 1914. Throughout the war there was cooking in the yard of the hall for up to 200 soldiers at a serving. Here the 8th Battalion Northants Regiment were fed whilst stationed in Sittingbourne.

After the war, the mixture of military and leisure activities which had taken place before hostilities resumed. The Hall remained the headquarters of B Company Detachment 4th Buffs. Their caretaker and recruiting officer was Sergeant H. G. Freeman.

Whist drives and concerts took place in the hall during the 1920s on evenings when it was not required for military use.

As the former Drill Hall sheds its layers of paint the inscription '4th Battalion The Buffs' can be seen again above the sign for the Net Church

Members of 10th Kent (Sittingbourne) Home Guard Battalion together for the last time at a farewell gathering 1956 at East Street Drill Hall.
Lt Col J. E. Wills commanding in centre. John Wills was the last managing director of Wills and Packham, brick manufacturers and barge owners.

It is believed that the hall was in use as a spiritualist church for a while in the 1950s and then by 1963 was the headquarters of Civil Defence in Kent. The Civil Defence Corps, established by central government in 1949, was an organisation of civilian volunteers authorised to take charge of an area during a major national emergency such as a nuclear bomb raid. The Corps was closed down in 1968. Doubtless, throughout the country at that point, a large proportion of the population had their fingers crossed. 50 years later, perhaps that still applies; we might wonder whether the risks and dangers have diminished.

In 1970 the drill hall was up for auction.

The hall for sale in 1970
The signage still reads 'Kent Division C.4. Sub-area, Civil Defence Headquarters'

During the early 1990s, the former drill hall stood empty for a while, before finding new life. Unlike its previous use it now has a peaceful purpose – as the Net Church, a Pentecostal Christian denomination affiliated to the Assemblies of God.

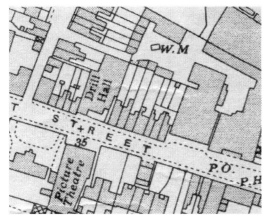
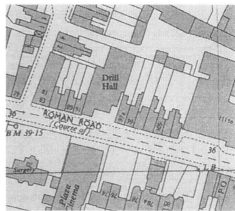

1960 Ordnance Survey map

Number 97 East Street

We can say little of the cottage that was number 97. In 1861 Stephen Crouch a widowed labourer lived there alone, in 1871 the cottage was empty and in 1881 it was not listed. The final mention of number 97 that we have found is in the 1891 census return which gives the information that it was a four-roomed cottage inhabited by widowed Maria Bartlett and her two children. The cottage was demolished a year later.

Although the Foreman family were listed at 97 in the 1908 directory, the 1911 census return reveals that they actually lived at 97a and 97 was no more.

Number 97a East Street

This was a residential property until recent years. The first resident we know of was John Impet, a man in his thirties whose job was to drive a mail cart. He had a wife and four children to support. In 1861 young Thomas Adams a coach painter from Maidstone was resident here with his wife Ellen, two little children and old father John Adams who was a farm labourer. Of the family only old John Adams remained in the house in 1871 and he shared the house with Evan Richards a Welsh pensioner from Cardiff and his wife.

The building seems to have been empty in 1881 at any rate it was not listed in the census. Jane Henham is the next occupant we know of and she was here by 1891. She died in January 1892 and this information about her appeared in the Gazette: '*Mrs Henham mother of Thomas Henham the High Street butcher died most respected by all who knew her in full possession of her faculties at age of 92. Her husband Thomas had been a gunsmith who died in 1868 aged 75. The couple had lived at number 64 High Street. She herself had lived in Sittingbourne for over 70 years having grown up in Tenterden'.* Jane Henhams daughter, Jane Henham junior, continued to live at 97a after her mother's death and was still here in 1901. She earned a living by sewing shirts.(11) She died in 1908.

In 1895 an agreement had been drawn up between Sittingbourne Co-operative Society and the owners of numbers 97a and 99 who were Mr and Mrs Henry Pell whom we meet at number 112. It was just a matter of access to yards and drains at back of their property for the Co-op.

Ernest Foreman a wheelwright and coachbuilder lived here in 1911 with his wife Rose and two young children,

By 1922 elderly Mrs Elizabeth Boorman lived here. She had run the Rose and Crown round the corner from East Street at number 2 Bell Road with her husband William. She died in 1926 aged 77.

An auction of the contents of the house was held before the building was put up for sale: '*97A East Street (was Mrs. Boorman deceased) three bedrooms, two sitting rooms, scullery, cellar and garden'.*(N01)

Joe's Hairdressing for Men at 97a in 2008 (CA)

Later occupants that we know of:

1933	Albert and Elsie Knightly
1947-1980	The Richardson family
1985	Marion and Ricky Duchesne
1989	vacant
1990	Leonard Bye, Gary Page, Bernard Tucker – of Hatton and Tucker – see above – and below at number 99
1997 to date	Joe's Hairdressing

97a, 99, 101 and Aldi supermarket (MHP)

97a & 99 in 2018 (CB)
Number 97a is a hair-dressing salon called Joe's and
99 is a beauty salon called Cerise's

Number 99 East Street *Laburnum House*

William Hunt, a farm labourer, was the tenant here in 1851; the house was full with five children, Mrs Hunt and a lodger. In 1861 this was the home of young Percy Lyon already married at 21, a banker's clerk who had been born in London and his 19 year old wife Selena.

It is in 1870 that we first see number 99 named as Laburnum House by Mrs Harriet Taylor. Widowed Harriet Taylor kept a boarding-house here. She was then in her sixties born in Chilham and had been married to a farmer. Her grandson lived with her and part of the house was let to a young widowed printer and his child. No doubt Mrs Taylor looked after the youngster and two lodgers. Harriet Taylor had moved next door to number 101 by 1881 when Jane Videan lived here with her son.

A notice appeared in 'The Era' in 1884 which gives the impression that number 99 then housed the office of a theatrical agent. It read: '*Wanted for six nights commencing Monday November 10th at Theatre Royal Croydon, Lady for Mrs Primrose in the vicar of Wakefield. Walking gent., Walking Lady, and two Utility Gentlemen. Address with lowest terms, cartes and references to Messrs Roberts, Archer & Bartlett, 99 East Street Sittingbourne up till Monday, afterwards Lecture Hall, Chatham.*' It is intriguing but we do not know who placed the notice. We imagine a 'walking lady' was one who had no words to speak and simply walked across the stage!

Mrs Frances Burton, the widow of John Chambers Burton the blacksmith at number 26, moved here in 1887 after the death of her husband, with her old father and daughter Mary and was still living here 20 years later.

By 1922 Edward Bradley a Sittingbourne man who had trained as a blacksmith moved here with his wife Mabel.

In 1931, when the Bradleys were still here, notice was served by the council on the owner's agent, Albert Turner, to make the house safe for human habitation by repairing the bedroom walls to prevent damp, and fitting efficient window frames in the bedrooms.

Later occupants that we know of:

1945	Mrs F. Ralph
1947	Charles Gill
1950	R. Antrichan
1951-1963	Drury family – at which time, this freehold, and that next-door at 101, were both held by Charlie J Howard, a property-owner from the Medway Towns. He acquired several commercial premises in our town centre – see HSI nos. 33-39.
1975-1985	Bernard Tucker – of Hatton & Tucker – see number 97a next-door
1990	John Hall and Elizabeth Turner
1991-1998	vacant

In 2000 a new business opened in the building this was Jaycrest employment agency which was still operating in 2005. Recruitment continued under the name TemPer from 2009 and then in 2014 Pharos Specialist Recruitment. This then became the premises of Hidden Gems – vintage and shabby-chic antique furniture, before being taken on by 'Cerise's' – a beauty salon.

'Temper' Agency at number 99 in 2008
and on the left, no doubt a door to the flat above (CA)

Number 101 East Street

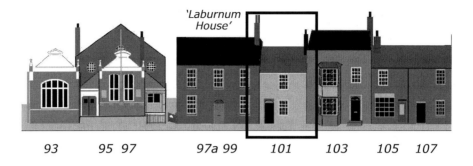

William Spendiff, an elderly widowed farm labourer, lived at 101 in 1851 – he was, perhaps, the first occupier; he was 79 when he died in 1860.

Charlie and Margaret Packer

The next resident of 101 was a man whose family we have come across several times in this book. He was one of the Packer basket-makers and lived his whole life in East Street. In 1861 when he and his wife Margaret and three young children left the Packer family home at number 10 and moved to 101 he was in his thirties. (see numbers 10 and 55)

The Post Office Directory for 1866 lists Margaret as running a school here. This enterprise did not last long, probably the combination of lack of space and a growing family of her own to look after proved too much. The family still lived at 101 in the 1870s. However by 1881 they had moved to number 55 and their place here had been taken by old Harriet Taylor from number 99. Harriet died in 1886.

A musical family – The Brooks

The Brook family had lived across the road at number 34 but by 1891 George Burton Brook from Canterbury and his wife Jane had set up home here with their children. George earned a living by teaching music. He did not live a long life but was cut off in his prime aged 46 in 1896. Widowed Jane was also musical and after George's death she gave piano lessons. She had three adult children in the house then and two young ones.(11) When George died the youngest had only been a baby whilst the eldest, a daughter, was grown up and could help at home. The two eldest boys were working as labourers in 1901.

As the years went by Jane remained at 101 in fact she was here until her death in 1934 in her eighties. It seems one or more of her children always lived with her. In 1911 there were three sons at home, the eldest, Archie, was a fish merchant by then whist the other two worked in shops. Son Leslie set up a motor haulage contractor business from the house. When she was older daughter Bessie returned to live at 101 and died here in 1954 bringing to an end over 60 years of tenancy of the house by the Brook family.

The Boomerang Milk Bar

It was then, in 1955, that a shop front was fitted, for the owner of the building Mr Charlie. J. Howard of Chatham (see above at 99) for 101 was to be the premises of that most modern of establishments – a milk bar – and boasted a juke box.(105) By 1960 it was called the 'Boomerang Milk Bar' and was a popular meeting place for those teenagers who considered themselves to be Mods whilst the Rockers congregated at the Plaza Café across the road. If they could afford them, Mods liked to wear suits and ride scooters whilst Rockers liked longer hair with quiffs, leather jackets and motor bikes.

The Boomerang Milk Bar and number 101 in 1961 (EKG)

We were told that the unusual name 'Boomerang' was chosen because the owners of the café had emigrated to Australia but came back again. A check of passenger lists on the Ancestry site revealed George and Lilian Chadwick, whom we knew lived at 101 in 1960, had set sail for Sydney from London in the spring of 1952. George was then 35 and Lilian 40. They had left their home in the High Street Herne Bay where Lilian worked as a hairdresser and George was an engineer. But for some reason Australia did not live up to its promise and so they returned to Kent and settled at 101.

The Chadwicks had moved on by 1969 when the café had the very downbeat name of 'Fiasco'.

By 1981 Bernard Tucker had opened numbers 99 and 101 as Hatton & Tucker which was a sports-gear shop and he lived above the shop. Bernard already had a sports-gear shop at 57 High Street which he ran with Michael Jeffrey who lived over the High Street shop.(HSI)

1981 Advert for Hatton & Tucker

By 1987 Goad maps show there was no longer a business here although the flat upstairs might well have been lived in. The shop remained vacant for a good ten years.

From 2000 until recently, this building housed the Sittingbourne branch of 'Abbey Cleaners', an independent dry-cleaning business. They still have a branch in Faversham, after whose abbey the firm took its name.

At the present time in 2019, the building stands empty – again.

Abbey Cleaners at 101 East Street in 2008. The front door to the flat upstairs is on the right (CA)

Number 103 East Street

'Laburnum House'

93   95 97   97a 99   101   103   105   107   109   111

Nowadays where number 103 used to stand beside the surviving number 101 there is a paved path on the west side of the Aldi store leading to the car park and shop. Number 103 was a six-roomed private house which never had a shop-front added to it and seems to have been demolished around 1960.

The 1840 tithe schedule has number 103, plot 235, on the plan, 'part of a house and garden' owned by John Hinde and occupied by Ann Murton. John Hinde was a member of the prominent and wealthy family of that name. The Hindes were renowned for their sharp attitude to business; based in Milton, they lived comfortably at 62 High Street – a substantial house of classical design known, until recently, as Hinde House. Having been converted for multiple occupation, it is known now as Burley's flats. Ann Murton does not appear in the Sittingbourne census, a year later; renting this modest house, it seems unlikely that she was a member of the wealthy Murton family of Tunstall.

It was widowed Martha Chittenden a woman in her sixties who was the tenant at number 103 along with her young servant girl when the 1841 census return was taken. Martha died in 1846 and the next tenant was Mary Fisher an elderly widowed charwoman.

In 1861 John Masters the shipwright lived here with his wife Amelia and family.

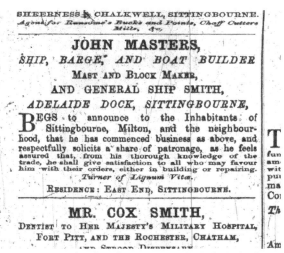

John Masters advertisement in the local paper in 1868.(N01) This must have been the year that he went into business on his own account rather than working for someone else.

By 1871 when the house was empty the Masters had moved along to number 65 where much more can be read about the family.

The next inhabitant we have discovered was young Londoner Robert William Speed, a clerk, who was at 103 in 1878. His stay in Sittingbourne was brief for by 1881 he had returned to London.(9)

William Broadbent

William Ralph Broadbent, a young chemist's assistant from Middlesex who had married Sittingbourne girl Jane Gambell, had moved in by 1881. The Broadbents later moved on to Station Street where William opened his own business as a 'drug and patent medicine vendor' which would have been a poor man's pharmacy. William had little time to make a success of it for he died in 1893 aged only 38.

Mrs Frances Binder, an elderly widow from Faversham lived here in 1890, able to support herself on her own means.(36) She had made the very short move across the road to number 108 a year later and Bill Ovenden a tin-plate worker with wife and four children had moved in to 103 in her place.(10)

The other residents we know of are listed here:

1895	Mr Brain	
1901	Edward Lewis	paper mill labourer

The Williams family from number 15

By 1908 Thomas Arthur Williams had moved into number 103 with his wife from number 15. (see number 15) The move to this smaller house marked the end of Thomas's enterprise as a job-master and the start of taking things easier as he got older though he was still the town carter in 1911.(12) Thomas died in 1923 aged 74. Annette lived the rest of her life here and their two sons Arthur and Harry continued to live here after her death. By the late 1940s they had sub-let to Alfred and Gertrude Harrowven who remained at 103 in 1956. However, the property was no longer listed in the 1960 electoral register or the 1963 directory and so we think that it was demolished by then.

Today the space where number 103 used to stand is a walkway (AJW)

Numbers 105, 107, 109, 111 East Street

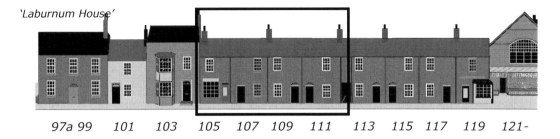

'Laburnum House'

97a 99 101 103 105 107 109 111 113 115 117 119 121-

Today the land where the houses later numbered as 105, 107, 109 and 111 stood is covered by part of the Aldi supermarket. In the tithe schedule of 1840 these properties were each described as 'part of a house and garden' and were parcel numbers 231 (111), 232 (109), 233 (107) and 234 (105). The Ordnance Survey plan, showing the site as it was about 25 years later, makes clear that, when the site was surveyed, there were just two structures here; this explains why, in the tithe schedule, each dwelling was described as 'part of a house and garden' These structures were altogether different in outline from those which appeared in later editions of the Ordnance Survey plans.

The cottages are seen on this section of the tithe map

In 1840, the old cottages belonged to Mary Tilley who owned some others, including numbers 23 to 29 East Street. Mary herself lived with her father Thomas Tilley at number 20 High Street. Her tenants were listed as John Hogben and Ann Popperwell with the other two noted as in use by Mary probably implying that they were empty at the time – or let to servants or short -term tenants.

At the time of the 1851 census, two of the dwellings stood empty and perhaps, not long after that, the old structures were pulled down and replaced by the four cottages, which, before the Second World War had been bought by the Sittingbourne Co-operative Society to demolish so as to make space to further extend their store. (see 113-125)

Number 105 East Street

In 1841 this four-roomed cottage was the home of John Sherwood a young vet who was soon to become established at number 87 High Street.(6) But in 1841 Sherwood was saving money by sharing 105 with one of the East Street Snelling tribe – Benjamin who was a bricklayer, his wife, three children, baby and nurse. After a few years Ben Snelling moved across the road to number 62. (see 62).

The house was empty in 1851 but by 1861 a shipwright named John Masters, his wife two sons and a servant were at 105 – perhaps occupying the new building. They soon moved next door to number 103 and then to 65 where you can read a lot more about their lives. George Handcock is the next tenant we know of. He was a married cement miller from Chatham with four children.(8) We know that Richard Trowel and his family lived here in the 1880s. He was a labourer from Borden and then came John Austin, a fisherman from Queenborough whose son fished with him.

Edward Shilling, thatcher

The first business run from the house that we know of was that of Edward Shilling a thatcher from Bapchild. In 1894 he advertised in the local paper:

18th August 1894: 'Thatching wanted. Apply to E. Shilling'

He advertised again in 1896: 'E. Shilling, thatcher and reed layer, 105 East Street.' The occupation of reed laying can be defined in two ways: someone who placed layers of reeds on a thatched roof (but as Mr Shilling was a thatcher he would have done that anyway). More likely in this case it was the other definition of a man who cut the reeds ready to dry in batches for thatching.

The 1901 census enumerator found Edward, who was 50 by then, still living at 105, working as a thatcher and his wife Frances and five children. The amount of thatch being used locally was diminishing and Edward struggled to earn a living so that by 1908 he had left East Street and returned to live in Bapchild where he was employed as a farm labourer, doubtless adding to his income when he could with thatching jobs.

We know that Edward's father was a farm labourer in Bapchild as was Edward himself by the age of nine.(7) After he got married he had worked in the brickfields. By 1891 he was labouring as a barge-loader whilst his wife Frances ran a corner shop and they lived in Shortlands Road.(10) Their eldest son, also Edward then aged 16, laboured in the brickfields too whilst even ten year old James worked there half time.

But Edward Shilling was a man who wanted to give his children a better chance in life and so he had learned to thatch, perhaps taught by an old friend in Bapchild, and started his own enterprise.

Bootmakers

In 1908 Alfred William Atkins made boots to sell at 105 and he was followed by another young bootmaker Arthur Hedley Watts.(12) At some point Arthur managed to purchase number 105 and rented out at least the living accommodation for a while whilst living in Teynham. We know from the electoral register that Edward and Elizabeth Weller lived here in 1922. Arthur continued to work here and is in the 1927 directory. It is the 1933 electoral register that tells us that Arthur owned the cottage whilst Frank and Lydia Wakelin lived here. By 1934 Arthur's directory entry was for Teynham.

The premises were empty in 1939 having been bought by the Co-op although later on they sometimes took tenants for the upstairs accommodation.

Number 107 East Street

In 1841 the next cottage was the home of Charles Wiles a shoemaker his wife, children and a lodger. In 1851, like next door, the premises stood empty and Charlie and his wife had moved on to Flushing Street. Maybe the landlord had asked them to make way for the rebuilding, or perhaps there had been too much competition in East Street for a man who wanted to work on his own.

William West a wheelwright from Hollingbourne with wife and child lived here in 1861. Other tenants followed including Joseph Holland a mail driver from Chilham with a wife and five sons, and George Reader a local labourer.

During the 1880s John Goddard moved into 107 from number 128 where he had previously had his hairdressing business. An 1887 advertisement he placed in the local paper reads: '*J. Goddard Hairdresser 107 East Street will grind razors, scissors, table cutlery and Doctors' instruments at short notice. Will return charge if not satisfied.*'

Hairdressing continued under young Edward Phillip Parr who was here by 1890 with his wife and child. Edward came from Croydon and remained in East Street until at least 1901 before returning to his home town.(11) By 1908 the business was in the hands of Edward Henry Knowles who had moved into the four rooms with his wife, children and brother.

Tenants during the 1920s included Edwin and Lilian Harris, Phillip Cherrison and by 1927 Ernest and Norah Milbourne. In 1933 Sittingbourne Co-operative Society gave the Milbournes notice to quit so that 109 and 107 which adjoined the furnishing department could be demolished and the department extended. Ernest had grown up in Shortlands Road and more recently been a tenant of number 113.

Number 109 East Street

In 1841 the five rooms of number 109 were occupied by Ann Popperwell, a widowed tailor and her son Henry whom she had also trained as a tailor, her daughter and two lodgers. It was unusual for a woman to be described as a tailor in the Victorian census returns. Ann and Henry were still working and living there in 1851 with a cousin who was a labourer lodging with them. In this census return Ann's occupation is given as the more usual needlewoman. She had been born in Fordingbridge, Hampshire. The Popperwells are the only family we know of who ran a business at number 109.

The following table lists the tenants we know of who followed them.

1861	Alfred Swinyard+ family	blacksmith
1871	John Hernden+ family	brickfield labourer
1881	Benjamin Smith+ family	mariner
1887	Thomas Lockyer	
1891	empty	
1896	Charles Attwood	
1901	Edward Bonnett+ family	bricklayer
1908	George Denne	
1911-1926	Reuben and Mary Smith	gardener
1927	Reuben Smith and Ellen and Charles Harris	
1933	Frances Smith	

Number 111 East Street

In 1841 John and Mary Cooper lived at 111 with their six young children. John worked as a gardener for one of the better off inhabitants of the town. He was then in his thirties and it was surprising to find that during this decade he moved along to number 49 with the family and set up as a baker.(see 49)

At 111 the Coopers were followed by George Thomas, a bootcloser, and his wife. Bootclosers stitched together all the parts of the shoe upper. As we know there were several shoemakers and bootmakers in the street whom George could have been employed by.(6) In 1861 labourer Stephen Neves and his wife Mary were the tenants.

Number 111 was empty in 1871 but by 1881 the Bragg family had moved in. William Bragg was a young blacksmith from Sussex with a wife and three little sons. By 1891 the Braggs had left and Mary Ann Carpenter a local woman was the tenant. She worked as a paper sorter at Lloyds Mill to support her six children for she was widowed. However her eldest child, William, was 15 and working as a labourer and Mary's mother lived with them to look after the children whilst Mary was at the mill. Mary's offspring included Harry who later ran a grocery shop in West Street. The Carpenters remained at 111 ten years later.

Martin Luther Wheeler, a paper mill worker rented the house in 1908 but it was untenanted in 1911. Catherine and Frederick Pope were the final occupants during the 1920s. By 1927 the building was empty and soon the Co-op purchased it to extend their premises whilst still taking the occasional tenant in the upstairs accommodation until the building was demolished.

For the next phase of the history of this site, we refer our readers to the next section which gives more details of the history of the Co-operative Society.

Aldi in 2018 on the site of 105-127 (CB)

Numbers 113, 115, 117, 119, 121, 123, 125, 127 East Street

107 109 111 113 115 117 119   121-127   Church

Numbers 113, 115, 117 and 119

These four small dwellings belonged to Thomas Hedgecock in 1840 and are each described on the tithe schedule as 'part of a house and garden.' The house had been partitioned into cottages and was occupied by four tenants whose homes were numbered 227, 228, 229 and 230 on the tithe map. Later they were known as 119, 117, 115 and 113 East Street. We don't know how old this large house was.

Thomas Hedgecock was the older brother of John Hedgecock who owned and lived in number 121 next door (see below).

Unfortunately Thomas had died some months before the 1840 tithe schedule was drawn up. As far as we can ascertain he had neither married, nor had children, nor left a will. He was only 39 and no doubt had imagined he had years of life before him. Presumably his brother John inherited the house.

None of these homes ever had their front rooms converted for use as a shop although a tailor did briefly work at 115.

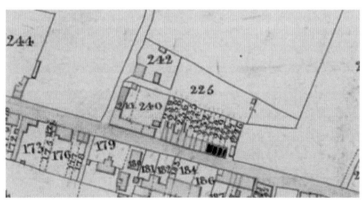

The terrace of cottages can be seen in the centre of the 1840 tithe map

In the museum archives is a photograph showing the cottages on this site – replacements for the big house described in the 1840 tithe schedule. We do not know when the redevelopment of the site took place. These cottages were demolished to make way for a new store for Sittingbourne Co-operative Society in 1928.

Number 113

Charlotte Philpott and her daughter Harriet lived here in 1841 and had sufficient money to be independent. They were followed by William Philpott who was probably Charlotte's son, his wife Mary and their two adult sons, Thomas, and the appealingly named Friend.(6) William and his sons were farm labourers and all the family had been born in Sittingbourne.

By 1861 Henry and Eliza Bonny and their children were in residence. Henry was a 'gas dealer' then who within a few years had been appointed manager of the gas works and moved to Murston with his family.(8)

Number 113 was rented in 1871 by James Philpott a young blacksmith from Chilham with a wife and five children who may not have been related to the earlier Philpotts who had lived in the house.

Labourer Thomas Howting was the tenant of number 113 by 1881 with his wife and children. The Howtings remained for a good 20 years.(10,11) Mrs Alice Foreman was the occupant in 1908. It was while Charlie Shonk lived here in 1911 with his wife and children that a scullery was added on the back of 113, 115 and 117.(88a) Charlie was paralysed and he and his wife Emma were supported by their 20 year old daughter who was a shop assistant and their 18 year old son who was a stoker. The final tenant before demolition was Ernest Edwin Milbourne who had previously lived at number 107.

Number 115

Elderly labourer Edward Bailey tenanted the house in 1841 with his wife and two young children who were probably the old couple's grandchildren. George Marden, a young carpenter lived at 115 ten years later with his wife Sarah Ann.

John Garrett, a Sittingbourne man, was the master tailor who lived and worked here in 1861 but he is neither listed in the 1858 directory nor in that of 1862. He died in 1865 and so perhaps was already ill when he came to number 115. It is not surprising if his health was poor for he grew up at number 2 High Street where his father was a collar maker. That was a spot known for its poor drainage.

By 1871 John James Russell had taken on tailoring here following in Garrett's footsteps. He hailed from Warwickshire and had come with his wife Matilda, daughter and stepdaughter. In 1894 Mr Russell died in his fifties. Matilda however still lived at 115 in 1901 with three of their adult children for two of her sons worked at the paper mill and her daughter had a job as a servant. By 1908 James Clements, a brickfield labourer rented 115 with his wife Louisa. He was followed by Ethel and Ernest Musk and the final tenant was Mrs Mary Ann Murton.

Number 117

In 1841 John and Jemima Hogwood lived at 117 with their children. John's occupation in that census return is illegible but ten years later, still at 117 he was listed as 'formerly a schoolmaster'. By then he was in his fifties. Where he had taught we have been unable to discover and when his daughters were baptised his occupation had in fact been given as shoemaker. Widowed Richard Baker was a labourer who was living at 117 in 1861 with three of his adult children. In 1871 William Baker continued his family's tenancy of the cottage. He was a widowed farm labourer who lived alone.

A young upholsterer's assistant, William Norris, had moved in with his mother and nephew by 1881. Later tenants included a brickmaker, Josiah Thomas, an elderly labourer, Edward Allen and his wife Susan who took in washing and finally Esther and George Mills who lived here until the row of cottages were demolished.

Number 119

James Payne, a labourer from Sheerness and his wife Charity occupied 119 in 1841 with their three children. Later they moved to the Butts.(6) Thomas Lee was a mariner and lived here with his wife Ann in 1851. Then came the Sage family who stayed here longer. Charlie Sage, a Borden man, was a brickmaker and he and his wife Ann had four children although by 1871 only three were at home and the place of the eldest had been taken by a lodger.

The 1881 census records John Carpenter a general labourer, his wife Mary Ann their two children and a lodger at 119. In May 1885 the 'Whitstable Times and Herne Bay Herald' carried a report which mentioned young William John Carpenter, then aged ten, being bitten by a monkey in East Street. He and some other children were standing watching the antics of the little animal who belonged to an Italian musician. The monkey snapped his lead and flew at William biting him on the thigh. William recovered. We can imagine the Italian with the barrel-organ trying to earn some pennies to keep body and soul together and the monkey wearing a brightly coloured jacket. No doubt the children were shouting and clapping and the monkey was nervous.

In 1891 it was George Nicholls a local general labourer in his forties his wife Elizabeth and two children who lived here and the Nicholls were followed by Albert Atkinson whose job was to deliver wine and beer. The Atkinsons must have found the cottage a squeeze with their six children. They were the final tenants for by 1908 number 119 was incorporated into the Sittingbourne Co-operative shop.

Numbers 121 to 127 until they became part of the Co-op

For years there were no houses to the east of number 121 up to the farmhouse later known as number 151. Cherry trees still draped their boughs over the fence and blossom floated on to the road until Sittingbourne Co-operative Society built their new store at 123 in 1877 and then extended it to number 127.

Number 121
The Hedgecock family

The Hedgecock family were considerably better off than their near neighbours in East Street for they owned this house and as we have seen the one to the west of it. The tithe schedule lists John Hedgecock as owning plot 225 which consisted of an orchard and garden. He also owned plot 226 which was the house he lived in and a workshop. The house was later numbered as 121 East Street.

In 1841 John Hedgecock, his wife Eliza, and their eight children lived in this detached house. They remained there for ten more years with John earning his living as a painter and glazier. However by 1861 with the town rapidly growing and the brickfields lying so close by he seized the opportunity to become a brick merchant assisted by his eldest son Thomas. They moved across the road to number 80, leaving younger son John junior at number 121 where he worked as a plumber and glazier living with his wife Susanna. (see number 80)

The family were Anglicans and parish records show that John junior served as parish constable in the 1860s. He and Susanna were still at 121 in 1871 with their five children and a servant. Another of John junior's brothers ran the Ship Inn in the 1850s before moving on to number 42 and working as a fruiterer. They were an enterprising family.

By 1881 John junior had moved his home and business to Faversham's West Street and the Tongs had moved into 121.

The final residents of number 121

Stephen Tong described himself as a 'gentleman' in the 1881 census return so he had sufficient money not to need to earn a living. He was then a widower of 69. He came from Sheppey and the household was completed by his son John who was a corn and coal merchant and Frances Tong Stephen's granddaughter who kept house for them. By 1891 the Tongs had moved along the road to number 151 where we meet them again, and 121 was left empty until it became part of the Co-op store.

By 1905 the Co-op had built into the spaces of 121 to 127

The rise and fall of Sittingbourne Co-operative Society

The part of East Street where Aldi's supermarket now stands was for many years dominated by the Sittingbourne Co-operative Society. By 1908 the local directory records that numbers 119 to 125 were departments of the Co-op Store. At 119 was the butchery department, 121 was the drapery and outfitting, whilst 123 and 125 constituted the grocery.

The Sittingbourne Co-operative Society had been founded in 1874 by a group of working men. Members opened their first shop that year at 69 East Street (see number 69). It very quickly became apparent that that little house was too small for the rapidly growing society.

So in 1877 new premises were purpose built beside 121 East Street on a plot of land which had hitherto been an orchard but would now be number 123. The new building was the main store and boasted bakery, grocery, furniture, drapery and an office. Further expansion took place in 1885 with a butcher's shop and coal depot added to the building. Soon piggeries were built in the yard behind the shop to supply the butcher.

The society then purchased other houses in East Street adjoining the shop to the west ready for expansion. During 1892 a new drapery department was built and the existing grocery/drapery made into a larger grocery. In 1893 a tailoring shop was added too.

In 1899 electric lighting was installed with the electricity being generated by the society. It was the first shop in the street to have this modern form of lighting. Other properties in East Street soon had electric lights to switch on with the electricity supplied by the Co-op's generator. The drill hall next door, at that time used by the Foresters, was one of these.

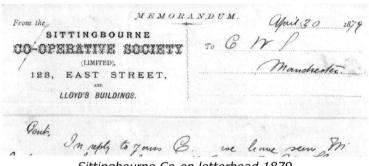

Sittingbourne Co-op letterhead 1879
Address: '123 East Street and Lloyd's Buildings'

Sittingbourne Co-op letterhead 1924
Numerous addresses!

By 1920 the society's central premises comprised not only 119 to 125 but also numbers 84, 86, and 88 East Street. In addition the Co-op had a greengrocery at 78a and, from 1924, a pharmacy at 81 and 83.

In May 1928 the new East Street department store opened at a cost of £12,000, adjoining the old shop to the west after demolition of the old cottages at 113, 115 and 117. It was a two storey building with a basement running the length of it and a long frontage to East Street. The building had been constructed of local bricks by the Sittingbourne firm E. Bishop and Sons Ltd. The East Kent Gazette reported that the new premises 'shone like white marble'. Over the entrance arch was the motto 'Perseverance'.

The store was much admired by local people who particularly liked the mosaic-work marble floors. Everyone was struck by the cash tubes radiating round the building from a central cash office; noiselessly and swiftly the money was carried round the building.

In 1928 a new East Street building was opened next to the existing one

But behind the new building all was not going so smart and modern for the slaughterhouse left much to be desired. The council sanitary inspector Mr Alexander Leslie's report of 1945 is included in the minutes and makes for queasy reading:

'This is where all animals for the whole of Sheppey, Sittingbourne and surrounding villages are slaughtered since 1939 when the Ministry of Food centralised slaughter and it was requisitioned. The building was constructed by the Co-op as long ago as 1882. In 1939 the average weekly kill was four or five cattle, 112 sheep, and 35 pigs. In 1941 some additions to the building had been made by extension into the garage on behalf of the Ministry.

On one side of the slaughterhouse is a corn store and stable, on the west is a clothing factory employing six. A store room of the factory is over part of the lairage.(a place of rest for animals on their way to the abattoir) On the south east 33 feet away are the main offices of the Co-op. Only 66 feet away is rear of grocery and drapery departments. Opposite the entrance to the lairage 14 feet away are stables and a warehouse. Female toilets for Co-op staff are 26 feet away opposite door to slaughterhouse. The yard is in constant use. The rear of the slaughterhouse is built into the large Co-op garage. Behind is a large Co-op dairy and bakery. The slaughterhouse is a combined killing and hanging area 379 square feet. There is another hanging room 592 square feet. The lairage accommodation is 661 square feet.

The floor of the slaughterhouse has channels connecting to the sewer. The floor is worn and sunken with joints between the slabs allowing blood and filth to accumulate in the centre of the floor. There is too little space and the number of beasts killed means that hanging carcases become contaminated with gut contents. Diseased meat can also infect other meat. Ventilation and lighting are unsatisfactory'.

Sittingbourne Co-operative Society Ltd Executive Committee and Officials 1940

You can feel Mr Leslie's distaste and alarm, nevertheless matters continued as before. The slaughterhouse was inspected twice a week with the results of numbers of diseased animals recorded in the council minutes. In April 1946 he visited no less than 58 times. That October he was able to report that Percy Wells the local MP had made representation to the Ministry of Health. The premises were visited by a regional medical officer and minor alterations made. *'But I again emphasise because of the absence of a separate cooling and hanging room for carcases and unsatisfactory ventilation and lack of facilities for storing blood, tripe, skins etc it is unsuitable'.*

The East Street Co-op with the new western extension, pictured in 1962 (EKG)

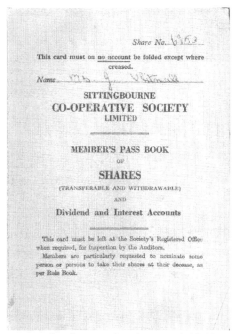

Member's pass book issued 1949

In the shop the Co-op tried to keep abreast of the times and in 1960 a large new extension to the East Street store opened making it a department store where the customer could buy everything under one roof. This lasted only 14 years before it was replaced by the newly built department store in the High Street which is now Wilkinson's. The East Street store closed and was used as a warehouse.

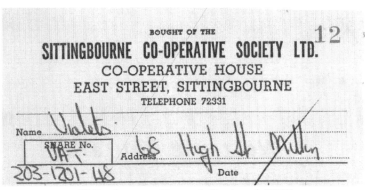

Sittingbourne Co-op letterhead 1973
'Co-operative House'

This was not quite the end of the story of the old department store, for work began in 1984 to transform it into a shopping arcade and upmarket banqueting complex. Upstairs was transformed into a banqueting hall called the Regis Suite, with seating for 220, and catering was provided by Co-op's own department. There was also a dance hall, lounge and smaller banqueting hall. Twelve shop fronts were created downstairs in an arcade to attract specialist retailers. It all opened in 1985 but failed to attract shoppers. In 1987 some of the shops closed and others were converted to offices.

In 1994 bulldozers demolished the Co-op building and Regis Suite in East Street. An Aldi supermarket opened here in 1998 and is still here now.

For those who wish to read a full history of Sittingbourne Co-operative Society the museum's publication is still available.

Aldi supermarket in 2019 on the site of the former Co-op and numbers 105 to 127 (AJW)

The Co-operative Society's expansion
at its main site 103–127 East Street

The Co-op 121 - 127

Begun in 1877

Circa 1910

The Co-op 111 -127

Opened in 1928

Circa 1930

The Co-op 103 -127

Opened in 1960

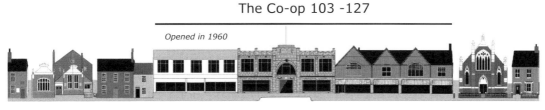

Circa 1962

It should be noted that Sittingbourne Co-operative Society didn't start with these premises and didn't end with them. They ran a large number of shops especially in East Street on both sides of the road at various times.

Bible Christian Church/United Methodist Church/Martial Arts Centre

113 115 117 119   *121-127*   *Church*   *129*   *131   133*

The building in 2016 (BA)

Today this building looks different and has a very different function compared with when it was new in 1888. Then it was red brick, now the bricks are washed a cream colour, then it was a church, now after years of housing a martial arts centre, it is for sale.

The Bible Christian Church

The architect who designed this building was William Leonard Grant, one of our town's more notable architects, who features in volume 1 of our High Street history at numbers 49-51 and 85. The builder was George Pavey of West Street.(WS) The building and the site cost over £1,300 and most of it had been raised before the building was finished. The worshippers were Bible Christians who had previously met nearby in their chapel in George Street off Canterbury Road. That chapel continued as a mission.(41) The new building here could seat the enormous number of 350 worshippers, with some in the gallery. What a lot of their hard-earned money they poured into building this church.

Bible Christians or Bryanites were a Methodist denomination founded by William O'Bryan in Cornwall in 1815 which by 1820 had spread to Kent. O'Bryan's followers were concentrated in the south-west but missionaries were sent all over Britain. They had built a small chapel in St George's Street in 1859 and 20 years later had made plans to build a new, far larger church in East Street.

This was a flourishing church and when the annual Sunday School tea was held here in 1892 there were no fewer than 327 children on the register.

The trustees of the chapel in 1906, as well as Reverend Thomas Nicholas the pastor who lived across road at number 76 (see number 76) were Francis de la Mare of Albion House Sittingbourne – a mechanic, William Swinyard of Milton – a gasworks foreman and Edwin Pearce of Halfway Houses Sheerness – a baker. Classrooms were put up behind the church in 1906 and became known as the Tiny Tots Temple.(N01)

The Bible Christian Church around 1900

The United Methodist Church

In 1907 a national change occurred when the Bible Christian Society amalgamated with the United Methodist Free Churches and the Methodist New Connexion to form the United Methodist Church.

This East Street church continued to flourish under the name of the United Methodist Church running a branch of the Band of Hope and a Christian Endeavour Society. Services were held on Sunday mornings and evenings with Sunday School in the morning and afternoon. Extra money was garnered for the church in the usual way with jumble sales and sales of work.

A ten day mission was held at the church in 1925 run by visiting Sister Ellen. Concerts were given regularly over many years.

East Street Methodist Church

As the years passed after the amalgamation of the branches of Methodism this church became known simply as East Street Methodist Church rather than the United Methodist Church.

Sale of Work c.1940

We are lucky to have the recollections of museum member Sheila Hepburn née Matthews who remembers attending Sunday school in the 1960s for such memories bring alive for us what it meant to be a member of the congregation:

"Up until the 1960s Sunday School was held in the large school room at the back of the church in the morning and afternoon. We sat on wooden benches, and the Sunday School would be taken by George Hales of the East Street garage who was the superintendent.(see number 13)

Church services were held in the morning and evening, and the organists were either Maisie Wiles or Roger Hales (George's grandson).

During the 1960s the Sunday morning services were changed to a family service, and the Sunday School was held in the mornings only, and it was incorporated into the family service. Everybody would meet in the church, and during the service the Sunday School would leave to go to their lessons in the school rooms at the rear of the church. They would then go back into church at the end of the family service to join in.

The Hales family were heavily involved in the church. As well as George Hales, his son Len and his children Colin, Roger, Pat and John all attended the church and were involved.

When we were teachers Wendy Parks (née Mullins) and I would go round and collect the children from their homes to take them to Sunday School. This would entail picking up children from the Canterbury Road Estate, Woodberry Drive Estate, Gaze Hill and Bayford Road. On the way we would call into my Nan and Grandad's home in Bayford Road where my Nan would give the children some sweets.

We used to teach the youngest class, and these lessons were held in a hut which was at the bottom of the alleyway at the rear of the church.

There were no indoor toilet facilities so regardless of the weather it was a case of going outside, and I can remember there was only one ladies' toilet.

The Sunday School children were encouraged to collect for overseas missions. This could either be done by putting odd coins into a money box which was shaped like the world, or by asking family members, friends and also people in the congregation to donate on a regular basis.

This would mean the Sunday School member would have a book with the people's names in and the amount of money they wished to donate weekly – usually one or two old pennies a week – and this would be collected on the Sunday.

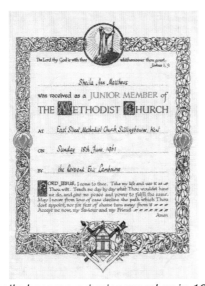

Sheila became a junior member in 1961

Sunday School Anniversary was held once a year, and the children would be dressed in their Sunday best which often meant a new dress for the occasion. All of the congregation would wear button holes.

Another annual event was the Sunday School outing which was a visit to the coast. A bus, or even a couple of buses, would be hired for the day. Sometimes we would go to Broadstairs or Dymchurch where a banner would be put up on the beach and a picnic enjoyed. We also went to Westgate and Margate where the beach would be followed by the Sundeck Café for tea and a visit to Dreamland.

Once a year at Easter an 'Egg and Flower Service' was held where we would take eggs and flowers to church, and at the end of the service these would be distributed to local elderly people.

The church was specially decorated for the Harvest Festival, and pride of place was given to a large loaf of bread which had been made in the form of a sheaf of corn by Barrows the bakers. The church would be full of produce which local people had donated mainly from their own gardens and allotments. This food was then sorted and divided up, and taken round to local people who were in need. I can remember going up to the allotments at the top of Gaze Hill with my grandad and his wheelbarrow, collecting vegetables off the allotments which would then be wheelbarrowed to the church. Following the Harvest Festival a supper would be held.

A toy service took place close to Christmas when the Sunday School children would go through their toys, and take any unwanted ones to the church which would be given to needy children in the area.

Every Christmas there would be a nativity play by the Sunday School scholars. And every year we would have a Christmas party in the school room at the back of the church.

A Christmas Fair was held there too. Stalls were put up round the room which were full of items which people had made to be sold. I can remember my Mum buying dolls which she used to dress to be sold, and my Nan would crochet doily sets. Wendy's mum would make delicious cakes which were also sold.

We would go out carol singing before Christmas. A small organ would be loaded on to a trailer which would be pulled round the local streets with the organist, Brian Davis, sitting in the trailer playing. The carol singers were given a jam jar with string tied round it to hold, and inside each glowed a lighted candle.

From the late 1960s onwards there was a crèche in the church on a Sunday morning which enabled parents to leave the babies and very young children under supervision whilst they attended the church service.

East Street under 12 Sunday School Choir who won at the 1957 festival. Choir practice was held weekly.

Once a year the District Methodist Youth Festival of Music and Drama was held in the Wesley Church in the High Street where local churches in the area competed for a place in the final. The events covered a large variety of classes from choirs, solos, duets, piano, readings as well as a handicraft section for embroidery, knitting, art and handwriting. The heats were carried out during the day in the Wesley Methodist Church in the High Street, and the winners would perform in a concert in the evening. The winners from this local festival would then go on to compete in an area final which was usually held in the Central Hall at Chatham.

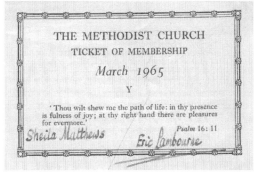

Sheila's card on becoming a full member of the church

East Street Church also had a scheme for visiting elderly people, and Wendy and myself used to visit a couple called Mr and Mrs Parr.
The senior youth club was held on a Friday evening. Various activities were arranged, and on one occasion Wendy and myself were taken blindfolded by car to a mystery destination. We were dropped off, blindfolds taken off, and we had to find our own way back to East Street Church. I can remember we were dropped off by Tong Mill pond so it was quite a walk back.
During the 1960s a trip was arranged to the theatre at Maidstone where the pop groups of the day would give shows. Members of the Methodist Church Junior Youth Club held a Christmas Social on New Year's Day 1960."

In 1977 with a dwindling congregation this church amalgamated with the Wesleyan Methodist Church in the High Street and the East Street building was sold to become a martial arts centre.

The Methodist Church building for sale in 1977

The Martial Arts Club/Sombo Centre

One man, Martin Clarke, who lived in East Street himself until his untimely death in 2018, was the driving force behind this sports centre since it opened in 1980.

Swale Martial Arts Club in 2008 (CA)

Martin Clarke 1950–2018

Born in 1950 to parents who both excelled at martial arts, Martin coached professionally when he grew up. He founded Swale Martial Arts club and also the British Sombo Federation. He won over 300 medals in Judo, Sambo wrestling, weightlifting, Jiu Jitsu and amateur wrestling. He represented Britain at Judo, Jiu Jitsu and Sombo Wrestling. Martin's widow and children are also experts in this field.

After 1980 he organised the IBF National Judo and Karate Championships on an annual basis. On occasion he organised the British Amateur Wrestling. He coached and managed Jiu Jitsu, Sombo Wrestling and Judo competitors at International and World Events and was awarded a Gold Medal for services to International Sombo by FIAS, the World Governing Body for Sombo.

It was fortunate that a good use was found for this building and so that it was well cared for, but since the death of Martin Clarke, the family are moving the club to the High Street and selling the premises. What future it has is unsure at the start of 2019.

Numbers 129 to 139 East Street

Church   *129*   *131*   *133*   *135*   *137*   *139*   *141*   *143*   *145*   *147*   *149*

These modest six-roomed houses are long since gone for they stood where the gap is now between the Martial Arts Centre (originally built as a Bible Christian Church and then renamed as the United Methodist Church) and the roundabout with St Michaels Road.

None of these houses had been built when the 1865/6 Ordnance Survey map was drawn, but, by the time the 1871 census return was taken, the terrace numbered 131-139 had been erected whilst the detached number 129 had not been built. In fact the odd numbers 121-129 were not listed in the 1871 or 1881 census returns.

By 1871 the land had been divided into plots ready for building and therefore the numbering of 131 was already worked out by 1871 before the construction of numbers 121-129.

In 1868 two important auctions of plots of building land were held at The Bull in the High Street. William Streeton, whom we encounter at number 169, purchased some of the lots and erected some of the houses. There were hundreds of lots available for this was the development of Shortlands Road, Shakespeare Road, Harold Road, Goodnestone Road, the west side of Murston Road, Cowper Road and some of the houses in East Street between numbers 129 and 173.

William Streeton kept the 1878 auction plan which was a revised copy of the 1868 plan and it has remained in the family ever since. We have been allowed to reproduce a section by Carole Corbett one of William's great-granddaughters. The 1878 plan reveals that, over the ten years, the vast majority of the plots had been sold off for they were coloured pink. The small fraction of the plots left to sell and develop were in Cowper Road and at the top of Shortlands Road.

Numbers 129 to 139 East Street were inhabited well into the 1980s. Only number 131a is listed in the electoral register of 1990 and not even that by 1998 and so we conclude that they were demolished in the early 1990s.

Number 129
A house for John Charles Cooper

In 1890 a detached house and shop was built for Mr John Cooper next door to the Bible Christian Church and numbered as 129 East Street. The plan submitted to the council reveals it had a basement, shop, parlour, living room, kitchen, scullery and three bedrooms.(105) Although the house was built with a shop we have not found a record of it being used as such. From the 1891 census we learn that John Charles Cooper was Sittingbourne born and bred aged 65 *'living on his own means'* with his wife Ann and a live-in domestic.

Unfortunately John barely had time to enjoy his spanking new house as he died in 1892 leaving over £2,000.

Cooper was far from being a stranger to East Street when he moved into the newly-built house a year before his death, in fact he had lived his entire life in the street at various addresses. In 1881 he had resided next door at 131 where we meet him below, earning his living as a fruiterer.(9)

Widowed Ann Cooper may well have moved out soon after John's death although she survived until 1900 when she died aged 80.

We know the Taylor family lived in the house by 1901. Philip Dalby Taylor was baptised in Sittingbourne 1870 but had been born in Suffolk, the home county of his parents. Philips's father was an engineer at Lloyd's Paper Mill and Philip followed his father into the mill when he left school and was employed as a clerk.

Philip married Clara Cooper in 1896 and perhaps it was then that the young couple moved into number 129. Clara was a Sittingbourne girl (although not a daughter of the Cooper family who had previously owned the house). The Taylors lived at 129 with their two daughters until at least 1919, later they moved to Bell Road.

In 1924 the property was advertised for sale: *'For Sale freehold house occupied by tenant, quarterly low rental £24 per annum'.* The tenants then were Emily and Frank Shrubsall. They were followed by the Reverend Munderford Allen and then Nellie and Walter Phipps.

By 1947 Ernest and Norah Milbourn were living at 129. Ernest had been born in 1892 and in 1913 had married Norah Louisa Hibbins who was two years younger. Ernest was a dairyman; sadly he committed suicide in 1953. Norah Milbourn continued to live at 129 although by 1970 she lived downstairs as the house had been made into two flats

Number 131
John Charles Cooper again

The 1871 census return records that number 131 was empty but by 1874 John Charles Cooper the fruiterer whom we have met at 129 lived there. He had moved with his wife Ann from number 179 which was owned by John's brother Fred the baker. (179 was later numbered as part of Canterbury Road). John and Ann still lived here in 1881 with a live-in servant but also had rented out a room by then to elderly widow Sarah Edwards. The Coopers remained at 131 until their new house next door was ready in 1891. Mr Cooper had started his working life as a baker, trained by his father, John senior, who had the bakery at 49 East Street which was later taken on by John's brother Frederick. (see number 49). Even in early married life in the 1850s and 1860s John junior remained living and working at number 49 baking bread for his father.

George James Reeve, painter and decorator at 131

In 1891 George Reeve, his wife Harriet and their seven children, all born in Sittingbourne (as was Harriet), moved in to 131 where George and Harriet were to spend the rest of their lives. George was a painter and decorator born in Pluckley. We have already encountered the Reeves at number 61 where George had carried on his painting business whilst Harriet ran the eating house or café. George always worked as a painter and we know he established his own business in 1879. (see advertisement below)

In 1901 George, by then 60, was still working and employed two of his sons. The sons had left home by 1911 whilst George was still working and two daughters remained at home. And so it was that George and Harriet were able to celebrate their golden wedding in 1915 which was reported in the local paper: '*Mr Reeve is 75 years and Mrs Reeve is 73 years. There have five daughters and two sons one of whom is Councillor William Reeve.*'

Within a month or two of the golden wedding George had died. The firm which he had founded was continued by his sons. Son William moved into 131 with his family in 1919. The Reeves owned numbers 4 and 6 Albany Road and these William advertised for sale in 1919. George's widow Harriet died in 1924 aged 83. Members of the Reeve family continued to live at number 131 until the early 1950s.

A 1930s advertisement from the local directory for Harry Reeve's business

J. and F. Sampson – wallpaper at 131 and 133
By 1959 number 131 had become the home of Joan Sampson who ran 'The Wallpaper Shop' at number 133 throughout the 1960s and into the early 1970s. It is not clear that Mrs Sampson lived at 131 but the upstairs was made into 131a, a flat, whilst downstairs was part of the wallpaper shop which extended into 133.

Michael Andrew, Gents hairdresser
In the late 1970s and early 1980s this was the hairdressing salon named 'Michael Andrew' whilst the upstairs flat was separately let to various tenants.

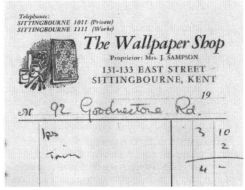

1972 receipt from the Wallpaper Shop

1981 Advert for Michael Andrew at number 131

Number 133

For most of its existence number 133 was residential. Here are the names of those we know of who lived there. Numbers 133, 135 and 137 all belonged to a member of the Cooper family in 1942 and were sold that year to Mr A Thomsett, a member of the family who had lived at 69 East Street. This is recorded in the account book of Hedley Peters & Son – the auctioneers, who carried out the transaction.

1871-1881	Elizabeth Smith+ lodger	annuitant
1891	Mark Burley+ wife	cement miller
1901	Jane Jackson+ daughter	needlewoman
1908	John James Ralph	
1911	House empty	
1922-1951	Adelaide and Frederick Drake	
1953	Thomas Milbourn	
1963	A White	
1975-1980	Beryl Keeler	

The only evidence we have discovered of a business being carried out at number 133 is in the 1985 photograph showing a shop front bearing the name Lime Kiln Joinery.

1985 – Private residence at 129, Michael Andrew Gents Hairdresser at 131 and Lime Kiln Joinery at number 133 (EKG)

Number 135
George Thomas – taxidermist and naturalist

The first known inhabitant of number 135, George Thomas, was a local man with an unusual occupation (albeit there was one other man in the town who practised the same craft.) George was a taxidermist and naturalist and originally a 'boot closer' too (someone who helped in the process of making boots by stitching the upper parts together).(6,7) For the 1871 census return George described himself as a naturalist. He was then in his forties and supporting a household of wife, three children (two of whom had special needs), a son-in-law, stepdaughter and granddaughter. George was a man to be relied upon and was elected parish constable in 1872 as the vestry minutes of St Michael's Church show.

By 1881 the Thomas household had shrunk a good deal consisting only of George, his wife, daughter Adelaide and granddaughter. The versatile George then described himself as a taxidermist and general agent. Daughter Adelaide was a dressmaker who must have had flair for, aged only 20, she was employing three 'hands' or workers, thus taking up the space which had been left in the house.

George Young of 47 and then 26 High Street was the other taxidermist and naturalist in Sittingbourne. He also made up his income with a third trade – in his case hairdressing.

Drawing on his experience as parish constable George Thomas found yet another niche for himself, for by 1891 he served as sub-bailiff to the county court. George died in 1900 in his early seventies.

We have found no evidence that the Thomas family used their front room as shop; rather it was probably the case that those with an animal they wished to have stuffed to keep and admire would have just knocked on the front door with the deceased creature.

For a few years after George's death number 139 was lived in by Edward Foster and his wife. Edward was a young grocer's warehouseman and the couple soon moved to 56 West Street.

Sylvanus Button

Then by 1908 Sylvanus Button (a name that Dickens would surely have liked for one of his characters) moved into number 135. Sylvanus had been born in Portsmouth where his parents had chosen that unusual Christian name for him in 1863. Sylvanus was the Roman god of the forest. However this was the obvious choice of name for the young Button since his father's name was Sylvan, shortened from Sylvanus.(7) Sylvan was a blacksmith who had migrated with his young family to Ramsgate from Portsmouth by the time Sylvanus was seven.

When he grew up Sylvanus worked on the Murston brickfields as a labourer and had moved to East Street from just round the corner in Shortlands Road. (11) His wife Annie had died in 1901 in her thirties leaving Sylvanus with their two children. In 1903 Sylvanus married again, this time to local woman Ellen Pilcher and they went on to have two sons. Ellen died in 1924 aged 60. One of Sylvanus's sons, Edward, had emigrated to Canada and lived in Hamilton. In 1930 the widowed Sylvanus set sail to Montreal to see if he would like to settle with his son and family. However it did not suit him and he returned to Sittingbourne where he died in 1932 aged 68. Sylvanus's son Frank then continued the tenancy.

The final years of 135

After the Second World War there were a number of different tenants of the house including Esther and Frank Ingall, Jane Ede and Ron and Jean Gilham.

A big change came in 1962 when a shop front was at last added to the house and L. C. Newby opened a television and radio shop here. How long this lasted in addition to the Newbys shop at 149 we have not discovered but by 1974 R. & S. Ralph had taken over the electrical shop in addition to their similar shop at number 161. (See HSI, 65 High Street)

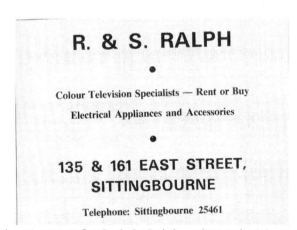

1977 advertisement for R. & S. Ralph, colour television specialists

Number 137

Number 137 was always a private house. William and Sarah Saywell were the occupants in 1871 with their two children. William had been born in Bredgar and was a farm labourer. The other early inhabitants of 137 that we know of are listed in this table.

1881	Maria Fever	laundress
1891	William Norris+ family	upholsterer's assistant
1901	George Baker+ family	naval pensioner
1908	Charles Beard	
1911-1915	William Beard+ family	farm labourer
1924-1927	Thomas William Phipps	insurance agent

Early inhabitants of number 137

Frances and James Jemmett

By the early 1930s Frances and James Jemmett lived at number 137. When Frances died in 1935 aged 71, an obituary was written for the local paper which tells of her great faith. Frances was a keen Salvationist. Born Frances Luck in Faversham she spent 14 years as a girl at the Salvation Army's Hadleigh Farm Colony in Essex where she 'distributed periodicals' She married James William Jemmett, a brickfield labourer, in the Wesleyan church in 1882. They had moved to Murston from Faversham in 1908 with their seven children and regularly attended both East Street Methodists and Sittingbourne Salvationists in Shortlands Road. Frances was well-known and deeply respected in the town a cheerful person who was very active in both congregations.

Ivy and Reginald Barden

The next tenants we know of at number 137 were Ivy and Reginald Barden who were here by 1947 and remained until the house was demolished.

Number 139
Arthur Bishop, draper

Arthur Bishop and his wife Eliza opened a draper's shop at 139 and they are the first residents of the building that we know of. Arthur had been born far away in Shropshire and Eliza in Staffordshire and they had one child. Later on the family moved on to Chatham. By 1881 number 139 had become a private house and continued so into the 1890s. George Hills Handcock, a miller from Ashford, his wife Eliza and their five children were the tenants in 1881. We know that when the next census was taken Stephen Brooker a labourer and his wife lived here.

George Fountain Cook, bootmaker

It was George Cook, a bootmaker who opened a shop at 139 by 1895. George was a Yorkshireman, born in Bradford in 1847, but had settled in Sittingbourne as a young man and been apprenticed to William Harnden at number 16 East Street.(7)

By 1881 George and his wife Sarah lived nearby in Goodnestone Road where George had his own shop. Ten years later they were to be found in Shakespeare Road with their four children.

Having made it to the better trading location of East Street by 1895 George and Sarah moved house no more. George died at number 139 aged 80 in 1923.

Albert Whitehead watch and clockmaker

After Sarah Cook moved out, Albert and Ethel Whitehead moved in and lived at number 139 where Albert had his watchmaking and jewellery shop for many years. This had not been an obvious craft for Albert to learn for he had been born in Teynham in 1892 the son of a brickfield labourer. He was a bright boy and by 1911 was working in Wood Green, Middlesex as a watchmaker's assistant.(12)

Clearly he felt most at home where he had grown up with his relatives nearby and so he and his wife Ethel moved in to number 139.

In 1915 we know that number 139 was owned by Richard Hadaway who also owned 141 and 143 whilst living at the other end of town on the London Road and having a tobacconist's in the High Street.(115)

A 1937 advertisement for Albert Whitehead's shop in the local paper states it had then been established for 12 years. So we know that the shop opened in 1925 when Albert was 33 and continued until he died in 1966 aged 74. Electoral registers show that Ethel was still living in the house in 1980.

A. W. WHITEHEAD
WATCHMAKER AND JEWELLER.
BEST PRICES FOR GOLD, SILVER AND ROLLED GOLD.
Established 12 years.   15 years' London experience.
We have no agents.

139, EAST STREET, SITTINGBOURNE.

1937 receipt from Albert Whitehead, Watchmaker and Jeweller

Numbers 141-149 East Street

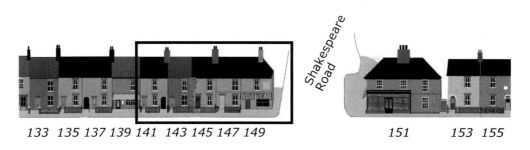

133 135 137 139 141 143 145 147 149   151   153 155

This terrace of five six-roomed houses was built, as was so much else in the town, between 1865/6 when the Ordnance Survey map was drawn up and 1871 when the next census was taken. They were demolished in 1973 to make way for the joining of St Michaels Road with East Street but appear to have been empty by 1970.(115)

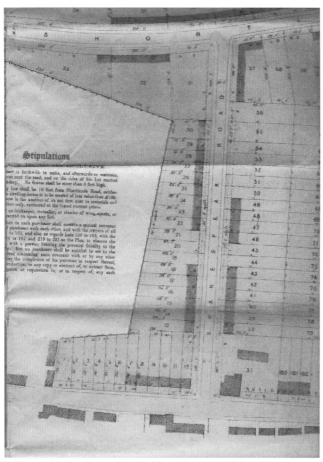

A section of the 1878 auction plan which belonged to William Streeton (see number 169) showing 149 East Street and 151 either side of Shakespeare Road in the foreground and the plots of Shakespeare Road which were already built.(CC)

Although we do not know who the original owner of the terrace was we know that William Knowles of Canterbury Road owned the terrace in 1930 because the council served notice on him to repair it.(105) If he did do anything to remedy the situation at that time it was not enough because in 1931 the council again served notice for him to repair the toilets and yet again in 1932 when he was also required to make 141 and 143 fit for human habitation by dealing with damp in the front rooms upstairs and down.

Mr Knowles died in 1949 but problems continued into the 1950s; the new owner Mrs Emily Hall (the neighbour at 149) was served statutory notice from the council via her agent, Hedley Peters, to provide proper drainage for 141 and 143.

Number 141

Number 141 at the western end of the terrace was always a private dwelling and these are the names of those we know of who lived there:

1871	Henry Duffin+ family	furniture salesman
1881-1891	James Fuller + family	tailor
1901-11	Richard Pierce+ family	cornfactor's car man
1915	Ellen Johncock	
1922-1926	Edward Snelling+ family	cement worker

Numbers 141 and 143 were owned by Richard Hadaway in 1915 along with number 139. Mr Hadaway had a High Street tobacconist's and lived on the London Road.(115)

In 1926 Edward George Snelling who was then the tenant at 141 was killed in a dreadful accident at work: *'Fatality at Smeed Dean Cement Works, Murston - Edward George Snelling of 141 East Street, was on cleaning shift with a rag which wound round and pulled him round the shaft. He had a wife and family.'*

Poor Mrs Snelling continued to live at 141 for a while longer.

Florence and Harold Jeffery were the next tenants and stayed in the house for many years (at least until 1963. Harold had been born just round the corner in 1911. Throughout their time here, the owner was Mrs Emily Hall of Bell Road – see below – numbers 147 and 149 East Street and HSI number 29).

Number 143 East Street

Some of the occupants of number 143 did try to earn a living at the house though it never had a shop front. In 1871 widowed Mary Smith, then in her fifties and living alone, described herself as a general dealer. No doubt locals soon got to know that they could knock on her door to see what cheap goods she had for sale.

By 1881 Henry Price, a shipwright, and his wife Mary Ann were the occupants with their children and in 1891 it was labourer Robert Bartlett and his wife Elizabeth.

The Atkinson family

From 1900 to the 1950s this was the home of the Atkinson family. Though born in far off Lincolnshire in 1842 Josiah Atkinson had spent much of his life in Sittingbourne. By 1871 he was trading as a baker and grocer in Shakespeare

Road where he remained ten years later but by then he had taken on a second job, that of being a coal merchant. An unlikely and rather worrying combination alongside the baking! In 1891 Josiah had stopped baking in favour of the coal, and lived in Bayford Road. Then we find the family at 143 East Street from 1893 and probably this was when he gave up selling coal in favour of the less dirty business of making ginger-beer. Certainly in 1901 when Josiah was 59 he described himself as a ginger-beer maker.

Mary Ann Atkinson, Josiah's wife, was not local either but from Bedfordshire. With them at this time lived their son Herbert who was employed by someone else as a baker and their grandson, young Albert Atkinson. The ginger-beer making was probably very small scale indeed as Josiah did not advertise it in the 1908 directory nor in the 1918. But the 1911 census return confirms that this is what Josiah continued to do assisted by his wife. By then they were getting on in years and it must have been a comfort to have their unmarried daughter Ellen, a cook, living with them. Young Albert was still there too, by then working in the paper mill. Ellen was probably Albert's mother.

On Josiah's death in 1927 he was able to leave £322 and probate was granted to Percy Willis, the outfitter of 14 High Street. Mary Ann Atkinson had died just before her husband, aged 89. Their daughter Ellen, who never married, continued on at 143 for many more years. She generally had lodgers who by 1947 were Irene and Thomas Morgan. Ellen Atkinson died in 1952 aged 80. Irene and Thomas Morgan continued to live in the house. Tom Morgan died in 1961 at the early age of 47 and Irene continued there alone,(at least until 1963).

Number 145
Number 145 was always residential.

Thomas Cackett and family
The Cacketts lived in this house for many years and were probably the first occupants. Thomas Cackett was a house-painter and glazier born in 1839 the son of a Charing clog maker. Charing was where he lived until his marriage to Jane Robinson, a Hollingbourne girl in 1864. They had one son William, who was born in Milton. We encounter the family at number 145 in 1871, with them lived Thomas' brother William who worked with him as a painter. When Jane died young in 1877 Thomas soon remarried, and he and his second wife Elizabeth Wratten had several children. Brother William moved on and his place in the Cackett household was taken by his mother, old, widowed Isabella Cackett. By 1891 old Isabella had died, William Cackett, Thomas's only child by his first wife, still lived at home. He was then a postman in his mid-twenties and was to remain in the same house in the same job for many more years. Thomas himself continued to work as a painter until his death in 1902. Perhaps his widow and children then left Sittingbourne, certainly they had gone from East Street by 1908.

The Gilham family
By 1908 George Gilham, a Sittingbourne man lived at 145 with his wife Jane, son Herbert, adopted daughter and elderly mother.(12) George and Jane Gilham both died in 1942. Herbert married in 1944 and continued to live in the house.

He died in 1948 aged 54. Other members of the family lived at 145 into the 1960s.

In this image taken in the 1920s, numbers 145, 147 and 149 are on the left with their neat front gardens enclosed by iron railings. The sunblind was out over the shop window on number 149. The junction with Shakespeare Road is just before Wade's shop at 151.

Number 147

In the 1870s the Bodley family lived at 147 and stayed at least 20 years. Henry was a carpenter. They were followed by 1901 by George Wood, a labourer born in Throwley and his wife Sarah. They remained for a good ten years and then came John and Ada Swan in the 1920s. The owner of number 147 at this time was Arthur Berriff who lived at 88 High Street where he had an outfitter's shop.(12,115)

A shop at 147 – A. & E. Hall

A big change took place at number 147 in 1933 when a plan for a shop front was approved by the council for the new owner Alfred Hall. Alfred and Emily Hall already owned and lived in number 149 and had a shop there (see below). They then opened their drapery and children's outfitting shop at 147 which continued until the Newbys took on both shops in 1946.

Newby & Sons

'Newby & Sons' run by Louis Newby sold electrical goods and remained until at least 1963. (see below for 149)

Number 149 East Street

Number 149's corner position can clearly be seen with fruit and vegetables for sale. The Odeon film poster dates the photograph to the late 1930s or soon afterwards. Note the horse and cart, and the distant spire of the Congregational church (adjoining 93 High St) which retains its prominent position to this day.

Number 149 was the end of terrace house built on the western corner made by Shakespeare Road with East Street. It differed from the rest of the terrace, for it was always a business as well as a home. It too had six rooms but unlike the rest of the row it also had another large room for use as a shop. In 1911 it was described as a: *'Six-roomed house and large shop'.*

The first occupants that we know of were James Fuller – a married tailor from Dorking, his wife, and a lodger, in 1871. Then by 1878 Edward Hinge a marine-store dealer was listed in the directory. Earlier in the 1870s Edward had been a publican at Minster, Sheppey. He died aged 60 in 1880 leaving his widow Mary Ann to continue the shop. Mrs Hinge retired to Park Road after some time, with her granddaughter where she was to be found in 1891.

Henry Elfick

So a new tenant moved in to number 149 and this was Henry Elfick. We know he was there in 1887 when, perhaps because he had just opened up shop, he placed a series of large advertisements in the local paper: *'Mr Elfick 149 East Street Sittingbourne also High Street. Clothes boots shoes etc. The Peoples Cheap Clothing.'*

The Elfick family had had great success in the High Street where they had moved from number 110 to larger premises at 96/98. They were a family with generations of experience of trading having had shops of various kinds from grocery to drapery in Milton for generations.(HSII) However this particular venture was short-lived and by 1891 number 149 had become the establishment of a confectioner, William Johnson. We do not believe the Elficks ever lived here but remained comfortably in the High Street.

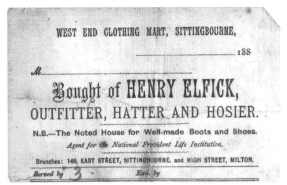

Elfick's 'West End Clothing Mart' at number 149 East Street!

William John Johnson

At any rate by 1891 William John Johnson a confectioner from Newington had moved in with his wife Elizabeth and started to concoct sweets to sell. We know William made sweets himself as in the 1901 census return he described himself as '*manufacturing confectionery at home to sell*.' He was then in his late fifties. Matthews in his memories of the town mentions: '*I also have recollection of Mr. Johnson's sweet shop*'.(69) It is a pity for us that he did not list some of the sweets that he bought there as a boy. Mrs Elizabeth Johnson is listed in the 1891 and 1895 directory as also having a shop at 102 East Street. She died in 1903 aged 58. William kept this house and shop going until 1911 when it was up for sale: '*To be sold old established confectionery business, six roomed house & large shop*'.

Percy Wise

It does not appear that Percy Wise was a member of the coach-building Wise family of East Street though he may have been related in some way. He had been born in Faversham in 1875, married Eliza Shilling in 1898 and they had several children. Percy turned his hand to a number of jobs – he had been a journeyman baker and a travelling crane driver.(11,12) He was only 46 when he died '*after a long and painful illness*' as the announcement said in the paper. We have not found any evidence that the Wises ran a shop whilst they were at 149.

Lily Burrows

In 1915 one Lily Burrows ran a shop here but we know nothing of her.(47)

Miss Ribbans and Miss King

By 1926 the Misses Ribbans and King, drapers, were trading here. We have not been able to discover anything about Miss Ribbans or Miss King, but noting their names, we wonder if perhaps one of them might have been known as Sittingbourne's ribbons Queen. A Hannah Ribbans, who was born in 1890, died in Sittingbourne in 1957.

Alfred and Emily Hall, fruiterers

Alfred and Emily Hall ran 149 as 'East Kent Fruit Store' wholesale and retail from 1930 (or slightly earlier) until at least 1947 and lived in the house. Emily had been born into the Knowles family who had had greengroceries in the town for generations. *(see 65 and 20 High Street)* Alfred Hall had begun his working life as a draper. He and Emily had one son, Robert Knowles Hall who served in the RAF and died on active service in the Second World War. During that war Alfred served as major commanding 'A' Company of Sittingbourne Home Guard. Later he was president of Sittingbourne Chamber of Trade. Alfred and Emily had two daughters Marguerite and Jeanne and in later years Emily opened a ladies fashion and children's wear shop with them at 29 High Street.(HSI) That shop did not close until 1967.

L. Newby & Sons

Louis Charles Ansty Newby was born in 1901 in Southwark and grew up in Wandsworth where his father was a shopkeeper.(12) He married his first wife Sarah in 1923 and they had three children Jean, John and Frank. Before moving to 149 East Street they lived in Murston Road and Louis sold wireless sets.(56, 57) We know they had taken on the shop at 149 by 1960 when their advertisement boasted: *'L. Newby & Sons a quarter of a century and still on the ball with our efficient service, tvs tape recorders etc.'*

In 1962 Louis made a late second marriage to Clara Back. By 1963 the shop at number 149 had been turned into a greengrocery by the Newbys whilst their electrical business continued next door at 147. Louis lived on long after number 149 was demolished. He died in 1985 aged 84.

Numbers 135 to 149 demolished by 1977 and advertising hoardings occupied the space before a roundabout was built some time just before 1980 (EKG)

1988: A roundabout forming the junction between St Michael's Road and East Street, was formed. A new entrance to Shakespeare Road was formed (EKG)

1980: the view south west. At the centre of the photograph is the roundabout connecting (clockwise from top), South Avenue, East Street St Michael's Road and Shakespeare Road. East Street runs left to right across the picture.
Bottom left is Bayford Road and the public house originally called the Shakespeare Hotel.

Number 151 East Street

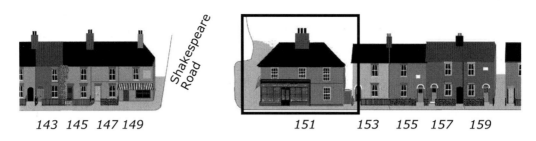

143 145 147 149   151   153   155   157   159

Nowadays the attractive old red-brick house which is number 151 stands in an unfortunate position, beset by traffic. Since the roundabout was put in for South Avenue on the other side of the road and St Michaels Road on this side of the road, this became the first house on the east side of the roundabout.

It is one of the few listed buildings in East Street and must be one of the oldest – perhaps dating back around 500 years. The brick string-course along the front elevation, indicates that, originally, the first floor used to overhang the wall beneath, forming what is called a jetty. In the statutory list of buildings of architectural or historic interest this building is described as timber-framed, of two storeys, re-fronted with stock bricks during the 19th century.(71) In fact our photograph shows the front wall is of red facing bricks not yellow stocks. Like every human endeavour, our statutory list of ancient buildings is not free from error. The roof is steeply pitched, and, (when it was listed) there was a 19th century shop-front, which is no more. At the sides, the upper levels are weather-boarded and at the back, there is exposed timber-framing – features which confirm that the basic structure is a timber-frame – as was normal, here in Kent, when this farmhouse was built. The left wall has two double sashes. The chimney is central, as is the door, which gives the house a pleasing symmetry. Originally there would have been an entrance lobby between the door and the chimney – a standard layout for Kentish farmhouses of the mid-16th century.

Originally this farmhouse with its garden, yards and outbuildings at the back, was surrounded on three sides by open land which by 1791, and perhaps even earlier, had been planted with orchards – total area just over six acres. This part of Kent was (and still is) renowned for its fruit-growing – hence the town's motto *'Known By Their Fruits'*. As historians, we should remind our readers that this apt motto was coined by George Hardy, Head-teacher at Borden Grammar School in the mid-20th century. Doubtless the farmers, who lived here, appreciated the convenience of the London to Dover road passing in front – ready access to the market etc.

After years of having a shop in part of the house it is once again back in use as a home in single occupancy, but nowadays, no orchards can be seen from its windows. Where, today, we have a busy roundabout, there was, long ago, the farm pond.

In his history notes, our old friend Canon Scott Robertson speculates that, in the late 16th century, this house and farm may have belonged to one Peter Naylor who was charged with the quit rent *'for the house late William Kypping's'*. Quit rent was a feudal land tax – abolished long ago. In 1574,

Kypping's house, says the Canon, belonged to Symon Potman – whose ancestors, doubtless, had something to do with pots and pans.

In 1791 the map produced for Valentine Simpson, landlord of the Rose Inn tells us that the freeholder of this property at that time was one Thomas Skip Bucknall Esq.(HSII) Since this gentleman appears, so named, in a formal list of Sittingbourne's landowners, Skip was apparently not a nickname – perhaps it derived from the family of one of his forebears. Imagining the occasion of his baptism, one wonders at the reaction of the vicar when it was proposed by his proud parents.

John Shakespeare's farmhouse

The tithe map shows that, 50 years later, in 1840, the house still had orchards on each side of it. The houses of East Street on the opposite side of the road extended beyond number 151, but the north side was less built-up and the orchards belonging to the farmhouse had not yet been sold off.

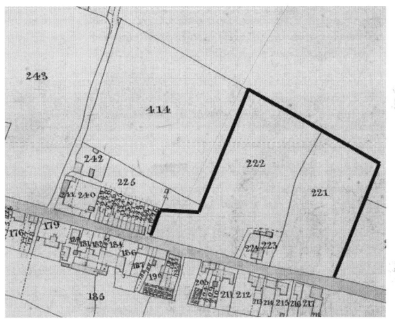

A section of the tithe map of 1840 showing the house and the fields on the right which are numbered 221,222,223,224. West Lane can be seen at the left-hand edge

At this stage in its history the house was partitioned and was numbered 223 and 224 on the tithe schedule. It belonged to a certain John Shakespeare and unfortunately we have not been able to discover anything about him. He owned nothing else in the parish, as far as we know.

The house was let to Jesse Cooper, an old gardener and his wife, and to Leonard England a young farm labourer with a family; the house had come down in the world and was rented out to two families.

The three orchards and some buildings were rented by one Philip Hammond, who was, for some 20 years, landlord of the Bell Inn (in Bell Road) before, it seems, moving to the Golden Ball in Murston. Perhaps Mr Hammond grew apples to make his own cider.

Rebecca and James Tyler

By 1851 local couple James and Rebecca Tyler, their six young children and a nurse for the baby lived at 151, which was back to being in use as one house. James was a carrier who employed three men. Ten years later the census records Rebecca here with six children four of whom had been born since the previous census whilst some of the older ones had left home, a niece and a servant. That night James Tyler was not at home but in Canterbury staying in the Northgate Street home of his friend William Banister a millwright and engineer whilst no doubt doing some business in the city. James described himself for the census as a flint merchant (and at his death he was also described as such in probate index). Rebecca however was recorded in the census as 'wife of town carrier.'

James was a man who could turn a skilled hand to many things and that year, 1861, despite being 60, he made an arrangement with John Burton who had the main smithy in East Street (see 26/28). Burton and his wife Mary moved a few miles to Tunstall leaving the East Street business in Tyler's hands. Directory entries of the 1860s refer only to James Tyler as the wheelwright, blacksmith and town carrier. Because the Burtons sold their furniture the implication is that the Tylers moved along to 26/28. The Burtons moved back to 26/28 in 1870 and the Tylers moved, not back to 151, but to the newly built number 157 which James owned along with the rest of the terrace. (see 157)

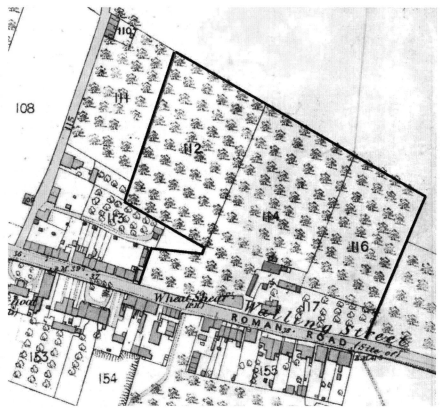

This part of East Street in 1865/6 – Ordnance Survey – showing the farm buildings and pond beside the house. The holding included the orchards numbered 112, 114, 116 117

Thomas Butler, labourer

So there was a new tenant of number 151 by 1871. The house was full with 12 people.(8) Here lived Thomas Butler, a general labourer born in Charing, his wife, two step-children whose surname was Sorrell, four Butler children and a brother in law. Also sharing the house were Leonard Sorrell, a young labourer from Sittingbourne with his wife and son. Ten years previously the Butlers had lived round the corner in West Lane and it is that 1861 census return which records that the Sorrells were Butler's nephews.

A coffee house

By the time the 1881 census was taken William Inchcomb, from Throwley had opened a coffee-house at number 151 with Elizabeth his wife and a niece. A year later in 1882 the directory tells us that George Sellen kept the coffee house. We can feel sure this was the George Sellen shown the year before in the census return living with his family next door-but-one to the coffee house at number 155. He was then a brewer's traveller in his thirties with a wife and five children to provide for.

Tong the butcher

The coffee-house did not prosper; perhaps it stood little chance with so many public houses so close to it. By 1891 John Thomas Tong had turned it into a butcher's shop.(10) Tong was a single man from Sheppey in his forties and his niece Frances Tong kept house for him. John's old father, Stephen Tong, also from the Island, completed the household. The Tongs had come to 151 from number 121 where John had worked as a corn and coal merchant.

The Tongs moved on again in 1894; first having had the household furniture, stock utensils-in-trade and other effects auctioned. In addition to the usual bedsteads and carpets their possessions included a treadle sewing machine and of course a sausage machine. Perhaps business had been poor and they needed the cash, or more likely, John's health was not good for they moved to Snodland where he was to be found with his niece in 1901, having taken up the less strenuous trade of selling confectionery.

Number 151 was advertised as 'to let' when they left – '*A good corner shop, convenient house, stable yard, slaughter house, cattle shed and outbuildings.*'

The Foster family

It was then that Edward Foster moved into the house and opened his greengrocery business, at any rate he is listed at number 151 in the 1899 directory.

We learn from the 1901 census that Foster who had been born in Bobbing was then in his forties, earning a living as a fruiterer and greengrocer with his wife Kate and five children, two of whom had been born in America. Edward's brother, Walter George Foster, had emigrated to America in 1874 and was living in Tennessee in 1880 (*information from Mary Breeds, a Foster descendant*). Edward and Kate Foster had themselves set off to join his brother for a new life in America in 1882 but returned home to Sittingbourne in 1893. Edward's greengrocery did well and by 1907 he had opened a branch at 54, West Street.

By 1911 Edward Foster junior, one of the Foster off-spring who had been born in Memphis Tennessee, lived at 151 running the shop with his wife Jane. Edward senior was then living at Hearts Delight, Borden cultivating his orchards with his wife and two other sons – George and Harry. Some of the produce from the Foster orchards naturally made the short journey to the Foster shop.

Number 151 is on the right-hand side with its lap-boarded upper structure and a shopfront

Butchery returns to number 151 – the Pittocks and the Wades

In 1919 Henry Pittock bought the house and opened his new butcher's shop here having long since had a shop in West Street where the family lived. (N01,24) Harry Langtry Pittock (born 1891) Henry's son, who had got married in 1915, ran the East Street shop with his wife Florence. The Pittocks were still here in 1951.

1936 invoice from Pittock the butcher

By 1963 the Wade family ran the shop which was known as 'H. M. Wade' and Mr and Mrs Wade still lived here in 1983.(115)

*1977 East Street looking east, Wade's shop at number 151
in the foreground on the left and the two terraces can be seen beyond it (EKG)*

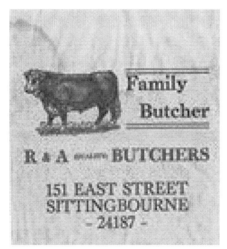

*R & A family butchers took over the business when Mr & Mrs Wade retired – perhaps the
shop was let whilst the old folk lived upstairs*

By 2009 the building had been converted back to a private house and so it remains, though apparently occupied by more than one household, as it was in the 19th century.

There remains a small yard behind the building, but the old farmhouse is bereft of its adjoining orchards, whose grass, blossom and fruit once supported wildlife in this vicinity.

Number 151 in 2016

Numbers 153 to 167 East Street

Garden Place

We know that these two terraces of four six-roomed houses, all of which still stand, were built between 1867 and 1870 for they do not appear on the 1865/6 map but are recorded on the 1871 census return. So those who lived in these houses in that year may well have been the first tenants. We have grouped the eight houses together here because in the 1908 and 1927 directories they were collectively named as 'Garden Place'.

The first owner of numbers 153-159 seems to have been James Tyler who probably had the terrace built whilst he lived next door at 151. He then moved into 157. In 1881 there was an auction sale of numbers 153, 155 and 157 'freehold houses with stables and yard' by the executors of James Tyler's widow, Rebecca, of number 157 where we shall meet her again.

153 to 159 in 2018 (CB)

Nowadays 153, 155, 157 and 159 remain residential. A narrow pathway to the back yard separates them from numbers 161, 163, 165 and 167 which also constitute a terrace. The original owner of this set of four dwellings was Samuel Willis a tailor of whom more below. Three of these houses have businesses running in them now. The front rooms of numbers 161 and 167 are both being used as tattooing salons by 'Skin Illustrations', and 163 has the 'Red Goa' Indian takeaway. Only number 165 remains a private house.

We know from an advertisement in the local paper that, in 1895, the rent on each home was six shillings a week.

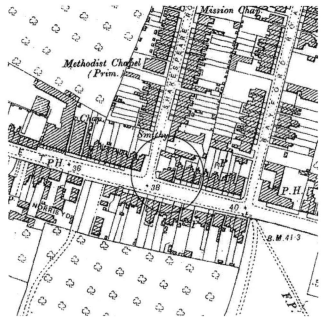

The Ordnance Survey map dated 1897 shows the location of the terrace between Shakespeare Road and Bayford Road. For reference, the shop at 151 is circled.

Number 153

Number 153 has always been residential; some of the tenants are listed here with dates when they were known to live at 153. We see that by 1970 the house had been divided into two flats.

1871	Jane Daniel (widow)+ family	annuitant
1881	John Matlock+ family	accountant
1891	uninhabited	
1901-1911	Henry Reuben	baker
1922-26	Edith and Thomas Sivyer	
1933	George and Mabel Herridge	electrical labourer
1947-51	Herbert and Margaret Chasteauneuf	
1960-63	Florence and Anne Fryday	
1970	bottom flat – Robert and Sandra Duff	
1970	top flat – Joan Lake	
1975	John and Anne Wade	
1990	top flat – Sinclair Thomson	
1990	bottom flat – Pamela Medhurst	
1998	top flat – Edward Louch	
1998	bottom flat – Carole Wood	

Residents at number 153

Number 155
Some occupants of number 155:

1871	uninhabited	
1881	George Sellen+ family	brewer's traveller
1891	Margaret Brett	living on means
1896	George Coombe	
1901	John Holdstock+ family	steam-engine fitter
1908-11	Horace Hunt+ family	journeyman butcher
1922	James and John McGarry	
1926-33	Rose and Samuel Buss	grocer
1947-75	Frank and Laura Broad	
1990	Marlene Day, Keith Taylor	

George Sellen moved in 1882 to run the coffee house at 151 (see 151)

Number 157
James and Rebecca Tyler

We have related something of the Tylers lives at number 151 before they moved to this terrace when it was built. The 1871 census records them here at 157 when James was 70 and still employed as the town carter but as we know he was in fact also a flint merchant, blacksmith and wheelwright which helps to explain how he could afford to buy the terrace or have it built. Five of the Tyler offspring were living with Rebecca and James in 1871; two of these were daughters with a dressmaking business at home.

James did not live much longer but died in 1873. The probate index reveals that he left Rebecca £455 as well as the four houses in the terrace. Rebecca lived until 1881 when she died aged 64.

A rapid turnover of occupants

William Hucksted, a local young man, was living here in 1891 and described himself as a 'traction engine and thrashing-machine proprietor'. William was married with three children and a young live-in servant. We can see from the 1881 census that it was William's father, William senior who had started the business because our William and his wife were then living with his parents round the corner in Shakespeare Road and William was driving his father's traction engine.

By 1898 Horace Savage another local man lived at 157. He had an oil and colour shop at number 100 but went bankrupt that year (see 100) due to his wife Sarah's ill health and competition from the Co-op.(N01)

In 1901 Frank Blake, a young engine-fitter from Murston, had moved in as tenant of 157 with his family, then came Mrs Rose Blake. By 1911 the house had been divided into two flats – upstairs and down. Ernest Back who worked at the paper mill had three of the rooms with his wife and child whilst old John Masters a carpenter lived in the other three rooms with his wife Elizabeth.

This division of the house does not seem to have occurred again.

Robert Wormington, gardener and verger

In 1921 this notice appeared in the local paper:

'Sad death of verger.
The death occurred on Wednesday morning after a very short illness of Mr Robert Wormington of St Michael's Church. The deceased lived at 157 East Street and was 70 years of age'

Some of our readers might welcome a few words on the distinction between the functions of sexton and verger at St Michael's. In High Street volume I we mentioned that some members of the Hogwood and Tidy families were sextons – they lived opposite the church in a cottage, which, Canon Scott Robertson recorded, was built originally for the sexton and the church clerk. Since a sexton was concerned primarily with the building and the churchyard, it was practical for him to live opposite the church, where he could keep an eye on things. The verger, however, was concerned with ceremonial, so he was able to live further away.

In 1911, ten years before Mr Wormington died, he and his wife had been living at Sittingbourne vicarage (which, in those days, stood on the north side of the churchyard) There he worked as the gardener for Reverend Adolphus Parry-Evans. Robert had been born far away in Worcestershire. When he died, he was able to leave his widow Hannah £255. He must have been missed in the church he had served for so long.

A shop is opened at 157

A shop front was added to number 157 in the 1920s and Rose and Samuel Buss who appear on the electoral register here in 1922 may have been the first to run a shop in the building.

Sarah and William John Reynolds had moved in to number 157 and opened a confectionery and tobacconist's shop by 1926 and were still here in 1949 with a council licence to sell their home-made ice cream.(115) William died aged 84 in 1962. Sarah had died in 1957 and it was probably then that William moved out for in 1958 it was Mr E. T. Wetherall who had the shop and lived here.(115)

Later residents of 157 included James and Evelyn Osbourne in the 1960s who continued the shop and Alfred and Shirley Blackwell in the 1970s.

Number 159

In the 1908 directory number 159 is named as 'Ebenezer House' and a plaque is still affixed to the front wall with the name 'Ebenezer Cottage'.

'Ebenezer Cottage' in 2018 (BA)

Ebenezer is a place name which appears in both books of Samuel in the Old Testament of the Bible. It cropped up quite often in the 19th century at different locations, including the names of nonconformist chapels. For those who are not sure, perhaps we should add that, in this context, nonconformist means Christian congregations who in some respect differ from the tenets and practice of the established Church of England. We have not discovered why this name was chosen here but we know from the electoral register that it was already called 'Ebenezer Cottage' in 1876 when it was owned by Samuel Foreman then of 6 West Street of whom more below.

Widowed Jane Wilson was the tenant here in 1870. She ran the cottage as a little boarding house with two lodgers in 1871 as well as having her nephew living with her.

Sergeant Major Samuel Foreman

The next occupant of the house was the owner Samuel Foreman, a sergeant major in the Yeomanry from Walmer who was recorded here in the 1881 census return. With him were his wife Mary who was a midwife, their five children and one grandson. The Foremans were still here in 1891 by which time Samuel in his sixties was retired and living on his pension.

There followed a number of tenants who did not stay long at 159, however the Foreman family retained ownership until the 1950s, when it was bought by Percy Hubbard, who, in the course of a long life, spent mostly in Sittingbourne, acquired many houses in the district. In volume one of our series on the High Street, we recount the circumstances of his arrival here in our community.

1895	Frank Williams	
1899	George Springthorpe	photographer
1901	Jesse Jarrett+ family	labourer
1908	William Holland	

A flurry of drapery at 159

It was probably Annie Budd who placed this advertisement in the local paper in 1921 for certainly she and her husband Samuel Thomas Budd lived here by 1922: *'To Let: Board & Lodgings two gentlemen or ladies. Quiet house 159 East Street'* and again that year she tried: *'To Let – Respectable lodging for working man.'*

Annie Budd was a woman with plenty of ideas as to how to earn some money and in the 1927 directory she was listed – *'Mrs Annie Budd fancy draper'* so she opened a shop in the front room. This was not a success and she was not listed in the 1930 directory. The Budds still lived here in 1933.

Henry J. Attwater and his wife Mary lived here from the 1940s until the 1970s. During their tenancy number 159 had been allowed to deteriorate by the Foremans and in 1954 council minutes record that notice was served on Hedley Peters (as agent for the owner Percy Hubbard) for repairs to be carried out as the conditions were prejudicial to health. Two years later, on behalf of the executors of Mrs F M Foreman, Hedley Peters sold the cottage to Percy Hubbard.

Later occupants of 159 in the 1990s were Carol and Iain Blake and Keith and Trudy Martin.

Number 161

This 2018 photograph shows 161-169 in the foreground and 153-159 in the background (CB)

Now we cross the narrow passage and start to look at the second terrace.

Samuel and Charlotte Willis

Samuel and Charlotte Willis were the first owners and occupiers of number 161, and Samuel owned the other three houses in this terrace too.(N01) Sam was then in his sixties; a journeyman tailor from Berkshire. He had opened his tailoring and outfitting shop at 14 High Street in 1858 (see HSII for more on the Willis family). Leaving the High Street business in the capable hands of their son Henry they moved along to enjoy retirement in the new house in East Street.

Sam died in 1880 aged 75 and Charlotte continued to live at 161 with her unmarried daughter Charlotte junior. Charlotte cared for her mother until 1889 when the old lady died aged 85. Charlotte then took in a boarder, probably more for company than to make ends meet for she could have had no financial worries.

With two parents who lived to a good age it is no surprise to find that Charlotte herself did not die until 1920 when she was 85. It was then that the four houses left the Willis family: '*1921 Sittingbourne property for sale: Lodging houses in the market. Block of four houses in East Street the property of the late Miss C. Willis of 161 East Street*'. This was sold for £300. Numbers 163 and 165 were passed over at £185 each but sold privately. Number 167 was sold at £300. In addition to the houses Charlotte was able to leave £1,518 between her nephew Percy Willis who by then had the shop at 14 High Street and his unmarried sister Fanny.

After 50 years of being occupied by the same family the house was let to Caroline and William Farmer who were there throughout the 1920s. They were retired and William had worked as a marine store dealer.(12)

Ernest Johnson, dairyman

Then came a change for the house when it was adapted to use the front as a shop as well as making a home for a family. Daisy and Ernest Victor Johnson moved in and lived here through the 1930s and 1940s running a dairy. They had lived in Shortlands Road previously.(54) Ernest died in 1949 leaving over £800.

A Mr J. Waterman then took on the selling and delivering of milk and moved into 161.(105)

Modernity was creeping in and a bathroom was installed in 1954 by the then owner, a Mr A. Wellard, who applied to the council for planning permission. No doubt other bathrooms were installed along the terrace at a similar date.

Ray's hair salon

By 1963 the front room had been refitted. It was no longer a shop but was now Ray's hairdressing salon for ladies. R. & S. Ralph had their television and electrical shop here for a few years in the 1970s. They had also been at number 61 and number 135.

Later inhabitants of the house in the 1990s included Andrew and Lisa Turrell and Sarah Gore-Philips. In 2009 tattooing had arrived at 159 which was called 'A2 Tat2.'

A2 Tat2 Skin Illustrations – tattoos
at number 161 East Street in 2009 (CA)

Number 163

The occupant of 163 in 1871 was young Robert Young who had been born in far off Edinburgh and whose trade was coach building. He had married Mary Ann Gray a Bredgar girl in the autumn of 1870 when no doubt they moved into this their first home. Mary was only 20. In High Street volume II we tell that Robert, the coachbuilder, devoted the coming 40 years to watchmaking; perhaps this major change was forced upon him by an accident.

Betsey Geere, a Yorkshire widow in her sixties was the next tenant of 163. She had her daughter and son living with her and her elderly sister in law too.

Samuel Ost a local mariner and his wife lived here by 1891 and we know of another local man; William Prentice, a young brickmaker who lived here with his wife in 1901.

In 1908 Joseph Laird Green an Irishman who had previously worked at the paper mill in Snodland was the tenant. Number 163 seemed to attract those born far away.

The last two tenants before a shop front was added to the house were William Dockree, a telegraph lineman who rented here in 1911 and Alice and Frederick Joyce who were here in 1922.

Edward James Landen cycle agent at 163

By 1925 a shop front had been added to the house and Edward Landen advertised bikes for sale, bicycles and wireless sets repaired.

Landen's advertisement of the 1930s

E. J. Landen, Chairman of Sittingbourne and Milton Urban District Council 1945-46

Landen did well and in 1930 were able to purchase the business of Frank Hadlow car and cycle salesman and engineer of 55 High Street.(N01) In 1937 Landen gave up 163 East Street to concentrate on the more lucrative 55 High Street where they remained in business until selling out to Sittingbourne Co-op in 1946. As recorded already in High Street volume I, Mr Landen was Chairman of Sittingbourne and Milton Urban District Council in the year of the victory celebrations, 1945-6, President of the Chamber of Commerce and a preacher at the Wesleyan Church opposite his premises in the High Street.

Grimsby Fisheries at 163

So in 1938 fish began to be fried at 163 by Grimsby Fisheries. Fish and chips continued to be served here for some years. Faith and Harold R. Arnold lived here in the 1940s and in 1947 Harold was granted planning permission to add a 'fish washing room and a bathroom' to the house.

Then by 1960 John and Winifred Payne lived here and ran the fish shop. John fried the fish, Winifred served the customers. They were a popular pair; their business thrived for some years enjoying a strong following of customers. In the 1960s they were in their sixties – about as old as the century.

The house was divided into a flat upstairs and one down by 1970 as recorded in the electoral registers. The shop may have continued and certainly by 1990 food to take away was once more being cooked and served at 163 when it became an Indian takeaway named 'Masala Magic' run by the Sandhu family. Today it is still a takeaway – 'The Red Goa'.

Masala Magic at number 173 East Street in 2009 (CA)

Number 165

Number 165 has always been residential and never had a shop front added. Here we list as many of the occupants as we can.

1870-81	Frank Usherwood+ family	clerk to county court
1882	William Inchcomb	
1891	Arthur Boulding	coach painter
1899	Esther Harris	let rooms
1901	David Mannering+ wife	ironmonger's assistant
1908	Empty	
1911	Percy Hassam+ family	insurance agent
1915-22	Edith and William Reeves	sergeant in Royal West Surrey
1926-37	William and Mary Shilling	
1947-75	Cyril and Florence Rouse	
1990	Ashley Wicks	

Arthur Boulding was the man who took on the Wises' coachbuilding business at numbers 38/40 when they sold it.

Number 167

Robert Wright, his wife Lucy and two infant daughters were probably the first occupiers of number 167; we know they were there in 1869. Wright was an excise officer, far enough from his home in Tiverton Devon for the authorities to be sure that no offenders would be relatives of his. By 1881 the Wrights had moved on to Oxfordshire as the job dictated and the Ward family had moved in to 167.

Henry Ward was not local either but hailed from London and worked as aa mechanical engineer. He was married with four children and a young live-in servant.

The next occupant we have traced was the Biblically-named Balaam Elijah Chambers, a gas fitter from Faversham who had moved in with his wife Louise and four children (with ordinary names) by 1891. Balaam is a Hebrew name meaning a diviner.

Another unusually named occupant of number 167 was Welcome Colyer, who had been born in Middlesex. He and his wife Sarah lived here by 1901. Welcome was a Metropolitan Police Pensioner (probably known as 'Not' to the criminal fraternity) and he and Sarah still had three children at home then. They were still in East Street ten years later but had moved a few doors along to number 171.

The 1908 local directory lists Thomas Henry Weller at 167 and then by 1911 Henry Tidd, a caretaker for the main Sittingbourne post office at number 85 High Street, had moved in with his wife and children. Tidd was a Londoner. He and the family had previously lived on the premises of the post office.(11)

Cooked meats for sale at 167

The next time that we come across number 167 it had for the first time come into use as a shop as well as a dwelling. Council minutes of 1921 reveal that the new owners of the house then were Messrs High the undertakers whose premises were close by. High had put in a plan for a rear extension for George Frederick Hughes who was opening the shop. Hughes put the following in the East Kent Gazette that year:

> 'G. F. Hughes begs to announce that he will open premises at 167 East Street on Tuesday next as a cooked meat & provision stores. Ham, beef, pork & brawn, salmons, sauces of all brands. Picnic parties catered for. All goods best quality.'

George had previously worked as a grocer's assistant in the town and had lived with his parents in Shortlands Road. He married Florence Hopson in 1913 when he was 33.

The Hughes venture at 167 did not last long in their hands and by 1926 one Fitzherbert Charles Barnard had the cooked meat store. He then perhaps took on other work whilst his wife Sarah ran the shop until her death in 1937 aged just 50. Sarah had been born Sarah Westley in Northants. She and Fitzherbert had married in Gravesend in 1913. Fitzherbert himself lived on into old age.

Cyril and Betty Bassett (née Moys) ran the shop next. They had married in 1944.(93) Cyril had worked as a postman in the 1950s.

Greengrocery at 167

When Delia and Brian Gallagher moved in at the start of the 1960s they changed the shop and it became a greengrocery.

By 1975 Barry and Susan Piesley lived here. We have not established whether there was still a shop at 167 then but it seems probable.

East Street Fruit and Veg at 167 already closed in 2009 (CA)
The door on the right marked 167a must be access to accommodation above.

In 2009 the shop was simply named 'East Street Fruit & Veg Shop' but closed down early that year.

Nowadays 167 is part of the tattoo business Skin Illustrations which also runs at the other end of the terrace at 161. Skin Illustrations is a chain with branches in Maidstone, Whitstable and Canterbury.

Numbers 169, 171, 173 East Street

This final short terrace of three houses brings this side of East Street to an end, with 173 standing on the corner of Bayford Road.

These homes were erected between 1866 and 1868. Whilst 169 had six rooms and 171 had seven, being the corner house 173 had the space to be larger with eight rooms and two cellars.

Today 169 and 171 remain private homes whilst 173 houses Magic Wok Chinese takeaway.

169 and 171 around 2006 (BA)

Number 169
William Streeton – a Jack of all trades

In 1870 the Post Office Directory for Sittingbourne listed William Streeton as a boot and shoe maker 'wholesale and retail' but a year later, in the census return, his job was recorded as farmer. Born in Northamptonshire he had already worked at many different jobs by the time he arrived here during 1867 to live at first at the newly built 21 Shakespeare Road before moving to number 169 East Street with his second wife Mary and three daughters.

Describing himself as a farmer in 1871 was probably just a passing phase for he was already a builder. Certainly he had acquired land and perhaps he briefly farmed some of it with the help of his son James who lived round the corner in

Goodnestone Road and was then a farm labourer but later helped his father in the building trade.

As early as February 1868 William had this notice placed in the local paper:
'A capital investment Sittingbourne for immediate sale Fourteen well-built freehold houses newly erected being numbers 1,2,3,4,5,6,10,11,12,13,14,15,16 and 17 Paradise Place, Shortlands Road Sittingbourne.

One of the houses has a Shop, in which a Butcher's business is carried on. The Property is well worth attention as it is very desirably situate in the most interesting part of the town. Two thirds of the purchase money may (if desired) remain on mortgage to be repaid in nine years by quarterly instalments. The Houses must be sold and may be had either together or separately. For further particulars apply to Mr Streeton, 21, Shakespeare Road Sittingbourne.'

This came so soon after William arrived in Sittingbourne that it seems most unlikely that he had been involved in the building of these houses. More likely perhaps is that he had borrowed money to buy them in the hope of a rapid sale and profit.

With the town expanding at a great pace William had seized the chance to become an entrepreneur, building and selling modest houses. The electoral register for 1868 records him owning land and a house in Shortlands Road and William continued to build more houses in that road during the 1870s and then later in Terrace Road.

He was a confident and articulate man as is shown by his being one of the prime movers behind the formation of Sittingbourne Ratepayers Association just two years after arrival in the town.(N01) Surprisingly he did not limit his enterprises to the local area but in 1873 made what must have been a prolonged visit to Stamford: *'the utilization work [for the drainage of the Town and disposal of sewage] has been carried out by Mr Wm. Streeton, of Sittingbourne.'* (The Stamford Mercury)

That year was a busy one for Streeton who also advertised 15 acres for sale to be sold in 18 lots in the town.(N01)

One of his descendants, Mary Connaughton, has thoroughly researched her ancestors and found that William was actually a tenant at number 169 East Street whilst he built and owned other properties nearby. The story passed down through the family is that he collected rents in East Street including that of number 102 where Solomon and Hannah Wood lived and so he met their daughter Emily.(115)

The family story is that Hannah Wood *'pushed her daughter Emily off on to William Streeton'* in spite of the fact that his wife Mary was still alive and he was 28 years older than Emily. However it could be that Emily was already pregnant by then and that Hannah was making sure Streeton would look after her daughter which he in fact did.

Emily Wood and William Streeton's first child was born in 1872. By 1876 Emily lived with her children in Shortlands Road in another house owned by William. What the neighbours thought of William and Emily we can only guess but we do know that Emily had a deep Christian faith. Her father Solomon Wood was a Methodist lay preacher and in later life Emily became a member of the Baptist congregation.

Being only round the corner Mary and Emily must often have encountered each other. How awkward that would have been!

After Mary Streeton died in her sixties in 1884 William did not marry Emily Wood but moved in with her and their three illegitimate children who had been born before his wife died. Then, from 1887 until 1891, he and Emily had three more children, all of whom bore 'Streeton' as their middle name. William proved a loving father to all his children.

Painting of William Streeton (CC)

His youngest daughter was only three months old when William died in 1891, worth only £62. He had fathered ten children in his life over a period of 41 years. Emily was virtually destitute with three children under 11; it was difficult to make ends meet even though she was a skilled dressmaker. She vowed never to have anything to do with a man '*not even if his skin was stuffed with diamonds.*'

The Cannells, chemists and printers

After William Streeton left number 169 to move in with Emily, the house became the home of George Cannell who came originally from Norwich but had moved around England a good deal as we can tell from the birth places of his children. The Cannells arrived in East Street in 1884 with George working as a chemist and printer. He was in fact both doctor and chemist. However Dr George Cannell no longer practised as a doctor. He had lost the use of his legs some years earlier due to a stroke but patients would come and see him for advice and medicine. He had ventured into printing in order to set his eldest son Arthur up in a new trade, for although Arthur was already a chemist he did not enjoy it.

Most of our information about Arthur Cannell who was born in 1866 comes from Richard Goulden's excellent publication; 'Sittingbourne & Milton Regis Book Trade 1770-1900'.

So George Cannell purchased the machinery required for a small press which was set up at number 169 in an outbuilding at the back but Arthur did not make a success of it although he was joined in the enterprise by his brother Walter who had just left the army.

George's wife Annabelle died in 1890.(61) Matters went badly for the brothers for after their father died in 1893 they took to crime and were arrested

241

in 1894 for receiving stolen goods which belonged to Fredrick Parrett who ran the East Kent Gazette. Arthur and Walter were arrested together with an employee of Parrett's. They were accused of stealing type and other printing materials from the Gazette office. The Cannells had just moved the printing side of the business to 84a East Street. They were sentenced to four months in prison with hard labour. They had a younger brother, Bertram at home and a sister, Lilian, who were 17 and 21 at the time their brothers went to prison. Sad to say Lilian could be found in Milton Union Workhouse in 1901 described as a 'field worker.' Walter and Bertram both settled in London but where Arthur went we have not discovered.

Mary Coe, dressmaker

After the Cannells had moved out less tempestuous times arrived at number 169 with Harry Coe a gardener from Lynsted and his wife Mary who was a dressmaker.(N01)

A private house

In 1908 Samuel Fosbraey was living at 169. Born in Borden, he worked at the paper mill.(11) A single man, he wanted wider horizons and on 2nd July 1910 an auction of his household furniture was held in the house because he was leaving for America. He sailed for New York a week later on the Lusitania, which was to become so famous when it was sunk by the Germans in 1915.

The next inhabitant of 169 was Arthur Dennett, also a paper mill worker in his thirties, with Mabel his wife, and his mother in law in the six rooms. Arthur served throughout the war as a gunner. In 1921 the Dennetts moved to number 53. (see number 53)

The tenants who followed them at 169 were Alfred and Emma Howland who were there into the early 1930s. Then came a number of different members of the James family who remained over 30 years well into the 1970s. The house has remained residential to this day.

Number 171

For just a few years after they were built 171 and 173 were separately occupied. The first occupant of 171 that we know of lived here in 1871 and that was Frank Whitehead a sawyer in his forties from Bredgar, with a wife and two children who shared the house and rent with young Bill Butcher, a brickmaker, and his wife. Three years later a shop opened at 171.

Henry Read, tobacconist

Henry Read a tobacconist moved in and set up shop and remained perhaps until 1880.

Number 173
Walter Greensted, grocer

Young Walter Greensted is the first occupant of number 173 that we know of and in 1871 he ran a grocery and butchery here.(8) With him until his death in 1874, lived his father Thomas, a retired miller. Walter owned the house as is recorded in the electoral roll.

Walter had been born near Faversham. His brother Percy had a butcher's shop along the street at numbers 81 and 83 and no doubt supplied Walter with meat as required.

Numbers 171 and 173 in joint occupation

By the time of the 1881 census Walter Greensted had expanded his business and home into number 171. He had married and he and his wife Sarah had three young children. Walter was respected in the town as is shown by his serving as overseer of the poor for St Michael's Church.

A life-changing tragedy struck Walter and Sarah early in 1887 when their seven year old son Claud died.(N01) It was very likely this event which made Walter ill and unable to continue his business. In July this notice appeared in the local paper: *'East Street W. T. Greensted Grocer & Provision Merchant 171 & 173 East Street begs to inform the inhabitants of Sittingbourne and the neighbourhood that in consequence of ill health, he is compelled to relinquish Business and has disposed of same to Mr Trayton Brand for who he solicits a continuance of those favours so liberally bestowed on himself for the past 18 years'.*

Underneath this:

'Trayton Brand Having succeeded to the old established business hitherto carried on by W. T. Greensted hopes by strict attention to orders and continuances of the support accorded to his predecessor.'

So the Greensteds moved out of 171/173. They went to Linton to make a fresh start and there Walter opened a butcher's shop and they lived with their remaining three children.(10) Although the announcement of the transfer of the business did not make this known, the East Kent Gazette of 1894 revealed that in fact Walter Greensted kept ownership of the premises of 171 and 173 and also the stock until that year. This meant that Trayton would not have required capital and was managing the business for Greensted.

Trayton Brand

The very unusually named Trayton Brand was born in Surrey in 1851 and had worked as a grocer's assistant in Doddington before moving to East Street with his wife. Perhaps he was later able to start his own business for just three years later the grocery was being run by James Buss. Trayton died in Canterbury in 1902.

James Buss

In 1890 James Buss took space in the local paper to tell the public he had taken on the grocery lately carried on by Mr Trayton Brand. He reminded the townsfolk that he had 19 years' experience in the trade.(N01) Buss was able to open a post office here too.(36) With him were his wife, five daughters, two sons and a niece who worked for the family as a servant. Matthews in his recollections of Sittingbourne in the 1880s and 1890s remembered Mr Buss and his grocer's shop.(69) From the auction details of 1895, we too can picture the inside of this shop which had been so beautifully fitted out by Walter Greensted. The counters were mahogany with twisted pillars and fitted with tea bins for the loose tea. There were marble slabs for cutting and slicing, brass hydraulic gasoliers (these were chandeliers with gas burners), three brass scales, 12 japaned black and gold tea canisters and six porcelain butter stands.

One of James Buss's daughters was named Kate (born in Sittingbourne in 1875). She was a second class passenger on the Titanic in 1912 and she survived. Kate was one of two passengers booked by Hedley Peters whose ticket agency was based at 93 High Street. As was his custom, Mr Peters accompanied the passengers for embarkation at Southampton docks. We can imagine his feelings after the catastrophe; one of his responses was to establish a benevolent fund for the widow and eight year old daughter of the other local passenger, Richard Henry Rouse, of New Road, who was drowned. Hedley's own daughter, at the time, was aged nine. Kate was on her way to meet her fiancé in the United States. She did eventually marry him but had lost her entire trousseau and all her wedding presents in the wreck. Speaking of her traumatic experience she said: "Never as long as I live shall I forget it, nor the brave souls who, I know, have perished."

It was 1895 when Walter Greensted decided to sell off 171 and 173:

'Relinquishing business, the entire stock of W. T. Greensted will be sold without reserve, at cost price, until cleared. Sale to commence this day (Friday) 171 East Street, corner of Bayford Road'

A few months later came the following:

'To be sold without reserve 171 and 173 East Street, grocery fixtures, shop fittings, utensils in trade etc. As the shops are about to be altered into two private houses the whole of the above will be sold without reserve.'

However the houses failed to sell and Walter Greensted hung on to them and still owned them in 1915.(115) He had them decorated:

'To be let the two private dwelling houses situate numbers 171 and 173 East Street. Number 171 contains seven rooms and cellars, and number 173 eight and two cellars, also stable and stores at the rear. Both houses have been thoroughly painted and papered throughout. For further particulars apply to John Peters and Sons, Auctioneers and House Agents.'

Greensted also enquired of the council whether they had any objection to the forecourts at the front and side of those houses in East Street and Bayford Road being enclosed by a wall. This would have given a little privacy from passers-by on the pavement now that they were no longer shops.

Number 171 – a private house again

At 171 in 1901 Rebecca Horton from Borden took in three lodgers to help pay the rent. By 1908 this was the home of the cheerfully named Welcome Colyer the police pensioner whom we have met a few doors away at number 167. Welcome died in 1929 aged 78.

The Lynch family then lived at 171 for many years.

Number 173

Although number 173 was now a private house without a shop front yet a small business operated from the house.

Thomas Hunt, chimney sweep

If your chimneys needed sweeping in 1901 this was where you could call on Thomas Hunt a sweep from Ramsgate whose household consisted of his wife, daughter, nephew and two boarders.

The Thomas family, dressmakers

By 1911 the house was the home of Edwin Thomas, an elderly shipwright from Rodmersham his wife and three daughters Emma, Clara and Hilda who ran a dressmaking business together at home.(12) Hilda Thomas, the youngest daughter was musical and took pupils for the organ and piano.

Edwin died aged 80 in 1922. None of the daughters married or left home but still lived here into the 1950s.

Howe painter and decorator

In 1963, A. Howe, a building contractor and decorator ran his business from 173.

Fast Food and Takeaway

By 1974 the premises at number 173 had been converted to a fast food outlet and, until 2007, was home to Kentucky Fried Chicken. In the following year David Wen took over the premises, trading as Royal China. He was succeeded, in 2010, by Mr Tongrong You trading as Magic Wok Takeaway. The business was taken over in 2017 by Mr Jiajia Chi who trades under the same name.

KFC in 1974 (EKG)

The Royal China at 173 in 2009 (CA)

173 in 2018 (CB)

The South Side (even numbers)

Number 2 East Street – The Three Kings

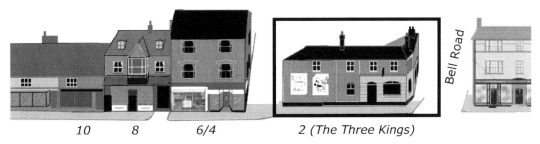

| 10 | 8 | 6/4 | 2 (The Three Kings) |

We do not know for how many centuries an inn named The Three Kings welcomed travellers on this corner of East Street and Bell Road but it is likely that it already stood there in pre-Reformation days when pilgrims tramped by on their way to Canterbury. Presumably it took its name from the Bible story about the three wise men who visited Jesus Christ at Epiphany.

This is the first of five inns or public houses in East Street – all on the south side – perhaps because land for their yards was more readily available on that side of the street – viz the Yeakell plan from 1791 accompanying our notes on Bayford South Field.

Yards were needed because some of these social gathering places were also what, today, we would call transport hubs, where carriages and vans called regularly en route to other towns. Folk awaiting the arrival of the vehicles would bring business to the public house – we can imagine the discussions and the competition that led to such arrangements. Establishments with the bigger yards for turning vehicles would have an advantage, yet we have found no notes of vans providing a scheduled service at the Plough, which had the largest yard of the five.

Here at the Three Kings in the early 19th century, we learn from the directories that, en route to London and Dover, *'Stephen Wrake's waggon calls three times a week.'*

The Three Kings and East Street, c.1908 in the time of 'Mike' Tucker

At one time the Three Kings was owned by John Allen – probably a member of the family prominent in Sittingbourne and Borden in the 17th century. In the early 17th century the inn was run *'by Mrs Linsell, an old servant of Sr John Honeywood* [High Sheriff of Kent] *who consequently always put up at that house'.*(62)

It is certain that when St Michael's Church was badly damaged by fire in 1762 some services were held at the Three Kings including christenings. The reason for the choice might have been the respectability and regular church attendance of the publican. However a more compelling reason would have been that the building actually belonged to the Dean and Chapter of Rochester until 1771 as a sale notice of 1771 in the Kentish Gazette stated: *'To be sold all that good accustomed Public House known by the sign of the Three Kings with the malt-house, buildings, stables, yard, garden and appurtenances; situate and being at Sittingbourne, in the occupation of Mr Boulden* [sic]*, and held by lease from the dean and chapter of Rochester'.* (Kentish Gazette – Saturday 24th August 1771)

The lease of the Inn was held by Thomas Boulding, who owned the premises next door. The Bouldings were closely associated with St Michael's, which more than one of them served as Churchwarden. Their butcher's shop adjoined the churchyard.(HSII)

In 1779 Thomas Boulding was giving up his lease on the inn:

'To be let and entered upon immediately, the well-known and good-accustomed inn known by the Three Kings in Sittingbourne in Kent with the Brewhouse, all the utensils and household furniture, with a garden, yard and stables thereunto belonging and now in the occupation of Thomas Boulding The further particulars may be known by applying at the said house.' – (Kentish Gazette – Saturday 6th February 1779)

In the 1830s when the inn was owned by Mrs Maria Louisa Crump (see Red Lion in HSII) a horse-drawn omnibus named 'The Warrior' left the Three Kings every morning at 6.45am for Gravesend where it arrived in time for the morning steam-packet to London Bridge. Weary return travellers arrived back in Sittingbourne at 8.30pm. (*South Eastern Gazette – Tuesday 25th November 1834*)

By 1840 the Three Kings was owned by John Brenchley along with The George and The Red Lion in the High Street.(4) Mr Brenchley lived in Brenchley House in the High Street employing Mr Oliver Saxby Davis as publican of The Three Kings.

A year later widowed Mrs Sarah Jackson was in charge of the inn and as well as coping with her six children she somehow found space for 11 lodgers. They must have been uncomfortably overcrowded and Sarah must have been desperately overworked.(5)

Publicans came and went in the 1840s and we know from the 1851 and 1861 census returns records that the income of the inn continued to be boosted by the presence of a handful of lodgers. By this time, with the end of the coaching days on which Sittingbourne's prosperity had rested, the Three Kings was not the respectable inn it once had been and many cases of petty crime occurring there which can be read about in the local paper.

In 1864 a customer broke in one night after closing time and stole brandy, raspberry cordial, cigars and tobacco from the landlord, Samuel Knight who had been in charge since 1861. (*Canterbury Journal, Kentish Times and Farmers' Gazette*) The thief made off to Chatham where he was able to treat several ladies of ill-repute to drinks and put himself up in an inn. Three further examples from 1865 will give the idea of what went on:

'25th February: William Poore a young man was wilfully accused of breaking a pane of glass value 1/- at The Three Kings Inn in Sittingbourne on Wednesday night last.

11th March: Edward Turner assaulted his wife Hester Turner on the 18th February in front of the bar in the Three Kings Public House He eventually dragged her into the passage.

9th September: Harriet Jackson (a deaf woman) was charged with stealing a saucepan and an ale glass of the value of 2s 4d, the property of Samuel Knight of The Three Kings Inn. On the 20th April Elizabeth Knight deposed that the saucepan and glass produced belonged to her husband and were missed by her on or about the 20th April and Henry Burley a tailor residing in Sittingbourne purchased them of the prisoner for 4d and the cost of a loaf. The prisoner was sentenced to 14 days imprisonment with hard labour.'

That February fire broke out in the inn early one morning. J. F. Dawson the licensee and his family had a narrow escape from death. (*Maidstone Journal and Kentish Advertiser*) The owners, Maidstone brewers Brenchley & Co., had the building insured for £400 and the contents for a similar amount. Henry Tidy whose building yard adjoined at the back in Bell Lane had a good deal of his house destroyed too. Dawson was bankrupted by the fire. (*Kentish Gazette – 24th May 1870*)

The inn was soon rebuilt and local man Charles Clinch was granted the licence. He was not new to the licensed trade. In 1861 he had been running the White Hart in Crown Quay Lane.

In October 1870 Clinch appeared before Sittingbourne magistrates to answer a charge of *'knowingly suffering prostitutes to assemble in his house contrary to the terms of his licence'*. It was not the first time this has happened. Police

Constable Kewell gave evidence that on passing the pub at 12.30 at night he heard some very disgusting language being spoken in the taproom. On entering the room he saw five prostitutes and 18 or 20 men sitting and drinking together. The house was not closed until one o'clock. The evidence presented was conflicting and it was difficult to prove that Mr Clinch had known what was going on. Mr Clinch's daughter Ann claimed to have had exclusive management of the taproom that evening. Mary Goldsmith, a servant at the pub who shared Ann's bedroom said all had been quiet, as did Mrs Ann Bentall, the lodger who also shared the same bedroom.

What swung the case in Clinch's favour was the testimony of two of his neighbours who were both respectable tradesmen. Mr Henry Tidy the builder who lived next door in Bell Road considered the Three Kings was well-conducted and never a cause of disturbance. Mr Brown the saddler diagonally opposite the Three Kings in the High Street had seen no impropriety. The summons was dismissed and Charlie Clinch's licence renewed. No doubt Messrs Tidy and Brown enjoyed a free pint or two.

The 1871 census return gives us the information that Clinch had been born at Otterden, was then 51 and lived with his wife Emma, daughter Ann, sister in law and two lodgers.

Perhaps there had been one clash too many with the forces of law and order for by 1874 the Clinch family had moved out of the Three Kings and into number 4 next door where they ran a butcher's shop. Charles Clinch died aged 59 in 1878.(110)

Having recorded some negative facts about Charles Clinch it is good to note from the 'Kent and Sussex Courier' 27th March 1878, that he was a member of the Sittingbourne Volunteer Corps from its inception in 1860 and was buried with full military honours. About 60 members of the corps including Captain Knight were present together with a contingent of the battalion from Dover. The report concludes that 'he was much respected by his comrades.'

Richard Wallis was the next licensee of the Three Kings. He was another Kentish man and ran it with the help of his wife Augusta and grown up daughter Ellen. They were still there in 1881 when two of their younger daughters were learning to be dressmakers. A year later they had moved on by which time Isherwoods the brewers owned the pub.

A tenant who was here for some years in the 1880s and 1890s was William Palmer who hailed from West Malling. By 1901 he was a widower whose son and two daughters helped him run the business. Perhaps it was Palmer who began to take the pub on an upward path to being a hotel. Certainly in 1908 when Walter George Tucker, known as Mike, took the Three Kings on it was called a 'hotel' it was an altogether more respectable place. He advertised 'Good stabling, good beds, good storage for Motors'. His motto was 'civility and respectability'. His advertisement in the local directory shows a photograph of him sporting a handle bar moustache and bow tie. It was a free house with a full licence. Tucker was a local man with a wife and four children.

Here were held the meetings of the Sittingbourne Branch of the Royal Antediluvian Order of Buffaloes.(43) The meetings of this friendly society continued to be hosted, definitely until 1962, and possibly until the pub was closed down.(87)

Although the painted signs on the outside walls continued to advertise 'Tucker's Tea Gardens, luncheons, dinners and teas provided', throughout the

First World War, Tucker and his family actually left in 1912 when The Three Kings licence was transferred to Sydney Arthur William Nokes, previously a shipwright, aged only 24 and newly married to Laura Lilian Coulman on Sheppey.(N01)

George 'Mike' Tucker in 1908

Although so young the magistrates must have felt that Sydney had sufficient character to run the inn and sufficient knowledge of how to do it as his brother Walter Nokes was the licensee of the Druids Arms in Sheerness and his father William had the Globe and Engine in Sittingbourne.(12)

Sydney enlisted in the Royal Navy at Sheerness in early October 1916, described as a licensed victualler, formerly shipwright. His skills as a shipwright were needed by the navy. We learn from his service record that he was 5' 9" tall with brown hair and eyes, of fresh complexion and sporting an appendix scar. His conduct was excellent during his service and the last ship he sailed on was the HMS Venus from which he was demobilised in June 1919.

All the pubs in the town were busier than usual during the First World War with troops stationed all around and making their way to the front. As the local paper reported in November 1914: 'Suitable billets had run out of space and the Inspector of Nuisances found eight men sleeping in a stable in East Street where there was room for three at most.' The building was described as unfit for human habitation but no action was required as the arrangement was temporary.

Whilst at the Three Kings Sydney and Laura Nokes were blessed with two daughters – Doris and Audrey, and three sons – Sydney, Roy and Reginald. Upstairs where the family lived were three large bedrooms and a club room.

Part of the Three Kings building seems to have been sublet by the Nokes in 1924 to fishmonger Henry Cullen who was also listed at number 2 that year in the directory.

Sydney Nokes was an ambitious, entrepreneurial man full of ideas and plans to make a good life for his family. His aim was to acquire the tenancy of the Billet and with this in mind he purchased a piece of land on the London Road opposite the Billet where he thought the family might eventually have a café which his daughters could run. He also bought a house under the railway arch in Milton intending it to be a base for a wholesale tobacconist's business that he was developing for his sons to run when they grew up.

Sydney Nokes continued in charge until his death in 1928 at the early age of 41. He had contracted meningitis and despite his father arranging for him to be attended by Sir Thomas Horder (later Lord Horder), physician to the king, he could not be saved.

The Three Kings, S. Nokes, 1930
East Street is to the left, Bell Road to the right.

Laura had to sell the piece of land and the Milton property. She continued to run the inn for Fremlins and to bring up the family. All the three sons learned trades and all served in the forces during the war. Laura carried on at the Three Kings until 1949 when she retired. The 1933 electoral register records her as the only adult living at the inn.(54,57)

Laura Nokes (PN)

Laura and Sydney's son Roy Nokes and his wife Muriel (née Couchman, daughter of the butcher at number 8) who were newly married, then took on the tenancy.

Sittingbourne Caged Bird Society held meetings at the Three Kings in the 1950s and early 60s and possibly before and after that period.(87)

1966 looking south up Bell Road

Muriel and Roy Nokes at The Three Kings (PN)

By the early 1960s town pubs were becoming less profitable. They were losing trade partly because customers were becoming more affluent and car ownership was increasing, resulting in trade migrating to country and out-of-town pubs – there being no breathalyser laws for drivers. As a consequence, Roy returned to his trade as an electrician for the South Eastern Electricity Board. Muriel ran the pub during the day with Roy joining her for evening and weekend opening hours. They eventually decided to leave the licensed trade and moved out on 5th November 1962.(87)

The Three Kings was taken on by Charlie Thompson and his wife.(N01) They had previously run the Foresters Arms in Berry Street near Sittingbourne Station. They vacated that pub because plans to build St Michael's Road and redevelop the area between the High Street and the station were being put into action.

A small side-line of the history of the Three Kings building is that for a time during the 1960s, a new address, 2a East Street was recorded.(121) This was the coach-house that formed an integral part of the building and was being rented by a firm called Alpha Engraving which was run by a Mr Fletcher. A further business which utilised the old stables for a time was that of photographer S. J. Newman who gave his address in the 1969 town guide as 'The Old Stables, 2 East Street'.

In the early to mid 1970s the Three Kings was acquired by Rex Boucher, the owner of Hulburds department store close by in the High Street. The pub was empty in 1975 and demolished a few years later, except for the perimeter walls which were retained to a height of about four feet to maintain the boundary with the pavements in East Street and Bell Road. Some of the etched glass pub windows were used in a fashion clothing section of Hulburds shop called the Three Kings Boutique.(87)

The pub's boundary walls retained, 1985

In January 1980 the local paper reported upon plans by the council to make the site of the Three Kings into a car park for a short period. The Sittingbourne Society objected to the idea. Rex Boucher had planning permission for a three storey office block on this corner site. He was quoted as saying it 'had taken him 30 separate deals to get the land together and that the block would be a Sittingbourne landmark'.(N01) However for some years the site was a car park, certainly between 1982 and 1995.(121)

The site of the former Three Kings Hotel and the widening of Bell Road, 1986

In 1986 the remaining boundary walls were demolished and the site was paved to make the current public open space.

Numbers 4 and 6 East Street

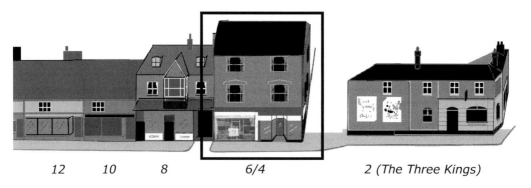

12   10   8   6/4   2 (The Three Kings)

The present building numbered 4 and 6 East Street was probably built around 1900 and is now the premises of Bourne Funeral Services with its double fronted shop which also has windows at the side.

W. G. Matthews, writing about his Sittingbourne childhood of the 1880s recalls that the building which then stood on this site was old and timber-framed.(69) On the tithe map of 1840 number 4/6 East Street is shown as quite a large building (parcel 152). A Thomas Gatland was the owner of the house then; he lived in the town and his tenant was one 'White.' The property stood alone with a sizable gap between itself and the Three Kings on one side which was the main entrance for carriages and horses to the back of the inn.

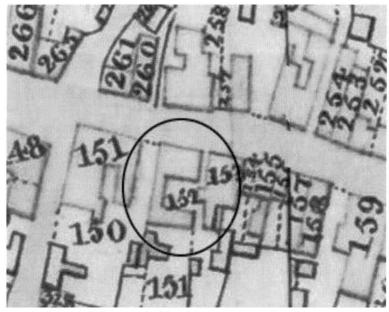

Parcel 152 in circled in this section of the tithe map

On the other side towards number 8 was a far narrower gap. By 1851 the building had been partitioned and remained so for many a long year.

Number 4 East Street

The 1851 census schedule implies a partitioning of the building into three, with two households on the west side and one (later number 6 on the east side) Here lived and worked John Wetherill, a hairdresser, born in Rochester, his wife and three children and also John Lee, a 60 year old greengrocer from Doddington his wife, and lodger. John Lee died in 1859.(110) Ten years later widowed Mrs Ann Lee who hailed from Harrietsham seems to have had possession of the whole of number 4 and continued the greengrocery trade supported by a nephew, two nieces and a lodger.

Number was 4 no longer a greengrocery by 1871, when a certain Edward Hurst a general dealer from Faversham had his shop here with his wife and four children.

At some point during the next three years number 4 became a butcher's shop run by Charles Clinch and his wife Emma. They had moved from the Three Kings next door.(32) (see number 2)

It is hard to see how the Clinchs came to acquire the skills to run a butchery because apart from a time as a servant as revealed by the 1841 census of Otterden, Charlie had spent his life running pubs. He died in 1878 and the directory for that year lists Mrs Emma Clinch, pork butcher, and so she continued to run the shop until her death in 1884 aged 61.(110)

The list of Sittingbourne's shop-keepers, who, in January 1887, announced in the East Kent Gazette, that, on Wednesdays, they would close their shops at 4pm, includes at number 4, Mr A. Fossey, House Furnisher. Very likely, this was Alexander Fossey from Limehouse, who, for some ten years, had been trading in the same line at 124 High Street – one of the new shops at the West End of the town. Perhaps Alec brought his family down here to this less desirable location near the gas works, because the rent was lower, but they did not stay here long.

Thomas Stroud

After the Fosseys left, a Thomas Stroud of Canterbury, came to live at number 4 with his Cornish wife and their two young sons. Following, to some extent, Alec Fossey's lead, Tom opened his own furniture and upholstery business here. His 1890 advertisement in the local paper boasted that he made beds which were 'cheap and good' and that he named the shop 'The Economic Furnishing Store'. The 1890 directory shows he had other skills too, for there he is listed as a cabinet maker and an insurance agent. Despite this diversification, Tom Stroud too was a short-term occupier.

Drapery at number 4
William Cook Gardener

Sometime between the 1891 census and the publication of the 1895 directory William Cook Gardener moved his drapery here from across the road at number 5 where he and his wife Kate had previously lived and run their business (see number 5).(10) He was then in his early thirties. Born in Thorncombe, Dorset, he had set off to improve his fortunes and had begun as a draper's assistant in Croydon.(9,10) Perhaps he and his wife never lived at number 4 and certainly the 1901 census listed it as an uninhabited draper's shop. This freed space for storage upstairs or for the milliner to work on the hats ordered by customers.

We know that by 1901 Gardener had done well enough to be living in Albany Road which lies an easy walk from the shop. His elderly widowed mother had come from Dorset to live with him, her daughter in law and the young family of three children. A young female shop assistant boarded with the family and a servant completed the household. Ten years later old mother Gardener, in her eighties, was still with the family in Albany Road.(12) By then two of Gardener's workers, a milliner and a shop assistant, lodged with the family.

Mr Gardener advertised regularly in the local paper; in 1908 he drew attention to his 'stock of millinery, straw and felt hats, jackets, gloves, umbrellas and underwear.' He continued to run the drapery until 1921.(49) In three of the census returns Gardener is spelt as Gardner but Gardener is correct for this family.

Herbert George Jones at 4 and 6

Herbert George Jones was the next draper to take on the shop at number 4, also moving into the living accommodation of number 6.(115) He had been born in Derbyshire in 1881 and by 1911 the census found him already a draper, though then working for someone else and living in Abingdon. The reason for moving so far away to settle in Sittingbourne was that he had wed Charlotte George, a girl from Teynham. They had married in 1908 and Charlotte must have missed her family when she lived in Abingdon. We know from directories, electoral register and advertisements that Mr Jones had the shop here by 1921. Advertisements make it clear the shop was **in** both 4 and 6:

1921: 'Jones 4-6 East Street. Requires young lady 3 years experience'

1925 3rd January: 'Ten Days Sale, H.G. Jones 4 and 6 East Street, millinery costumes, coats, coat frocks, skirts on Thursday 1st January to 12th'

Herbert Jones had a dry sense of humour as this announcement of 1933 makes plain: *'We are very pleased to be able to say that the Open Air Bath Scheme for East Street was only a Rumour. The holes in the surface of the road hereabouts have now been filled in and ladies can view our window displays without fear of a muddy shower bath.'*

Charlotte worked at the business with her husband. In the 1939 listing he described himself as general drapery manager and she as part time draper.

Herbert G. Jones died here in 1957 aged 76. Mrs Jones then moved to Albany Road, though later she went to live with her daughter and son-in-law at Fox Hill, Bapchild, eventually dying at Blair Park Residential Home on 26th October 1989. (111). She had been born in Faversham in 1883. Therefore, she would have reached the great age of 105 or 106 at her death.

John Peters & Sons

It was in 1957 that John Peters & Sons, the long established High Street furniture business took on number 4 as their drapery department. After the Jones moved out nobody lived upstairs and no doubt those rooms were used for extra storage.(115)

Peters continued here until 1979. The building was empty in 1980.(121) Advertisements show that they had another premises in East Street – number 50/52 which was their second-hand department. (see number 50/52) The building was owned by Laurence Easton at this time.(87)

Number 6 East Street
Boots and shoes at number 6

In 1851 Moses Sidders, a 35 year old shoemaker from Sittingbourne lived in the eastern end of the building later known as number 6, with his wife and five children. Moses died young in 1853 no doubt leaving his wife struggling to keep the family together. She remarried in 1858.(110)

It may have been when Sidders died that William Fisher, a single, local shoemaker in his forties came to live and trade at number 6.

The next we know of the fortunes of number 6 is the presence of Benjamin Hackshaw who in the 1866 directory described himself as a dealer in second-hand clothes. This did not prove a profitable venture and so he returned to his trade as a shoemaker by 1870.(31) Mr Hackshaw and his family never lived at number 6, their home was a few doors up the road at numbers 30/32 where it seems his main business was also (see 30/32). He died in 1882 aged just 56. (110)

James and Anette Inchcomb

In 1871 James Inchcomb, a coachbuilder. was living at 36 West Street with his wife and nine children and in 1881 (by which time he was widowed), he had moved to Crescent Street. He had premises in the yard behind 110 High Street. His two sons Caleb and Tapley took over the main business of coachbuilding in the High Street. So what has James Inchcomb to do with number 6 East Street?

At that date perhaps number 6 was a place where you could call to arrange for work to be done by either Mr Hackshaw or Mr Inchcomb. When Benjamin Hackshaw died in 1882 it is likely that James Inchcomb junior (a coach-builder like his father), or at first perhaps just his wife Anette née, Dorrell (see number 12) whom he had married in 1882, started to use number 6 as a 'fancy repository' – a place for buying knick-knacks, gifts, and, in the right season fireworks.(N01,36) James and Anette who were in their thirties, had come to live above the shop at number 6 by 1891.(10)

Coach-building was by then in steep decline and ten years later James' skills were no longer required and he described himself as a stationer and newsagent and so he continued for at least another ten years. It is the 1911 census which records that number 6 had six rooms.

Central Pie Shop at number 6

From 1932 until 1973 this is where the George family had their pie shop called 'Central' because in those days it was deemed to be in the centre of town. This shop has been part of the commercial life of Sittingbourne as long as anyone can remember.

Gordon White recalled his memories of the origins of the shop for Shirley Mannouch in 2016:

"My great-aunt, Mrs Rhoda George, opened the shop with one of her sons, Freddy. Another son, Roy, had a pie shop in Ashford and eventually became landlord of the Tickled Trout in Wye, near Ashford. The third son, Don, ran the pie shop in Sheerness. Freddy opened another shop in Maidstone in 1948 so in the 1950s and 60s there were four pie shops in all.

My mother, Grace née George, was Rhoda George's niece, she worked with her aunt and eventually took over the Sittingbourne business. In the early days closing time was a movable feast often staying open late to accommodate cinema goers and workers on late shifts. Mum and Dad married in 1931. During the war Mum ran the business single-handed and throughout those long six years she cooked the meat late at night for the next day's pies and then got up at 4am to light the ovens, make the pastry, cook the pies and serve in the shop. The ovens were fuelled by coke which needing kindling wood and paper to set the coke alight not an easy thing to master.

My Dad, Arthur White, joined her after the war when he was demobbed from the Navy. I remember the staff lining up each morning for a hand and nails inspection.

I only became part of the firm after doing an apprenticeship with Wraight Ltd, the builders, and my national service in The Royal Artillery. On demob I returned to Wraight's. It was in the mid 1960s that I became part of the family business eventually taking over the Sittingbourne shop in 1973 which was when the business relocated to number 30/32 East Street."

Carry out bag pre-1973 for number 6 East Street

Staff at Central Pie Shop – Mrs White is on the right

For the later history of the Central Pie Shop see number 30/32

Numbers 4 and 6 are combined again
John Peters & Sons

When the pie shop was relocated number 6 became the china and glass department of John Peters and Sons who as we have seen were already occupying number 4 and so the two halves of the building were reunited and internal access created between them. Numbers 4 and 6 have remained as one unit ever since. The property was empty for some time after the closure of John Peters and Sons.

Lockeyears and Sittingbourne Flooring Centre

In 1982 Lockeyears, the flooring contractors replaced Peters & Sons and sold carpets, vinyls and tiles. The firm had been established in 1945.

In 1985 the name of the shop was changed to the 'Sittingbourne Flooring Centre' and so it remained in 1991.(121)

Kentish Carvery

The Kentish Carvery was opened here in 1995 by a Mr Lawrence and a Mr Clapp but did not last long for the premises were vacant in 1997.(59)

Busy Bees

In 1998 Busy Bees another carpet retailer opened their business here which later moved into premises in the High Street. It closed during 2002.

Bourne's the undertaker

The shop then became the premises Bourne's Funeral Service run by T. Horlook & Son Ltd. The company, originally a family firm, was established in West Kent where, under the banner of Dignity, a much larger company, there is still a Dartford branch using Bourne's name. The Sittingbourne branch is still known as Bournes, though Martin Bourne is no longer involved.(121) Bourne's had moved here from number 8 next door.

Bourne's Funeral Service 2008 (CA)

4 and 6 East Street in 2016. The Three Kings used to stand next door where the tree and planters are now. In the foreground is Bell Road with East Street to the left.(BA)

Number 8 East Street

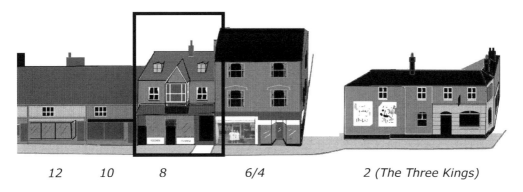

| 12 | 10 | 8 | 6/4 | 2 (The Three Kings) |

Today number 8 East Street houses the florist 'Flowers by Beatrice'. It has a shop window on each side of the door and three large bedroom windows. The central window belongs to a large reception room, rather than a bedroom. The two full-length windows on the right of the ground floor replace an open passage which gave carriage access to the rear yard. Above the bedroom windows is another storey with dormer windows. The present building dates from the late 1880s.

Unfortunately the ancient deeds of the premises were destroyed (without permission) in the 1980s by Barclays Bank who had made a loan to Oscar Gallaon, the owner at that time.

The tithe map of 1840 depicts the previous number 8 East Street as 153 on the schedule; a house then owned by William Gascoyne a well-to-do Bapchild farmer who owned another house and land in Sittingbourne as well as Bapchild Court and its acres. Number 8 was tenanted by William Jay, a cornfactor in his fifties, as the 1841 census also records. He had a wife and three children, his eldest son George was a tailor perhaps employed by the Burley family opposite. At the back he was renting a quarter of an acre from Michael Eaton, who owned all the land behind the shops and houses at this west end of East Street – stretching from number 6 to the Wheatsheaf Public House number 90.

William Matthews recalled 'Jay's little old building here' – that was here in the 1880s – evidently the previous structure on this site.(69)

By 1851 William Jay was earning his living in two ways – as a baker and a cornfactor.(6) No doubt baking was his original trade and he had tried to improve his family's lot by trading in corn. He had been born at Southminster in Essex and his adult daughters and son George (having given up tailoring) helped him in the bakery and shop. His wife had already died in 1845.(110)

From the obituary of William's daughter Elizabeth in 1896 we learn another reason for William's involvement in the corn trade. *'She was the second daughter of the late Mr William Jay who formerly carried on business as a baker and cornfactor at Sittingbourne for many years. Miss Jay's brother, Mr. William Thomas Jay, deceased was formerly in business as a miller at the Tide Mill, Milton, and afterwards at King's Mill, Milton'.*

So William had another son who was a miller locally and would have supplied the flour for the bakery.

Old William was still baking at the age of 78 with his three daughters and son George still living with him.(7) He lived on until 1867 when he died aged 84. (110)

Son Frederick was listed in 1861 as head of a separate household, though alone, in the part of the house nearest to number 10. Here Fred ran a butchery business. The premises at 8 East Street were a single building, but the retail space on the ground floor was then and for many years divided into two units. An archway (now bricked up and glazed) to the side of the right hand unit gave access to a rear yard and outbuildings including the slaughterhouse.

Directories record that George continued the baking business until 1882. None of the Jay siblings ever married. By 1881 Frederick had given up butchery and joined his siblings in the bakery business.

William Goodhew of the local farming family had taken on the butchery shop whilst the Jay siblings continued to live in the rest of the building.

George Jay died in 1884 aged 68 and no doubt he and his siblings had begun to feel their age by 1882.(110) At any rate after that year the Jay bakery came to an end and the whole of number 8 was given over to butchery.

Fred Jay later moved with his three unmarried sisters along the road to number 112 to enjoy retirement. (see 112)

The Goodhews – butchers

William Goodhew was a local man, born in Milstead, in his thirties with a wife and young family when he arrived in East Street in the 1880s. He had previously run a grocery shop at Key Street.(9) It seems that William was able to buy number 8.(*information from Muriel Smith née Couchman whose father later rented the butchery from the Goodhews*).

William Goodhew made a success of the butchery business and was able to have the old number 8 pulled down and the new building constructed in the late 1880s.

By 1899 he had purchased Key Street Meadow (also known as the Grove Meadow) in the parish of Bobbing fronting the London Road, from the Barrow Trust for £1,200. He was to build himself a house on it and then sell off the rest for building purposes.(97)

This receipt dated 1914 draws attention to the fact that the meat came from the Goodhews' own farms and that they were government contractors for meat.

As it turned out, William Goodhew never moved away from number 8 East Street, but his wife did. This is revealed by the 1911 census return which gives us the information that the new number 8 had as many as 11 rooms; evidently this was not enough for William and Eliza, who, it appears, could not live harmoniously together and had sufficient funds to live apart. In 1911 Eliza could be found as head of household at Bobbing Hill with two of her unmarried daughters and a servant. Meanwhile William continued to live in East Street with his son Lawrence James Goodhew, who was also a butcher and Lawrence's wife Gertie née Andrews.

The Goodhews continued to keep a butcher's shop here for many a year with nearly ¾ an acre of land at the back – rather more than the Jays had in 1840 – a slaughter house, paddock, cattle pen and sheep pen.

A 1920s advertisement for Goodhew

When Lawrence Goodhew died in 1934 he requested that his ashes be scattered in his rose garden so we learn that he was a keen gardener.(N01) Lawrence's son Oscar, then a young man of 21, returned from America to take on the business but in fact it was Charlie Couchman who ran the butchery for him. (110) Oscar Goodhew was not interested in the retail side preferring to leave that in the hands of others whilst he concentrated on his farming interests.

L. J. Goodhew, Sittingbourne Urban District Council Chairman 1922-1925
Died 1934 aged 48

The left hand (eastern) half of the front of the building was a greengrocery, separately tenanted, but both shops were known as Goodhews. Eventually the Couchmans also took over the tenancy of the butcher's and greengrocer's though from 1973 to at least 1977 the left hand side became a general grocery store run by Mrs Violet Pattenden, whose husband ran the butcher's shop at Bredgar. Previously, they had run the Rose Inn in the High Street.(N01,89)

The Couchman Family

From 1933 Charles Perry Couchman, known as Charlie, was in business as a butcher on the right hand side of number 8 and remained there for 43 years. (N01) He and his family had the whole of the upstairs accommodation. Charlie had been born at Aldershot in 1905 for his own father, Charlie senior, had served as regimental Sergeant Major in the Durham Light Infantry although he came from Faversham as did his wife. The 1911 census found the family at Colchester Barracks minus father as the regiment were away. The youngest three children had been born in Cork when the regiment was stationed there. The Couchmans returned to Faversham while Charlie junior was just a small child.

On leaving school at the age of 14 young Charlie joined Burgess & Boulding the local butcher, then the Faversham Co-op butcher before moving to Sittingbourne where he worked for Lawrence Goodhew who then owned number 8.

Charlie had married Doris Radley in 1926 after meeting her when they both worked in the same shop in Teynham. After their marriage Doris worked in the East Street shop with Charlie for many years, stopping only for a few weeks when each of their younger children were born. Overall they had eight girls and one boy, but there was plenty of room for the family in the two storeys above the shop.

Every Monday morning until the late 1960s Charlie went to Sittingbourne stock-market at the rear of the Bull Hotel to buy a pen of sheep. On more than one occasion animals escaped when being delivered to the shop and had to be chased along East Street or up the High Street before being captured. Clive Gascoyne, the Bapchild farmer, used to supply him with seven or eight pigs a week and a couple of bullocks.

On Monday afternoon and evening the slaughtering was done with only one animal ever in the slaughter house at any given time. Charlie served in the Home Guard during the war and it was during that time that the council supplied an asbestos roof to go over the yard next to the slaughterhouse, so it complied with the blackout, for up until then it had been open to the sky.

Charlie and Doris Couchman
relaxing in the Three Kings

The Couchmans' cash register now in the
care of Sittingbourne Heritage Museum.
They never did use decimal currency.

The Couchmans continued to use their old set of scales marked up in prices from 2½d to 2s 6d and Mrs Couchman had the job of converting them into decimal currency.(N01)

The Couchmans retired in 1976 in their early seventies, and looked forward to their first real break in 50 years and perhaps their first holiday together. They moved to a new home in Beechwood Avenue, Milton.

Oscar Gallaon's off-licence

After the Couchmans left the building it ceased to be a residence. It was sold to Alan Whitehead an investor from Tenterden; soon afterwards it was bought by Oscar Gallaon and his wife Patricia, née Peters, a Sittingbourne native, daughter of Hedley Peters jnr., the local auctioneer – and sister of Michael Peters, one of our contributors.

A native of the Veneto in Italy, the eldest of eight children, with ten times that number of cousins, Oscar had 'escaped' to Rome where he was employed at the five star Excelsior Hotel in the Via Veneto. There he met Pat who was employed as a house-keeper. They were married in 1961 at the Church of the Sacred Heart in Sittingbourne's West Street and returned at once to Milan where

Oscar was working at one of the chain of hotels run by the 'Jolly' group. After ten years in that city, where their daughter Isabella was born in 1963, Pat brought her husband home to Gore Court Road, Sittingbourne. Oscar by now was a qualified sommelier – an expert in wines – particularly Italian ones. In England he was employed by two successive wholesalers before starting his own business in 1975 at 11 Station Street.

The shop was divided – the lock-up shop at number 8 (the eastern part) was taken by a Mrs Pam Akhurst who ran a delicatessen and outside catering business. This shop, trading as The East End Sandwich Bar sold lunchtime snacks for workers such as prawn salads and fresh-made rolls and sandwiches. (N01)

1981 Advert for the East End Sandwich Bar

The larger unit – known thereafter as 8a – was transformed by Mr Gallaon into an off-licence called 'Vino Vino Italian Wines'. Before taking occupation, Oscar had the ground floor totally re-modelled. At the back, the slaughter-house and other outbuildings were demolished. The main building was extended to form a warehouse, with parking space on the remainder of the yard beyond. The archway leading from the street to the yard at the back was blocked and the floor space was incorporated into the shop area.(87)

Oscar Gallaon (MHP)

The interior of the shop was transformed with arched vaults of red brick creating the appearance of a wine cellar and a warehouse was constructed at the back, extending the building over part of the yard. Oscar's status and reputation in the field grew fast; he soon acquired an international standing, which came to the notice of the government of Italy. He was honoured with the rank of Knight of the Italian Republic – surely the only person of that particular status who has ever been in business here in Sittingbourne.

Vino Vino occupied two rooms on the first floor and let the remainder of the two upper floors as offices occupied by, amongst others, the local Conservative party, an accountant and a small firm of publishers.

When the business closed down in 1985, 8a was used as a second-hand lock-up shop known as 'Daley's' selling pine furniture. The next occupier was Michael Leake from Northampton who, together with his wife Elizabeth from Northumberland, ran 'Michael Leake Interior Design'. After a few years the Leakes retired to Park Farm Doddington.

In 1997 the name of the shop was 'Selective Furniture.' Meanwhile number 8 was occupied briefly by Chicks leisure wear.

Soon after this, the two retail units were combined again into one shop, occupied by Selective Furniture.(121)

Vino Vino at number 8a and East End Sandwich Bar at number 8 in 1981

Bourne's funeral service and Beatrice the florist

The next occupier, by the year 2000, was Bourne's Funeral Service, an independent family business, founded in Gravesend. After a few years, it moved to the adjoining premises at 4-6 East Street.

Martin Bourne then introduced the property to Beatrice Clark Florist, who is still in occupation.

Flowers by Beatrice

Flowers by Beatrice was established in December 1998 in Milton Regis. After building a reputation for quality and reliability that shop became too small and in 2003 the decision was made to move to the present, larger premises at 8 East Street. Here there are rooms for wedding and funeral consultations away from the busy shop. The owners, Beatrice Clark and her husband Rodney, are both natives of our district. Beatrice is a qualified florist who employs a team of three other qualified florists.

The upper floors have been converted to flats.

Flowers By Beatrice 2008 (CA)

Numbers 10 to 14 East Street

18/20   16   14   12   10   8   6/4

Numbers 10, 12 and 14 East Street consist of one medieval, grade II listed building. Mario's Café at the west end is number 10, and Beauty Zone takes 12 and 14.

It is a re-fronted timber-framed building, two storeys with painted brickwork, dating perhaps from about 400 years ago (or maybe older) of two storeys with painted brickwork. The roof is tiled and steeply pitched with one brick chimney stack.

It is remarkable that this structure, undoubtedly one of the oldest in our town centre, has survived largely untouched for centuries so close to the principal cross-roads – at the very heart of historic Sittingbourne. This raises the question of who resisted the tidal flow of redevelopment – who amongst the owners of this important site, through the centuries, has stood in the way of 'progress'.

On the 1841 tithe schedule the building is shown as parcel 154 being 10, 155 being 12, and 156 being 14. The whole partitioned house along with number 16, belonged to one Richard Shirley and the occupants are each listed for 10,12 and 14 as being in 'part of a house'.

Since the 1841 census return does not record any Richard Shirley who had been born in Kent or then lived in Kent we cannot identify him. Perhaps he was the young Corporal Richard Shirley in the regimental barracks at Kensington on the night that the census was taken.

Number 10 East Street
The Packer family, basket makers

When the 1841 census was taken John Packer and his family were the tenants at number 10 where they were to remain for generations. The Packers had established their Sittingbourne basket-making business in 1812, two generations after they began working nearby in Milton.

At first John Packer only rented this one section of a house in Sittingbourne. Later on, as the business flourished, the Packers also had a workshop round the corner in Bell Road, and used the East Street premises as home and shop.

John Packer had been born in Faversham in 1785. He married Frances Lucas in 1808 in Faversham where their first three children were born, but, during 1812, they moved home and business to East Street where the last five children were born. By 1851, when John was in his sixties, only unmarried sons Fred and Charles and unmarried daughter Fanny remained in Sittingbourne working at basket-making. Ten years later old John was still making baskets assisted by his son Fred and grandson, also named Fred. Daughter Fanny still helped her mother to keep house.

Son Charles also still worked at the basket making but lived separately further along the other side of the street (see number 101) with his wife Margaret and young family. Here Margaret Packer briefly tried her hand at running a little day school.(28)

Old John never owned his house, and his will showed that all he possessed was worth under £100 but, with the continuation of the business to consider, he wrote a will in 1863 when he was 78. There was by no means enough to give all the children something. His 'dear wife Frances' was bequeathed all cash, household furniture and stock in trade for the rest of her life. Eldest son William Edwin (1809–1880) was left all of John's clothes. William had probably already moved to work in Medway by this time.

Advert from 1908 directory

Sons John junior who moved to Canterbury and Elijah are not mentioned. Fourth son Frederick (born 1814) and his unmarried sister Frances Rebecca (born 1826) were to continue the business together. After their mother's death they were directed to pay their youngest brother Charles, who worked for them, £5 a year out of the business for four years, provided that he continued to work there, in addition to his earnings. Charles was comparatively young still at 33. Old John died in 1865 aged 80.

The 1867 directory lists only his widow Fanny: 'Mrs F. Packer basket maker East Street'. Fanny died at the good age of 84 in 1869.(110)

Son Fred and his sister Frances continued to live at number 10 over the basket and brush shop.(8,11) Fred did not long outlive his mother for he died in 1872. Brother Charles and his family had moved to 55 East Street with Charles's own oldest sons Frank next door at 53 and Charles junior at number 51 in 1891. All were basket makers as was Herbert, Charles's youngest son. Sisters Kate and Emily were dressmakers at home in 55 East Street. Frank and Charles junior each had wife and children.(see numbers 53 and 55)

As well as baskets the Packers made sieves, bassinets (cradles) and garden chairs. In the early years they made all that they sold but as time went on and cheap osiers were imported they sold foreign and English baskets, and a large assortment of household and fancy brushes.

For the 1881 census return, Frances, by then in her fifties, described herself as 'basket shop keeper'. Her niece Emma lived with her at number 10.

They remained the only occupants of the house ten years later when Frances chose to call herself a 'basket manufacturer' and her niece as shop assistant. Nothing had changed by 1901, but in 1904 Frances died aged 78. The 1908 directory records Miss Emma Packer, basket-maker, still at number 10.

The younger generation of Packers had taken the business on. These were Charles's sons Charles junior and Frank. So the firm became Packer Brothers whose advertisement in Kelly's 1911 and 1913 directory listed them as basket and sieve manufacturers of Bell Road. The 1918 entry is more informative: 'Packer Brothers, basket and sieve manufacturers, bassinettes and all kinds of square hampers and laundry baskets, Bell Road.'

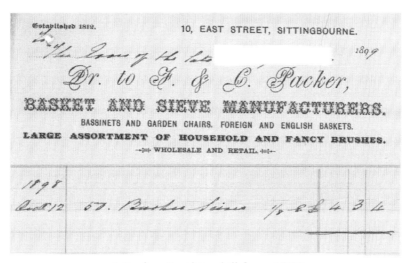

A Packer Brothers bill from 1899

By 1911 Emma Packer had left number 10 to live at 124 Park Road but still owned the East Street property.

Herbert and Alice Roberts

Number 10 was then used as a tobacconist's shop run by Herbert E. Roberts from Strood, a man in his thirties who lived above the shop with his wife and two daughters. Sadly he died aged just 38 in 1913.(110) In 1933 the electoral roll recorded Alice with her adult children Edith, Ena, Herbert, Julia and Phyllis Roberts. Alice Roberts continued to run the shop until at least 1940.(57) She died aged 73 in 1949 but had left number 10 by then.(110)

In the Second World War a couple of the Packer children were evacuated to Canada. One married a Canadian and remained there. Her sister came back to Sittingbourne and lived, with her husband, at the top of Park Road, beside the Gore Court Arms. In 1942 the Packer family sold number 10 East Street to Mr Herbert Byfleet for £300. This transaction is recorded in an account book of Hedley Peters & Son, who were the auctioneers.

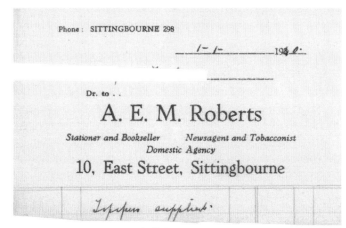

Phone: SITTINGBOURNE 298

/- /-   194 l-

Dr. to . .

A. E. M. Roberts

Stationer and Bookseller   Newsagent and Tobacconist
Domestic Agency

10, East Street, Sittingbourne

A bill from 1940

Ice cream and sweets

By 1947 and into the early 1960s Johnny and Betty Vasellina lived here and ran the shop along with the owners Herbert and Marie Byfleet. John Couchman recalls Betty Vasellina made and sold ice cream. According to another of our contributors, the late Gerry Cassell (founder of New Appointments Group) the Byfleets sustained the Italian flavour – Gerry remembered Mary as 'a rotund Italian'.(115)

Of equal interest to local children was the next trade to come here: Gerry Cassell's brother Will, made it a sweet shop. For years Will's parents had been selling their home-made sweets at 57 East Street, so here, Will adopted a different trading name – Eileen's. See also 46, 57 and 67 East Street.

By 1974 the Cassells had left and nobody lived at number 10.(115) The shop was vacant from at least 1975 to 1985.(121)

'Eileen's' sweets shop at Number 10 in 1966

The freehold of this building, by the way, had been acquired by George Dutnall, a property investor, living in College Road. He also owned number 16 and numbers 23–37 East Street.

From then to the present day number 10 has been a café and sandwich shop under various ownerships. Between 1991 and 1997 it was called the Good Taste Restaurant.(121) Then A la Carte catering had the premises until 2002.

From that year to at least 2013 its name was Sittingbourne Café run by Ismail Eydin. The name of the café remained the same from 2009 to 2013 but it was run by Azila Ltd, again the name of the café remained the same for the next two years when it was run by Mr Mahmut Boztemir. Today it is Mario's Café run by Mr Amarildo Harizaj.

Numbers 12 and 14 East Street
Robert Sargent – shoemaker

At number 12, next door to John Packer during the 1840s lived Robert Sargent (occasionally spelt Sergeant) the shoemaker and his family.(5) Mr Sargent and his neighbour on the other side, William Harnden must have begun by working together because Harnden was also a shoemaker although it is clear that later they worked separately. (see number 16)

By 1851 Robert Sargent was renting the other end of the property – number 14 – where we shall meet the family again.

The Dorrells – booksellers and stationers

The 1851 census for number 12 records John Ackland Dorrell, aged 32, book seller and tea dealer with his wife, stepson and baby daughter. Dorrell had started life at a disadvantage for he had been baptised in Sittingbourne in 1819 the illegitimate son of Jane Dorrell, a single woman, and John Ackland a lieutenant in the Royal Navy. John A. Dorrell remained a poor labouring man on Sheppey until he married Ann Reeve a bookseller's widow in 1850.(61)

Ann had been born in Tenterden in 1815 and married Jeremiah Reeve in 1838. She and her young husband were running a public house in Flushing Street Milton in 1841. This was short lived and by 1845 the directory lists Jeremiah Reeve as a stationer of Sittingbourne. So we can assume that at some point between 1841 and 1845 the young Reeves moved to 12, East Street. Late in 1849 young Reeve died and within six months Ann had remarried to John Dorrell.

John moved into number 12 and the business continued. Ten years later they were still there – 'John Dorrell, aged 41, bookseller and newsagent' with his wife and two daughters Jane and Anette, but by that autumn John had died.(7)

Widowed yet again, Ann, having been so long in the trade, was able to continue to earn a living from the shop, although she left the books and concentrated on stationery and newspapers: 'Mrs Ann Dorrell stationer and newsagent' and by the 1871 census describing herself simply as a stationer.(28)

The 1870 directory entry for Mrs Agnes Dorrell dressmaker and Mrs Ann Dorrell 'news vendor and stationer' may be incorrect and may refer to her daughter.

Ann Dorrell died aged 58 in 1873.(110) Her will left the business to her daughters but stated that her son by her first marriage, George Reeve, was to receive £50 paid in ten instalments over ten years from the business. If one daughter quitted the business the other was instructed to buy her out.

Directories show that the sisters continued the trade and in the 1881 census Jane described herself as a 'fancy stationer' denoting a number of extra special goods which could be purchased as presents.

In addition Jane and Anette had taken the sensible step of adding to their income by taking on two boarders, one male and one female. By the end of 1881 Jane had married in south London. Anette then married James Inchcomb in Sittingbourne and left number 12 and the stationery business closed. As Anette's husband was a bookseller she continued in the trade at number 6.(61)

In 1890 the directory lists Denham Charles Milway baker and confectioner, which proved to be a short lived venture here. The accommodation above the shop was uninhabited.(10)

Evidently Mr Milway belonged to the local family of that name, more than one of whom were bakers; his first name would, surely, associate Mr Milway with the Jordan family – auctioneers and plumbers of Milton. Denham Jordan (1836-1920) gained fame as an author under the pen-name *'Son of the Marshes'*. His book about Milton *'Annals of a Fishing Village'* was published in the year when his namesake was in business here at number 12.

Drapery and baby linen at number 12

By 1895 number 12 was known as Giraud's Drapery. The only George Giraud recorded in England in the 1891 census was a young printer in Deal whose father Edwin was also a printer, so this appeared unlikely to be the same person. Nevertheless by 1901 that same young George Giraud of Deal was running a draper's shop in Ramsgate and as we know had added an outpost in Sittingbourne.(11)

In 1895 this notice was placed in the local paper: *'Wanted an apprentice or improver to the millinery and fancy drapery. E. Giraud'* (this was George's wife Ellen). Giraud's shop here was still open in 1899 and we know it had closed by 1903. It is doubtful that the Girauds ever lived here. Probably related to the Faversham family of that name, George was a restless soul and, by 1911, had changed his occupation yet again and earned his living as a 'collector and salesman' in Ramsgate.

The Misses Roberts and Bockham

It was the Misses Roberts and Bockham who turned the drapery at number 12 into one which specialised in baby linen. The 1908 directory calls it 'baby linen warehouse'. We discovered from the 1911 census who Miss Roberts and Miss (actually Mrs) Bockham were. They were sisters; Miss Ellen Roberts, who was much the younger of the two, and her widowed sister Emily E. Bockham, aged 68, from Gloucestershire, ran the shop with the help of Edith Bockham, Emily's daughter. By 1911 Mrs Bockham left the running of the shop to her sister and daughter and acted as their housekeeper. She died aged 71 in 1914. (110)

It is from the 1911 census return that we learn that number 12 had five rooms.

Number 14 East Street
Shoemaking at number 14

The shoemaker William Harnden lived with his family in the third section of the building later known as number 14. He worked with his neighbour Robert Sargent. Both men had young families to feed.

Number 14 was bursting with life in the 1840s for William Harnden and his wife then had eight children at home. In addition there was William's brother, a tailor who probably worked for the Burleys across the road, and another brother who was a watchmaker. We know that by 1851 Harnden had moved to number 16 and worked on his own account. By then he and his wife had a dozen children to fit in the house as well as a brother and an apprentice.

So by 1851 it was the Sargents who lived at number 14. Robert Sargent flourished in his trade and employed two men and a boy by 1861. He carried on working into old age. The census of 1881 found him still at number 14, widowed by then and with his son George working with him. Robert died in 1884 aged 80 and just a year later George followed him to the grave aged 54.(110) Brother William, also a shoemaker with a shop in Charlotte Street took on the business at number 14 letting out the accommodation but keeping the shop.(9,36) The 1891 census records only a brickfield labourer, wife and child living here. In 1901 it was an uninhabited boot shop.

Then we have a confusion in that George Atterbury is listed as draper at 14 and 16 in the 1903 directory and yet in the 1908 directory William Sargent is still listed as having a shoemaking shop at number 14. Above the shop the accommodation remained empty of people though doubtless full of stock.

Baby linen at 12 and 14

During 1916 or 1917 numbers 12 and 14 were combined into one double fronted shop and home where Emily Agnes Howland and Ethel Mills lived.(49) Miss Howland had previously boarded above Easton's drapery store shop at 122, High Street where she worked as a milliner, no doubt saving up as much as she could with the aim of setting up her own shop which at last she achieved in her forties.(12) She opened 12 and 14 as a baby linen warehouse and ladies' outfitter and here she remained until 1934.

The electoral register for 1933 records Emily still here with Ethel Mills. Emily retired to Ashford where she had been born, and died there in 1943 aged 69. (110)

Ivy Bartlett

It was Miss Ivy Bartlett who was the next owner of the business. She had been born in 1911 in Sittingbourne, the youngest of six children of a brickfield worker and his wife. On leaving school she went to work for Miss Howland at the shop. Ivy's family possess a character reference which she was given when young. It reads: *'Miss Bartlett has been in my employ for just over seven years and during that time I have always found her perfectly honest and truthful and very willing and conscientious over her work signed Miss E. Howland, 12 East Street.'*

When Ivy took on the shop herself in 1934 she had the following advertisement placed in the local paper: *'Under new management, Miss I. Bartlett former assistant to Miss Howland announces that she has acquired the business at 12 and 14 East Street and will re-open with complete new stock on Thursday March 29th.'*

Ivy Bartlett when young, in Girl Guide uniform. The lanyard shows she was a patrol leader. The stripes on her pocket show she was a company leader, and she is wearing a guide leader's tie. On her left arm she has two badges one is either first aid or child nurse. They were distinguished by the colour She has at least seven badges on her right arm (DJ)

Ivy Bartlett's shop at 12 and 14, 1960s

David Jackson, Ivy Bartlett's great-nephew, recalls the shop which was the front room of number 12:

"Great Aunt Ivy (Bartlett) had a large baby doll in the shop window. There were glass cabinets and chairs for customers. Most of the stock was kept in the front room of number 14. On a high shelf in the opposite corner to the street door and next to the door to the stock room and living room, was a grey clock obviously given by a supplier or manufacturer and advertising their goods. I don't think Aunt Ivy employed anybody full time but occasionally my Mum looked after the shop for an hour or two. I think a Mrs Vandepeer may have worked there sometimes. Ivy's parents both lived with her until their deaths. I remember them sitting each side of the hearth when Mum and I visited. Flooding was a frequent problem as the house and shop were at a lower level than the land at the back of the house, so when it rained heavily water came in at the back and ran through the shop and out at the front."

Ivy never married and in 1945 was able to purchase numbers 12 and 14 for £800. The family have retained the solicitor's bill which reveals that the owner of the property had been Miss E. Packer of 124, Park Road, one of the Packer basket making family from number 10.

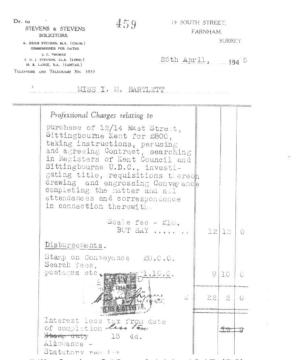

Bill of sale of 12 and 14 in 1945 (DJ)

Ivy had a talent for music and as a child she sang in Murston Church choir and decided to learn to play the organ; this she did at Faversham and then in London. She played the organ in Bredgar church for seven years before taking up the post at Murston instead which was much easier for her to reach on her bike. At Murston she used to practise for an hour every morning with either

Mr Fred Wanstall the official organ pumper or a choir boy pumping for her, then she would open the shop at number 12. In later years she appreciated the organ being pumped electrically.(N01)

Ivy in 1963 after 25 years as Murston organist

Ivy Bartlett's musical ability not only gave her a good deal of pleasure but benefited the community too. Another newspaper article appeared when she had completed 40 years as Murston organist in 1978 and the congregation presented her with a pound for every year she had been there. More than 500 Murston brides walked down the aisle to music played by Ivy. She was also the choir mistress and secretary of the parochial church council for 33 years.

In 1972 Ivy retired and separated the shop from the living accommodation. She let the shop to Bomar Fabrics, (who were here from 1973 until 1985) whilst continuing to live on the premises. Ivy died in 1996.

After Bomar Fabrics the next business in the building was Apollo Blinds.(121)

James Charles the tailor

From the early 1990s until 2011 the premises housed a tailoring business known as James Charles. Initially it was run by Mr J. H. Blogg and in later years by Alan Robertson. Both were said to have come from London. At the time, Burley's across the street having closed, the business here seems to have been our town's only bespoke tailor – able to create suits and other clothing from rolls of cloth.

James Charles, tailor, at number 12 and 14, 2008 (CA)

Beauty Zone

In 2012 Miss Nicola Rafferty opened the 'Beauty Zone' salon here which remains open in 2019.

Numbers 10 to 14 in 2019 (MHP)

Number 16 East Street

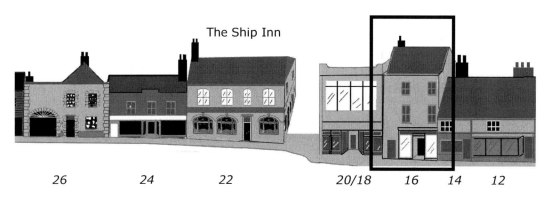

Today number 16 is a modern building which replaced the previous structure, which had been gutted by fire. The older building dated, perhaps, from about 200 years ago. Like the present structure it had two upper storeys but the second floor was of full height with a parapet wall and gutter – no dormers.

The present building houses a hairdresser's salon named Hair Zone with two storeys of living accommodation above. Photographs show that the previous building on the site was of similar height giving space for a double fronted shop and two floors above.

In 1966 number 16 at the forefront of the photograph housed Bryan Kite's electrical equipment shop.

The 1840 tithe schedule records that the building (numbered 157 on the tithe map) then belonged, along with three others in Sittingbourne, to one Richard Shirley and was occupied by John Packer the basket maker. It appears that Packer sublet number 16 whilst living at number 10 because the 1841 census contains the information that a needlewoman, Elizabeth Hutchins and a single man lived here. From being under-occupied the building was soon to burst at the seams with people.

The Harnden family

By 1851 the census recorded William Harnden, a Sittingbourne man in his forties; a bootmaker who employed one man and one apprentice. With him lived his wife Sarah, their 12 children (ranging in age from 20 to three years old), William's brother who was a sailor, a journeyman, and finally the apprentice. William and Sarah were non-conformists whose children were baptised at the Paradise Chapel, Milton.(111) The Harndens had moved here from next door. (see number 14)

William died in 1858 aged only 52. Sarah, a local woman, took charge of the household employing three men and two boys.(7) Six of her children still lived at home and these included her eldest daughter who would have supported her in the running of the house and shop, and her eldest son George the only one of the sons who was a bootmaker. Then there was a boarder, an apprentice, Benjamin Hackshaw who was a shoemaker employed by Mrs Harnden and Benjamin's wife and child. (see number 30/32)

This little enterprise continued for years. In 1871 Sarah described herself for the census return as a 'boot manufacturer'. Son George made the boots, (he was still unmarried at 37) and one daughter was still at home. Mrs Harnden no longer employed others but let rooms to an Irish farm labourer, his wife and three children. She died in 1875 aged 69. In later life she had managed to purchase the house.(115)

George Harnden continued to live at number 16, he married late in life, in 1878, to a London woman Susannah Brown. They had no children.

It seems to have been in 1895 that George and Susannah took the decision to retire to Albany Road a short walk away from George's family home and there George filled in his census return in 1901. He retained ownership of number 16. (115) In 1910 he died at home aged 78 leaving over £2,000.(111)

Drapery at number 16
Charles Harmer

A young draper named Charles Harmer, was the next occupant of number 16 and made his requirements for workers known in the local paper in 1895: *20th April: 'Dressmaking – wanted good general hand, also apprentices. Business thoroughly taught. Apply on Tuesday next to Charles C. Harmer'.*

Then the following year: *14th March: 'Drapery – Wanted a young lady apprentice for the Fancy Counter. Apply Harmer 16 East Street'.*

He also advertised his wares as follows: *'Cash Drapery Stores. Dresses, mantles and jackets made to order. A large stock of all the newest materials. Prices exceptionally low. Special attention given to mourning orders'.*

Charles Harmer did not remain long at number 16 and by 1901 he and his wife were to be found up the road at 43 High Street where he described himself as a 'draper's manager'. It seems he preferred the security of working for someone else.(HSI)

George Atterbury

Number 16 remained a drapery but it was widower George Atterbury who had the house to himself that census night in 1901. He was a draper in his forties who hailed from London. Unlike Mr Harmer, Atterbury was to remain in East Street for many years to come.

Requiring little of the living accommodation for himself George let out rooms as an office to a Mr Mills an insurance broker, as we know from this advertisement of 1908 in the local paper: *'Wanted two or three smart energetic young men on salary & commission to represent British Home Insurance corporation Ltd Write to W.J. Mills 16, East Street.'*

By 1911 George Atterbury had a widowed housekeeper and a shop assistant lodging with him and filling the small six roomed building. When fire broke out in the shops opposite (numbers 17 and 19) in 1912 the heat was so intense that Atterbury's plate-glass windows were cracked, the wooden fascia over the shop blistered and began to smoke. In 1922 the electoral register records George with three lodgers and this continued into the 1930s.(115)

The last directory entry we have for George and his drapery is 1938. He died in 1946 aged 89.(110) By then Mrs Warman, secretary of Sittingbourne Lawn Tennis Club lived at number 16.(N01)

George Atterbury's drapery shop at number 16

A wool shop

We know that by 1951 Mrs Corrie Mead lived here with her husband Walter and a lodger. Corrie had a wool shop.(115) In 1959 the local paper announced that Miss Christine Bills had transferred her stationery and wool business <u>from</u> number 16 to number 30 East Street. At what point in the 1950s Corrie Mead left the business and Christine Bills took it on we have not been able to discover.

Bryan J. Kite's electrical shop

Christine Bills had arranged to swap premises with Bryan and Sheila Kite who moved their television and radio business here from number 30.(N01)

The 1960 electoral register records two couples living at number 16, the address of one of the couples being 'Flat One number 16'. So this was a way of gaining a bit more income from the building. But by 1970 nobody lived in it. In the 1965 Sittingbourne town guide is this description of the business:

> 'This business is under the personal supervision of Mr and Mrs Kite. No job too small – no job too big. A special feature of the business is its after-sales service. There are especially favourable terms for the after-sale maintenance of television sets. We claim that there is no better value in Sittingbourne. Do not hesitate to call, write or phone Sittingbourne 2606'.

Bryan and Sheila Kite had left by 1968 when number 16 was in use as 'Gordon's Greengrocery'.

A fire destroyed the old building in the early 1970s. This is confirmed by the fact that 16 is not listed in the 1971 Goad data and remained unlisted through the 1970s.(87)

At the time of the fire (about 1968-70) the building was owned by George Dutnall of 92 College Road, who also owned number 10 and the terraces across the street, numbers 23-37. The Kites and the greengrocers were his tenants. After the fire, the site stood empty for some years.

The old number 16 being demolished. The date of demolition must be before 1973 as 'I. Bartlett' is still over the shop next door and Bomar Fabrics replaced Bartlett from 1973

In 1985 Goad had brought number 16 back into the list as 'vacant'. So the new building had arrived.

By 1991 these were the premises of the salon Hair Zone, owned by Mr A. Robins as it still is, although in 2017 the salon and the living accommodation upstairs were for sale. They are now occupied by people trading as Oliver & Lee. The current business is run by Lee Watts (known by his clientèle as Oli) who trades as Oliver & Lee Hair Design. Having lived in Sittingbourne all his life, Oli was previously at Tiffs Hair Design in Chatham.

Hair Zone at number 16 in 2018 (BA)

Numbers 18 and 20 East Street

'Forge House'

26   24   22   20/18   16   14   12

Number 20, which now houses 'La Pizzeria' take-away is a building whose design seems to be more concerned with function than style. It occupies the space where the houses numbered 18 and 20 used to be. There has been no number 18 since the old building was demolished. When the new number 20 was built during 1921 it would have looked smart and modern – a purpose built shop with large plate-glass showroom windows upstairs as well as down.(N01) Such glory days are long gone.

In the tithe plan of 1840 and the Ordnance Survey plan dated 1865/6 the building shared by 18 and 20 is shown as a single unit. However, we know that, until their demolition shortly after the First World War, numbers 18 and 20 were separate dwellings, perhaps an old building that had been partitioned. In 1908/9 the Ordnance Survey and the local directory show that 18 and 20 remained separate from each other. The buildings at the back, beside the inn yard, may well have been associated with the Ship Inn, which like 18 and 20, belonged to the Vallance family, the local brewers.

How old the first 18 and 20 were we have no idea for we have no photographs but we do know that they were small with four rooms each.(10)

Number 18 East Street

Being small, number 18 was more often just a private house rather than a shop as well, but several people did try to earn a living there in the front room. Most of these ventures were short-lived and we can see that the inhabitants of number 18 never had much money. However one or two of those who rented number 20 were able to run a business in the front room for a longer period of time.

From private house to shop and back – again and again

In 1841 number 18 was the home of William Rutter, a bookbinder from Dover then aged 30, his wife Caroline and their three young children. He is also recorded as the occupant in the 1840 tithe schedule. By 1851 the Rutters had moved a short distance up the road, to The Butts off the High Street and Rutter described himself as a bookbinder and printer. Benjamin Bourne, a brick-maker from Hollingbourne, in his thirties had become the tenant of number 18 with his wife and two sons. The house also contained an elderly labourer from Lynsted with two children.

Number 18 was quiet ten years later with only unmarried Sittingbourne woman Esther Gibbon in her thirties living there describing herself as a 'juvenile clothier'. She was using the front room as a shop for children's clothes. She married local tailor William Snelling in 1863 and they made their home in Station Street.(110)

The Smith family lived here in the 1870s and 1880s, John Smith was a bricklayer's labourer and his wife Mary came from Teynham.(8,9)

By 1890 the front room had become the hairdressing salon of old Thomas Morris. Tom fell on hard times, perhaps too infirm to work, and a year later aged 72, was in the Milton Workhouse.(10) Young 19 year old Henry Hall, another hairdresser, then continued the business until he relocated across the road to number 31 where he set up shop and lived for the rest of his life.(10) (see number 31)

By 1901 William Tassell a brickfield labourer from Maidstone, his wife Henrietta and their three children were renting the four rooms.

A few years later the local directory records that shopkeeper Edward Jury was trying his hand here.(43) This came to nothing and by 1911 he and his wife were lodging in Harold Road without jobs and number 18 was uninhabited. As far as we know nobody else lived at number 18 and it stood empty until demolished,

Number 20 East Street

In 1841 Ann Wilcock ran a greengrocery at number 20 with her daughter whilst her son, who also lived at home, worked as a labourer.

By 1851 number 20 had reverted to being a private house where Ebenezer Paine a Sittingbourne carpenter, in his thirties lived with his wife and two children. The house was overcrowded in the 1860s with labourer James Browning from Canterbury his wife, and five children.(7) Another labourer and his family lived here ten years later – Sittingbourne man William Millen who laboured in the brick-fields, his wife and three children.(8)

A change had occurred by the time the 1881 census was taken for Mrs Lydia Lee, a widow in her forties who described herself as a hawker, was here with her son and daughter and we know from the following year's directory that she had opened a shop at number 20: 'Mrs Lydia Lee shopkeeper.'

By 1884 Maidstone woman Eliza Stone had moved in with her son. (N01,10,36) She was a wardrobe dealer, which means she sold second-hand clothes.

Number 20 had reverted to being used as a private house by 1901 when Henry Marsh a widowed blacksmith from Sturry lived here with his son and daughter. The house was to let again in 1905 at four shillings a week.(N01)

Mr Moses Goldsmith junior is listed as living here as a private resident in the 1908 directory. He seems to have been the final inhabitant of the house although it continued in use as a shop for several more years before demolition.

The design of the new building which replaced 18 and 20 was approved by the council in January 1921. 'A New store: The surveyor reported that in accordance with the bylaws plans have been deposited by Messrs F Moore & Sons. For the erection of store at 18-20 East Street. Plans were passed.'

There was no living accommodation. It was built for Messrs F. Moore & Sons who were already established on the other side of the road.(N01) Frederick Moore is recorded in the 1911 census return at number 15. He was then in his forties, from Portsmouth, a manager for a dealer in iron, and was married with ten children. The family soon moved to number 41 whilst Fred and a son or two took on the new shop opposite. *(For a full account of Fred Moore's undertakings see number 41 East Street)*

Fred Moore's shop when new

For reasons now unknown the Moores soon rented out the new premises to the Teynham Engineering Company who moved to 20 East Street in 1924.(N01)

However they did not remain long either for by 1926 John Wilson, a butcher, was advertising in the local paper at number 20.

Dean's bicycle shop

Four years later the shop had become George Smeed Dean's and this business did endure. Dean, (born 1900) was a great-grandson of George Smeed the wealthy local brick-maker and barge-builder. His grandfather, of the same name, had an unfortunate end – he died, aged 44, on Chatham Hill after his penny-farthing bicycle jammed in the tram lines. Contrasting with this tragedy, the younger George made bicycles (of more modern and safer style) a main feature of the motor engineering and bicycle business that he ran at number 94 High Street for a couple of years, and, for much longer, here in East Street.(54) The shop did well selling not only bicycles but televisions, radios, electric shavers, fishing tackle, air rifles and mopeds.(N01)

George Dean lived just a walk away in Park Road.(115) He died in 1969 but the shop continued as Deans Ltd run by members of the family. George had sold the business to Edwin (Ted) Boulding, who had married one of George's cousins – Georgiana, née Doubleday. Georgiana was one of nine children of Reverend John Doubleday, long-serving Pastor of the Baptist Church. He had married Jessie, a daughter of George Hambrook Dean. We mention Reverend John across the street when he was a new arrival in the town.

Deans bicycle shop c.1960 (AP)

We wonder if George Smeed Dean and his cousin Georgiana ever knew that the Ship Inn, next-door to their place of business, had once been in the hands of their brilliant great-grandfather George Smeed. If so, given their Nonconformist Baptist background, we cannot be sure of their attitude. Doubtless of more significance to Georgiana would have been the location of her home. When Gore Court Park was fragmented for building development, Georgiana and her cousin,

Donald Dean, acquired some of the land on the corner of Park Drive (now Bradley Drive) and Park Avenue, which, long before, had been owned by their great-grandfather George Smeed.(82) On the corner site Georgiana and Ted built a house called 'Cordoba'. After the demolition of the mansion, Georgiana decorated her garden with treasured remnants of its ancient stonework. Nextdoor Donald gave his home the name 'Woodcourt' – perhaps deliberately echoing the old name of the park. At the back of 'Woodcourt' Donald laid out some tennis courts which he made available to the public – notably members of the Congregational Church. The access drive to the tennis court is now incorporated in the driveway of number 11 Bradley Drive. In the early 1970s the tennis court site was developed as Woodcourt Close.

Georgiana's husband, Ted, was a scion of the Boulding family of butchers, of whom we have written in High Street volume II. Ted's sister Nellie had married Nelson May of May & Sayers.(HSI,HSII) Nellie married Nelson – confusing similarity of names – scope for teasing! Ted's first name, Edwin, had passed down the family from a great-uncle. Ted's son Steve was involved in the cycle business at 18-20 and the last of the line in the shop was Ted's nephew Michael, son of Cuthbert Boulding, Ted's brother. In the 1960s, Michael's mother, Margaret, served as Chairman of the Urban District Council (the local equivalent of Mayor) She was deeply involved in the twinning of our town with the Belgian town of Ypres. Her branch of the family lived at 169 Park Road opposite 188 where George Dean had lived.

1981 Advert for Deans (EKG)

The cycle business at 18/20 was still known as Deans in 1980, but in 1987 the premises were empty and then came C & S Bikes owned by J. H. Cordingley who changed the name of the shop to John's Bikes and, in the year 2000 to the Raleigh Cycle Centre. The last bike was wheeled out of the building in 2004.

Fish and chips

A refit followed and then came a time when a good fish and chip supper could be bought here, certainly in 2005.(121) 'Kingfish' was run by Messrs Cosar and Bali for a year. In 2006 Ali Celiki took it on, changing the name to Sittingbourne Fish Bar.

La Pizzeria

In 2008 the final fish was fried here for number 20 housed the takeaway 'La Pizzeria' which was run by another member of the Celiki family – Ozkan. By 2016 it was owned by Mehmet Altaarian and is still open in 2019.

"La Pizzeria" in 2019 (MHP)

The Ship (number 22 East Street)

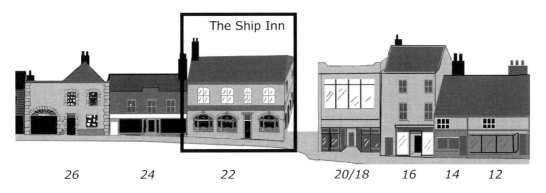

The present handsome Ship Inn building was converted for residential use in 2016. It had been erected in 1899 on the site of an ancient inn of the same name which served travellers as far back as 1582. Deeds of the inn dating back that far survive at the Kent History & Library Centre.

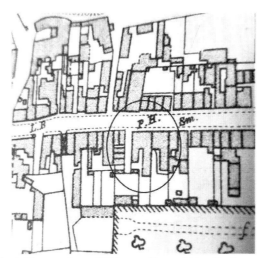

The Ship is (circled) at the centre of this section of the Ordnance Survey map dated 1865/6

Over the centuries The Ship had numerous owners including, during the 1700s, the Sittingbourne Tonge family who owned the brewery in the High Street. In 1806 Thomas Tonge bequeathed The Ship to his nephew William Vallance and it was owned by that prominent and wealthy family for many years.(HSI,HSII)

We know nothing of the men of earlier centuries who presided over the inn. A later host, here only briefly, became famous throughout Kent and that was George Smeed the self-made owner of brickfields, barge yards and farms who, in later years, became famous as England's most productive manufacturer of bricks. In his youth before he moved on to far larger projects, George managed The Ship. This tells us something of the calibre of the man – who amongst us could have run a town-centre public-house in Sittingbourne in those rather more rumbustious days? Even so, after a few years, for reasons unknown to us, young Smeed moved along the street to number 44 where he ran his business as a coal-merchant.(4,5,19,21,22)

More frequent than the carriage service provided at the Three Kings, a few doors away, by the waggon of Stephen Wrake calling thrice a week, here at the Ship, during Smeed's time, Stapleton's Directory (1938) tells us that a van owned by Stanbury & Co called every day. In the 1820s Young & Co provided a similar service – to London leaving *'every morning at 9 o'clock'* and to Dover *'every morning at two o'clock'* – at that time in the morning, we can imagine the disturbance to those on the premises – and their neighbours!

Sometime during 1841 a certain James Faught became licensee but probably it was during George Smeed's tenure that year that a branch of the National Charter Association met at The Ship.(5) The aim of the Chartists was to gain political rights and influence for the working classes. It was a short-lived branch. (81)

Harry Hedgecock ran the Ship in the 1850s. He came from an East Street family and had been born along the road at number 121. His father later moved to number 80 whilst Harry and his family left the Ship for number 42. What a lot they must have all seen of each other!

There were a number of other publicans at The Ship before the old building was demolished.

When the new building opened in 1899, still owned by the Vallance family, it was under the experienced eye of Henry Vandepeer. He was not new to the town, nor to the trade, having been host of the Golden Eagle in Station Street for ten years. The new Ship was a step up for Henry at the age of 50. He placed an announcement in the local paper in May 1900: *'Notice to dealers and others Henry Vandepeer late of the Golden Eagle is now of Ship Inn East Street'*.

The new Ship in 1902.
No doubt it is Henry Vandepeer standing proudly at the door

The 1901 census records the Vandepeers at the Ship: Henry a Sheppey man and his wife Dorcas a Sittingbourne woman. All their children were born in the town, the older ones worked for their father, but there were five younger children at home as well as Henry's old father and one boarder.

The Packers – probably 1922

The Vandepeers left before 1908 when the local directory appeared and the 1911 census enumerator found them living in Shakespeare Road, perhaps enjoying the chance of a quieter life, Henry was 60 by then and working on his own account at home as a marine store dealer.

Some later landlords of The Ship are listed in the table below. The dates given are dates when we are certain they were there but they could have been there well before or well afterwards too. This was a pub owned by the brewery Courage, known also as Courage & Barclay (1955) & Courage, Barclay & Symonds (1960).

1915	James Taylor
1922-45	Jessima and William Packer
1946-1951	Albert and Nellie Dennis
1960-63	George and Patricia Hawes
1970	Reg and Liliana Moore
1980-1998	Mike and Rosie Page

Reverend Bill Shergold, rector of Tunstall, known as 'the biking vicar', established the 79 Club at The Ship in 1981 for bikers. However it did not flourish as the 59 and 69 clubs, which he had founded in earlier years, had done. Reverend Shergold had occasionally made the national newspapers during the 1960s as the 'ton-up vicar' or the 'biker priest' He had ministered to the rockers of East London as leader of the 59 Club.

1981 Advert for The Ship

The Ship in blue and cream, rebranded as 'Page's' in 2011 (CA)

An attempt to revitalize the business as 'Page's' (but without losing the original pub name entirely), was short-lived. It was still in business in 2014 but after a period of standing empty building work began to convert The Ship to flats in 2015.(77)

The Ship Inn, painted red and cream, boarded and bricked up in early 2016 (BA)

The former Ship Inn at 22 East Street in 2019 (MHP)

Ship Yard

It is the 1841 census return which gives us our first glimpse of those who lived behind the Ship Inn in the cottages in the yard. At that point in time only one dwelling was inhabited and four were empty.(5) Edward Paten, who looked after the horses which the inn hired out and those of any travellers who came to stay, lived there with his wife and three children. No doubt the four empty homes were simple old cottages in need of modernisation. It may be that they were all originally part of the stabling and had been adapted to living accommodation. At any rate ten years later there were only three two-up two-down homes in the yard so it seems that two had been demolished. Successive census returns record the labourers, porters and bricklayers who rented them.

The dwellings disappear from our records after 1908 and it is perhaps surprising that they were not demolished a few years before when the new inn was erected.

Ship Meadow

The 1791 map (about which we have written elsewhere – notably in HSII) shows a parcel of land, just over four acres in extent, located north of East Street behind the buildings which then faced the inn. This field was owned at that time by William Drake of Bayford Farm, but its name, Ship Meadow, tells us that, at one time, it was linked with these premises almost certainly providing grazing.

Numbers 24 – 56 East Street

58   56-54 52-50 48   46 44 42 40   38-36 34 32-30   28-26 24   22

According to Canon Scott Robertson this stretch of East Street, between the Ship (number 22) and the Plough (number 58), was part of the Manor of Bayford.(62) He tells us that it was divided into four tenements. Any attempt to identify the extent of each of these four holdings would be pure speculation.

The tithe map and the Ordnance Survey map dated 1865/6 both show a multiplicity of properties here – at least a dozen. Scott Robertson makes clear that they were all held by a succession of owners but he says nothing about occupancy – some if not all of the property could have been let to various tenants.

> Henry Cocken
> Mary Sole (his granddaughter) who married Captain Trevor,
> their daughter who married Francis Redman
> before 1786 bought by William Bax
> before 1793 one part bought by John Garrett
> before 1811, one part was sold by William Bax Garrett to William
> Cleaver
> the remainder by George Garrett to Robert Hinde.

From this, we might infer that perhaps the Bax family and the Garretts were connected in some way – see HSII – the Rose Inn and 2, 4, 6 High Street.

Number 24 East Street

The Ship Inn

44   42   40   38-36   34   32-30   28-26   24   22

This building is about 300 years old, a fact concealed by the frontage added during the 1860s or 1870s when Charles Gibbon who we meet below, was doing well here. The building is a fair size with seven rooms according to census returns.

Thomas Snelling – shoemaker
Between the Ship Inn and the smithy at number 26 stood number 24 where in 1841 Thomas Snelling a Sittingbourne man made shoes.(5) His wife Amy had been married before and her young son Charley lived with them. The building was numbered 160 on the tithe schedule – a house, yard and garden. The Snellings were still at number 24 ten years later with two live-in apprentices.(6)

Charles Gibbon, clothier
Sometime during the 1850s Charles Gibbon moved into number 24 and sold clothes and shoes with his wife Charlotte.(7) Here they lived and worked for many years and regularly advertised in the local paper. Gibbon was a Sittingbourne man, born in 1821. Opening the shop was a step up the social scale for him for in 1851 he had been a sawyer living in Mud Alley – the name given at that time to Berry Street off the High Street with Charlotte and his old father John who was a wood-dealer.(6,HSII)

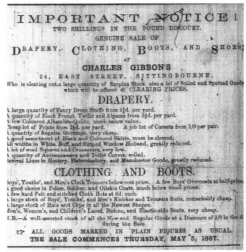

1887 advertisement for Charles Gibbon's sale

Charles and Charlotte had no children which must have enabled them to make savings and to afford a servant to help Charlotte with the housework whilst she worked in the shop.(8) At some point Mr Gibbon purchased number 24, a fact we know because it was sold by his executors when he died. The Gibbons remained here well into the 1880s, then Mr Gibbon retired, in his mid-sixties, and moved with Charlotte to Park Road.(N01,9,10)

Certainly John Hancock had moved here by 1890.(36) Charlotte Gibbon died in 1892 and Charles lived on at 7 Park Road looked after by a servant until 1904 when he died aged 83.(110) His executors then put number 24 up for sale describing it as double-fronted and let to Mrs E. Hancock who was paying £45 rent a year.(N01) Gibbon's other properties were auctioned at the same time and comprised six houses in Shortlands Road, two in Harold Road, two in Park Road, one in Bayford Road and one in Terrace Road – he had been quite a landlord.

John Hancock, boot and shoemaker

John Hancock then bought number 24 and moved in.(115) He had been born in Fulbourn, Cambridgeshire and continued the same business as Charles Gibbon, selling clothes and shoes.(10,34) John and his wife Ellen were in their fifties and had four children still living with them. A look at the 1881 census return reveals that the family had then lived in Newport, Essex where they had a grocery cum drapery and that there were two older sons who did not come to Sittingbourne with them.

Sadly one of their daughters, Ellen, known as Nellie, died aged 19 at number 24 in 1895.(N01) By then the Hancocks were putting the emphasis on boots and shoes in their advertisements and not mentioning the clothing. The 1899 directory entry reads 'John Hancock boot and shoe dealer'.

The following year John died aged 66, but Ellen continued the shop and lived at number 24 for many more years assisted by her two unmarried offspring by then in their forties – Mary Jane and Percy, as well as daughter Alice Goldsmith who had married locally in 1902.(11,12) Alice's husband was absent, perhaps he was a mariner or they may have been separated. Alice's young son Geoffrey Goldsmith was also living in the house in 1911, aged six and there he and his mother remained for many years.

The advertisements from 1903 to 1924 read 'Mrs Ellen Hancock Boot & Shoe dealer' Then as she reached her ninetieth year in 1926 it became 'Mrs Ellen Hancock.& Miss Mary Jane Hancock Outfitters and boot merchant'.

Old Ellen eventually died in 1928 aged 91.(110) She had done well with the shop and was able to leave nearly £5,000 to her children.(111) Members of the family continued living here and running the business. Geoffrey Goldsmith, Ellen and John's grandson, decided to keep the well-known Hancock name for the shop. It was he and his wife Gladys who were living here in 1933 whilst shop advertisements were for Mrs Hancock's.(115,56)

Geoff Goldsmith and his wife did not leave Sittingbourne but remained here for the rest of their lives, Gladys Elizabeth Goldsmith died on 24th November 1944. Geoff later moved to 46 Albany Road, however he maintained a shoe business after leaving number 24. This shop was in one of the two units that are now combined to form the Central Pie Shop – numbers 30/32. Geoff lived on until 1981.(87)

Gorman's shop at number 24 in 1966

Lily Gorman

Mrs Lily M. Gorman and her husband Henry who had married in 1941 moved in to number 24.(110) Lily sold fancy goods toys and gifts from the right hand side of the shop. Her husband sold bicycles and cycling accessories from the left hand side. The Gormans lived on the premises. Lily Gorman was the daughter of Jack Brett who ran and lived at, the adjoining jewellery shop. An advertisement in Tunstall parish magazine for 1977 reads: *'L. M. Gorman, sheet music instruments china, glass'*.

Indian restaurant

In 1980 a Mr Zobel ran a shop called Silhouette here which sold gifts and toys, but by 1982 the shop was vacant. China and glass was given another try in 1984 when Lee Kemp had the shop. A year later the shop was empty again for quite a period before being converted for use as an Indian restaurant.

The Empress of India restaurant in 2008 (CA)

In 1991 Ibrahim & Mahsure Deniz opened the Empress of India Restaurant which is still in business now. In 1998 the electoral register records Askik Ali and Abdul Alim lived here to run the Empress. The Empress is owned by Daily Spice Ltd.

Numbers 26 and 28 East Street

The East Street Forge and Forge House

Today this building is the 'Old Forge House' museum and tea room. The frontage of the building is 19th century with modern shop windows beneath it but the building is at least 400 years old. The faint shadow of the old arched entrance-way for the carts and horses can be seen beneath the whitewash at the eastern end of the building way above the shop front.

Blacksmiths – John and Mary Burton and John C. Burton

A certain John Clifford owned this building in 1840, along with another house a malt-house and cottages in the street.(4) (see 81 East Street et seq.) Clifford had been in business as a blacksmith in the mid-1820s (14) – apparently 2nd or 3rd in that line – two generations of the family appear as blacksmiths in Finch's local directory for 1803.(13) Clifford's tenant here in 1840 was the blacksmith Richard Burton. The 1841 census records that Burton was around 30, unmarried, and that his household comprised another blacksmith who worked for him, a whitesmith and a female servant. Numbers 26 and 28 were one building which was partitioned at that time and in the half later numbered as 28 lived Burton's sub-tenant, yet another blacksmith, Thomas Ransom with his wife and two children.

Business at the forge was 'exceedingly brisk in those days' because the situation on the London to Dover road could not have been bettered for passing trade.(N01)

Richard Burton died young in 1844 and his brother John took on the smithy. (N01,110) The 1851 census enumerator found that John Burton worked the forge where he lived with his family and employed three men. John and his wife Mary had a son, John Chambers Burton, who turned 13 that year. With them in the East Street house lived John's sister-in-law and nephew. The other end of the building housed labourer James Heath and his family as well as the Ransoms.

John Burton was a man of considerable means for as well as owning 26/28 in 1854 he purchased the elegant house up the road – number 70, The Chestnuts, to rent out. It cost him £450. This is recorded in the deeds of Chestnuts.

The Burtons remained here in 1861, until then John had also worked as a wheelwright. It was that year that the local paper advertised an auction of his wheelwright tools: '23rd February, Household furniture & effects, to be sold by auction. Goods belonging to Mr John William Burton Wheelwright.'

The Burtons had moved to Tunstall and lived there during those years whilst Tyler paid them rent for 26/28 East Street.

James Tyler began work as the wheelwright next to the forge, working too as a blacksmith. Directory entries of the 1860s refer to Tyler as blacksmith, wheelwright and town carter. Wheelwrights often worked in partnership with the blacksmith making the iron rims to go onto wheels. Sometimes one man had the training and experience to take on both tasks as in the case of both John Burton and James Tyler.

Tyler was in minor trouble with the law in 1863 charged with causing an obstruction to the highway in Sittingbourne after having been warned not to. There were two offences one of allowing a cart of timber to stand in the road for 12 hours and another for allowing a cart of timber to stand in the road for 36 hours. In mitigation he said that the load had not arrived in town until after midnight, the horses were knocked up and one had died on the road. The magistrates fined him two shillings plus 18 shillings costs.(*South Eastern Gazette*)

Directories of 1866 and 1867 record John Burton as the Tunstall blacksmith 'also at Sittingbourne'. Burton took the risk of the little business at Tunstall, paying a rent of £15-10-0 a year. Finding it uneconomic, he closed it down by 1870 and returned to East Street.(31)

By 1871 when street numbers were allocated the property was known as numbers 26 and 28 and there was only John himself, Mary and a servant living in the house. Aged 59 John must have been weary of the hard physical labour his work entailed. He died aged 66 in 1878.

Widowed Mary Burton continued the business. We learn this from the 1881 census for Mary is listed, employing four men and described as head of the household in spite of the fact that her son John Chambers Burton his wife and daughter lived with her and John C. Burton was himself a smith. John C. Burton's obituary in the local paper explains that when his father died '*Mr J. C. Burton conducted the business for his mother and then recently for himself.*'

John Chambers Burton was a talented and keen cricketer, known throughout Kent for his prowess on the field as his obituary related:

> '*Mr Burton's cricket career dated from the time when he practised in the meadow where the ground of The Gore Court Club is now situated*'.

(This was the field in Bell Road – now used by Borden School – where, after leaving Gore Court Park, the club was located before George Andrews gave them their present site at the Grove, Key Street.)

> '*He soon made rapid strides in this game and his proficiency becoming known to the County Club authorities, he was chosen to play in the English Colts trial match at Lords in 1861 where he made his appearance at the same time as the famous professionals Jupp and Humphreys. He subsequently played for Kent County Team and on several occasions made some good scores, particularly distinguishing himself against Notts at Crystal Palace cricket ground and also at Trent Bridge Nottingham, in another match. Mr Burton was also a member of Captain Hardy's eleven at Chilham Castle, where he made large scores in matches played there more than once. He constantly played for Gore Court from 1873 up to about 1881 when he retired. He was a good and safe bat, particularly strong on the off side and was the first cricketer to introduce round arm bowling in this district. He was possessed of*

considerable nerve and was often backed for stakes in single wicket matches in the presence of crowds of spectators.'

Burton's sporting talent and physical strength as a blacksmith failed to prevent him from dying aged only 49 in 1887 of heart disease from which he had suffered for five years. During those years the name of Milton man Alf Buggs appeared in the directory showing that he was working for Burton.(34)

Burton left his widow Frances, and young daughter Mary and '*numerous friends to miss his cheery manner'*.(N01)

It was then, in 1887, that a notice appeared in the paper announcing that Alf Buggs junior was taking over the shoeing and smith business from Mrs Burton. (N01)

Within months of the death of her husband Mrs Burton and her daughter moved across the road to smaller and doubtless quieter premises at number 99 East Street after an auction of the household furniture. The auction notice in the paper listed the piano, the clock, John's double-barrel centre-fire gun in its leather case and single-barrel gun (he had been a good shot), beds chest of drawers and easy chair. By August Mrs Burton realised that her husband's dog that he used to take shooting with him should also be found a new home and she placed an advertisement: '*Black Retriever. The widow of the late John Chambers Burton offers for sale his young dog well trained for his work and soft mouth. 99 East Street.'*

The probate index shows John C. Burton left an estate worth £343.

Alf Buggs

Although he was still living and working here four years later with his wife Emma and four children, life took a new and more advantageous turn for Alf soon afterwards when he moved up into the High Street to take charge of the Red Lion.(10,HSII)

The Barry family

By 1899 George Edward Barry had taken on the business as the directory records. The 1901 census shows he was married, then 28, born in Strood and had two children and a servant. George continued here for many years.

By 1911 the eight roomed house (numbered 26) was home to George his wife Charlotte their sons Alfred and Edgar (who was 11 years younger than his brother) their little sister and a cousin. The First World War meant a shortage of labour and George placed an urgent advertisement in the local paper:

3rd June 1916: '*Strong boy wanted about 16 years for forge at once G. E. Barry, The Forge East Street.'*

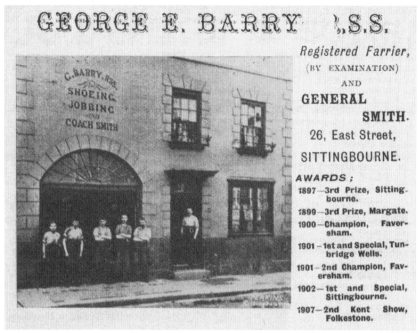

George Edward Barry, farrier, and his men (1908 directory)

1907 invoice showing some of the variety in George's work

George and Charlotte Barry in the garden at East Street

Young Alfred would have been 16 and had probably passed himself off as older and enlisted leaving his father short-handed like so many others.

George and Charlotte had four sons – Alfred, Edgar, Harold and Herbert and one daughter Edith.

During the 1930s the name of the business was changed to 'Barry and Sons'. (51)

One of George Barry's invoices. This one of 1929 proudly displays his awards as a gold medallist in many Kent competitions and member of the Worshipful Company of Farriers of London

By 1935 the Barrys advertised as 'G. E. Barry Assoc. Farriers & general builders'. Charlotte died in 1932 aged 57 and George died in 1940 aged 68. (110) Members of the family continued to live at 26/28.

In the age of the motor car the need for blacksmiths was fast dwindling and adaption was vital to survival. The Barrys had adapted and did work on cars and on buildings too but they no longer prospered and in 1946 the ancient art of the

307

blacksmith ceased to be practised here. However, the eldest Barry son, Alfred, continued to work under the new owners across the road

G. Hales & Son – motor-body works

1946 transfer of business notice:

> 'G. Hales & Son, East Street, have acquired the old established business of G. E. Barry & Son, welders & general smiths, added to their own modern facilities for oxyacetylene & electric welding. We will maintain same high standards of workmanship, orders can be left at the forge. Mr A. Barry in disposing of the above business to G. Hales & Son wishes to thank his customers for their patronage. Mr Barry will continue to work on as an employee'.(N01)

The Hales had premises at 13, East Street for many years. (see number 13)

When Hales bought the Barrys' business in 1946 they continued to work on the north side of the street at number 13, merely adding the Barrys' customers to their own. However it appears from the notice of transfer of business that they intended to work on both sides of the road 'orders can be left at the forge' but if they did so it was probably not for long.

The Bunting family lived at number 26 during the 1940s as the electoral registers show.

Jewellers at number 26 and 28

So the building was partitioned and by 1950 number 28 had become the premises of jeweller S. H. Brett & Son run by Sydney, known as 'Jack', Brett. (N01) It was he who installed the shop-front to the forge at 28 in 1950.(87)

Jack and his wife May lived on the premises. In 1958 the council approved Brett's application for the display of a clock on the face of the building.(105) Later photographs of 26/28 show that brackets still exist for a clock above the shop entrance to number 26, where it was moved in 1964 when Jack Brett expanded his shop into number 26 giving the building its present appearance – more or less.(87) Until then, number 26 had remained a dwelling, retaining its Georgian window and front-door, installed, probably, in the early 19th century, by Mr Clifford. (*The old door was moved to 8A Gore Court Road, where it remains – undoubtedly the oldest front-door of hundreds now located on the site of Gore Court Park.*)

Probate registry records show Sydney Harold Brett of 26 East Street died on 7th April 1965, with probate granted to his widow May and Sydney Harold Jack Brett (Jack's son, who, in his father's time, was known as 'Jackie').

The shop front at number 28, probably 1950s

Geoffrey Vaughan Luscombe, watch and clockmakers and jewellers, then took on the shop.(60) Mrs Brett continued to live behind the shop for some time after Mr Brett's death and then Geoffrey and Mary Luscombe lived and worked here and were still here in 1982.(N01,115)

26-28 East Street in 1966
Geoffrey Luscombe (NMR)

1981 Advert for the jeweller at number 28

By 1984 these premises were vacant. Geoffrey had been born in 1918 in Kent. He died in 1987 aged 68 having transferred his business, briefly, to London Road, Teynham.

By 1991 until at least 1995 the premises were in use as the Slender You beauty salon with living accommodation and an entrance at the back of the building at 26 (26a).

'Trophys & Signs' were at 28 by 1987 and into the early 1990s.

By 1995 number 28 was occupied by Abbey Dry Cleaners of Faversham, founded and owned by David Boughton. They remained here for four years until they moved to number 101 East Street.(121)

There were further changes with Mutts Cutts dog grooming at 26 from 1995 to 2001. At 28 Green Leaves for gardeners opened for just a year in 2000.

The fancy dress hire shop Character Costumes opened at number 26 in 2001 and then from 2005 were able to expand into 28 too. The business was started by Mrs Deborah A. White. The attraction of a museum in the form of a house during the Second World War has been imaginatively added by using the old living accommodation. Here enactors regularly give visitors a flavour of life during the war.

A change came at the end of 2016 when Mrs White decided to let number 28 out as Forever Hair Salon. Character Costumes has now been closed and the frontage tastefully changed to 'Old Forge House'. A tearoom fronts the premises with the museum behind. Forever Hair Salon has moved to premises in the High Street and number 28 has now been absorbed into the tearoom and museum.

26-28 East Street in 2016 (BA)
26 and 28 East Street, about 100 years after George Barry, the blacksmith stood there with his men. Compare this image with that of the forge.

Numbers 30, 32, 34 East Street

The Ship
Inn

44   42   40   38-36   34   32-30   28-26   24   22

Numbers 30 and 32 East Street

One house stood where the modern number 30/32 is today. In 1840 the property was depicted on the tithe map (plot 162) and belonged to one John Cowland who also owned what were later known as numbers 34, 36, 38 and 40. Perhaps he was related to the ladies of that name who lived at number 24 High Street. The tenant of 30/32 was Mary Tucker who was a governess, presumably out of work at the time. Her daughter who was a dressmaker lived with her and they had a lodger. Mary was still there with one lodger in 1851, by then in her fifties, she had found herself a job as a schoolmistress.

In 1861 30/32, 34 and 36 were being sold:

'Sale by private contract, six freehold houses. Three situate at the top of the High Street leading to the railway station, in the occupation of Messrs Inge, Millen and Harms: and three at the East End in the occupation of Messrs Snelling, Butterwick and Nichol. For further particulars apply to Mr White, wine merchant, Sittingbourne'.(N01)

This is a very useful for our history because the 1861 census records Messrs Snelling, Butterwick and Nicholl living respectively at 30/32, 34 and 36 East Street. So we learn that Richard White the wine merchant of 28 High Street then owned these three properties. Messrs Inge, Millen and Harms appear in volume II of our account of the High Street at number 82.

Young Frederick Snelling, one of the many Snellings of East Street, was the joint tenant of 30/32 along with an old carter and his wife. Fred was only 21 and was trying to make a go of dealing in second-hand clothes.

By 1871 Benjamin Hackshaw, a bootmaker, lived in the six-roomed house. He had moved along the street from number 16 where he had lived with the Harndens and worked for them. Ben Hackshaw had been born far away in Great Marlow and had married a local girl there. All did not go well with their marriage for we know that Jane Hackshaw entered St Pancras workhouse in London in 1854 with three children.(111) She entered again in 1857 with the two surviving children. However by 1861 Benjamin, Jane and their younger son were reunited and had moved to the growing town of Sittingbourne to make a fresh start at number 16 working in the Harndens shoemaking business. The Hackshaws' older son Benjamin junior had joined the Navy by that time.(111)

By 1871 Benjamin's marriage had again broken down and he lived at number 30/32 with five boarders one of whom was a woman, as well as one servant. Jane Hackshaw had returned to Great Marlow where she ran a second-hand clothes shop in the 1870s. This was a time when Benjamin was faring well enough to rent number 6, East Street and sell shoes there.(32) He died in 1882 aged 56, leaving bequests totalling a modest £30.(111) We cannot know now whether he had a problem with drink or a roving eye, but his life and that of his wife certainly had a good deal of sadness in them.

George Cook, a bootmaker lived here in 1890, he had been trained by the Harndens but by 1891 this was the home of Valentine Tyler a 'bargee hoveller' and his family.(36) Hoveller was a Kentish dialect word for an inshore boatman. By 1899 one William Willis had a shop here.(39)

Shipp's shop

Number 30/32 was buzzing in 1901, for here lived George Fowle, a middle-aged Hollingbourne man who worked as a carter on a local farm, his wife Annie who ran the shop, their five children and a boarder. The shop remained a newsagent's when Mrs Emma Shipp a London widow moved in accompanied by her two children and aunt.(12,43) Emma was a resourceful woman; already widowed ten years earlier, she brought up her four children the eldest of whom, Charles, was already working as a shipwright and no doubt helping to support his mother and siblings.

In 1920 the freeholder, Frederick Moore, sold the property to William Charles Taylor of Chillman House, 75 Murston Road, family home of Chilman Ladd Taylor a local builder.

In the following year Taylor sold to William Bramwell Booth, whose father had founded the Salvation Army. Presumably, this acquisition was purely for investment purposes generating funds for the Booth family or for the Salvation Army at large.

By 1921 Charles Shipp had taken on the newsagent's shop with his wife Alice and lived at 30-32.(49) In 1927 the property was sold to Mrs Martha Gwynneth Passby, doubtless as an investment; The Shipps remained in occupation at 30-32 until at least 1935 when George Shipp was running the shop. Their surname is sometimes spelt Ship rather than Shipp in the records.

Later tenants included John & Rose Healy during the 1940s. In 1953 Mrs Passby sold the premises to the adjoining owner, Sydney Harold Brett, who had been renting the premises since 1945

The old building is demolished

It was in 1957 that council minutes recorded that S. H. Brett of number 28 was permitted to pull down the existing 30/32 and rebuild as two single-storey shops. Bryan J. Kite was the first tenant and he was here very briefly before moving along to number 16.

He was followed in 1959 by Miss Christine Bills who had transferred her business from number 16 to number 30. She sold stationery and wool and was also here only briefly before, during 1960, this became the town's branch of the Singer Sewing Machine Centre.

1958 advertisement for Bryan Kite's shop

Mid 1960s to 1973

Then in 1963 the directory records our friend from number 24, Geoffrey Goldsmith, selling footwear at 32. *(see number 24)* Mr Goldsmith arrayed the outside of the shop with many pairs of shoes hanging down it. In the 1950s Michael Peters recalls Mr Goldsmith, in late middle-age, quietly-spoken and amiable. He lived at 46 Albany Road. (see Handcock HSII)

In the mid-1960s the sewing machine shop was taken over by a firm dealing in a different kind of machinery – Crestvale Motors, whose successor, Fred Hart (according to Goad data of 1968) took over Number 32 as well. Mr Hart, who sold motor parts and accessories, called his business 'The Car Shop', and he remained here until the pie shop opened.

This 1966 photograph shows Crestvale Motors on the right at number 30, Goldsmith at 32 and then Reed's hairdressers at number 34 on the left

Central Pie Shop

In 1973 the two shops were combined and occupied by the Central Pie Shop, which moved from 6 East Street.(see number 6 for details of the White family who still run it today)

Gordon White retired in 1997 leaving his son Malcolm and granddaughter to run the business. Now in the hands of the fourth and fifth generations of the family, the pie shop is still very busy with regular customers, passing trade and daily orders. The most popular pies are meat and bean on the savoury side and cherry and apple for sweet. Sausage rolls are always in demand but new lines are introduced to tempt the customers.

1981 Advert for the Central Pie Shop

Number 30-32 in 2018. These are the premises of The Central Pie Shop and were built in 1957. At the left side of the photograph the gable end of number 34 can be seen. Number 34 is at least 200 years old. (BA)

Number 34 East Street

The Hairdressers at number 34 in 1966

Number 34 is a small, two-up two-down house which is far older than 30/32. When the adjoining number 36 was demolished a new end wall had to be built for number 34.

In 1841 a tailor named George Sargeant lived here with his children and ten years later John Butterwick a tin plate worker from Sunderland and his local wife were the residents. Edward Nicholls, a local labourer, lived at number 34 in 1861 with his wife and five children.

He was followed as tenant by a blacksmith who worked on his own account behind 34, though later in the yard of number 15.(33) This was William Chapman who must have found home rather crowded with his seven children and wife. Two of his sons were also blacksmiths. William Chapman remained there in 1891 with his wife and the two sons who became blacksmiths, by which time the sons were in their thirties but by 1895 they had moved to number 15. (see number 15)

Men's hairdressers

By 1901 the front room of number 34 was transformed into a barber's shop. Richard Evans, a Welshman, was the hairdresser and he lived here with his wife and three lodgers. Frederick G. Scott the next hairdresser to live at 34 stayed much longer, well into the 1930s, with his wife who was a nurse.

Doris and Lewis Bunn were the next to take up residence at 34 where Mr Bunn continued the tradition of hairdressing. Had he been a character in the card game 'Happy Families' Mr Bunn might have been a competitor for the Pie Shop next door and Mr Barrow the baker at 38 High Street.

They were followed by Charles and Mary Reed by 1945. Then from the late 1960s to 1999 it was 'Ian's hairdressing for men' run by Ian Mantle.

In 2005 the building was in use as Broadway Dental Laboratory but this was gone by 2011.(121)

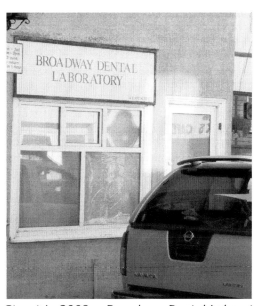

34 East Street in 2008 – Broadway Dental Laboratory (CA)

Currently 34 is occupied by a dog grooming business called Dip Snip & Clip. This is run by Patricia Ivesen from Sussex who, in 2017, replaced a similar business named 'Moon Beam'.

Moon Beam dog grooming salon at 34 in 2016 (BA)

Numbers 36, 38 and 40 East Street

Today the land where numbers 36 to 40 stood has been redeveloped. Number 40 was joined at first floor level to number 42 by a room which was part of the larger number 40. Underneath was vehicular access to a yard and outbuildings to the rear of both properties. This was important as the coach-builders who would have required constant vehicular access to the rear.(87)

This 1960s photograph reveals that numbers 36/38 were part of the same building at the centre of the photograph. For long periods over the years it had been partitioned into two but was then occupied as a whole by F. Crowder's shop whilst the weather-boarded number 40, also Crowder's, is in the foreground. Both properties could well have been medieval.

Number 40 and 42 with the vehicle access which can be seen as the dark entrance-way

Number 36 East Street

As we have reported next door this western end of the house was numbered 165 on the 1840 tithe schedule. It was occupied in 1841 by a young wheelwright Henry Norrington and his family and owned by one John Hunt who owned no other property in the town. Norrington worked for William Wise at number 40.

This notice appeared in the local paper in 1861:

'6th April 1861. By sale by private contract six freehold houses. Three situate at the top of the High Street leading to the railway station, in the occupation of Messrs Inge, Millen and Harms: and three at the East End in the occupation of Messrs Snelling, Butterwick and Nichol. For further particulars apply to Mr White, wine merchant, Sittingbourne.'

This is a very useful announcement for our history for the 1861 census records Messrs Snelling, Butterwick and Nicholl living respectively at 30/32, 34 and 36. So we learn that Richard White the High Street wine merchant owned these three properties. At number 36 was Edward Nicholls a labourer from Lynsted with his wife and five children.

By 1871 Augustus Fairbrass a clothier from Faversham lived here with his wife Caroline. They had fallen on hard times and no longer had a shop due no doubt to the mental health problems which Augustus suffered. By 1881 he was a patient in the Chartham Asylum and Caroline was keeping house for her widowed brother in Faversham.

Some later inhabitants of number 36:

1881	George Burton Brooks (see 101)	teacher of music
1891	Albert Williams	groom
1901	Fred Tong	carter
1911	William Hambrook	blacksmith
1922–26	John and Emily Campbell	
1933–38	Robert Cheeseman and Maurice Jeffrey	
1945	Ernest and Violet Witt	

The first date at which we know there was a shop at number 36 was 1937 when a fruiterer's was mentioned in a report in the local paper naming Thomas Otterway as the fruiterer.

From the 1950s number 36 was combined with 38 and 40 as a shop.

Number 38 East Street

The tithe schedule records that what was later known as number 38 was, like number 40, part of parcel 166 which was owned by John Comber and occupied by William Wise. By 1851 widowed Sarah Jackson a charwoman and her family lived at 38. After this the Wise family expanded their living space into 38 from 40 and occupied and later owned both.

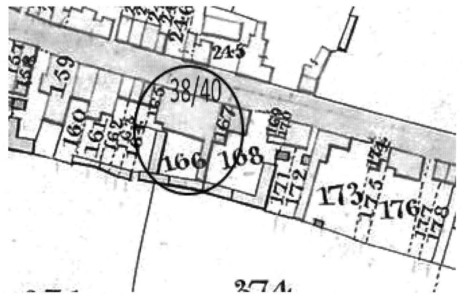

The large building which was parcel 166 is circled in this section of the tithe map

Number 40 East Street
The Wise family – coach builders

According to the obituary of William Francis Wise, the Wise family arrived here during the late 1830s and William Wise, who hailed from Doddington, set up his business as a wheelwright.(N01)

The 1841 census return records William aged 39, his wife Frances their children William, Matilda, Rebecca and Mary and a female servant. William's business could not have been better placed for trade on one of the busiest roads in England and during the 1840s he established himself as a coachbuilder.

Mrs Frances Wise died sadly young in 1847 and by the end of the following year William had remarried.(110) So the 1851 census enumerator found William, with his second wife Harriet (née Palmer), son William Francis aged 20 who had learned the trade from his father, two younger children and one servant. William no longer employed his next door neighbour.

Although the railway had arrived in Sittingbourne in 1858 and coach travel was declining, yet there was still a demand for carriages of many types and so we find by 1861 William Wise employed five men and nine boys His elderly mother in law, Mary Palmer, lived with the family.

The local paper carried this advertisement in 1861 'Coach Implement Factory East End. W. Wise makes basket carriages on premises also very convenient horse to hire'.

Here are two other advertisements, both from 1865:

'For Sale. A very handsome new phaeton, seats for four. A double seated basket phaeton; and several full size pony carriages, second hand and new. Apply Mr W. Wise Coach Builder Sittingbourne'

————————

'Wanted, Journeyman Wheelwright for light and heavy work and constant employ. Apply to Mr Wise Sittingbourne.'

————————

It must indeed have been a thriving business during the 1860s for in October 1863 we read:

'On Saturday evening last the workmen in the employ of Mr Wise coach builder, were liberally regaled by their employer with an excellent supper after which they were supplied with cigars and Payne's ale ad lib. Songs and toasts, loyal and patriotic were given, and a vote of thanks passed to Mr Wise for his liberality. A brass band was in attendance and played a selection of music.'(N01)

There must surely have been more than five men and nine boys working in the business to warrant such an elaborate occasion complete with brass band.

By 1871 William and Harriet lived alone in both numbers 40 and 38 other than a female servant. However next door but one at number 44 lived William Wise junior who continued to work at coach building with his father. A year later old William died leaving effects worth nearly £800.(111)

William junior, his wife Jane, their two sons William and Sidney and one servant moved into 38 and 40 where they were listed in the 1881 census. William junior died in 1887, his wife followed him to the grave two months later. Both were only in their fifties. An obituary appeared in the local paper:

'Another tradesman is removed from our midst by the death of Mr William Francis Wise which occurred at his residence in East Street Sittingbourne yesterday week.

The deceased who was 56 years old never enjoyed good health. He died from Consumption a disease which he is said to have inherited. Mr Wise was a coach builder by trade and carried on business at the well-known premises in East Street for 18 years, having succeeded his father the late Mr William Wise who first started business there 50 years ago. The deceased never took part in any public business; he was very quiet and unassuming in his manner and was respected by all who knew him. He leaves a widow (who has been an invalid for many years) and two sons. The Funeral took place on Tuesday when his remains were interred in the Cemetery. The burial service was conducted by Vicar Rev. H. Venn.'

After their parents' deaths the Wise brothers; William III and Sidney continued at 38 and 40 along with Sidney's wife and daughter. Sidney had followed his father and grandfather's teaching and become a coach builder. Younger brother William Wood Wise was a 'coach trimmer' who painted and upholstered the vehicles.(10)

The era of coach building was coming to an end and diversification was vital to keep the business going. Bicycles seemed to be the way forward and in 1892 William placed this advertisement in the local paper:

'Bicycles, bicycles, bicycles, from 30 shillings upwards. W. Wise agent to Coventry Machinists Co. All kinds of repairs carried out.'

Nevertheless in 1894 the Wise brothers sold up and moved out of the home their family had inhabited for so long. The advertisement for the auction gives us the useful information that by this time the Wise brothers owned number 40, the yard and workshops and also 38 and 36.

'Messrs. Wise Brothers, sale by auction an old established coach and builders business. House with carriage builder's shop, cottage and premises.'

Unfortunately this was not a good time to buy a coach builder's business and it failed to secure a bid. However as we shall see one of their workmen took it on. Sidney's wife Emily died in 1898 aged only 37 and he moved to Chatham with his children still working as a wheelwright.

William Wood Wise had not got on with his brother and they had not been able to agree on matters at all. This William had married Helena Forman in 1892 and she had lived for two years in Sittingbourne with him. When the business was sold she returned to her parents whilst William sought a new job in Newbury. However he then made his way to Ireland and in Derry in 1901 he bigamously married Elizabeth Platt. This was discovered and he served 15 months in prison.

Arthur Boulding

The workman who took on the business was Arthur James Boulding, a Milton man who had worked for the Wise brothers. He could not buy the premises and still lived down the road at 167 East Street in 1891 described as a 'coach painter'. No doubt he had the full support of his fellow-workers who would have been keen to keep their jobs. He placed the following announcement in the local paper:

'1894 Arthur J. Boulding having taken over the business lately carried out by Messrs. Wise Brothers, coach builders, 38 East Street, trusts by strict attention to business to merit a continuance of the patronage received by them.'

Well the directory records the business still trading in 1899, but it was in its final months, for by 1900 numbers 38 and 40 along with 36 were for sale as an advertisement in the local paper shows. Mr Boulding went bankrupt. *(Dover Express – Friday 15th June 1900)* The times were against him and he was not a businessman. The 1901 census recorded 38 as uninhabited and 40 as being used as an auction room.

The Swift family

William Albert Swift, who was much more comfortably off than Mr Boulding, had purchased 38 and 40 by 1903 when in his fifties. Swift was a Sittingbourne man who had run a house painting and plumbing business from his home at 31 Milton Road Sittingbourne assisted by his son Albert Edward and two daughters. (11) William and his wife had 12 children in all to bring up and support but the older ones were by then well able to work for their keep.

William Swift and his daughter Maud in the garden. This scene raises a few queries – what were they doing? Was this a celebration? Did they always use their best furniture from indoors? Who carried it out for them? Why only one cup & saucer ? What a big tea-caddy! Perhaps this was simply a picture to advertise some furniture and other chattels that William had for sale.
(JSH)

Swift did not sell the Milton Road house and in fact it is doubtful that he ever moved into East Street. Instead, his daughter Bertha, who was then in her thirties, lived there in the ten rooms and managed the shop with her younger sister Lilian. They looked after their 11 year old brother Stanley too. This is revealed by the 1911 census return which was filled in by Bertha on behalf of her father who was the official head of household. Mr and Mrs Swift remained at 31 Milton Road where they could have been found that census night with their daughter Gertrude. Nearby, in Station Street, their eldest son Albert had set up home with his wife and two children and still worked for his father as a house decorator. By 1908 the versatile William Swift had added furniture-dealing to his occupations.(43)

Mr Swift died in 1912 aged 65.(110) Probate of his will was awarded to his widow Sarah, his son Albert and his brother George who was a jeweller in

Sheerness. William had prospered and left assets valued at £3,081. The family erected a handsome headstone for him in the town cemetery.

The Swift family memorial in Sittingbourne Cemetery commemorates William, Sarah and three of their children. (BA)

After his father's death William's eldest son Albert continued the business at 38 and 40 as a decorator and plumber moving from Station Street where he had previously lived with his wife Ethel.(11)

In 1916 Albert joined up but must have had ideas of starting in some new trade if he survived for he placed this advertisement in the local paper:

> *'Mr A. E. Swift is joining the forces and his stock in trade as decorator and plumber to be auctioned off and also household furniture including blacksmith's bellows, hearth and anvil'.*

Presumably Ethel and the children moved out to live with her parents for the duration of the war. Mention of a blacksmith's anvil and bellow are surprising – Albert had always been a decorator. An announcement in the local paper towards the end of 1916 shows that part of the house was used by the forces:

> *'New recreation room for soldiers & sailors The C.E.T.S at Mr Swift's Store 40 East Street entrance through passage.'*

Albert Swift did survive the war and moved back into 38/40 with his family. Newspaper advertisements and directory entries record his furnishing and decorating business continuing here up to 1936. He owned a few small houses including 3, 4, and 5 The Wall. We know this as the council served an order in 1930 for him to improve these properties. In 1931 the council ordered him to repair the roof of number 38.(105)

In 1935 Albert's mother old Sarah Swift died aged 84 in the family home at 31 Milton Road where her daughters had looked after her. Unhappily once probate of her will was granted and after a long delay caused by dispute, Albert and Ethel were required to move out and sell the business or at least live in number 36. The 1937 newspaper announcement read:

> *'Notice: By orders of the executors of the late Mrs Swift. Sittingbourne in the main thoroughfare. The important property occupying a prominent position on the main London–Canterbury Road known as*

36/38/40. East Street. Available for business (with dwelling accommodation) or as a site for rebuilding, frontage 67 ft depth 108 ft. With vacant possession except number 36. Sale by A. J. Turner & Son Bull Hotel 17th Sept.'

Albert went to court to contest the selling of his home and business which arose from his father's will. He lost and was given three months to vacate number 38/40:

'24th April 1937 Executors in Court Action. At the Sittingbourne Court on Tuesday before his Honour Judge A. F. Clements. Sarah Annie Farrow of Brook Road Thornton Heath, and Percy Ward of 32 Park Road Sittingbourne claimed possession of a shop and premises 38 & 40 East Street Sittingbourne from Albert Edward Swift, carrying on business at that address. Mr Geoffrey Smith appeared for the plaintiffs while the defendant was represented by counsel Mr W. J. C. Tonge, Mr Smith pointed out that the plaintiffs were executors under the will of the late Mr William Albert Swift and they wanted possession of the premises so they could sell them and clear up the estate. His Honour made an order for possession within three months.'

For those of us who know the background, this report has an intriguing aspect: Percy Ward was a clerk at Winch Greensted & Winch and Geoffrey Smith was a new partner at the town's other principal firm of solicitors, Harris and Harris. Relations between the two firms were never particularly cordial. Why was Mr Ward represented by Mr Smith?

The weather boarded number 40 pictured here in 1937
Just about the time that Albert Swift was leaving

Numbers 36, 38, 40 East Street

In January 1944 numbers 36, 38 and 40 were auctioned, described as a cottage, a private house and a large shop total frontage 108 feet. They were purchased by a Mr C. J. Howard of Chatham who sent the council plans to change the frontage.(80)

In February 1946 a Mr W. G. Kennett and his wife Olive were the tenants living at 38 and 40. They found the house had been badly neglected as Mr Kennett wrote to the council:

'I wish to draw your attention to the conditions under which my wife and family and self are living which I consider to be a menace to health. The roof leaks badly causing the rooms to be damp, the chimney smokes badly but the great menace is there is no drain to the sink it having been broken.

The place is in poor condition generally owing to its great age.

I first reported it in December, the sanitary inspector called but nothing was done. The position is desperate.'

The 1947 electoral register records Mrs Olive Kennett still living there along with Eugene and Leonard Dicks. The Dicks were there alone in 1951.

During 1950 Mr Howard applied to the council to change the external appearance of number 38 by removing roof tiles and replacing them with corrugated asbestos.

All three of the premises 36, 38 and 40 were then converted to a ladies' and children's clothing shop by a Mr and Mrs Crowder who bought the premises. Mrs Florence Crowder ran the shop, followed, we believe, by her daughter. The family were in business here from at least 1953 to 1984.

Initially Mrs Crowder also had a hair salon at number 40 whilst she and her husband lived at number 36. Mrs Crowder added to the shop income by doing alterations to garments for customers.

Crowder's Ad from 1981

F. Crowder is the name above 36 and 38 and 40 here in 1985

Demolition of the old building and the building of Ronald's Court

We believe the old buildings were demolished in 1986. Ronald's Court flats were then built on the site by local builder Clive Tucker and named after his late father Ronald Edgar Tucker who, probate records show, died on 11th April 1986. Clive himself died a few years later.(87)

A modern pair of semi-detached homes in traditional style and a part of the three storey building stand where 36 and 38 were, whilst the site of number 40 is covered by the near part of a block of flats and the structure with the archway.

The sites of 36/38 and 40 as redeveloped with Ronald's Court. (MHP)

327

Number 42 East Street

The Plough

58   56-54   52-50   48   46   44   42   40   38-36   34

Where the old cottage which was number 42 East Street once stood, are now the modern block of flats called Ronald's Court.

In this 1906 photograph the original number 42 is the building in the forefront on the right then selling confectionery. The attractive arched window above the shop can be seen. It probably dated from the 18th century. At first glance the front wall appears to be faced in brickwork, but the window being flush with the front rather than set back a couple of inches, suggests that this was more likely to have been a thin timber-frame structure, possibly centuries older than the elegant window. If this is correct, the appearance of brickwork would have been created by mathematical tiles – hanging tiles which resemble bricks. This deception, common in the 18th and 19th centuries when brick buildings were considered superior to timber ones, can be observed elsewhere in our town centre – for example at number 50 High Street.(HSII)

Home and shop

Number 42 was a modest four roomed cottage with an additional room used as a shop (the number of rooms is given in an 1897 description of the property when it was available to let). We believe that it too was part of parcel 166 on the tithe schedule along with neighbouring 40, 38 and 36 – properties all owned by a Mr John Comber (or perhaps Coomber, that being a more familiar name in our local records). In 1841 young George Patterson, a bootmaker lived here with his wife Sarah and their babies next door to William Wise, the tenant, at number 40. Since, according to the tithe schedule in 1840, Mr Wise was the tenant of all of parcel 166, we might surmise that Mr Wise had sub-let 42 to the Pattersons. Ten years later this was the home of Matthew Cornford, a farm labourer, and his wife.

The Hedgecock family

In 1861 one of the Sittingbourne Hedgecock families was the tenant of number 42. Mrs Mary Hedgecock, from Rochester, then in her thirties described herself as a painter's wife and had two children. Her husband Henry was away that night but we know from directories that by 1866 he had abandoned painting in favour of selling fruit and vegetables at number 42 and this continued into 1874.(8,28,32) Henry and Mary had run the Ship at number 22 during the 1850s. Henry had been born at 121 East Street where his brother John still lived whilst his father lived at number 80. (for more on the Hedgecocks see number 121)

Henry Bennett

By 1876 the Hedgecocks had moved on and Henry Bennett who sold paints at 110 High Street had opened a branch of his business here.(N01,33) He had purchased the building as we can see from the electoral register of 1880 but he still lived at 110 High Street. The Bennett shop came to an end by 1881 and was followed by a number of short term tenancies.(N01)

Confectionery

When next we learn who lived at number 42 it was 1890 and young Andrew George Geering a confectioner from Whitstable with his wife Ellen and children had moved in.(10) Geering's Christmas 1894 advertisement boasted '*The largest and best stock of confectionery in the district, also a picture framing department.*' Mr Geering's main shop was at 47, High Street. He was doing well there and thought a branch should flourish in East Street. By 1901 the Geerings were living above their High Street shop and employing a Richard Laid to run the East Street shop.(11)

The only people at home on census night 1901 were sisters Elizabeth and Ruth Laid, daughters of the absent head of household. Elizabeth Laid was trying her hand at running a dressmaking business from home assisted by her younger sister Ruth.(11,39) Although number 42 is clearly recorded as a confectionery shop in the 1901 census, Elizabeth and Ruth's father, Richard Laid, was a gardener who was at home in Milton Road that night with his wife who ran a general shop assisted by another daughter.(11) So running the shop at 42 probably fell largely to the Laid girls.

Confectionery continued when the Laids moved out with James Mungham taking on the shop, and then from 1910 Mrs Lydia Hollands ran it whilst her husband James worked as a market gardener.(see number 17) There followed a succession of short-lived attempts at making a go of confectionery at number 42. It must have been hard to make a living in such a small space if you had no other income. In 1921 Mr A. Brook was declared bankrupt and his stock of sweets, fittings, utensils, household furniture & effects had to be sold off.(N01)

Nonetheless there was one final attempt at selling confectionery because Matilda and William Hammond took the shop on and lived there until 1927. (115,53)

Many changes

Then a change came when Valentine William Turvy opened a greengrocery. (53) Annie and Lachlan MacKinnon were the tenants by 1933.(115) Then a Miss Mary Brown sold second hand clothing and shoes here: *'Wanted urgently ladies and Gentlemen's cast offs clothing, footwear. Household furniture, bedding etc. Miss Mary Brown 42 East Street'*.(N01,57)

Frances and Jesse Goodhew lived here by 1945 and throughout the 1950s but it was just a private dwelling at that time. In the late 1940s when their son Monty got married in 1948 he and his bride June Gray lived there with them too.(115,87)

By 1961 the front room was converted back to being a shop again, first briefly a cake shop and then a pet shop named this time 'The Bird Shop'. The retailer A. V. Nash, combined running the shop with being landlord of the Anchor in Ospringe.(87)

1961 advertisement in East Kent Gazette

From 1971 to 1980 the shop here was Southern Domestic – who specialised in the sale and repair of white goods for the kitchen.(121)

In 1985 number 42 was made vacant prior to demolition and the building of Ronald's Court flats.

40-42 East Street 2018 (BA)

Numbers 44 and 46 East Street

Numbers 44 and 46 were two parts of one old house which, in modern times, has again become one property; a newsagent's shop with accommodation above. It is timber framed and at least 300 years old. Into the 1930s it still retained a large yard at the back with stables and other outbuildings.(N01)

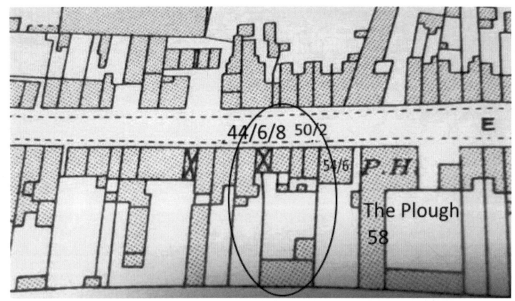

1938 Ordnance Survey map showing the yard behind 44 and 46

The tithe map of 1840 records that at that time the two halves of the house were in separate ownership and were shown as parcels 168 and 167. Parcel 168 (number 46) a 'house, yard and offices' belonged to Elizabeth Reason. The Reason family did not live here but in their elegant Georgian house number 45 High Street.(HSI) Parcel 167 (number 44) was owned by Rachel Reeves, an elderly lady who lived at 85 High Street and was tenanted by one Henry Gasson. It was described as 'part of a chapel.' We have been unable to discover any more about this use of the house as a chapel but imagine it was rented for a time by a branch of a non-conformist sect. We know from the 1841 census return that labourer Edward Sumnard and his family lived in one half of the building (number 46) and, in number 44, the young George Smeed and his family (with William Jeffrey an old labourer). George had yet to make his fortune and was working as a coal merchant – having lately left the 'pub trade'. As mentioned already, the directories for 1838, 1839 and 1840 tell us that Mr Smeed was, in those years, the landlord at the Ship Inn (22 East Street). We do not know why there was this change in his career, but he was still only 30 years of age.

Ten years later Eliza Hadlow a single dressmaker lived alone at one end of the building (number 44) and James Gibbon a young carrier and his family in the other (number 46).(6)

In this 1985 photograph we can see numbers 42 to 54
Number 42 is in the foreground – minus its stylish Serlian window shown in the
1906 photograph

In 1861 one of the East Street Snelling family – William Forster Snelling, a master tailor in his twenties lived at 44 over the shop with his wife Emma and children. William was a brother of Alfred Snelling the shoemaker who lived a few doors away at number 54/56 where he and William had grown up. William and Emma shared number 44 with a needlewoman and her younger siblings. This announcement appeared in the paper in 1868: '*W. F. Snelling of East Street, tailor, has been there seven years and is now moving shop to Station Street.*' This was a step-up to better premises. At the other end of the house, at this time, in number 46, lived James Lambert a saddler who made good use of the yard and outbuildings and was able to employ one man and a boy. Lambert hailed from Surrey and was married with a child. The household was completed by a boarder and the shop boy.

The next occupant of 44 after William Snelling also had relatives in East Street; this was William Wise junior, the coachbuilder, who moved into number 44 with his wife and two sons. William had only to go next door but one to work at coach building with his father. (see numbers 38,40) William junior had previously lived at 78 East Street.(7) So at this point this end of the house became a private home.

Esther Smeed, a single woman in her thirties who lived here with her niece, ran a tobacconist's at 46 whilst the Wises were at 44.(8) Number 46 remained a tobacconist's in 1881 when James Hickmott from Frittenden lived in the house and ran the shop with his family. Hickmott's neighbour at 44 was John McCartney an engine fitter from Scotland who had moved in with his wife Margaret and five children. Then Sidney Nathan Smith a young newspaper reporter in his twenties lived at 44 briefly in the mid-1880s. Born in Wiltshire, he had married a Faversham girl. Whilst living at 44 he was working for the local paper, and then by 1887 he and his wife had moved to Faversham. He eventually became editor of the Faversham News.(61)

Newspaper advertisements reveal that a coal merchant John Tong was the next occupant of number 44, with its conveniently large yard, and so once more these were business premises as well as a home.

> 18th June 1887: 'J. T. Tong will sell coal in partnership with his brother: Tong Bros Coal, Coke Merchants. 44 East Street Sittingbourne where orders will be punctually attended to.'

There came a time in the 1890s when the two parts of the building were united for the Tumber family lived and worked in both halves. Initially, in 1890 David Tumber sold coal as Tong had done but the Tumbers lived at 46 and later took on the tobacconist's shop at 44. One Robert Glandfield, a confectioner who had previously been a foreman at the cement works, briefly made his home at number 44 and was followed by 1891 by old Thomas Sage who was also a confectioner. Since we know that at this time Andrew Geering had his confectionery shop next door at number 42, we can assume that first Glandfield and then Sage (or more likely his wife Elizabeth who was 21 years younger) worked for Mr Geering.(10)

When he arrived in East Street David Tumber was unmarried and his sister Mary Ann who was deaf and without speech lived with him. The household also included David's widowed cousin James Tumber who was a labourer in his thirties with two children, Jane Austin their housekeeper and also a lodger. Jane Austin died in 1894 in her sixties and then in 1896 David Tumber married Elizabeth Mitchell.(110) Their marriage was a very brief one for Tumber died in the autumn of 1898 aged just 38 following his baby son to the grave. He left Elizabeth to bring up their surviving infant, and keep the shop going.

A puzzling notice appeared in the Gazette early in 1894: 'J. Ingram has taken the shop lately occupied by W. Wise, 44 East Street for the sale of English and foreign fruit, new milk, fresh butter and eggs daily.'

This is strange since we had no evidence that William Wise had used number 44 as a shop and we know the Sages lived there in 1891. Could it be that the Sages only lived upstairs at 44 whilst working at number 42 and that downstairs at 44 the female members of the Wise family ran a shop?

At any rate matters did not work out for Mr Ingram and number 44 was advertised to let during much of 1895: 'House and shop, 44 East Street, to let. Apply J. Ingram, 63 East Street'.

By 1901 nobody lived above the shop at 44 which was then known as East Street Bazaar and we know that Oliver Chambers sold china and glass here in 1903.(11,40) The 1901 census recorded that he lived over his main shop in Preston Street, Faversham with other members of the family. Peter Stevens' book about Preston Street describes Oliver Chambers' Sixpenny Bazaar selling glass and kitchenware so 44 East Street was for a few years a branch of Chambers' business but not one that lasted, unlike the Faversham shop, which continued for many years.

As the years passed some directories recorded Mrs Tumber living and having her shop at 44 and others at number 46. Certainly she did not rent the whole house nor the yard and outbuildings. Number 44 was to let in 1908 *'To let house & shop with large yard containing stable & large out buildings situate East Street apply Mrs Tumber 46, East Street.'* It came up to let again in 1912. When the war ended Elizabeth Tumber remarried at last but had already left East Street.

It was Wallace and Annie Mercer who were the new tenants at 44 and who continued the news-agency there. Wallace was a Sussex man who had originally been a printer.(10) His 1915 advertisement showed he was getting his own calendar and almanac printed.

> *'Mr W. J. Mercer of 44 East Street has again published an almanac. The utmost care has been given to compiling and illustrating of the Almanac and Calendar price 1d per copy.'*

Messrs R. White & Sons, the London lemonade manufacturers, were renting the stable and yard to keep their horses and bottles for local distribution by 1915 which was when the firm wrote to the council who had refused their request to widen the crossing outside the yard. They therefore asked the council to put the work in hand and send the account to them, keeping the cost as low as possible.(N01)

White's use of the yard was interrupted by the army during the First World War. How large the stabling was is shown by a list in Sittingbourne library's local studies collection. The list sets out where soldiers and their horses were billeted. It includes *'stabling at rear of Tumber's yard for ten horses 8th Battalion Northants Regiment.'*

Mrs Eva Woodruff, wife of the vicar of Iwade, owned numbers 44 and 46 at this time and in 1921 she sued R. White & Sons Ltd for £15 which was half a year's rent of number 46 with its stable and yard. White's yard was supervised by the foreman Albert Atkinson who lived at 46. Mrs Woodruff got rid of Whites though the Atkinsons remained. She put both 44 and 46 up for sale within months.(N01) They could be purchased separately: *'Shop & dwelling house no. 44 East Street in the occupation of Mr W. J. Mercer as a quarterly tenant at a rental of £20 per annum. House and yard 46 East Street. Yard & buildings in hand.'*

In 1921 the yard and perhaps number 46 itself were taken on by the builder A. C. May who was still there in 1932.(105) Meanwhile the Mercers continued at 44 until Wallace died in 1935 and Mrs Mercer carried on the business alone for a time.(90,N01)

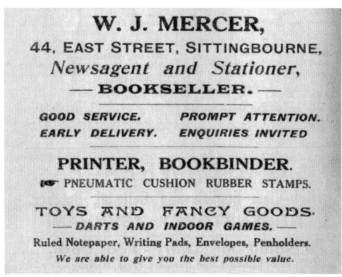

1927 advertisement

Number 44 continued as a newsagent's shop. In the late 1930s and until at least 1948, John and Margery Rate ran it and lived there followed by Doris and John Salisbury in the early 1950s.(115)

It is interesting to note that in 1949 the East Kent Gazette carried a notice advertising numbers 46 and 48 for sale jointly. I imagine this actually included 44 too. The description reads: '*Business premises and yard, a shop, living accommodation at the rear, a lock-up shop with three rooms over, yards and buildings.*'

The lock-up shop with three rooms above refers to number 48.

By 1953 until at least 1975 the shop at 44 was run by Wally Barnes and his wife Valerie.(N01) Wally actually rejoiced in the splendid and surely unique name of Walsingham Charles Barnes.(115) We can picture his mother as a devout and childless woman, whose prayer for a baby was answered after a pilgrimage to Walsingham! Wally was born in London in 1909 and lived on in Sittingbourne until 1980. The shop sold toys and paperback books as well as newspapers.(N01)

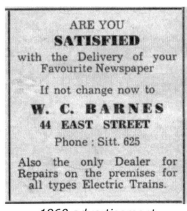

1960 advertisement

Number 46 was a fruiterer's in the 1930s run by Frank Barnett. Margaret and Thomas Sheehan were recorded living here in 1947 in the electoral register. Council minutes record that the shop had been closed 'due to the war' and that in 1947 when Sheehan opened it up the rates went up accordingly.

By 1954 the council had concerns about the state of number 46 and inspected it.(105) They found that a couple (unnamed in the report) were tenants there with their two children and paid a weekly rent of 17 shillings and 11 pence for this they had three bedrooms, a living room, scullery and shop. The owner by this date was Sittingbourne Co-operative Society who had long since bought up properties in the street in case they needed to expand into them. The housing inspector listed 20 or more external repairs which he considered necessary. The window frames were rotting, weather boarding was falling off and tiles were missing. Inside, all the rooms were damp, the cellar was boarded over to prevent access, the staircase was dark and steep and mice roamed the scullery. Months later no improvements had been made so the council rehoused the tenants and closed down the living accommodation leaving just the shop which was still permitted to continue.

In the 1950s number 46 was in use as a florist's shop named 'Stems and Petals' run by Arthur and Catherine Cassell, who at the time, were also running a sweet shop at number 57. Although the shop was still named 'Stems and Petals in the 1963 directory it is listed as there as 'second hand furniture and glassware etc.' By 1973 the shop at 46 was empty and so it stayed for many years, but the name remained painted above the shopfront.(92)

In 1977 number 44 was vacant but by 1979 it had been taken on by Don and Joan Smith and renamed 'D' n 'J Smith'. They acquired number 46 and incorporated it into their business as the greetings card section with access from the main shop.(92) Later, their son Nicholas joined the business. After Don's death, Joan and Nick continued the business until the current proprietors took over a few years ago when the shop was named Chris's Newsagent.(92) The name is now East Street News.

44 East Street D'n'J Smith 2008 and (Chris's News), in 2011 (CA)

East Street News in 2018 (CB)

The Smiths closed number 46 as a card department and by 1995 let the property to Bassant who were financial advisers (later of West Street).

At time of writing number 46 is in the process of conversion to residential use.(92)

Number 48 East Street

In this 1906 view number 48 is the boarded up building, on the right.

At number 48 we have a tale of one small and inconspicuous building which had a variety of uses over time. It was not yet built when the tithe map was drawn in 1840, but does appear on the 1865/6 map. Perhaps it had begun as a one-up one-down cottage with a passage way to the yard and then at some point the upper floor was extended over the passageway to make a second bedroom. As time went on it was altered and on the left a narrow, glass-fronted shopfront was installed whilst on the right the passageway remained, secured with a large wooden door at night.(87)

In 2011 the old building was demolished and was replaced with a new house in 2015.

In 1871 labourer William Lee and his wife lived here. A report of an 1875 meeting of the Sittingbourne local board (from the Whitstable Herald) tells us that number 48 by then belonged to William Wise the coach-builder who lived at number 38/40 and that water was laid on to the cottage that year. Nevertheless number 48 was not listed in the 1881 and 1891 census returns. This means that it was not lived in but perhaps it was in use for some commercial purpose.

A chapel for the Particular Baptists

By 1901 the census records that number 48 was being used as a 'Baptist meeting room' and the 1908 directory tells us it was a group of Particular Baptists who worshipped here. The Sittingbourne group had formed during 1900 (there was no place of worship for Particular Baptists in the town in 1899 when that directory was printed). No doubt a preacher had come to Sittingbourne from a nearby congregation such as Chatham to make converts.

More is revealed by our local directory of 1908 which tells us: *'this sect have a small meeting house in East Street, Sunday services are at 11.30 and 6.30. Preaching service on Wednesday at 7.30 pm'*. The deacons were Mr G. Baynes and Mr J. Martin. The secretary lived at 16 Shortlands Road and turned out also to have been John Martin who was disabled in some way as the 1911 census records. George Baynes who was the other deacon then, was an elderly army pensioner who had moved away to Gillingham to live with his daughter by 1911.

The Particular Baptists still exist and are a sect of non-conformist, evangelical Christians who do not form part of the Baptist denomination but do share their belief in adult baptism. They emerged as a separate body early in the 19th century. One of their differences in belief is that they have no centralised headquarters nor a governing committee. To worship they require just a room.

As we can see from the 1906 photograph the downstairs of number 48 was boarded up at that time awaiting a new tenant, and the Particular Baptists hired the upstairs rooms. We can imagine the little building resounding to hearty hymns and impassioned sermons every Sunday morning and evening. Directories show they remained worshipping here until at least 1934 but the group did not last much longer for by 1938 there were no Particular Baptists listed as meeting for worship in the town.(57)

Fred Rumble, wheelwright

In 1924 number 48 was also the premises of Frederick Rumble who must have used the entrance way from the street to the yard behind to access his workshop. That year he placed a for sale advert in the local paper for a governess car in good condition. *'Apply Rumble Coach Builder, East Street'*. Fred Rumble was trained as a wheelwright and in 1911 had lived along the road at number 80 with his parents. At that time he was 18 and already fully trained as a wheelwright. Fred married Daisy Moore in 1920 and she became very well known locally as an accomplished pianist and had her own dance band in which Fred played the drums.

Fred Rumble on the left, Daisy Rumble on the piano – picture taken in 1963.
By 1939 they lived in Albany Road

By 1927 these were the premises of East Street Haulage Contractors.(53) – perhaps Mr Rumble was still in charge there.

In 1930 a new shop was proposed to the council for A. C. May at number 48. (105) A.C. May already had a licence to keep temporary buildings such as garages behind numbers 46 and 48.

In 1933 Alfred and Rosina Cook lived here and the building was owned by a Louisa Matthew who lived in Harold Road.(115)

By 1935 Mr Mackinnon had a sweet shop here. Ernest and Florence Crump lived here in during the 1940s as the electoral registers record.

In 1949 the East Kent Gazette carried a notice advertising numbers 46 and 48 for sale jointly. The description reads: 'Business premises and yard, a shop, living accommodation at the rear, a lock-up shop with three rooms over, yards and buildings.'

The lock up shop with three rooms above refers to number 48. From at least the mid 1950s until 1996, number 48 was a rather ramshackle second-hand furniture and junk shop run by Mr and Mrs Farrimond who lived on the premises.

Ronald Farrimond was born in 1916 and he married Margaret Reeves in Croydon in 1943. Mr Farrimond died in 1982 and the 1990 electoral register records that Margaret stayed on. She died in 1996. The shop was called 'Copper & Brass' although the Farrimonds did not have a sign on the fascia.(121) This troubled their neighbours – the Easton family, whose shop next-door, trading as John Peters & Sons, was also selling second-hand goods. "People think that old place next-door, with no name, belongs to us" said Mr Easton "they're giving the wrong impression and pinching our trade."

By the year 2000, number 48 had become the premises of a charity shop. (121) In 2005 it was back to being a second-hand shop this time named 'Etc Etc'.

The building was demolished in 2011 and during 2015 was replaced with a new house in traditional style with dormer windows. A great improvement, though perhaps the front elevation at ground floor level would have benefited from a little more attention to architectural detail.

Number 48 East Street – the second-hand shop in 1985

Number 48 (Etc Etc) awaiting demolition in 2008

48 East Street today is a modern home (BA)

Numbers 50 and 52 East Street

The Plough

58   56-54   52-50   48   46   44   42   40   38-36   34

Numbers 50/52 today form the premises of the shop called 'The Carpet Centre'. It is probably timber framed and about 300 years old. For very many years the old house was partitioned into two four-roomed cottages numbered 50 and 52. In 1840 the tithe schedule records the property as parcels 169 and 170 which like number 48 belonged to Daniel Winch. The only Daniel Winch in the 1841 census of Kent lived in Dover with his wife, and was of independent means, so it is likely he was the owner. The residents of the two sides of the building then were Sarah Wilcocks and her son and on the other side David Sergeant, a seedsman.

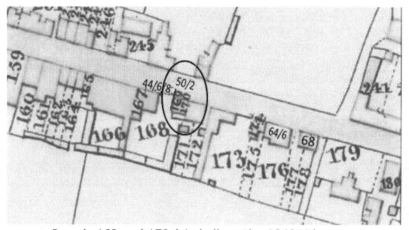

Parcels 169 and 170 (circled) on the 1840 tithe map

Number 50

Number 50 continued to be residential in 1851 when John Higgins a waterman from Frindsbury, his wife and three children lived there. The next tenants we know of were the Gibbs family. William was a grocer's warehouseman and he and his wife also had three children.(7)

There were just a few years when tenants attempted to run a shop in the small space at number 50. In 1871 this was the home and shop of Thomas Burgess, a young draper from Gravesend his wife and three daughters.(8) By 1881 the cottage had reverted to being a private home where Francis Simmonds a labourer from Hollingbourne lived with his wife.(9)

Mrs Mary Ann Tong advertised herself as a dressmaker at number 50 in 1890 whilst her husband Frederick worked as a groom and coachman for one of the better off inhabitants of the town.(10)

At times number 50 was overcrowded such as during the time of the Bottle family. Bill Bottle was a furniture porter from Tong who shared the cottage in

1901 with his wife, daughter and a lodger.(11) The Bottles stayed longer than most previous inhabitants and ten years later had been blessed with a further three children leaving no room for a lodger.(12)

In 1919 the overcrowding at numbers 50 and 52 had been brought to the attention of the local medical officer who reported to the council: '*With reference to numbers 50 and 52 East Street the rooms of each are so small that it would be better to make the two houses into one*'. The surveyor also reported that he considered the rooms too small to be used by families. The inspector of nuisances said they had calculated 300 cubic feet of air space for each adult person and as one of these rooms had only 500 cubic feet it was not large enough for two persons. The council decided that they could not agree to the alterations suggested by the owner and the clerk was instructed to send a copy of the medical officer's report to him.(N01)

This seems to have brought the occupation of the two cottages to an end and by 1924 number 50, which was owned by Stephen Snelling, was being used as the office of the local branch of the Labour Party.(N01) Here Charles Shepherd, Labour's local agent worked. In 1926 both 50 and 52 were empty.(52)

There followed a few years (up at least to 1935) when M. & S. Bensted, fruiterer, had a greengrocery and flower shop which according to the directory was only in number 50 and indeed there would have been much more space for a shop with nobody living on the premises.(N01,53)

Mr Snelling still owned the premises in 1931 when council minutes record that he proposed making changes to number 50 but these, whatever they were, were turned down.

By 1938 John Peters & Sons the furniture dealers were using both 50 and 52 to sell second-hand furniture (see also 4 East Street). This part of the business was run by Monty Easton, who had acquired the John Peters & Sons in the 1920s.(HSI,HSII) In his latter years, Monty could keep himself busy here without being 'in the way' at the firm's principal shops. Later on, the second-hand business here was run by two of the firm's porters Lew Ravensdale and 'Snowy' Snashell. By 1959 John Peters had renamed their shop here as 'Home Bargains'.(N01) In the 1970s they sold china and glass here and it survived as the last remaining element of John Peters's retail business – with a new side-line: the historic postcards, postage stamps and other 'collectibles' which Christopher Easton, the firm's last proprietor, had begun to trade.(121) The soft furnishing, china and glass departments at 4-6 East Street closed in 1979 and, in the same year, the furniture business in the High Street had been hi-jacked across the street by a former manager – a Mr Wilson and renamed 'Wilson Peters'.(HSI,HSII)

John Peters & Sons at 50 and 52 East Street, 1985

At some stage, in the late 1980s, David Bushell, who been manager of the shop, took over the second-hand business – though, in his early years there, he retained the Peters trading name, perhaps because there was goodwill attached to the old name or because the ownership of the premises remained with the Eastons, owners of John Peters. Previously they had employed David as a furniture porter.(87)

In 1997 number 50/52 stood empty and then by 2000 was the premises of Barker's home entertainment shop. This was a brief enterprise and the following year a new business moved in; the Carpet Centre which is still there today.

The 'Carpet Remnant Centre' at number 50 in 2008 (CA)

Number 52

Before being combined with number 50, number 52 was never a shop but was home to a series of working people. Generally it seems to have been less crammed with inhabitants than number 50. There was William Woodhurst a young brickmaker from Strood with wife and son in 1851, widowed Mary King working as a charwoman to support her daughter in 1861, George Bunting who laboured in a cement mill and had a wife and daughter. By 1881 old widow Maria Hobbs from Sittingbourne and her granddaughter lived here.

Labourer John Grant from Thurnham seems to have tenanted number 52 for the longest period of time. He and his wife Rebecca had moved in by 1891 when John was in his sixties. By 1901 he was 73 and crippled and the old couple must have struggled to make ends meet. John Grant died in 1909 aged 81. Rebecca lived on until 1914 in the alms houses down the road receiving out-relief from the workhouse.(12)

After the death of John Grant and Rebecca's move, the new tenants were young Ernest Wood a Milton man who worked at the paper mill, his wife and two children.(12)

They may have been the final inhabitants of the cottage and as we have seen 52 was combined with 50 during the 1930s.

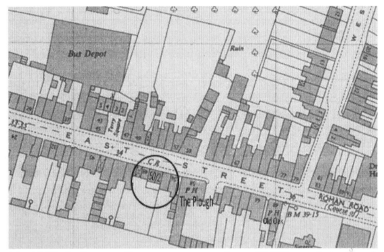

On this 1960 Ordnance Survey map numbers 50/52 can be seen circled

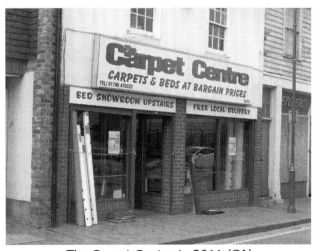

The Carpet Centre in 2011 (CA)

Numbers 54 and 56 East Street

Numbers 54 and 56 used to be one house partitioned to allow for two dwellings, a shop and workshop, next door to the old Plough Inn. The family lived at 54 and worked at 56.

Numbers 54 and 56 on the left of this image between the furniture shop and the pub. The door and window on the right are the (Snelling & Ward) shoemaker's shop and the left hand door, the residence

The old house was demolished around 2007. Today there stands in its place a traditional style, red-brick, double-fronted, terrace house with dormer windows and, alongside it, a tunnel passage.

The Snelling family

The Snellings of East Street were quite a tribe. Old Stephen (1767-1850) lived on the north side of the street. He was a bricklayer – following the same trade as two other members of his family recorded in the local directory for 1803. Stephen is recorded in the 1841 census as a widower in his seventies. He and his wife Elizabeth had had several children and one of these was Stephen junior (1798-1868) who was taught the bricklaying trade by his father. Another son of old Stephen Snelling, William Forster Snelling was a tailor who lived for a while at number 44.

Stephen Snelling junior, bricklayer

The 1840 tithe schedule records Stephen junior renting the eastern part of a house and garden, owned by Robert Hinde. The other part (also owned by Robert Hinde) was let to one Edward Gibbs.

Mr Hinde was a solicitor based in Milton – one of the family that did well from lending money and the ownership of property. Until the early 20th century, successive members of the family owned the fine double-fronted building in Milton, number 60 High Street – known as Hinde House (renamed Burley's Flats).

Hinde's partitioned house here in East Street is numbered 171 and 172 on the tithe schedule.

Stephen junior did well at his trade of bricklaying for the 1851 census, taken when he was in his fifties, records that he employed five men. Seven children out of the 13 of he and his wife Susannah were then still at home. The eldest, James, had left home as had daughter Emma and son Stephen (b1825).

Alfred Snelling, shoemaker

Stephen and Susannah's third son, Alfred, a shoemaker aged 24 in 1851 was to spend his whole life at number 54/56 where he had established a shoe shop by 1851. Whilst Alfred's father was still alive, through the 1860s they were both listed in directories, Stephen for his bricklaying and Alfred for his shoemaking.

The 1871 census records Alfred Snelling, bootmaker, Ellen his wife and their four sons- Thomas, Alfred junior, Harry and Stephen.

Alfred lived on until 1893 when he died aged 66. Looking back at his life and his skills an East Kent Gazette article of 1928 noted: '*Alfred Snelling, what a bootmaker he was, and further, how well did he hand on to those who followed him, both his reputation and his skill for a fit and quality. He made a name both for himself and for his town, because many a seaman in distant ports has advertised the fact to a sodden-footed sailor that there are no boots so strong and so truly watertight as Sittingbourne boots made by Mr Snelling'.*

What a lovely memorial to a bootmaker!

Alfred did hand his high standards of craftsmanship on to one of his younger sons – Harry who continued the business.

Thomas Snelling, a ne'er do well

Alfred's eldest son Thomas, whom his father had trained as a shoemaker, took to drink. The Plough Inn next door was only ever one step away. Early in 1879 when he was 23, he came up before the magistrates in Sittingbourne. His father had in desperation given him into custody for striking his brother. Mr Snelling had requested that his son be bound over to keep the peace. Mrs Snelling might not have agreed with this drastic action but she was not there to ask having died in 1877 aged only 44.

Thomas' brother did not appear against him so the magistrate told him he was a disgrace and discharged him.(N02) However matters became much more serious a few months later when Thomas turned to arson.

On 24th May the Whitstable Times reported that a fire had broken out in a thatched lodge behind William F. Wise's premises in East Street. It burnt to the ground and the cab inside it was destroyed too. The same lodge had caught fire a few weeks previously. This time Thomas came before Sittingbourne magistrates charged with wilfully igniting straw against a wooden building on the premises of Mr William F. Wise with intent to burn it and also with setting fire to farm buildings at Trotts Hall Farm down the road the following night.

The Wises lived just a few doors away from the Snellings and the gardens of the two properties adjoined. Thomas was the prime suspect straight away as 'his conduct had been very loose lately'. He had been seen within yards of the Trotts Farm fire. After being arrested he confessed he had started both fires and was sent for trial.

At Trotts Hall four horses perished in the fire. One of these belonged to Messrs Rugg, veterinary surgeons, who occupied some of the stables. Property destroyed included a wagon and harnesses.(N02) For this very serious offence the magistrates remanded Thomas to appear at the Kent Midsummer Assizes in July when he was found guilty and sentenced to 18 months hard labour.

This must have been an anguishing time for the rest of the family who were respectable and hard-working and had a good reputation in the town to maintain. Nevertheless Alfred did not forsake his errant son and allowed him to return to the family home when he was released during 1881 when he was described on the census return as an 'unemployed shoemaker'. At this stage his father was not employing him.

Thomas' brother, Alfred junior, was a cooper and still lived at home as did young Harry who was working with his father as a shoemaker and the youngest Stephen, only 12, was being trained by his father too.

For a while Alfred Snelling sublet number 56 to a local woman, Mrs Emma Young who had the unusual job of fur and feather cleaner. She advertised her services in the 1878 directory and in 1880 announced she was moving from 56 but the 1881 census enumerator found her accompanied by her son and a boarder between 54 and 58 East Street in a dwelling mysteriously numbered 9. Perhaps this was a refurbished out-building behind number 56.

By 1891 Alfred had his son Thomas working with him (having got over his love of setting fires) as well as son Harry. Stephen, the youngest son, was still at home too but had become a plumber. Harry had married and so his wife doubtless cooked for them all.

Alfred died in 1893 having made a will which appointed his friend the baker, William Cremer his executor. The total value of his goods was £82.(111)

Harry Snelling and Ernest Ward

After Alfred's death, Harry continued the business at 54/56. Apart from the absence of old Alfred the household remained the same for the next 20 years since neither Thomas nor Stephen had married and Alfred and Fanny had no children.(11,12)

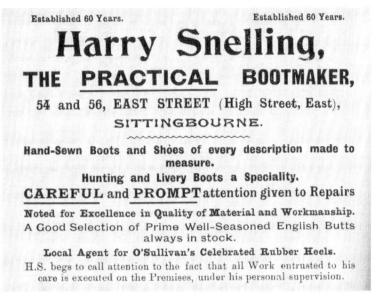

Advertisement in the 1908 Directory

Thomas died in 1915 aged 59.(110) Harry, Fanny and Stephen continued to share the house until her death in 1928.(115,110) Harry carried on the business and his brother Stephen continued to live with him in the old house until Harry died aged 78 in 1938. When he got old, certainly by 1935, having no children to continue the trade, Harry had taken on a business partner Ernest Frederick Ward, a Milton man born in 1897, another bootmaker, and the shop name was changed to Snelling and Ward.

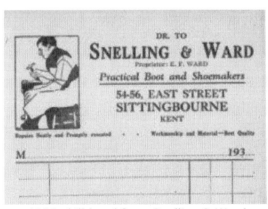

1930s bill head from Snelling & Ward

Harry's will had appointed his brother Stephen and Ernest Ward joint executors. Harry's effects were valued at nearly £1,000. The last Snelling to remain in the house was Stephen who died in 1940. Whether the Wards were related to the Snellings we have not discovered.

Goad of 1968 gives the business name as 'Snelling' at 54 but 56 as a private home.(121) Ernest Ward and his wife Hilda lived at number 56 with their family. Ernest Ward was still in business there in the 1960s – a polite gentleman of the old school, he was highly-regarded in the community. He and his wife still lived at the shop during the 1970s. He died in 1983.

The 1985 Goad map shows the 'Snelling & Ward' shop still open but by 1995 until at least 2000 'Marshdown' insurance broker was listed – it was a partnership, between Messrs Down & Marsh. Neville Marsh, who lived in Hillbrow, Sittingbourne with his wife Avril and their family, had been an inspector for the Royal Insurance Group. Until the late 1960s, it was customary for the larger insurance companies to employ staff to visit their agents regularly. The Royal's inspector visited the company's agents in our town every week; the company had a strong local following, derived to some extent, probably, from the Kent Fire Office whose business had been taken over by the Royal in 1901. Readers of High Street volume II will have noted that the Kent Fire Office had been founded in our town in 1802. Neville Marsh's predecessor at the Royal, Mr Morton, was perhaps the last professional gentleman to wear a bowler hat in our town for business. In those days – the 1960s – the bowler was standard headgear for underwriters at Lloyds of London – and for staff of various organisations in the City. When the Royal decided to close down their team of inspectors, Neville Marsh went into business with Mr Down, but they did not stay here long – perhaps they'd have done better had they adopted the correct headgear!

In 2005 the building was empty and, by 2011, had been replaced by a new house. Behind the house another new building, named Hedley Court, hugs the east and back boundaries. Access at the rear is from Fairview Road, which cuts through what, in 1840, was Michael Eaton's orchard.

Number 56 c1995-2000 when it was an insurance broker's. (MHP)

A 2016 photograph of the modern building which replaced the old 54 and 56 East Street (BA)

The Plough (number 58)

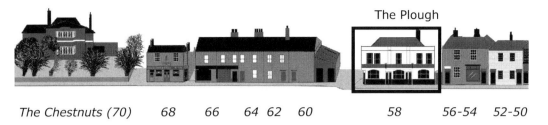

The Chestnuts (70)   68   66   64 62   60   58   56-54   52-50

The Plough stood on the south side of East Street for centuries until it was demolished in 2005. The magnificent roof structure, which survived all the changes during three centuries, gave a flavour of the quality of what would have been provided on the floors below – before successive alterations in keeping with the times.

When The Plough was built in the 17th century it was not as a public house but the home and workplace of a 'wheeler' or wheelwright and belonged to one Robert Smoothing. There was a good-sized yard which survived into the 20th century with outbuildings offering plenty of space for a wheelwright's business at the back as well as the horses and carriages that would have frequented the inn.

The Plough can be seen on old postcards of East Street, this one from 1904

Alan Abbey made many interesting discoveries in his study of the premises including that the original timber framed rectangular building stood at right angles to the road.

It was not licenced as a public house until 1769, when it was given the name 'The King Henry VIII'. This did not last long and in 1786 the sign was changed to the 'The Royal Oak'. The final and lasting name of 'The Plough' was chosen in 1793 when the inn belonged to the Chatham Brewery Company.(62)

Successive owners, in the 18th and 19th centuries, according to Scott Robertson, were John Banks (before 1800), William Reason and then James

Best, who, the tithe schedule tells us, owned the freehold in 1840 when, as noted below, the tenant was William Pay.

The building itself underwent great alterations over the years and during the Victorian era the entire frontage was modernized giving an appearance which belied its age.

Victory decorations at the end of the Second World War

We learn something of the men and women who presided over the Plough Inn from census returns. We have not listed them all here but simply include some whom we know something about.

William Pay was in charge by 1840 and remained for at least a further ten years. This was never a grand establishment and Pay was able to run the place with the help of his wife and two live-in servants in 1841.

By 1855 James Hammon had the Plough licence and his wife Matilda and daughter Jane worked with him as well as a live-in maid. James Hammon had previously worked and lived across the road at number 15 as a wheelwright. On census night in 1861 there were two working-class visitors who had paid to stay the night as well as William Pay who no doubt was a friend. The Hammons left during the 1860s.

Two other landlords made brief appearances before John and Ann Noble arrived in 1871 and settled in for a long haul. By this date the Plough had gone down in the world and there were no more paying guests staying the night. Instead there were five lodgers who provided a steady additional income for the Nobles who did all the work themselves. John Noble died in 1876 aged 52 and Ann was allowed to take on the licence. By 1881 it was her son George Noble who presided over The Plough with his wife Fanny who was also busy with their six children. As for George's mother Ann Noble, she remarried in 1879 to labourer James Sellen, and they boarded at 98 East Street.(9)

The Nobles left the Plough in 1882 and William and Charlotte Hubbard moved in.(34) They must have felt they were on the up as they had previously run The Prince Alfred in Hawthorn Road which was a smaller set up altogether. However

William died miserably young in 1886 aged only 38. Charlotte was granted the licence but the work was too much for her with four young children. So within a year she moved across the road to number 25 where we meet her again, running a shop.

The Sage family

By 1891, Sittingbourne born and bred Alfred Robert Sage had moved in to take charge of the Plough with his wife Louisa (née Denne). The Sages were in their thirties with five young children. Louisa continued the tradition of taking in lodgers and had six that year.(10) Alfred had started his working life as a labourer and it turned out that running a pub was not how he wanted to spend his life after all. By 1901 the family were living in Milton and Alfred was working at the paper mill. However his younger brother Edwin George Sage took on the Plough in his place.

Edwin and his wife Elizabeth also had a young family. Whilst at the inn Edwin, with another brother, young Ernest Charles Sage, successfully continued the business which their father Edward had already established. During the 1890s Edwin and Ernest began to hire out waggonettes, carriages, brakes and four-horse drags from behind their parents' home at 52 Shortlands Road.

Edward Sage was the father of Edwin, Ernest and Alfred and he was in business as a general carrier as this invoice of 1887 shows. He had done well as earlier he had simply been a carter.(9)

The Sage brothers now continued at The Plough which had plenty of stabling and space for the vehicles at the back. Ernest was still single in 1901 and lived round the corner in Shortlands Road with his old parents, describing himself as a 'carriage & stable proprietor'.

Percy Hubbard described the pleasure of outings from the Plough in his memories of Sittingbourne:

'*The Old Plough still stands, once the home of the Sage family, where on an Easter Monday, or Whit Monday, or August Bank Holiday, one would hire a coach with either two, three or four horses for the day and travel with friends as far as Leysdown or Sutton Vallance, or perhaps Wateringbury. One could rest and have refreshments, probably a picnic and perhaps a game of cricket, arrive home late in the day, tired after a thoroughly enjoyable day. I remember that Mr Sage once told me he was returning from the Isle of Sheppey in a bad fog. He could hardly see the two back horses, let alone the two front ones so he gave the horses the reins and they brought him home across the marshes with dykes on either side of the road. The horses knew and perhaps could see better'.* (70)

In the capable hands of Ernest and Edwin Sage the vehicle hire business thrived. In 1907 they took over Messer's Ongley & Sons' bus and carrier business which ran from Sittingbourne to Maidstone and by 1912 could offer the public outings in motor buses.(N01)

It was during 1911 that the Sages' decision was made to leave the Plough. Edwin, Elizabeth and the four children were to move to Crescent Street and this was announced in the local paper in December 1912: *'E & E Sage are moving from the Plough Inn to Crescent Street phone number 69'.* There they continued their job-master and motor engineer services for many years. Edwin died in 1935 and Ernest in 1944 aged 77.

George and Rebecca Datson

It is likely that George Datson took on the Plough when the Sages left. We know he was here by 1915. We learn from the 1911 census that he was a mariner, captain of the sailing barge 'Hope', a Milton man then in his forties with wife Rebecca and daughter Jessie.

During the First World War the Plough was required to provide stabling for ten horses of 8th Battalion, Northants Regiment. Later on the stables were converted into garages some of which were rented to neighbours such as Jack Brett, the jeweller, who kept an ancient Rolls Royce there.(87)

George Datson died in 1935 aged 69, Rebecca continued on at the Plough and still lived there in 1947.(115) The Sage family retained some involvement with the premises for Herbert Sage was running a haulage contractors business there in 1938.

Invoice from J. H. Sage operating from 58 East Street in 1940 as haulage contractor, furniture remover, car hire, garage and repairs

Frank and Bess Raffe, licensees of the Plough Inn, in 1958 (EKG)
Behind them are antique wine barrels (out of sight) which Frank refused to sell to a film producer

The millennium found The Plough run-down and empty. Having heard of proposals for its demolition, Michael Peters, as Secretary of the Kent Historic Buildings Committee, made an inspection and was able to confirm that, though much of the interior had undergone successive changes during the long life of the building, the range of rooms at the front on the first floor of the main building seemed to have retained its original form. Remarkably, the roof structure above those rooms, over 300 years old, was intact and in sound condition.

Just before demolition, 2004

Michael lodged an application with English Heritage for the building to be added to the statutory list of buildings of special architectural or historical interest – now called the National Heritage List for England. Sadly the application was rejected but, just before the building was demolished in 2005, Michael invited Alan Abbey to lead a team to survey the building for Sittingbourne Heritage Museum.

They made an exciting discovery under the floorboards. It was a large cache of 17th century clothing. It is considered to be the best (and, according to some experts, the most ancient) find of its kind ever discovered in England. The collection is displayed at the museum.

This corset, found concealed in the Plough, seen here exhibited at the Ashmolean Museum in 2018, is from about 1630

The site is now occupied by Plough Court – a development of 14 flats arranged in two buildings – one on the East Street frontage, one at the back, fronting Fairview Road, separated by an open space – a central courtyard. The developers were Propan Homes of Sevenoaks.

The front elevation is in two parts – apparently the aim being to recreate the historic appearance of the street – a frontage of separate dwellings. This block is another example of a tendency in our town centre to copy past styles when constructing new buildings on sites that have been cleared of authentic old buildings. The new ones are not always architecturally inferior to what was there before.

As can be seen from the picture, the larger part of the façade is Victorian style – masquerading as a pair of substantial mid-19th century three-storey houses, coated in pale cement stucco, with double-hung sliding sashes. There are three triples and two singles, complete with horns to each end of the bottom rails of the upper sashes – a style-feature of the period. Some readers might be interested to know that horns were added to prevent the upper sash being lowered to the cill, where it could be difficult to slide up again separately from the lower one. There are two doors, each with six panels, a letter-slot and knocker. Doubtless to avoid encroachment onto the pavement, their entrance steps are all but eliminated, creating a dangerous hazard, were these doors ever to be used – hardly likely given that these twin elevations mask far more than two dwellings. It appears that the doors are there simply for decoration. At eaves level, a shelf-like projection is provided, emphasising the difference in scale of this part of the frontage from the remainder of the front.

With good architectural manners, the remainder of the front resembles the front of the block of flats next door – where two small houses – numbers 54-56 East Street – used to be. This style, is rather simpler than the stucco design and from an earlier period. Known loosely as Georgian, it was fashionable in Britain during the 18th and early 19th centuries, during four successive reigns of Hanoverian monarchs, all named George. Here the appearance of the front, like the block at 54-56, is of one single dwelling – also three-storey – the policy of the developers being to maximise the number of dwellings on the site.

Dormer windows have been provided on the top-floor and double-hung sliding sashes below, with a single six-panel door, complete with letter-slot and knocker – and another hazard step. Apparently it is a fake like the other pair of doors on this frontage.

The real street-entrance to the block is the gated alley-tunnel between the two parts of the frontage.

Plough Court – These flats have replaced the old Plough Inn (AJW)

Numbers 60, 62, 64, 66, 68, The Old Oak

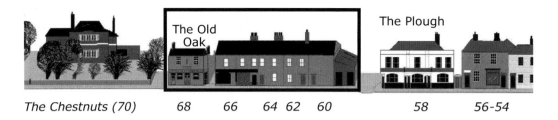

The Chestnuts (70)   68   66   64 62   60   58   56-54

Canon Scott Robertson refers to one house that stood here between the Plough and the alley flanking what, in our time, was the Old Oak public house – see below.(62) The house to which he refers was probably that which, in 1840, appeared on the tithe schedule map as parcel 176 – being the most substantial in that row. In 1840 it was in the hands of Edward Hogwood. By 1865/6 (the Ordnance Survey plan tells us) this house had been divided – numbers 64 & 66. Not long after that, the present buildings on that site were constructed.

Before 1742 Thomas Homan sold it to John Johnson, whose widow sold it to Peter Reason. The next owner recorded here is John Porter, whose heiress, Elizabeth Porter conveyed it to Bryan Faussett – a name which crops up elsewhere in this series – notably at 26 High Street in HSII. In 1811, George Monk Tracey lived there – perhaps as tenant. Lawyer Faussett's daughter, Mrs Hasleden, sold it to Mr Hogwood.

Next door, on plots 174-5, the 1840 tithe map shows here, on the corner beside the yard of the Plough public house, two cottages, (later numbers 60 and 62) This site now has part of a block of eight flats (nos. 60-66) constructed in the 1990s (N01)

In 1840, the corner site at the east end of this row, beside the alley, was occupied by a single building occupied in two parts. In the 1860s, the census and the Ordnance Survey plan tell us that the two parts had been combined and, by the end of that decade, it had opened its doors as a beer-house called the 'Old Oak'. As far as we can tell, much of the old structure is still there but around 1900 reconstruction seems to have taken place at the front of the building and, at about the same time, a two-storey structure was added at the back.

60 and 62 East Street

The 1840 tithe map depicts the cottages beside the Plough as very small (numbers 174 and 175). They were occupied then by James Fry and Sarah Hogwood. Mrs Hogwood, a widow, is identified in a deed dated June 1878 referring to the marriage in that month between Sarah Ann Hogwood and one Henry Pell of Chartham near Canterbury. We write more about them when considering numbers 110-118 East Street. The freehold of numbers 60-62 and the larger house next-door had been acquired in 1837 by Edward Hogwood a Sittingbourne man, who owned a number of properties in the district.

In 1841 the census tells us that these premises at 60/62 were occupied by Harriet Keeler and her sister Ann.(5) By 1851 Harriet had moved to the High Street and was running a grocery with her niece. In 1851 it was George Eley, a mariner, from London, who rented one of the cottages with his wife and two children whilst, in the other one, lived one of the many members of the East

Street Snelling family – Benjamin, a bricklayer with his son and daughter in law and two younger children. By 1861 these Snellings had moved within the town to Railway Terrace.

In 1861 William Hucksted an agricultural engine driver lived at number 60, one of the pair of cottages beside the Plough, with his wife and family. He was foreman for S. Shrubsole who announced in 1856 via the local press that William Hucksted could take orders for the hire of new Clayton, Shuttleworth & Co.'s improved steam threshing machine as well as new improved drills.

The Jarvis family were the next inhabitants of number 60 and then for many years the house was filled with hats; hats being made, hats being repaired and hats being trimmed, for from the 1860s to the 1890s this was the home and workplace of the Jarvis family. Sarah Jarvis was a Sittingbourne woman who had lived with her husband George, a whitesmith, in the High Street in 1861. By 1866 they had moved to number 60 East Street where she advertised her skills as a straw-bonnet maker. Sarah described herself as a milliner for the 1871 census return and she had trained her daughter Emma who was 16 by then, to help her in the business. Sarah died during the 1870s but Emma continued to make hats. In 1894 she was still advertising her skills as 'Miss Jarvis, straw hat and bonnet maker. Hats cleaned, dyed, altered and feathers curled.'

Nevertheless she was making life-changing plans at that time for during 1895 she took the bold step of emigrating to Canada, aged 40, where she was soon married to a Charles Burrows.(111)

Emma's father, George Jarvis, was a whitesmith; this meant he worked with tin and made household utensils.

In 1890 he went into partnership with George Brown another whitesmith who lived in Berry Street. They advertised that year that they could hang bells and change locks.(36) Then in 1891 came this announcement in the local paper:

'G. Jarvis & G. Brown are starting shop as whitesmiths, bell hangers, locksmiths, and workers in iron. They have both worked for Mr White, ironmonger, for many years'.

Mr White was Richard White of 28, High Street who had a long-established ironmongery.(HSII)

By 1901 the Jarvis family had left number 60 and Sydney Brown had moved in with his wife Susan and six children. Perhaps he was related to George Brown though he was not his son (George did have a son named Sydney but he was much younger). Sydney of 60 East Street was a sail-maker who had been born in Milton.

At that time number 60 was by no means the most salubrious spot to live in East Street, for squeezed in between the Plough and number 60 were public conveniences, which, for the inhabitants of number 60, were definitely an odorous inconvenience. Probably it was the Brown family who organised a petition to the council to have those toilets closed in 1909 as a menace to public health. The petition did not succeed and the toilets were still causing problems in 1958 when they were vandalised.(80) They remained until at least the late 1970s. Hopefully this long-standing health hazard was not responsible for the early deaths of Mr & Mrs Brown: Sydney died in 1914 aged only 47 and a year later Susan followed him to the grave aged 49.

By 1922 the council water inspector, Albert John Kenwood had moved in and no doubt the public toilets were well kept whilst he lived next to them.(115)

The later inhabitants of number 60 that we know of are listed here:

1933	Alfred and Lydia Dickinson	
1935	J. Adams	motor engineer
1939	William Daynes	
1945-1951	Eva and Thomas Daynes	
1956	Robin Daynes	

In 1949 the council served statutory notice on Mr Hugh Wynn Turner to improve the drainage as it was in a state 'injurious to health'.(80) Mr Turner (principal of A J Turner & Son, auctioneers and estate agents, 2 Park Road) was the managing agent for the owner. In that role, as agent rather than owner, the law made him liable to receive such notices because, as 'person in control of the premises' he received the rent from the tenant.

The Goad map of 1968 gives no names as occupiers of 60 and 62 (and 64) implying they may well have been demolished by then and the blank space is still recorded 18 years later.

We do know that the building stood empty long before it was demolished. By 1987 the present block of eight flats had been built.(121)

The modern 60-64 in October 2018 (MHP)

The women of number 62

In 1861 Sarah Terry from Bapchild and her daughter, Sarah junior, lived at number 62 which as we have noted was by then one of a new pair of cottages. Sarah, who luckily had an annuity to live on, was still here ten years later, by which time she was 81. Sarah junior was still with her and they had been joined by old Sarah's son, his wife and child. Old Sarah lived on until 1875.

We have already met the next occupant of the house for she used to live at number 60. This was Mrs Harriet Keeler, a widowed, elderly tea-dealer from Maidstone, whose home was shared with nieces and a nephew. It was still a private house without shop front, where those who wished to purchase a little tea could knock and ask.

Harriet and her unusually-named husband, Adman, (whose first name is perhaps derived from the Anglo Saxon word meaning 'noble protector' – a person of military status) had formerly run a grocery shop on the south side of the High Street. Adman died in the late 1860s leaving Harriet £200. She lived on until 1890 when she died aged 85. Her unmarried niece Ann Austin continued to live at number 62 a while longer. She was a dressmaker.

The Gandon family at 62

By the time the Ganden family moved in it had been quite some years since there had been any children in the house. William Gandon (spelt Ganden in some records) was recorded in the 1901 census as a coal-heaver from Tong. He was married and he and his wife had been blessed with six children whose ages ranged from 20 to four. The eldest son worked with his father delivering coal. Somehow the Gandons found house-room for two adult nephews who were carters and no doubt made a useful contribution to the household budget. It is doubtful whether the house had ever been more crowded for the 1911 census return reveals that there were only five rooms.

At night a Gandon or two must have slept in every room. As he got older, coal heaving must inevitably have become harder and by 1911 William had found less strenuous work as a 'water-fitter's labourer' which involved helping a plumber fit pipework to houses so that they had their own water supply. William Gandon lived on until 1923 when he died aged 70. His wife Charlotte then took in lodgers to make ends meet: '1924 Board and lodgings for working men number 62 East Street'.

A year later Charlotte decided to aim for more refined lodgers: *Bed sitting rooms to let with board suit two gentlemen, apply 62 East Street.*

Charlotte survived until 1935 but she had left East Street before then, no doubt to live with one of her children.

These are the later occupiers of number 62 that we know of:

1933	Frank Simmons
1945	Kathleen Dormedy
1947-1956	Bernard and Myra Law

64/66 East Street

As reported previously, the 1840 tithe map shows that a much larger house than 60/62 on this spot belonging to Edward Hogwood. The house is numbered 176 on the map and, in that year, it was occupied by Mrs Frances Bunyard, who, in the 1878 marriage deed, to which we have referred previously, is identified as a widow. The 1841 census return records that the tenant was James Bradly who ran a grocery here with his wife Margaret and four children. With them lived old Lucy Hogwood obviously related to Edward the owner. Lucy died in 1847.

The house still boasted a shop in 1851 when Thomas Henham from Teston lived here with his wife Jane and children. Thomas was a gunsmith and cutler and the family remained here for many We can see from the 1861 census return that Thomas Henham junior was working with his father who had trained him as a gunsmith too but by 1866 young Thomas had branched out into butchery and opened a shop at 53 High Street.(HSI)

The Ordnance Survey map dated 1865/6 map shows The Plough (parcel 152) with 60-62 next door

Old Tom died in 1868 in his seventies. Widowed Jane then took on number 66 whilst remaining living at 64 and became a lodging house keeper. The 1874 directory shows that she also kept the shop at 64 open as a butcher's shop. Her task was not too onerous as she had the help of her unmarried daughter Jane and they only had three elderly ladies lodging with them.(8)

By 1881 old Jane and her daughter lived in quiet retirement at number 64. Old Jane moved across the road in her last years to number 97, outlived her daughter, and died in 1892 in her nineties.

By 1890 Jane Henham junior had left number 64 and it was the home of Mrs Emma Sharp who took in laundry.(36) Emma's husband was not at home on census night 1891; very likely he was a mariner. As for Emma herself, her life had begun 50 years previously in Somerset. In the East Street cottage she had the company of a live-in servant who no doubt was kept constantly busy helping with the washing.

By 1896 Stephen Moys a gas and water fitter lived and had his business at number 64 and was here until 1903.

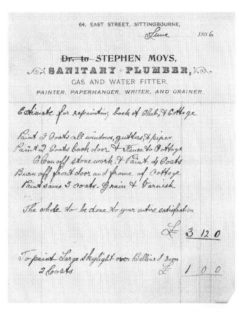

An 1896 invoice from plumber Stephen Moys who lived at number 64

Stephen also undertook painting and decorating as we can see from the invoice. He was a married man from Canterbury and he and his wife Edith had four children.(11)

The table shows some later inhabitants of number 64 when it was residential with six rooms. The dates given here not certain – these people lived in the house, but they may have arrived sooner or left later.

1903-1926	Charles Stanley	road foreman
1926	Thomas Wallace	
1945-1963	Beatrice Mills	

The Williams family at number 66

Amy Williams was a widow in her forties when the 1891 census return was taken. Living with her at number 66 and helping to run the drapery and china shop were her eldest two daughters. One son worked as a bricklayer's apprentice whilst the remaining four offspring were too young to be of much help. *"Mrs Williams, mother of the outfitter, had the same premises now held by her son. It was then a toy and fancy shop"* said Matthews of number 66 in the 1880s.(69)

Amy Williams' husband Henry had been a mariner and died in his forties in 1881 leaving Amy at their home in Charlotte Street with nine children to support.(9) Luckily the eldest were of an age when they could earn something and Mrs Williams was clearly a resourceful woman. Born in Bredgar, she had the example before her of her own mother, who similarly widowed, had run a grocery shop on the London Road.

Amy Williams' eldest daughter Ada died in 1895 aged only 29 after years of assisting her mother in the shop.(N01) This was when Amy handed the shop over to her eldest son Harry who was married with a young family, and retired to the comfort of 65 Park Road with four of her children.

Harry placed an advertisement in the local paper:

'1895 14th September Special Notice - Harry Williams, begs to announce he will on Saturday 14th September open the premises at 66 East Street, as a gentlemen's hosier and hatter. All goods cash only.'

Harry and his wife Annie were still running the shop and living at number 66 in 1930.

Percy Norris and the Plaza Café

By 1933 there were at last new occupants at number 66 and the Williams family had gone. Percy W. Norris and his wife Mabel had moved in and were converting the shop to a café. The council gave Mr Norris permission to add a projecting sign to the front of the building in 1933. The Plaza Cinema had opened a few doors away in 1910 and so Plaza Café was an ideal name for the establishment. The Norrises were followed in 1948 by a Mr G. Howell.

The Plaza Café in 1961 (EKG)

In the 1970s it was run by Mr and Mrs Carl. It continued to be the Plaza Café in 1991.

By 1995 there had been a change of occupancy and the Plaza Café was no more. 'Peter's' fried fish was the new name, though who 'Peter' was, we do not know. Elvyn & Maurice Back lived here and ran the fish shop; perhaps it was they who, a couple of years later, gave it a new name: by 1997 it was the plain 'East Street Fried Fish Shop'.

Number 66 in later years

In 2005, 'Sittingbourne Fried Chicken and Kebab' was trading at number 66 but in 2008 work began to split the premises into two shops. In 2009, the eastern side next to the Old Oak was trading as 'Sittingbourne Kebab and Pizza' numbered 66. Since 2018 the owner has been A. Celebi.

At the western end, now numbered 66a, we had 'Starz Tailors'. The tailors had closed by 2010 and in May of that year 66a at the west end had become 'Kent 7 – Gentlemen's Barber', which by 2018 had become 'K7 Barber'.

Starz Tailors at 64 East Street in 2009 (CA)

66 (left) and 66a – K7 Barber in 2019 (AJW)

The 1909 Ordnance Survey map for this section of the street with The Plough labelled PH on the left. The Old Oak, at that time, seemingly did not merit the same designation. Probably it still had a restricted licence defining it as merely a 'beer-house'. Comparison with the Ordnance Survey map dated 1865/6 displayed previously indicates the additions that have been made at the back. The 1957/1960 map seems to show the present outline of the building. Note also that the archway at number 66 has been filled-in and the building enlarged overall.

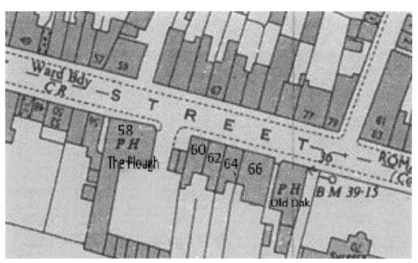

The 1960 Ordnance Survey map with numbers 60 to 66 in the centre – numbered by us for clarity. Note also the changes to the small building at the entrance to the Plough Yard the public 'convenience' which caused so much fuss and bother – see above.

68 – The Old Oak Inn

The Old Oak, 1940s

The Old Oak opened at number 68 under a beer-house licence some time between 1868 and 1870. It closed for the last time in 2013, when it was auctioned.

It still stands today but has been converted into flats. For comment on the name & other history see T*he Inns, Taverns & Public Houses of Sittingbourne & District.*(77)

The passageway on the eastern side of the building helps to identify it on the various old maps.

As mentioned already, we believe that different sections of this building date from different periods. The front appears to have been substantially remodelled around 1900. The main back addition is thought to date from about the same time but the sections in between appear to be rather older. The building as extant is almost certainly the structure that was described in the 1911 census return as having seven rooms.

The tithe schedule in 1840 described it as a house and garden in two parts. At that time it was owned by an elderly coach-maker named John Maplesden, was living in the western end. The eastern part was occupied by his tenant Margaret Brenchley. John Maplesden was already a widower in 1841 and retired to live with his son Richard a Rochester baker.(6) John died there in 1855 in his eighties. By 1841 Margaret Brenchley had been followed here by old widowed Susanna Blake, her two daughters and a servant.(N03) Ten years later, the two halves of the house were the home of the Chapman brothers, Thomas and William, blacksmiths from Lenham in their thirties, both of whom were married with children. No doubt they had come to Sittingbourne because of its position on the London to Dover Road and soon brother William moved just down the road, to number 34, and worked in the yard behind number 15.

Brother Thomas was a lively character who also soon moved a few doors down the road but, in his case, it was to run the Wheatsheaf public house. (for much more about Thomas Chapman see the Wheatsheaf).

In 1861 the census recorded a young sawyer, Frank Bird living with his wife and children in what was probably both parts of the house.

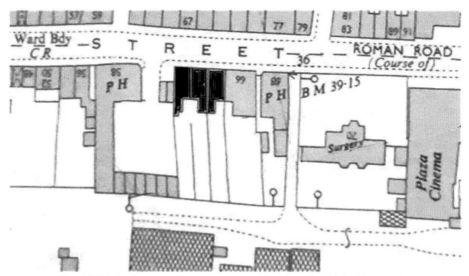

The 1960 Ordnance Survey map with 60, 62, 64 in the centre

The Old Oak at old number 68

The use of the building as a beer-house began not long after that – shortly before 1870.

The licensees of the Old Oak changed frequently in the early years suggesting that they found it hard to make a satisfactory living here in between the long-established Plough and Wheatsheaf.

1871	Thomas Brown
1874	William Chapman
1878	George Goldfinch
1881	George Kite
1885	R. Sage
1887	George Norman

It seems very likely that the William Chapman who was the licensee in 1874 was William the blacksmith, whom we have met here already.

When we look at 1891 we find that the next publican, George Gilbert Coleman, described himself as both 'beer seller & shipwright' showing that he needed two incomes. He and his wife had two boarders lodging with them.

In July 1894 there appeared in the local paper a report on a sale of the premises by auction – on instructions from the trustees of James Taylor the deceased owner. The report tells us that *'The beerhouse is a small one'* – suggesting that the sale took place before the reconstruction of the large back addition and the reconstruction at the front. It contained 11 rooms – four more than those counted in the census of 1911 but the room-count in that census specifically ignored such rooms as a 'scullery, closet, bathroom, warehouse, office or shop'.(N01)

The 'Old Oak beer-house and premises' was 'occupying a capital position in a popular neighbourhood at East Street.' The report continues *'This house was also licensed prior to 1869'.* However, we have no evidence that it was licensed at an earlier date.

> *'....bidding started at £450 and rose at such a rate that eventually the property was sold for no less than £1,700, the purchaser being a local brewer. One commentator stated it is a long time since such a good price has been secured for similar property in Kent'.*(N01)

The premises were sold whilst George Coleman was licensee – he was retained by the brewery and stayed until 1900. Perhaps it was then that the old building was restructured.

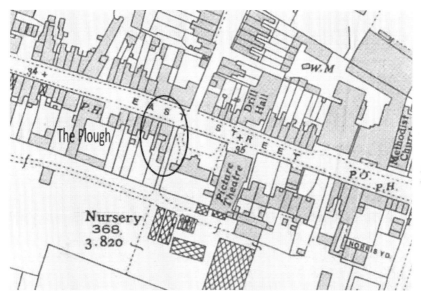

1938 Ordnance Survey map with Plough on left. The position of the Old Oak is indicated

The Argent family at the Old Oak

Samuel James Argent, a young man from Sheerness, was running the Old Oak with his wife Alice by 1900. They were still there ten years later when the number of rooms in the building were recorded – there were seven rooms providing further proof that this was the present building.(12)

The Argents had just two children and seemed only to take in two lodgers. Directories record that Samuel ran the pub until his untimely death aged 52 in 1925. Alice, his wife, had already died two years earlier.(110) Their daughter, Alice, aged 24, who had doubtless long assisted her father behind the bar, was granted the licence to continue. Alice had been born in 1901, her parents were patriots and commemorated the British victory at Pretoria by having their daughter christened Alice Maud Pretoria Argent under which splendid name she ran the pub until 1926. Alice had married Albert Cox in 1923 but directories show that she retained her maiden name – at the Old Oak she was Mrs Alice Maud Argent.(52)

Alice's only brother Samuel Sidney Argent then had the licence for a few years but a new family had arrived at the Old Oak by 1930.(54)

Albert and Audrey McCartney

Albert and Audrey McCartney then moved into the Old Oak still owned by the brewers Frederick Leney & Sons.(105)

A considerable robbery occurred at the pub in 1948. Somebody must have found out that the McCartneys kept their life savings in their bedroom and £3,500 was stolen. (*Dundee Courier – Monday 11th October 1948*)

Some of the more recent licensees were:

1951	Dorothy & Leonard Colchin
1960	Alfred & Ena Court
1963	F.S. Bucknell
1980	Derek & Edna Lee

We know that during the 1960s the regulars of the Old Oak had their own football team.(N01)

The Old Oak football team presented three cheques at the Old Oak public house to the Kent Association for the Blind, the Medway Old People's Welfare and the Friends of the Sittingbourne Hospitals, June 1966 (EKG)

Rod Nicholls and his wife Rita became licensees in 1980 and were still there in 2002. They gave the pub an excellent reputation for serving Real Ale and home cooked food.

Originally the pub's sign showed an old oak tree but, around 1980, Whitbread, the brewers who owned it by then, changed it to a picture of the rotting hulk of an old ship on the seashore. In its final years a new sign showed an old oak tree once again. Last orders were called in 2013 and the pub has now been converted into flats.

On the front elevation, there remains one reminder that this building used to be a public house: on the entrance door near the alley, there is a small brass plate about four inches wide bearing the single word 'Bar'.

The Old Oak, was renovated in 2008, this picture taken in 2011 (CA)

After conversion to residential use, 2018 (MHP)

Numbers 70-82 East Street
The French Houses and The Chestnuts

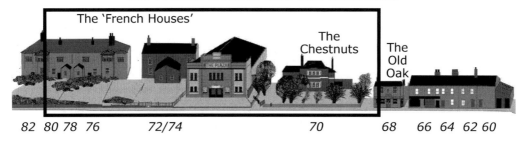

As long as anyone can remember, the doctors' surgery, known as 'The Chestnuts', number 70 East Street and some smaller houses, numbering 74-82, which once stood nearby, were known collectively as 'the French Houses.' Nobody seems to know why, but in recent years, it has been suggested that they might have been built or occupied by Huguenots – Protestant refugees from France, thousands of whom took refuge in this country, to escape religious persecution in their homeland. However, this cannot be – the Huguenot refugees came to England largely in the late 17th century and the early 18th.

These houses were built more than 100 years after the main Huguenot influx, by which time, following the French revolution of 1789, there was religious toleration in France offering Huguenots full freedom to worship in the way they chose.

Another theory put forward is that these houses might have been constructed by, or to accommodate, French refugees of a different kind: those who fled from the repercussions of the Revolution and the Napoleonic wars.

The only records of the early years of these houses of which we are aware, provide no basis whatever for such notions and we consider it far more likely that the name given to these houses derives, not from their builders, or their occupiers, but from their architectural style. As can be seen in the following pictures, the principal front windows on number 70 are ornate, latticed casements of a particular kind and every house in this row had particularly deep, projecting eaves below roofs of a distinctive low pitch. Such features were fashionable around the time that these houses were built - the period of the Regency 1811-1820. Often described as *'cottage orné'* this style of architecture is said by some to have derived from the paintings of some 18th century French artists. Maybe the use of this 'posh' French phrase describing these houses gave rise to their association with our Gallic neighbours.

If our readers are unconvinced by this suggestion, we at the museum shall be pleased to hear of any relevant facts or records – or alternative theories – which could be mentioned in subsequent editions of this book.

Number 70 East Street – The Chestnuts
In 1812 Mr John Leach, a businessman from Boughton, purchased a plot of land beside the Wesleyan School from the trustees with a frontage to the street. He complemented this by acquiring an adjacent strip of land from farmers Michael Eaton and John Hedgecock whose orchard occupied the area behind the school field. Leach then had a large detached house constructed in a fashionable style. which was completed a year later. The architectural design was most unusual – perhaps unique – in the area, and set back a fair way from the street.

John Leach never lived in the completed building, but sold it to two local men Thomas Alexander (who had been born in Strood) and William Walker Bentham. The new owners immediately rented out the house to Mrs Susanna Blake, the widow of a Captain William Blake formerly of Lymington, and her daughter, also named Susanna. The two women lived comfortably with three female servants. (5) Mrs Blake was a wealthy woman who drew up a long and complex will in which she made it clear that her daughter could stay in the house for a year after her death, inheriting all her mother's jewellery, books, plate and linen. There was a sum of £3,000 to be invested too and then the income from it would be divided between Mrs Blake's other children. The will was witnessed by the two Sittingbourne surgeons, Dr John Grayling and Dr William Castle, who were already attending Mrs Blake in her illness when she made the will four years before her death in 1846.(HSI)

The Chestnuts in 2019 (AJW)

For the next nine years after Susanna Blake's death, the house was inhabited by its owner Thomas Alexander and his family. They had returned from Port Louis, Mauritius where Mr Alexander had worked for the government as a munitions officer. The 1851 census return recorded Thomas at number 70 as *'late storekeeper civil department HM Ordnance in the Mauritius superannuated'*. He lived here with his wife Grace, four daughters and two servants.

However on his death in 1854, with her income reduced, widowed Grace decided to sell the house and move away. Surprisingly it was not purchased by a member of the gentry but by John Burton, the blacksmith from number 26, for £470. Despite owning the property for the next 70 years it appears that no members of the Burton family ever took up residence in the building but instead rented it out.

Tenants included Reverend Henry Lodington the retired curate of Graveney, a single man with three servants in the 1860s and William Francis Drake a brick merchant from Aylesford and his family during the 1880s. The name 'The Chestnuts' had been given by 1884 due to the two large chestnut trees in the grounds.(N01)

When in 1889 John Burton's widow Mary let the premises to Dr Robert Maxwell Boodle a surgeon and GP she had made a decision which permanently affected the fate of the building. Dr Boodle moved in with his father Dr Robert Hockin Boodle who was a retired surgeon. Young Dr Boodle turned the ground floor into a surgery where family medicine was practised as it has been ever since. Old Dr Boodle died here in 1895; Dr Boodle junior married Mrs Lucy Eliza Paine in London in 1898 and she moved in with her young daughter Gladys.(9)

Dr R M Boodle, his wife and step-daughter in the garden about 1907 (MHP)

The Boodles were prominent members of the local community over the next 21 years and leading members of the temperance movement in the town. Dr Boodle was also a key figure in the development of the first swimming pool in the town funded by local businessman Frank Lloyd; he served on the Urban District Council for a number of years.

Dr Boodle provided care for much of the east end of town and this included many of the brick workers who lived and worked in Murston. He had built up a loyal following of patients during his time in the town. All health services prior to the 1911 Medical Insurance Act were purely private with all medical contacts demanding a fee.

In 1907 Dr Boodle sold the practice to Dr John Sawers Clark, a young Scottish doctor recently qualified from Edinburgh University. The Boodles moved away to Caversham in Reading in 1909 where Boodle continued to practice.

Dr Clark rented the premises from Mary Burton who still owned the property, for a fee of £44 per annum. The agreement continued throughout the period of the First World War until 1925 when Dr Clark finally purchased the building for the sum of £1,075 and named it 'The Chestnut Surgery'.

Early in his time in Sittingbourne Dr Clark invited his brother-in-law Dr James Crerar down from his native Ayrshire to share the expanding workload. The two doctors practiced in different parts of the town, with Dr Crerar living and working out of a large house near Milton High Street called Blair Park (now a care home). Both were extremely popular practitioners and continued working until Dr Sawers Clark retired in 1935 as his health started to fail and Dr Crerar worked until his death in 1948.

However the surgery continued to prosper as in September 1935 Dr Clark sold the practice to a Dr George Llewelyn Smith for the sum of £2,000.

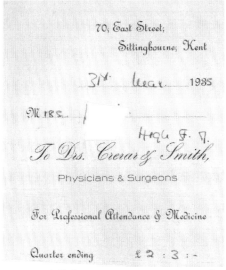

1935 bill from Doctors Crerar and Llewelyn Smith

Dr Llewelyn Smith

This ambitious young man expanded the practice further in 1938 by employing a local recently qualified doctor from St Barts Medical School in London to share the added burden. This new partner in the practice was Dr Raymond Birch. Tragedy was to befall the surgery in the early war years with the untimely death of Dr Smith, who died in a motoring accident along with his good friend and fellow GP colleague from a neighbouring practice Dr Francis Ind (HSI).

Both young doctors died instantly after colliding with a concrete bollard as part of a wartime road block on the Thanet Way (A299).

Doctors Crerar and Birch with the help of several local doctors managed the health of the patients for the remainder of the war years. Dr Birch was the Medical Officer to the Sittingbourne Home Guard. He had contracted TB just after qualifying as a doctor, which put an end to his chances of enlistment to the front line.

In March 1941 Dr Birch leased the building for a period of 21 years. He had the option in the first seven years to purchase the property for £2,000. It was on 17th September 1945 that Dr Birch took up that option of purchasing the surgery.

Dr Birch in Home Guard uniform

Number 70 East Street continued to serve both as a family home and a doctor's surgery. This state of affairs lasted up until 1952 when the Birch family moved out to live in Bredgar. By this time the partnership had further expanded to four doctors, and each of the partners took an equal financial share in the practice and the building was solely used as a surgery. Whenever a partner retired the new incoming doctor was expected to raise funds to buy out the outgoing partner. This was always a difficult time for a newly qualified doctor often with a new family and a new mortgage having been to new area, and then added financial stress of 'buying in' to the practice. One of the new partners was Dr Mary Budleigh, who was the first full time female GP in Sittingbourne.

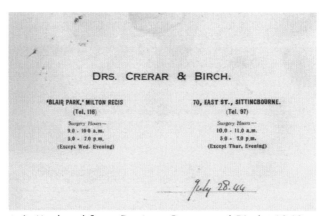

Letterhead from Doctors Crerar and Birch, 1940

In the late 1940s a full time practice manager and fully qualified nurse was employed at the practice. This was quite an innovation at the time since most of the administrative tasks had historically been performed by the GP's wife.

Rear of the building before the 1970s extension

The next major change came in 1970 when the building was becoming too small to accommodate the expanding practice with 10,000 patients and five doctors.

Dr Roy Taylor oversaw the development of five new consulting rooms constructed at the rear of the property. The surgery always tried to keep up with new technology even from the time of Dr Clark who was one of the first GPs to install a telephone. His telephone number was Sittingbourne 97.

Front of the building in the 1970s

The turnover of GPs in the first 125 years at the practice has been low with most GPs retiring after 40 or 50 years of service to the patients of the town. The last four partners doctors Garlant, Thompson, Cantor and Hall giving a combined total of 135 years of service.

Over the last 15 years there have been several plans to move the surgery to more modern purpose-built premises, however none have been successful. It looks as though the surgery will continue at its current site for many years to come with further improvements being made to benefit the patients.

The Chestnuts Surgery in 2018 (MHP)

Number 72 – Wesleyan School and Empire/Plaza Cinema

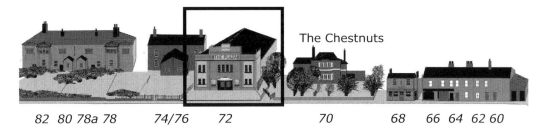

The Chestnuts

82 80 78a 78   74/76   72   70   68   66 64 62 60

A group from the Wesleyan School.
In this photograph we have all the proud children who had gained a medal
Mr Roper is on the left

The Wesleyan School

The school log book which is the basis for most of the material here is in the care of the Kent History & Library Centre.

Methodism, a sect of Protestant Christianity, separated from the Church of England in the 18th century. Its founder was John Wesley. From time to time, sections broke away; some adopted the Methodist title, others called themselves Wesleyans.

The Wesleyan School in East Street was built in 1834 as a Sunday School and enlarged in 1873 to become a day school. It provided 296 places. The enlargement seems to have involved the demolition of a cottage, numbered 72, where in 1871 the census enumerator recorded the occupants as Stephen Robinson a labourer in the cement works and his family.

Towards the end of May 1873 Sittingbourne Wesleyans gathered for the laying of the foundation stone of their new school. The ceremony was performed by a prominent Methodist – William McArthur, MP for Lambeth, an Alderman of the City of London who, seven years later, became Lord Mayor and was honoured with a knighthood.

Lewis Shrubsole, a Faversham builder, was to erect the building from plans by Charles Pillow of Milton. A good start had already been made with the classroom at the rear nearly completed. For several years the Wesleyans had been hiring additional rooms elsewhere, so this work was a necessity. The old schoolroom was 43 feet by 23 feet; this was to be double in size. The new building to the rear would consist of an infant schoolroom 28 feet by 19 on the ground floor, and a male Bible classroom 28 by 17, the upper part divided into five rooms the largest of which was to be used as a female Bible class room.

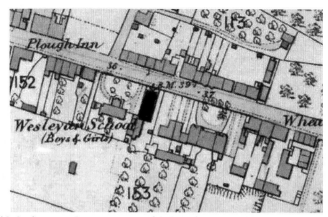

On this 1865/6 Ordnance Survey map the Wesleyan School building is labelled (and shaded solid), on the right of the doctor's surgery with its semi-circular drive on the left of the image.

Reverend James Wray of Kilburn led a procession of ministers, teachers, friends and upwards of 200 children of the Sunday School to the site of the new school. A crowd of onlookers gathered. Hymns were sung and prayers offered. This statement was read out: '*The Sittingbourne Wesleyan Sunday school was commenced by the late Mr John Bate in 1803. The old building was erected in 1804, the present enlargement in 1873, suitable provision being made for both Day and Sunday School.*' Then the paper was placed in a sealed bottle in the cavity of the stone.

John Bate was a local notable who appears repeatedly in this series of histories – see HSI & HSII. He lived at number 38 High Street and was a trustee of the adjacent church. He was also, for a while, tenant of 93 High Street.

During the evening a public meeting was held in the chapel, speeches were made and Wesleyan Schools were compared favourably with Anglican National Schools and British Schools. The Wesleyan Conference of 1841 had established a committee on education and pressed on with establishing Wesleyan Schools which were open to all children, Methodist or not, but each teacher had to be a Methodist recommended by a minister. By 1857 there were over 400 schools and of course far far more Sunday Schools.

Autumn 1873 found the local paper reporting that special services were held for the Wesleyan Schools opening and collections made for the building fund. It described developments: '*The hall of the building immediately facing the street viz the old schoolroom, enlarged to double its size, is 43 by 46 feet it will seat between 400 and 500 and is we believe the largest room in town. Then there is a classroom and the third room is the boiler house with two coppers fitted up for endless supply of hot water for the gigantic tea parties often held. Water is laid on from the public main. The Wesleyans have taken on a heavy responsibility.*'

On 5th January 1874 the Wesleyan School opened its doors for the first time and 132 children poured in to be educated by the young but fully qualified teacher William Henry Roper from Blankney, Lincolnshire. William Roper had trained at the Methodist Westminster College London. This was not his first post for he had taught for two years in Devon before arriving, but here he was in charge of a large new school at the age of 25. It was he who kept the log book from which we learn a good deal about the school and of Roper himself who was to stay here for all the rest of his working life, seeing generations of children pass through the school. He was in fact to be the only head that the school ever had.

Young Roper was keen and able and had soon fashioned a good school which consistently pleased the inspectors who visited. In the first week he noted: *'The greater part of the children are unable to do anything but read and most have been to dame or private schools.'* A dame school was one for very young children run by a single lady, sometimes with help, usually in her own home. (See Twyford School, 1 Crescent Street – HSII) Though widespread for hundreds of years, Britain's dame schools, like many other established institutions, seem to have died out in the mid-20th century. Michael Peters, one of our contributors, believes that he was among the last of Sittingbourne's children to have started their schooling in such a place. In the sitting-rooms at 58 Park Road, the 'Fröbelian School' run, single-handed, by Kathleen Howard (whose husband Jim taught French at Borden Grammar School) Michael was taught basic subjects including arithmetic, geography, history, elementary French, handicrafts and what, in those days, was known as nature-study. Mr Roper would surely have approved.

Back at East Street, the inspector's first report read: *'This is a new school. Mr Roper deserves credit for the results he has already brought about. The children passed a very fair examination and are in good order.'* The following year the discipline and the work were praised again. Mr Roper required his pupils to be clean and had a daily boot inspection, sending children back home to clean them if not satisfactory. He found a few such errands cured them.

Word spread and the second week 176 children came although the desks had not arrived yet. Attendance proved to be irregular at first with the children often kept away and a few children only came for the first week or two, after that they were *'at work or running the streets.'* Within three weeks the desks, copy books and reading books had been delivered and Mr Roper had created order assisted by his pupil-teachers and a monitor. As he wrote: *'This week some actual teaching done.'* Roper's own class were always the oldest children and he was soon trying to instruct them in how to add weights and measures. He seemed to have an enthusiasm for giving the children new songs to sing; within months a harmonium was acquired and a globe for geography. Grammar, recitation of poems, drawing and history were all part of the curriculum. Subjects for writing that first year included the 'Manufactories of England' and bees. Drill was soon added to the weekly mix and this was in the capable hands of Sergeant Williams who came in for the purpose. Drill was the Victorian term for physical exercise and involved formal movements all done at the same time by the whole class.

Just now and then you sense in the log book Roper's satisfaction at a job well done. In 1889 he wrote *'The boys were delighted with their drawing lessons which have been beneficial in making their written exercises neat and exact'*. An innovation in the curriculum came in 1904 when, as he wrote: 'Falling into line with other schools a number of the boys and girl visited the swimming baths at fixed times in the week.' The town swimming baths were in the Butts.(HSII) Grubby children could wash there as well as swim.

The school had a committee of managers, who had the same kind of role as school governors do nowadays. They visited regularly to see that all was going smoothly as did the Methodist minister. Committee members included Henry Elfick the High Street draper and Amos Buley the High Street plumber who was the most frequent visitor of the committee for some years.

The first pupil-teachers were William Parham the 15 year old son of a Milton teacher, Frank Datsun also 15 and from Milton and Henry Pavey. Parham passed his exams and stayed on as a teacher. However, years later, in 1882, after insulting Mr Roper in front of all the boys Parham was dismissed by the committee. Henry Pavey had to leave after two years as he could not make the grade.

The school grew rapidly with well over 200 pupils after two years, so an assistant teacher was appointed. Children had to be turned away for the school was full. In July 1878 a new young infant teacher the charmingly named Clara Gosling was appointed. She was but 18 and lodged with Mr Roper and his wife Sophia whom he had married in 1876. Clara remained at the school for six years. There were 270 pupils by 1879 with new children being admitted all year round. Nevertheless the inspector found discipline well maintained.

By 1884 the staff, including pupil teachers, numbered six. Staffing was at times inadequate and when in 1903 Mr Garner the assistant teacher was incapacitated for a few weeks by an accident Mr Roper struggled. He wrote: 'As the staff is too small when all the teachers are present I have had a difficult week.'

In fact the school was becoming overcrowded which caused problems. Inspectors were noting by the end of the 1880s that improvements to the building were required – a proper playground, more toilets, cloakrooms to hang coats. Attendance peaked at 295 in 1884.

As the years went by Mr Roper always recorded when teachers were appointed and when they left. Sometimes he mentioned how well a particular teacher was doing. On just one occasion he wrote severely of how badly one teacher did: 'He is positively useless as a teacher. His services have been very disastrous to the work and discipline of the class.'

A reading of the log book reveals a man who cared about his pupils and did his best for them, In 1902 he wrote: 'This week I have been busy with examination work, so far I have found the lower classes most backward, although the teachers have worked very hard. These are mostly children who came up from the infant department in a very backward condition and I am afraid will be a difficulty throughout each successive class.'

William Roper and his wife Sophia lived just a walk away at 29 Park Road where they raised their four children.

It was a fact of life that there were always some older pupils absent because they were at work. From March to October the boys laboured in the brickfields of Murston. Factory Act legislation allowed them to attend school half time. Mr Roper adjusted the time that the registers were closed in order to mark working boys in, for some could not arrive before 9.30. Other families worked at harvest time and took the children with them to earn their bit. Older girls were kept away to look after their younger siblings whilst their mothers worked in the surrounding orchards.

As with all Kentish schools the summer holidays were timed to coincide with hopping and so commenced toward the end of August with a return date around the last week of September. Often this had to be postponed for it was of little use starting a new term if all the children were still in the hop gardens. Many a year Roper noted with resignation in October that, they had forgotten almost everything they had learned.

Classroom scene from about 1905
It looks as if the walls could have benefited from a lick of paint. How unfortunate that nobody thought to straighten the picture on the wall at the back – perhaps it was knocked by enthusiastic children shuffling into place for the picture.

Other reasons for pupils to be absent came round with the calendar – there was May Day and Guy Fawkes, and each July the fete at Gore Court. The Volunteer Camp at Bobbing each June meant most of the children were away for a day. Gore Court was owned by Sittingbourne's major man of business, George Smeed. When he died in 1881 most of the children missed school to go to his funeral. In 1901 there was a Welcome Home Day for the volunteers who had fought in the Boer War. Annual Sunday School treats were another reason for a day's closure each year when the children were taken on such outings as a train trip to Whitstable. General elections meant a half day closure in order for the school to be used as a polling station. By the 1890s the annual Co-op Festival caused an afternoon's closure too. On 13th July 1900 Roper wrote: '*Closed on Wednesday afternoon as the attendance was so bad. The average for this week has been the lowest of the year, Fruit gardens, orchards and Sunday School treats are the chief causes*'. Nationally the first Empire Day took place in 1902 (on 24th May commemorating the anniversary of the birth of Queen Victoria who had died in the previous year) Mr Roper mentioned it in 1910 when he noted that the children sang patriotic songs and one of the managers presented the eight best behaved children with half a crown each and everyone had the afternoon off.

In later years Mr Roper himself closed the school for an afternoon in August to take a party of the oldest boys to London to see the main sights and go to the zoo.

The schoolroom was used by the Wesleyan community for various fund raising events which were usually held on a Saturday; these might be concerts or sales of work. Much more rarely the children themselves put on a concert. The local paper reported in 1895: 'an attractive entertainment was given by the children of the Wesleyan School at the schoolroom in East Street, on Monday evening. A capital two hours' entertainment was given under direction of Mr W. H. Roper, the headmaster. Proceeds of the entertainment were given to the school fund.'

The poverty of many families affected attendance when the weather was wet, for some children had no shoes good enough to keep the rain out. Inevitably illness meant absences from school and these were serious matters for children then could and did die of scarlet fever and measles. Mr Roper himself became dangerously ill in 1875 (but did not record in the log book what the nature of the illness was). He had to convalesce for six weeks during which time the school was in the hands of the minister and the pupil teachers. Diphtheria was the problem in 1900 with an outbreak in July causing the medical officer to close the school on 26th July. When it re-opened on 13th August Mr Roper found that most parents were not going to send their children back for the ten days before the hopping holiday. In November the diphtheria returned causing a further closure over the winter.

Roper was always ready to devote extra time to slower children in the hope of bringing them on but some defeated his efforts. In 1886 he wrote 'Four children have to leave as to all appearances they have not the slightest capability of learning anything.' At the opposite end of the spectrum two boys passed the entrance examination for Borden Grammar School in 1887.

Roper hardly mentioned the parents, just giving the occasional comment such as 'many of the parents are rough and consequently there is some difficulty in getting order at times.' Once he recorded that a parent would not let his child 'learn such muck as geography.'

More than once as the years went by he would write in December; 'several of the parents out of work and cannot pay the fees.' Parents were still obliged by law to contribute to their children's education. They paid 3d a week for a child or 2d each if they had more than one child at the school.

In 1888 there were 20 cases in the school of chronic irregular attendance but the committee hesitated to prosecute if a child attended half-time. In 1890 there was great distress in the town due to strikes. Roper wrote 'During the past month the school has suffered on account of the strikes of barge men and the lock out of brick makers. Fifty families paid no fees but no children have been refused admission.' The local population was by no means static there was a good deal of moving into the town and moving away again amongst those workers whose lives were precarious. This meant that new children arrived whilst others left throughout the year.

Mr Roper did not record in the log book any instances of caning boys, though he may have used that punishment. He did use the phrase 'severely punished' which might have indicated caning. Truanting was one offence which merited severe punishment. William Bugden and William Goodhew kept truanting and their parents were also fined by the attendance officer. A boy was dismissed for insubordination. In 1887 Roper sent another boy home for his 'defiant attitude' with a letter to the parents that he would not be readmitted without a promise of obedience. No further mention was made. Mr Roper's personality seems to have been enough to quell most bad behaviour and he certainly would not tolerate his staff striking a child. Over the years two were dismissed for this.

The difficulty of running the school in unsuitable premises was noted by the inspector in 1891. He suggested removing the large gallery and placing desks there instead to make more space. Mr Roper noted the problem of doing drill in a playground that was too small making the lesson ineffective. In 1904 the inspector wrote: 'Considering the very awkward and inconvenient premises and somewhat weak staff Mr Roper continues to produce some very creditable results. The tone and discipline is satisfactory.'

A year later Roper again recorded his frustration at staffing levels which made it difficult for him to leave his large class to see how the others were faring: 'The class (his) consists of upwards of 90 children and I am without qualified assistance. The other classes are not quite as large and have good and fairly good assistant teachers.'

In 1899 William Roper completed 25 years as headmaster of the school and a public presentation was made to him of a purse of gold to which many Sittingbourne people had subscribed. The presentation took place in front of a large crowd in the town hall.(N01)

Pupils and teachers of the Wesleyan School, East Street
Some of the boys are wearing medals
Headmaster William Roper is on the left, another teacher on the right

In February 1905 the first Kent Education Committee medals for regular attendance were presented by the managers who felt moved to record the occasion in the log book: 'We the undersigned managers have this day attended the school for the purpose of presenting to 27 successful pupils the medals and certificates awarded to them by KEC for perfect attendance in four cases and regular attendance in 23 others. It has been a most interesting occasion and one to be especially recorded in the history of the school.'

As the years passed by Mr Roper continued to be admired by the inspectors. In 1900 they found the school 'well-ordered and conducted with satisfactory energy and success'. In 1902 the building was improved with a new staircase, new classroom floor and furnished with new desks. Fresh maps were provided for the walls.

The log book finished early in 1910 without mention of the new building to which the school was about to move. Mr Roper's last comment was that he had a bad leg and the doctor had ordered him to rest.

The old school building was then immediately converted for use as the Empire Picture Theatre, later renamed the Plaza.

The Wesleyan School was replaced by the Canterbury Road Council School just up the road, with 410 places, which is still in use today. Mr Roper continued as headmaster in the new building until 1919 when he retired at the age of 70 and was given a silver tea service by the managers. Altogether he had served as headmaster in Sittingbourne for 45 years and was remembered fondly by his old pupils. A number of them had emigrated to all parts of the Empire, and receiving letters from old scholars in far off places was a delight to Mr Roper. (N01)

As well as his hard work at the school Roper, with his strong faith, was always active in the Wesleyan congregation and held every possible office in the circuit over the years including superintendent of the Sunday School.

In old age he suffered from rheumatoid arthritis and could only go out in a wheel-chair, but his mind remained as lively as ever and he lived on until 1932 when he died peacefully in his sleep aged 83 having given a life-time of service to the children of Sittingbourne. A lengthy obituary appeared in the East Kent Gazette as befitted a man who was so well liked and respected in the town. It is worth quoting from it:

'He was a born teacher; he made educational work interesting and attractive, so that the scholars who came under his care found their labours lightened by his effective methods. Mr Roper knew the value of character, and he never lost an opportunity to instil into the minds of his scholars the value of having a good character, the priceless heritage of honour and integrity; in short, Mr Roper laboured throughout his life in moulding true citizens'.

The Empire Picture House

Early in 1910 Sittingbourne Urban District Council discussed the future of the Wesleyan Schools. The clerk had reported that an application had been received from Mr Walter Charles Wilson of the Bull Hotel Tonbridge for a cinematograph licence for the building. The surveyor said he had made an inspection and that Mr Wilson had promised to make the necessary alterations. It was agreed to grant the licence subject to the alterations being carried out to the satisfaction of the surveyor. Successfully converted to a cinema, the old school opened at the end of July as The Empire Picture House.

The cinema, with, in the foreground on the right, the Old Oak and a Maidstone and District bus passing by

Initially the cinema was a success. Mr Wilson owned other cinemas including one in Faversham and employed a resident manager, Mr C. Foster Wicks. The building was given its own generator run from a five hp gas engine and to begin with the seating consisted of crude wooden benches. The floor sloped upwards from the entrance and the screen was on the front wall, behind the ticket office. The cinema's frontage opened directly on to the footpath where cinema-goers had to queue prior to being admitted. With so many people queuing it often blocked the footpath, and at times the road as well. The problem could not be resolved until later rebuilding works took place which set the façade back several feet, thus creating a forecourt where patrons could queue.

A 1912 advertisement

By 1924 The Empire had changed hands and belonged to Hugh Reginald Butler. As well as popular films there were sometimes free promotional events such as the 1925 'cinematograph display and illustrated lecture "Your Chance in Canada" by Major W. H. Hayward. Splendid series of films featuring agriculture, dairying and fruit raising, cattle ranching and mountain scenery.' The intention of this was to inspire people to emigrate.

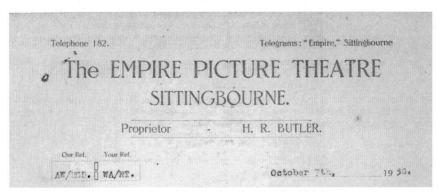

Letterhead from the Empire in 1930

In January of 1925 all records of attendance were broken with 1,100 persons coming on one day.

The Plaza Cinema

The Empire was sold to East Kent Cinemas in 1930 and in 1937 the name was changed to the Plaza. The new owners changed the cinema's frontage to give it a modern 1930s look, the seating capacity was increased to 469, and a ten-feet-deep stage and two dressing rooms were added for live performances.

The Plaza, probably 1937, advertising a film with Greta Nissen – On Secret Service (1933). On the left are the railings along the front garden of one of the 'French houses'

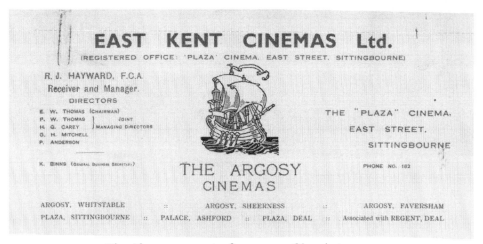

The Plaza was part of a group of local cinemas

Staff at the Plaza Cinema, 1937
Staff l to r: Olga Silburn (Usherette), ?? (cashier), Ken Binns (Manager),
?? (Commissionaire), Susan Caine (Usherette)
Poster advertises William Powell in 'Man Of the World' (1931)
also starred Carole Lombard

The manager was Kenneth Binns. Despite these changes and improvements, the Plaza was never one of Sittingbourne's popular cinemas, not helped perhaps due to it being towards the outskirts of town and the rebranding occurred just as a plush new rival cinema, The Odeon, was opening just further into town. However, location was not the only factor – like the Queens (one of its rivals, located just off the High Street) the old Plaza was avoided by many locals as a 'flea-pit'.

The Plaza, long closed and awaiting demolition, 1972

The cinema closed on 9th August 1952 and it was suggested it could be converted to a sports hall. This did not happen and in 1959 it was purchased by Mr E. G. Pritchard with the idea of converting it into a car showroom. Ernie Pritchard ran two large garages – at Bapchild (on the site now shared by a BP Filling Station and Perry's) and at Chalkwell (on the site now occupied by Tesco Extra – immediately north of Chalkwell Tannery). Mr Pritchard had planning permission but did not carry out the rebuild.(N01) The old cinema gradually became derelict and was sold to the council in 1972. After standing empty and derelict for almost 20 years, it was demolished in 1975 so that houses could be built on the site. The cinema was remembered in the name of the block of flats on the site – Plaza Court. These flats were in turn demolished and replaced with a new Plaza Court some short time after 2010. (You can read more about the cinema and other local cinemas in John Clancy's book *The Long-Gone Cinemas of Kent*).(74)

Residential flats named Plaza Court, built on the site of the old cinema and number 74 pictured here in 2010 (CA)

Plaza Court, new flats built on the site of the old cinema and number 74 replacing the previous flats of the same name (MHP)

Numbers 74, 76, 78, 80, 82 East Street

'The French Houses'

82 80 78a 78   74/76   72

The Yeakell map of 1791 shows that there were no houses as yet here and that the land belonged to one John Gibbons – his was a local family of some prominence, with several property holdings; we encountered them more than once in our study of the High Street.(HSII) However all the properties had been built by 1840 when the tithe map was drawn and we may presume that they were erected around the same time as The Chestnuts, 70 East Street. Notably, all of them had low-pitched roofs and deep over-hanging eaves, fashionable in England in the early 19th century.

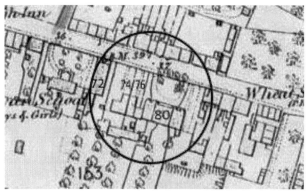

Section of Ordnance Survey map dated 1865/6 showing numbers 78-82 with the forecourt and driveway

Section of 1908/9 Ordnance Survey map showing number 80 divided into two parts, now called 78a and 80

The Ordnance Survey map dated 1865/6 shows 74 and 76 as a pair of semi-detached houses and number 80 dominating the row, with numbers 78 and 82, rather smaller, attached to its flanks. Number 78 was butted onto number 76. Like number 70, numbers 78, 80 and 82 each had a bay window with lattice panes. Set back from the street they had a forecourt, planted with trees and a loop driveway with two entrances.

The 1909 edition of the Ordnance Survey plan shows number 80 divided into two – as described below, when the western section became number 78a – the library of Sittingbourne Co-operative Society sharing the building with living accommodation.

These five houses have long since been demolished and replaced by modern housing which includes some flats.

Number 74 was demolished in the mid-seventies to make way for the first Plaza Court – see below

Numbers 78, 80 and 82 were demolished in the 1970s to make way for the Fairview Road development, where a terrace abuts the East Street frontage.

The last to go was number 76 (see picture below) which was demolished in 2016 and replaced by the present building, completed in 2017.

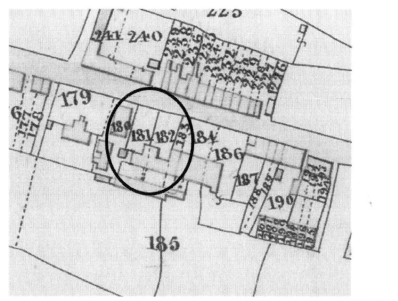

On the tithe map numbers 74 and 76 appear on parcels 181 and 182 attached to number 78 on parcel 183.

Number 74 was owned at that time by John Bate a leading Methodist in the town whom we have come across already in our study of the High Street. The Wesleyan Sunday School, next door, at 72 had also been built on his land.

Though Mr Bate is recorded on the tithe schedule as the occupier in 1840, we cannot be sure that he lived there. Until 1839 he had been living as a tenant in a more substantial property – 93 High Street.(HSI) He owned several premises locally and could have made this one available to an employee or to a short-term tenant, whilst as owner of the freehold, retaining liability for the tithe. (HSII) Quite possibly the tenant in that year was John Peters. In the census of the following year, John (great-great-grandfather of one of our contributors

Michael Peters) was recorded there with his wife and family; they remained for more than a decade.

As mentioned above, Mr Bate's house at 74 East Street was one of a pair. The other one (number 76, parcel 182) was let to Mercy Ann Tonge, who lived in this vicinity for the rest of her days – latterly next door at 78. Mercy was described in the census as an annuitant – indicating that she was blessed with funds of her own. She was probably a member of the wealthy family of the same name – Brewers, Maltsters, Grocers etc, they had substantial property holdings in the town – viz HSI & HSII.

Mercy Ann's landlord was a Michael Eaton, who was recorded in the tithe schedule as owning all the other French Houses (numbers 78, 80 & 82 East Street – parcels 183, 184 and 186). In the tithe schedule Mr Eaton is recorded as occupying what became number 78 East Street, but this small property may not have been his home. Probably, like the adjoining owner Mr Bate, he lived elsewhere and had let number 78 to an employee or a short-term tenant, who did not have to pay the tithe. Number 82 was let to John Mitchell and number 80 let to Mary Hassell together with another house behind it and an orchard of just over an acre (Parcel 185). Mr Eaton also owned three other adjoining orchards extending along the back of East Street – tithe parcels 374, 375 and 434. These seven parcels held by Mr Eaton, were, in our own time, all built on. They now comprise the entire Fairview Road development, including the row of houses at right-angles to East Street, where 78, 80 and 82 used to stand, almost opposite the Aldi supermarket.

Records traced so far about the Eaton family are rather sketchy. In 1804 a Michael Eaton married an Elizabeth Willett at St James's Piccadilly in London. Between 1811 and 1818, Michael & Elizabeth Eaton brought three children (Caroline, Emily & Edwin) to St Michael's Sittingbourne for baptism. In 1819 a Michael Eaton of Sittingbourne (formerly of London) died, making his wife Elizabeth his executor, and, in his will, mentioning his son Michael. The churchwardens' accounts for St Michael's parish church tell us that, in 1839, Michael Eaton owned four properties and some land (presumably the various premises listed above) but, in 1840, the churchwardens tell us that the properties were owned by his heirs rather than Mr Eaton himself. According to the 1841 census return there were no men named Michael Eaton living in Kent then, but probate records tell us that a Michael Eaton 'the elder' of Sittingbourne died in 1836.

Having dredged up these stray facts we set them out for those who might be interested. As we have said more than once in this series, we are happy to leave these genealogical queries for others to pursue.

Our old friend Canon Scott Robertson, writing in the 1870s, tells us that, by 1846, Eaton's land belonged to Maria Downs and John Maplesden. This land not being part of East Street, we have not researched them.

Number 74 East Street
A private home

In 1841, as mentioned already, this seven roomed house was the abode of John Peters, a cab driver in his forties, his wife Sarah, four children and their young lodger Edward Carman the sailmaker of whom we hear so much at number 67. Sarah Peters (née Walter) originated from Marden, but John's family had lived hereabouts for generations. This property is thought to have been the family's first home in Sittingbourne, following their return to this district from Bedfordshire, where John and Sarah had lived since 1822 and where all their four children had been born.

Having been employed as a groom at the Rectory at Barton-le-Clay, it is understood that John, back home in Kent, worked with his younger brother Benjamin, a Van Proprietor, based, from the early 1830s onwards, on the London Road at the far west end of the town – in a house once known as Hillside – now the Beaumont Guest House, 74 London Road. It may interest some readers to note that this house (and the adjacent site now occupied by the Coniston Hotel) stood, at that time, outside Sittingbourne, in the district of Milton, beyond the border that then existed between the two towns. For that reason, Ben's home, though some distance west of Chalkwell Road was identified in the 1851 census as being at 'Chalkwell'.

Pigott's directory entry for 1832 tells us that Ben's van left his house at 8.30 every morning (Sundays excepted)....naturally!(32) Later on, perhaps when John joined the team, Ben's business expanded – a second van was provided.

Stapleton's Directory of 1838 provides considerable detail of the service provided by Ben's coach-van named '*Surprise*' to '*Gravesend, through Rochester and Chatham*'. It left Sittingbourne from Benjamin's '*house every morning (Sundays excepted), at half-past six, and arrives at Gravesend in time for the morning steam packet for London; returns from Gravesend immediately after the arrival of the last packet from London. Another van also leaves Sittingbourne from the same place at nine every morning (Sundays excepted), and arrives at Gravesend for the half-past twelve boat*'.

Nine years later, in 1847, Bradshaw's directory qualifies this information slightly, telling us that, in winter, Ben's van left an hour later – at 7.30. If he was on that early shift, John, having to set off from the east end of the town before dawn, in winter, might have appreciated the opportunity to lie in for that extra hour. However, being the boss's elder brother, he might have been allocated to the later run starting at 9 o'clock. We do not know how often Ben made the run himself.

Though a mile or so from the setting-off point for the journey to Gravesend, John's home at number 74 East Street was quite handy for Plough Orchard – the half-acre of pasture and buildings (now fronted by street numbers 51-57 East Street *qv*) which Benjamin, in 1840, was renting from one Betsy Milner, together with the house adjoining. Very likely this house was occupied by another of Ben's van drivers. A horse pastured and or stabled there might well have provided transport for John on his way to and from Ben's place in the London Road.

Journeys to Gravesend and back in all seasons and all weathers, taking at least 3½ hours in each direction, will have taken up much of the day and been rather taxing at times – doubtless the drivers needed some time to rest. Apart from looking after the horse/s, we have not ascertained where John and other drivers might have rested on arrival at Gravesend.

Stapleton also confirmed that '*Vans and Omnibuses*' – provided by others – ran as follows:

To Canterbury – Thos. Ashtell (HSI) from the Bull Inn

To Maidstone – every afternoon at one – alternately from:
the Three Kings, East Street

the Wheatsheaf, East Street returning in time to catch the *'Tally-ho!'* coach to Canterbury.

Stapleton also tells us that coaches from Sittingbourne *'To and from London, Canterbury, Chatham, Dartford, Deal, Dover, Gravesend, Margate, Ramsgate and Rochester pass through Sittingbourne almost every hour of the day, calling at the Rose, George, Bull and Lion Inns'.*

The coach was a superior form of vehicle, offering more comfort than a van or omnibus; we note that Benjamin Peters claimed that his vehicle *'Surprise'* was a *'coach-van'*.

John and Sarah were still at number 74 in 1851. Their oldest son Walter had joined the household of his uncle Ben where we was employed as an ostler. Doubtless this move was necessary because Walter had to be available at all hours to help with the horses. Ben, by the way, had promoted himself to the status of 'Coach Master'.

George, John and Sarah's second son, was living with his own employer – Theophilus Smith, the bootmaker, beside the yard of the former Rose Inn, the premises lately acquired and occupied by the great George Smeed.(HSII) By 1861, George, by now an upholsterer's assistant, had moved in with his uncle Ben and aunt Clara Eliza; George had married their daughter (his cousin) Mary Ann. In the following year, George and Mary Ann moved to 124 High Street, where he established himself as a dealer in new and second-hand furniture and ironmongery.(HSII)

Back here at 74 East Street, in 1851, John and Sarah, in their fifties, were still sharing the house with John, their youngest child – aged 19. Whereas Walter, the eldest son, had followed his father into the coach trade, engaging himself with the horses, John, like his elder brother George, preferring to work indoors, had furniture in his blood. In 1851, described as a 'shopman', young John was employed by George Bassett at what became number 5 High Street, where Mr Bassett was in business as *'auctioneer, appraiser, furniture-broker and ironmonger'.*

We have recounted in (HSI) that, within a few years, Mr Bassett had moved away, being replaced at number 5 by John Reynolds and his wife Hannah. Not long afterwards, following her husband's death, Hannah Reynolds also engaged her employee's father. This change of career by John senior, coming indoors after a lifetime in the open air with horses, seems to have coincided with the removal of his brother Ben from Chalkwell to a new home and business premises beside the railway station – the brand-new Railway and Fountain Hotel. For a brief while, Ben had transferred his business from Chalkwell to the East End: probably to the land and premises which he had been renting – Plough Orchard and its buildings, where 51-57 East Street are now. This was a convenient location for John at number 74. Then having re-established himself at the Fountain and Railway Hotel, Ben sustained his Job-Master business – hiring out coaches and other vehicles – for the rest of his days – latterly at 34 Station Street, working for a while with his son Henry.

It is understandable that John, by now, well into his sixties, could have found working with horses was too rigorous. Hence, as mentioned, he followed his two younger sons indoors – to the world of furniture – becoming a furniture 'broker' to help Mrs Reynolds to run the furniture business. In 1859, John junior, in his late twenties, was promoted to the role of auctioneer – a profession that he and some of his descendants (eldest son, two grandsons and one great-grandson –

Michael, one of our contributors) followed for almost one and a half centuries (HSI)

John Peters Snr 1795-1866

Sarah Peters nee Walter 1789-1863

At number 74 East Street the next occupiers we know of were Henry Hughes, a cow-herd, his wife and three lodgers.(7)

In 1871 number 74 was empty as were 76 and 78 and this could have indicated a change of ownership. During the early 1870s Milton man Edward Bigg moved here with his wife Ann and two daughters from further up the street at number 112. (see 112) He worked as an inspector of weights and measures, bailiff to the Sheriff of Kent and constable of the Hundred of Milton. Around 1890 the Biggs moved to Pembury Street where Edward died in 1893.

Widowed Sarah Ann Rugg moved into number 74 when the Biggs left. She was here with her two daughters and a servant when the 1891 census was taken. Sarah was originally from Luton and was in her sixties at this time.

Susanna Ditchman, the next tenant of 74, did not arrive in Sittingbourne from London until the 1890s when she was getting on in years. She had no known connections with the town but perhaps the move was made to bring her nearer to her sister who lived in Faversham.(111) Miss Ditchman lived here until her death in 1904 leaving the considerable sum of £1,500 to Ditchman relatives.

The next residents we know of were David and Adelaide Glandfield who lived at 74 by 1908. Born in Milton, David worked as a commercial traveller and the couple were still here in 1951. He died the following year whilst Adelaide died in 1959.

Nobody was registered here on the electoral roll in 1960 and by 1975, as recorded above, Number 74 had been pulled down to make way for the block of flats known as Plaza Court. This block was itself demolished in 2016 and replaced by the present structure, which bears the same name.

Number 76 East Street
A private home

In 1841 Sarah Cooper aged 16, could be found at number 76. Sarah was the eldest of five children in the house whose parents were absent on census night.

A female servant was in the house with the young Coopers. We have not been able to discover who the parents were.

The Reverend John Smith, a Wesleyan minister, lived here in 1851 with one servant. We can assume a series of ministers then lived at 76 until each was posted elsewhere because in 1861 Reverend Edmund Lockyer from Dartford, a family man with six children a wife and a sister in law to support on his stipend inhabited 76.

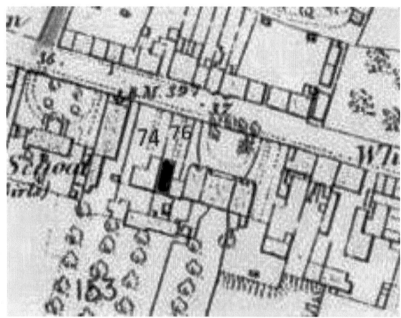

Section of Ordnance Survey map dated 1865/6
Number 76 is shaded

Charles and George Rugg, veterinary surgeons

By 1880 Charles Octavius Rugg of Rochester owned number 76.(115) He was a retired farmer and lived at number 76 with his son Charles junior in 1881. Charles junior was a young vet, a member of the Royal College of Veterinary Surgeons. Along with Charles senior and Charles junior lived young Charles's wife Cecilia, their son, Cecilia's sister and a servant. Charles had a brother George who was also a vet and in business with him. That census night he was down the road in the High Street visiting the Boulding family at number 6. He was to marry Ellen Boulding in 1884. In 1887 Charles junior placed an announcement in the local paper that he was moving to West Street.

Young William Henry Brown, a saddler and harness maker, lived at 76 in 1891 with his wife Ellen. He was the son of John Brown the High Street saddler and no doubt worked for his father.(HSII) Some years later Brown senior was in occupation of number 78 next door – and granted a tenancy of part of the property to the Co-op – see below.

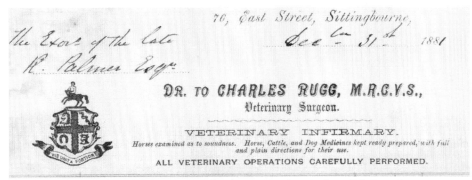

1881 Letterhead from vet Charles Rugg (junior) at 76 East Street

Phoebe Rossiter's boarding house

Widowed Phoebe Rossiter was running number 76 as a boarding house in 1901 and advertising her *'lodgings for respectable young men. Terms moderate'* in the Gazette. Phoebe was in her fifties, her three children were working as shop assistants and pupil teachers. Her four boarders were clerks and apprentices. Ten years earlier she had run a general shop in Teynham; that year her husband Robert died aged 42 and she had worked hard to bring her children up alone.

More Methodist Ministers

By 1906 number 76 had reverted to being the home of Methodist ministers, and it was Reverend Thomas Nicholas who lived there.(N01) It appears the Methodists had purchased the house because Mr Nicholas was succeeded by three or four more ministers. In 1911 Reverend Richard Squire, a widower from Devon lived here with his four children. In 1922 it was Reverend Richard Percy Cole and his wife Gertrude and they were still here in 1927.

Number 76 after number 74 was demolished to make way for Plaza Court. An entrance porch had been added and the windows had been changed

The later inhabitants of 76 that we know of:

1933	Catherine and Thomas Green
1938-1960	Ernest and Florence Field
1970s and 1980s	David and Muriel Bruce-Jones

East Court at number 76 in 2019 (MHP)

Numbers 78 and 78a East Street
A house divided

In 1841 Louisa Edman and her 20 year old daughter Louisa had sufficient income to live at number 78 with a servant and a female relative.

By 1851 it appears from the census return that number 78 had been partitioned into what was later known as 78 and 78a with Sittingbourne woman Miss Mercy Ann Tonge in one part and Sarah Hogben who owned some houses and rented them out in the other. Old Mercy (whom we met in 1840 at number 76) was 80 and very comfortably off. Her brother John, a retired grocer was with her, and we know he needed care as one of the two servants was a male nurse. Mercy died in 1853 leaving a will which instructed her executors to invest £500 for her niece Elizabeth Tonge from which she would receive an annual income. Various nephews were left £50 each and the residue of her estate was to be shared equally between her 12 nephews and nieces. Sarah Hogben in the other part of the building was in her fifties and had a lodger and a servant with her.

We have found no further mention of 78a for some years so it seems to have been a temporary division of the building which was later reinstated

The next occupant of 78 that we know of was Charles Cooke who lived here in 1861 with his wife, nephew and servant. He was the manager of the cement works at Murston.

In 1871 the house was empty and perhaps was not being kept in good repair for the following tenants were of a lower social class. By 1881 Albert Henry Hart a young grocer's assistant from Faversham lived here with his wife. By 1884 the Harts had moved and the house was to let again.

In 1890 one John Rossiter was the tenant and he was to be found a year later round the corner in Goodnestone Road working as a brickfield labourer. The house was empty again when the 1891 census was taken. In 1895 the occupier was one Henry Hooker.

William Kemsley, fruit merchant

William was a young man when he started his fruit business here in the 1890s. By 1901 he, like Mr Rossiter, had moved round the corner to Goodnestone Road where he was listed as a market gardener who worked for someone else.

John Brown the High Street saddler then moved in. Widowed and in his sixties he retired here from his business at 2 High Street and let part of the building to the Co-op. (see above number 76 and HSII)

Co-operative greengrocery and reading room at 78 and 78a

It was listed in local directories as being at 78a East Street from the 1880s certainly until the Second World War. This was a room in the house let to the Co-op leaving the rest available for living accommodation.

In 1901 number 78a (evidently part only of the structure) was let to Louisa Kemsley the mother of William the fruit merchant. Louisa was the widow of William Kemsley senior a High Street butcher. She had her daughter and granddaughter living with her and two visitors.

In 1908, Parrett's directory tells us that number 78a, as well as housing the Co-op library, was then inhabited by Richard Phillips.

Until 1909 the Co-operative Society paid to rent the library room but that year they purchased number 78 which the society documents noted as 'a cottage belonging to a Mr Brown'.

Blacksmith George William Curd from Faversham was the Co-op's tenant in 1911 and inhabited the six rooms along with his wife Mary. But that was only part of the house. In 78a dwelt Samuel Crayden, a local brickfield labourer, his wife and son. This part of the building had five rooms. It appears that the Co-op had extended the house when they purchased it so that both 78 and 78a had plenty of room even with the shop which opened at 78a by 1920. The Curds ran the Co-op's greengrocery here. George Curd died in 1929 aged 63 but Mary Curd was still here in 1933.

Later tenants of 78a included Frances & Philip Cherrison during the early 1920s, followed by Edith & Harry Cain who lived here into the 1930s and Herbert & Hetty Baker in the 1940s. Then came Mabel and William Mount and their family. Mr Mount was a long serving Labour councillor for the town. The Mounts were still here in the mid-1960s.

In 1959 Sittingbourne Co-op Works department showroom opened at 78a selling wall papers paints power tools and doors.

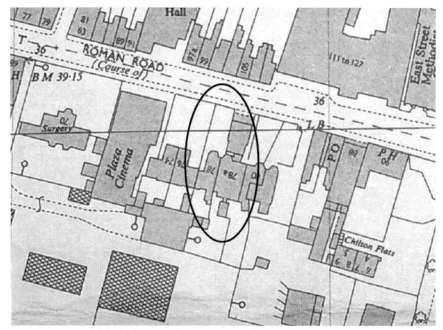

1960 Ordnance Survey map showing 78 and 78a

No one was listed on the electoral register for 78 or 78a in 1975. The building was demolished in the early 1970s, as were numbers 80 and 82 to make way for the Fairview Road development.

In the final phase of these buildings the forecourts of the French Houses and the premises occupied by the Co-op building department were used to display garden sheds and greenhouses, manufactured by Allwoods, a firm based in Whitstable, for whom the Co-op were local agents. There are still some Allwoods' sheds in this district, with their emblem at the apex of each gable – a triangular piece of wood, shaped like a capital letter A.

A row of houses, Lavender Court, in 2019, built on the site of the French Houses 80 to 82 (MHP)

Number 80 East Street
Helen Hassells

By chance we know a good deal about the life of Mrs Helen Hassells who had moved into number 80 by 1840. The tithe schedule for that year tells us that this house and the adjacent dwelling, with an orchard at the back extending to just over an acre, were let to a Mary Hassells who had a long-term tenancy. We might suppose that Mary was Helen's mother-in-law or sister-in-law, but we cannot be sure.

1840 was the year in which Helen became a close friend of Mrs Louisa Thomas of Eyhorne House Hollingbourne. The women were of similar age, Helen had been born Helen Jardine in 1805 in Scotland.

Louisa kept a diary for most of her long life and often mentioned her friend. (83) They were both comfortably off and well educated although Louisa had far more wealth. Though Mrs Hassells' fellow residents in the house were only a male and female servant for she was unhappily married, had no children, and her husband, Charles only made rare appearances, doubtless, causing on those occasions, plenty of 'hassle'. Helen Hassells and Louisa exchanged visits in their carriages, spent days with each other and attended events such as flower shows and cricket matches together. Mrs Hassells made a prolonged visit to keep Louisa company when one of her babies was born for in those days ladies were confined to their room for six weeks to recover from the ordeal of giving birth.

Sadly Helen died aged 42 in 1848 of stomach cancer. Louisa wrote in her diary: *'The vicar of Sittingbourne Reverend Walford read the service. It was a most melancholy ceremony. She herself had written the inscription for the plate on the coffin omitting altogether the name Hassells.'*

The house was then empty for some time and the next tenant we know of was John Hedgecock.

John Hedgecock, brick merchant

Being a brick merchant was a new venture for John Hedgecock who had spent most of his life as a painter and glazier living across the road at number 121 where more can be read about the family. But by 1861 John Hedgecock had moved to 80 with his wife Eliza and set himself and his son Thomas up as a brick merchants thinking to sell some of the bricks made nearby. Misfortune struck in December 1865 when the Gazette reported: *'A barge run down and loss of life. The Barge laden with bricks to the value of £50 to £60 belonging to Mr J Hedgecock. Walter Cullen drowned.'*

Nevertheless the enterprise continued and 'John Hedgecock brick maker' was listed in directories up to 1874. The electoral register of 1873 shows that he had purchased the house. He died in 1875 leaving effects worth about £450.

After the Hedgecocks left the house took a downward turn. It began to be inhabited by people who were working class and had little money to spare. The implication is that it was no longer lived in by its owner but rented out and little spent on its upkeep.

John Seagers, market gardener

By 1878 this was the home of John Seagers a market gardener from Tonge his wife Elizabeth and their four children. Perhaps he also had the use of the acre of land at the back.

Edwin Webb a stationary-engine driver lived here in 1891 with his wife. A stationary-engine was an engine whose framework did not move. They were used to drive equipment, such as pumps, generators, mills or factory machinery.

Richard and Mary King lived here in 1901. Richard was a Sittingbourne labourer who worked in the gas yard. The Rumble family were the next tenants we know of and they had moved in by 1908. William Rumble came from Wiltshire and worked as a caretaker. He lived with his wife Harriet and son Fred who was a wheelwright.(12) William had formerly been a police constable in Dover.(11)

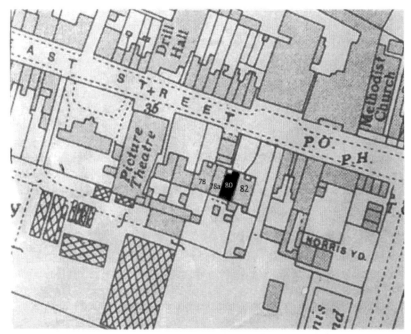

1938 Ordnance Survey map with number 80 solid-shaded

Richard Evans, a retired farm labourer, lived here next and died at the house in 1915.(N01) He was then 74. He had been born in Goudhurst and he and his wife Elizabeth had moved to East Street from Park Road after 1911.

Hannah and Walter Mills lived at number 80 in 1922. Walter was a local man, who laboured in the brickfields. The couple lived out their lives here, Hannah died in 1941 in her seventies. Walter remained at number 80 in 1947.

This may be the only photograph in existence showing the French Houses numbers 78-82 marred by the plain, functional extension constructed by the Co-op in the front garden of 78a. Latterly, as agents for Allwoods of Whitstable, the Co-op were selling sheds here and some samples of the sheds and greenhouses are on display

Later occupants of number 80:

1951	Charles and Jessie Taylor
1956-1960	Alfred and Violet Gambell

Nobody was listed here in the electoral register in 1975 – the block was pulled down to make space for the Fairview Road development.

Number 82 East Street
A private house

This end house of the French Houses had a good sized yard with stabling. In sales particulars produced in 1895, the orchard at the back is also mentioned, so it seems that, by then, this house had been combined with the adjoining dwelling, which had been listed separately in 1840, when both were let to Mary Hassells – see above.

In 1841 George Bushell was living here; then in his fifties he had enough money not to need to work even with a wife and seven children to support.

Ninety year old widow Ann Hedgecock lived here in 1851 – she was perhaps related to John Hedgecock the brick merchant who lived next-door. For company and income she had young labourer Charles Sage and his family lodging with her. Ann died in 1854.

George Allen White's evening school

By 1861 there was a new venture at number 82; an evening school. It was run by George White a schoolmaster who was then 32 and his wife Mary a schoolmistress who was 28. George had been born in Middlesex but Mary in Kent. They had two young daughters and with them lived Mary's widowed mother Sarah Elvy who was also a schoolmistress. An 1862 advertisement for the school in the local paper tells us something of it: *'French House seminary &*

academy East End now nearly 50 pupils. An evening school for children and adults run by Mr & Mrs White at 15s per quarter. Music & singing 10s, drawing 4s, book keeping 2/6.'

The January 1863 advertisement reads: *'French House evening school for children and adults 6.30 - 8.00, East End.'* A month later Mary White gave birth to another daughter. It is unlikely that this was the reason that the school came to an end although Mrs White would certainly have been busy.

We have not discovered any advertisements for the school in 1864 or 1865 and so it seems it was a short-lived affair. The most likely reason is that the early enthusiasm of local people dried up because they could not afford this extra expense either for themselves or their children.

There were quite a number of men named George White in England at that time and so it has not been possible to discover where George and the family went after they left East Street.

James Sellen, pig and cattle dealer

A very different family had moved into the house by 1866. James Sellen was a pig dealer in his fifties from Newnham and a niece lived with him and his wife Sarah.

We know James was able to buy the house as he was listed as the owner in the 1871 electoral register. He died late in 1874 aged 54 and the National Probate Index was useful in revealing that he was formerly a grocer in Lynsted but latterly a cattle dealer in Sittingbourne. He was survived by Sarah and left effects of over £450.

William Kite's dairy

The next occupant of the house opened a dairy here. This was William Kite a thatcher from Bapchild. An advertisement in the local paper in 1878 drew attention to the 'East End Dairy' where new laid eggs and fresh butter could be bought. William and Ellen Kite had moved into number 82 and were making good use of the land that went with the house. A notice in the paper in 1880 saying there were furnished apartments to let and good stable shows the Kites were trying to find a way of getting more income. This was successful as we can see from the 1881 census return that they had two lodgers with decent jobs – a gas fitter and a shop assistant. William Kite described himself as a thatcher again for this census return, he was 60 by then. A year later he was in the directory as a cow-keeper.

Ten years later the old couple lived in Terrace Road and William still got some work as a thatcher.

Jasper Dean mineral water manufacturer

Jasper Dean who is listed in directories at number 82 between 1884 and 1890 has proved elusive, but the pictured bottle shows that he was involved in more than just mineral water.

In 1891 the house was uninhabited.

'Williams & Dean Brewed Ginger Beer, Windsor and Sittingbourne'

Robert and Sarah Mace and their dairy

Robert and Sarah Mace had moved to number 82 and taken on the dairy by 1895. Robert had been born in Uxbridge in 1836, whilst Sarah came from Tonge and they had lived in Sittingbourne since the 1880s. In 1891 they had been living round the corner in Shakespeare Road and Robert had worked as a carter.

In 1895 number 82 was for sale:

> *'Valuable freehold property to sell by auction at Bull Hotel. All that substantially built freehold dwelling house, seven rooms situate and being number 82 East Street, with orchard at the rear, large stable, yard, outbuildings and good carriage entrance, the whole farming capital business premises. Now in the occupation of Mr. R. Mace at the rental of £37 per annum, the tenant paying rates. This property is situated in one of the busiest parts of the town, and is well adapted for a contractor, dairyman or any business requiring large premises'.*(N01)

Bidding for the house began at £350, and it was purchased for £800 by Henry Baker a market gardener who lived at Chestnut Street. Mr Baker did not move to number 82 and Robert Mace continued the dairy. Mace was still listed as dairyman in the 1908 directory by which time he was over 70. He added to his income from the dairy with some carting and was helped in his business by his son.

A sad event was reported in the Gazette in 1908. An inquest was held into the death of Henry Hammond who lodged at 82 and was employed by Robert Mace. Hammond was thrown from the van he was driving when the horse shied and he was killed.

Robert Mace was still working in 1911 when he was 75. When he filled in the census form he described himself as a 'farmer & dairyman.' He died at home in 1916 aged 80 and Sarah died in 1918 but their son Albert Joseph continued the dairy business in the 1920s with his wife Kate. Albert did not long survive his mother for he died in 1926 but Kate was still running the dairy in 1938 and did not die until 1947. It seems that she was the last person to live here before its demolition about 30 years later, making way for the Fairview Rd development.

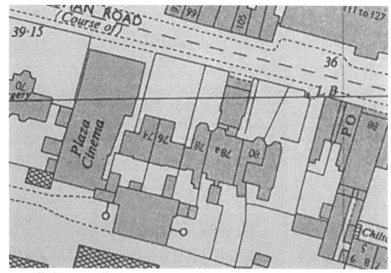

All the so-called French Houses, except 82, are numbered on the 1960 Ordnance Survey map above

The modern flats and houses on the site of former numbers 74 to 82 today (AJW)

Numbers 84, 84a, 86, 88 East Street

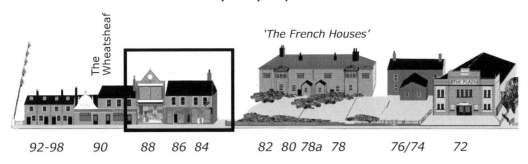

Why the street numbers in this group were changed

The pair of semi-detached houses which today are numbered 84 and 86 were built in the late 1880s to replace an earlier cottage, 84, which had burnt down. The fire is mentioned in Matthews' memories of Sittingbourne: '*There was a chemist's shop belonging to Mr. Gordelier. Mr. J. E. French had charge of this branch on occasions, when he was a very young man. The place was burned down one Sunday evening, and new premises were erected which are now the Co-operative Confectionery Department, and the East Street post office*'.(69)

The Mr J. French of this account was John French who already had his own chemist's shop at 128 High Street by 1891, though he was only 23, so the fire occurred before this. The 1890 directory records Gordelier's shop at 84 but a year later when the census was taken it was recorded as empty. Perhaps at that point it was a burnt shell. By 1895 it was listed as a post office so we can conclude that the present 84 and 86 were erected in the early 1890s. To add to the confusion the new buildings were numbered 84 and 84a.

Beside this to the east stood a pair of five-roomed cottages which, when the street was first numbered in 1871, were given the numbers 86 and 88.(N01) At the close of the 19th century this pair of cottages were demolished to make way for the tall, red-brick Co-op building which was given the number 88. The newly built number 84a was then renumbered as 86.

Nowadays number 84 is in use as a Coral betting shop whilst the eastern end, 86, is empty and boarded up. Number 88 has been converted into flats but still proudly boasts 'CO-OPERATIVE SOCIETY' inscribed in the plaster work above the front door.

This table may clarify the rebuilding and renumbering:

1840	84		86	88
1890s	New 84 and 84a		86	88
1900s	Same building renumbered as 84 and 86		New 88	New 88

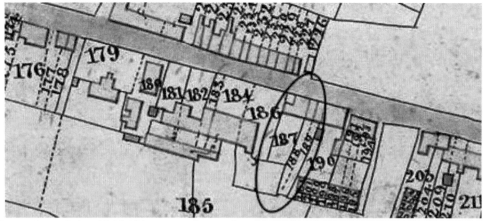

This section of the 1840 tithe map shows the original buildings none of which now stand. Parcel 187 was number 84, parcel 188 was number 86 and parcel 189 (beside the Wheatsheaf shown as 190) was 88.

Number 84 East Street

The old number 84 was a residential property which in 1840 was owned and occupied by John Mitchell and his wife Ann. In the 1841 census return John is recorded as 'independent' meaning that he did not need to work for a living.

Richard Whibley the draper from 10/12 High Street had retired to number 84 by 1851 with his wife Esther and three adult daughters. This allowed his son to move into the High Street home and take on the shop.

The next resident we know of was Thomas Mapleston Green from Aldeburgh Suffolk who was employed by the county council as a 'superintendent' although what he superintended is not clear from the 1861 census. Green was a widower in his forties who had been left with six children whose ages then ranged from 12 to two. Thankfully his cousin had moved in with him to look after the children whilst he earned enough to keep them. His wife had sadly died in 1860.

In 1870 Jacob Batch the town sweeper lived at number 84. Batch is not a Kentish name and in fact Jacob and his wife had both been born in Norwich as had their two older children. The birth places of their children as shown on the 1871 census return reveal that the family had lived in Sittingbourne for less than three years. By 1881 they had moved on to Lambeth.

Frederick Nichols, photographer

For a few years in the 1870s a photographer named Frederick Nichols set up shop here and also had premises at 54 High Street. We believe we have identified Fred as the FW Nichols, photographer, living in Hadlow in 1881. Then in his forties he was married and his 16 year old son Arthur was assisting his father with the photography. Fred had been born in Hampshire.

Fred Nichols advertised his portrait, landscape and architectural photography

Joshua Oliver Ockenden, photographer

By 1876 another photographer, young Joshua Ockenden from Bapchild, had replaced Mr Nichols. Joshua was married with children.(9) Ockenden remained until at least 1882. Photography was not a lasting success for Joshua and by 1891 he and his wife Dorcas were settled in Hastings with the children and Joshua was working as a builder.(10)

William Gordelier, chemist

By 1887 William Gibbs Gordelier, a chemist, was listed in the directory both here and at 39 High Street. Born in 1855 he was the son of Paul Gordelier a chemist who was well established in the High Street.(HSI)

By 1891 the building had been destroyed by fire and William Gordelier was living with his widowed mother at 39 High Street. Then the new building was erected and numbered 84 and 84a.

George Handcock, a cement miller from Ash and his wife moved into 84a but 84 was not yet inhabited when the 1891 census was taken. Briefly in 1894 the premises were in use as a printing office by Walter Cannell (see number 169).

James Dawes, baker

We know from advertisements in the local paper that James Dawes 'high class baker & confectioner' opened at the new number 84 in1897. Dawes hailed from Suffolk and was in his fifties when he and the family arrived in East Street. His son Jonathan Dent Dawes, (sometimes recorded as Dent Dawes) had been trained as a baker by his father and was listed in the 1899 directory.

In 1902 the Milton Workhouse records note that Ernest Williams aged 15 was sent from the workhouse to 'be placed in service with Mr Dawes of East Street to learn the trade of bakery'. He was provided with an outfit by the union guardians to start him off.

On the right in the foreground is number 84 when the Dawes family were baking there. The sign advertising teas and refreshments can be seen as well as the Hovis sign.

When James retired, he and his wife Ellen lived in Valenciennes Road and another son, Fred, who was also a baker lived with them.

Co-op Bakery and Confectionery at number 84

Sittingbourne Co-operative Society's bakery shop

The records of Sittingbourne Co-operative Society reveal that during 1903 a new lease of number 84 was drawn up between John Augustus Thomas the owner, described as 'a gentleman, of Burley Road', and Jonathan Dent Dawes of 84 East Street. Mr Thomas leased the building to Dawes for 15 years at £25 a year. Then, a year later, Dawes leased it to William Webb who was a confectioner of Lydney Gloucestershire for £50 for the remaining years of the lease. However in 1905 William Webb, decided to move his business to the High Street and assigned the remainder of the lease to Sittingbourne Co-operative Society. By that time it was Miss Elizabeth Hope of Great Chart, Ashford who owned the property, John Thomas having died. Elizabeth Hope had been born in Newnham and lived with the farming family of her married sister, acting as housekeeper.(12)

So it was that the burgeoning Co-op took on number 84 in 1905 for their confectionery and bakery. The building was no longer lived in. Miss Hope extended the lease to the Co-op in 1918 for three years at £40 a year but in fact they stayed far longer and were still there in 1963.

In 1921 the Co-op built a shop in the garden of number 84 and we think that the greenhouse and the rather temporary structure shown beside it in the 1960s photograph are the new shop, which sold greengrocery.

The greenhouse building in the garden of number 84 East Street c.1960

Today this area forms the gardens of the houses in Lavender Court (AJW)

Betting Shop

It was during the 1960s that number 84 became a betting shop as it still is today.

Numbers 84 and 84a in 2016 (BA)

Number 84a East Street
Edward Frank Handcock watchmaker, tobacconist and sub-postmaster

During 1895 George Handcock's son Edward advertised as watchmaker and tobacconist at 84a.(N01) He had been learning his craft working for a jeweller and watchmaker in Strood.(10) That year poor Emily Handcock died in the house, aged 32. She was Edward's sister and had been ill for two years.(N01)

It was during the 1890s that Edward was able to add sub-postmaster to his role in the shop.(39)

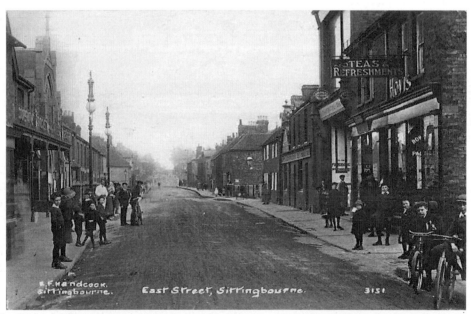

On the right of this picture which is looking east towards Snipeshill, are the Co-op Bakery shop, Handcocks, and the Co-op Furniture Store. Note that Mr Handcock published this postcard, doubtless offered for sale in his sub-post office

Whilst Mr Handcock was running this business and living here a dramatic incident occurred, although thankfully this time it was not a fire. In November 1900 a burglary was committed in the early hours. One of the shutters was pushed out of the way and the plate-glass window broken. Stock to the value of £200 was stolen. A neighbour living opposite was woken at 3.30 in the morning by loud tapping in the street and on looking out of the window saw a man with a bicycle near the kerb doing something to the shutters. The man then rode off. Later he returned and robbed the shop. A postman discovered the burglary at six in the morning and a jemmy left behind. This value of the stolen goods was high (£22,500 in value today) and merited reporting in the Manchester Courier and Lancashire General Advertiser. Edward Handcock slept through the break-in. It was reported that he kept a loaded revolver with him, as did most jewellers.(N01)

Edward, born and bred in Sittingbourne, was only 32 when the 1901 census was taken the following year. He and his wife Rose had a daughter, Winnie, and Edward's mother Elizabeth, widowed by then, lived with them. Poor Rose died aged only 29 in 1902. Edward remarried in 1905 to Olga Homewood and they had a daughter Mary.

A rather pathetic little crime committed due to poverty occurred at the shop in 1904 and was reported by The Whitstable Times and Herne Bay Herald – 'Two tramping tailors James Henry and James Higgs were charged at Sittingbourne Petty Sessions with stealing a pair of boots valued 4/11 of Mrs Brown of East Street and Higgs was charged with stealing a pipe from the shop of Mr Handcock, tobacconist, The men were seen by a neighbour taking the boots and the police found James Henry wearing them. Higgs afterwards entered near Handcock's shop and asked for some food. On being taxed with the theft he fished the pipe out of his pocket and was taken into custody. Higgs served 21 days hard labour and James Henry 14'.

By 1908 Edward Handcock had expanded his business and had both parts of the building – 84 and 84a – (now 84 and 86) one side being jewellery and the other the post office and tobacconist.

During the First World War the premises were used as a local War Munitions Bureau.(N01) 'All enquiries from local firms who are willing to assist in manufacturing munitions of war can be made at 84a East Street Sittingbourne The War Munitions Bureau which is open daily Sundays included.' Edward Handcock himself sat on the Sittingbourne tribunal.

The shops continued at number 84 and 84a (by then numbered 86) after the war but at some point Edward and Olga moved to number 75 West Street and then finally to the London Road.(115) Edward became a Justice of the Peace and served for many years on the town council. He served as chairman from 1917 to 1920. He gave his time and energy generously to the community and when he died aged 68 in 1937 his obituary in the local paper stated that he was 'probably the most outstanding personality in the public life of the town in the past 25 years.' As well as starting his East Street business about 45 years earlier, he had also opened a shop at 16 High Street later.(HSI) He was a governor of Borden Grammar School and a devoted follower of the town's football club to which he gave many trophies. He left his widow Olga to mourn him as well as three daughters.

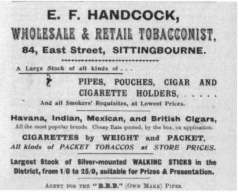

Although Edward Handcock's advertisements in the 1908 directory give the address as 84, his listing in the directory is 84a.

Councillor E. F. Handcock, Chairman Sittingbourne Urban District Council 1917-1920

Thomas H. Tyler, sub-postmaster at 84a

By 1933 Thomas and Elizabeth Tyler lived here and ran the shop but Thomas died in 1941.

The Embleton family

Frank and Margaret Embleton were the next tenants and lived here with their sons John and Roy and ran the post office. We know they were here by 1951 when Frank and Margaret were on the electoral register. The 1963 directory lists the Embletons at 84a and 86. By 1970 the register listed Roy, Frank and Margaret Embleton. Roy Embleton still lived here in 1990 although it was during the 1980s that the post office closed.

The old numbers 86 and 88

In 1840 a certain James Hunt owned the two five-roomed cottages which stood where number 88 is now. The tenant recorded in the 1841 census at 86 was postman, Thomas Payne from Newnham with his wife Esther and their eight children whose ages ranged from 19 to three years old. The Paynes were still here 20 years later by which time Thomas was 74 and living on his post office pension. He lived to be 84, dying in 1870.

Shops on the left include (coming nearer to the camera), 84 Sittingbourne Co-op Pastry & Confectionery, 84a East Street Post Office, (sub-postmaster E. F. Handcock) and Edward Frank Handcock, jeweller & tobacconist

In 1841 Henry Burley a tailor in his thirties lived at 88 his wife Maria, their six children as well as their lodger, blacksmith Thomas Chapman. This Henry was one of the Burley clan of tailors of number 7, one of the sons of Thomas and Ann Burley. To begin with he must have worked with the rest of the family at number 7 but by 1851 he had his own business in Milton.

David Sargent a local man in his forties lived at 88 in 1851 with his wife Jane and earned his living as a gardener. At 86 was young William Exton a printer compositor and his wife Ellen. They remained only a short while because Exton was working on an ill-fated venture in journalism – a new newspaper set up by Thomas Edwards which lasted no time at all. (see 86 High Street in HSII)

Jane Sargent the widow of David still lived at number 88 20 years later but, widowed by then, she died early in 1873 in her seventies. The probate index records that her effects were worth under £100 and Dr Fisher was her executor. It was the East Kent Gazette which gave us the information that the Sargents had owned their cottage and the adjoining number 86 too for this notice was put into the paper after Jane's death: '*Two houses each with five rooms in the occupation of John Sellen & Susan Baker as weekly tenants for freehold sale, owner the late Mrs Jane Sargent.'*

John and Mary Sellen lived at number 86 when this notice about the sale of 86 and 88 appeared in the Gazette. The sale did not mean that the Sellens needed to move however. After John Sellen died young in 1880 Mary Sellen took in laundry to support her two children and remained here in 1881 with a boarder completing the household. Nor did Susan Baker change her abode after the 1873 sale of 88. She was still there in 1881 a widowed laundress in her sixties from Tunbridge with a lodger.

The tenancy of both houses seemed to have changed ten years later when Henry Lambkin a blacksmith lived in one and Elizabeth Wilson in the other. But actually Elizabeth was Susan Baker's granddaughter and old Susan Baker still lived there too until her death in 1894.

Numbers 86 and 88 were then demolished to make way for the new Co-op building.

The Sittingbourne Co-operative Society's butchery department in the new number 88

This tall, attractive, red-brick building beside the Wheatsheaf replaced numbers 86 and 88 and is numbered 88. Built during the 1890s for the Co-op it was listed in the 1901 census return as an 'uninhabited butcher's shop'. It had a slaughter house at the back. With two floors above the shop the Co-op always planned to make good use of the space and the furnishing department was upstairs.(43)

Co-op Butchery Department in 1920

After the opening of the Co-op's new department store across the road in the 1920s the upstairs was used as a function room known as the Assembly Rooms.

Wedding receptions and parties took place and the Co-op Senior Choir had their weekly rehearsals. The rooms are fondly remembered by Heritage Museum founder, Peter Morgan who met his wife June there. She was the choir's leading lady and he a bass.

The Co-operative Society's butchery department closed in the 1970s. The shop was then rented by a plumbing and bathroom retailer who were not connected to the Co-op called Action Plumbing. They opened in 1977 and were still here in 1997 when the shop was known as Sittingbourne Plumbing Centre.

Sittingbourne Plumbing Centre, 1989 (EKG)

In 2003, following conversion from retail to domestic use, local estate agent Quealy and Co were offering for sale four apartments which had been built in the former shop and functions room, describing them as 'London loft-style living'. The agents believed this to be '*the first apartment development of its sort in Sittingbourne and the kind of accommodation that would suit young professionals or similar*'. Prices started at £125,000.(N01)

The building in 2018 (CB)

East Street South Avenue Junction

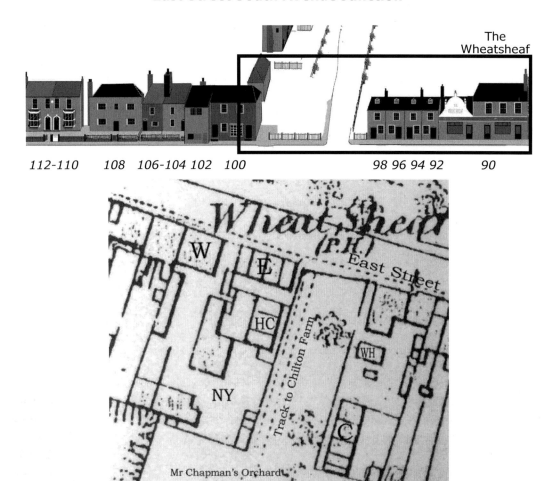

The Wheatsheaf

112-110   108   106-104 102   100   98 96 94 92   90

Ordnance Survey map dated 1865/6 of the area around The Wheatsheaf

The map is a section of the Ordnance Survey map dated 1865/6 of Sittingbourne showing the junction of the old Roman Road now East Street with what was to become South Avenue. The track itself is probably one of Kent's ancient trackways. In the 19th century it entered East Street as part of the orchard but was protected from the road by a wooden picket fence. There are two parcels of land on either side of this track, which led to Chilton Farm across '*Mr Chapman's Orchard*'.

The land to the West is fronted by what is now, numbers 100-102 East Street, and contains a number of buildings. The forerunners of which became known as '*Chapman's Cottages*', (C). These were built before 1840 and existed until the mid 1960s. The only other significant building, (WH), known variously as the White House, Plantation House and Chapman's Orchard Cottage was built after the tithe Survey of 1840 and it too survived until the area was redeveloped.

The parcel of land to the West of the track is self-contained with the Wheatsheaf Public House and Yard, (W) and properties numbers 92-98, (E), on

East Street. To the rear of these houses is Norris Yard which contained a number of buildings including Hope Cottages, (HC).

South Avenue was developed in two tranches. The western end was laid out before the Second World War in the 1930s. On the eastern side, Chilton Avenue was extended through the recreation ground to link up with South Avenue after the war in the early 1960s. By this time, Norris Yard had been redeveloped but Chapman's Cottages and the White House survived a few more years.

90 East Street – The Wheatsheaf Public House

The Wheatsheaf with its rear yard and coach house, was built near the beginning of the 19th century, possibly earlier. John Smith was the landlord in 1832. The 1840 tithe schedule for Sittingbourne shows that William Vallance was the owner but it was occupied by George Richardson who was the landlord. By 1847, Isaac Hogben was the landlord followed by William Apps around 1850. On 12th February 1850 the Kentish Gazette reported that *'Mr Apps, landlord of the Wheatsheaf, was robbed of a box containing £32'*. The crime was perpetrated by a guest who had been sleeping in a bedroom adjacent to Mr Apps' room who emptied a cash box hidden under Mr Apps' bed, before making his escape. The money belonged to a local benefit club held at the house. Thus giving some credence to the saying that, 'charity begins at home'. But this was not the only landlords concern. There were sanitary problems with the cottages in the inn's yard.

SITTINGBOURNE.—The magistrates were engaged for some time on Monday, in hearing cases prepared by the board of guardians of the Milton Union, against several parties, for nuisances. The first was against the owner of certain cottages at the back of the Wheatsheaf Inn, where there were three foul and offensive privies and an offensive cesspool. The nuisances being proved, an order to remove it within 48 hours was made.
Another nuisance was

South Eastern Gazette 15th November 1853

Year	Occupants	Year	Occupants
1832	John Smith	1891	Thomas Quinell
1840	George and John Richardson	1899	Edward James Allen
1847	Isaac Hogben	1908	Mary Anne Allen
1850	William Apps	1933	Mary Allen; Alfred and Blanche Bartlett
1858	Thomas Chapman	1939	Alfred & Blanche Bartlett
1870	Charles John Chapman	1960	Blanche Bartlett
1871	George Wilson	1970	George and Margaret Calver; Margaret Stepto
1872	Henry Hoile	1990	Derek, Edna, Jane and Richard Lee
1874	Joseph Hodgkin	2010	

Wheatsheaf Landlords

Thomas Chapman

On 23rd September 1856, the *Maidstone Journal & Kentish Advertiser* reported that at the Sittingbourne Petty Sessions, the General Annual Licensing Meeting renewed all the licenses of inns and beer houses submitted by several victualers with one exception; the Wheatsheaf Inn, against which several complaints had been made. The Inn's licence was suspended.

It is not clear whether or not the Wheatsheaf was licensed as a public house at the time Thomas Chapman occupied the premises some two years later, together with his wife and four children. It is likely that he would have made a living by alternative means. In addition to taking in eight lodgers, Thomas provided facilities for a coal dealership, a blacksmith and a grocer whose activities must have relied on the space provided by the Wheatsheaf's Yard. In the yard possibly in the coach house and near to the stables, accommodation was available for four or five families. These dwellings were referred to as 1-5 Wheatsheaf Yard, although number three does not appear to have been inhabited. Perhaps it was used as a store. The occupants in 1881 were Robert Batchelor, John Gregory, John Johnson and George and Eliza Goldfinch. All the occupants were poorer members of society mostly general labourers.

A horse and carriage of Chapman's time

Thomas Chapman also ran a licensed horse and carriage hire business, the horses were stabled in the Wheatsheaf's yard. But Mr Chapman's credibility as a horseman and carriage driver may be brought into question. On the 18th August 1866, the *Kentish Chronicle*, reported an accident with serious consequences:

'...Mr Chapman of the Wheatsheaf Inn, Sittingbourne, had taken Superintendent Green in his horse and cart, with a prisoner, to Maidstone. The horse, which was reactive, had backed the cart partly on to the pavement and on the animal being led off by a man, the cart suddenly swerved and both its occupants were thrown out on to the road. Mr Chapman was unhurt but Mr Green was so shaken that he has since been obliged to refrain from active duty...'

He later recovered, and, undeterred by this incident, Thomas continued his carriage hire business. The *Whitstable Times and Herne Bay Herald* reported two further incidents. On Saturday 12th January 1867:

'...a child of Mr George, living in Dover Terrace, Sittingbourne, was run over by a coal van in Pembury Road.....driven by Mr Chapman, the owner. The child is not seriously injured.'

And on Saturday 22nd June 1867:

' ...a horse and trap, owned by Mr Chapman of the Wheatsheaf Inn, Sittingbourne...was standing in the High Street at Rook's wine stores taking up a quantity of wine, when the animal, a colt, ran back, and the boy who was holding him, in endeavouring to stop him pulled the bridle and bit completely off. Through this great piece of negligence in harnessing, the horse started off, and after proceeding at a sharp gallop for a short distance came into contact with the delivery van of the London, Chatham and Dover railway. This caused a great crash, the wine being thrown out on to the pavement, the shafts were broken, and the horse of the cart, as well as the one in the van, were injured....'

Thomas provided a complete service to the newly built magistrate's court which was completed in 1856. He not only provided a prisoner transport service but he also provided accommodation in the Wheatsheaf's rooms for prisoners but not without incident. This is somewhat surprising as there is no evidence of other licensed premises being used for this purpose. Perhaps, the few cells at Sittingbourne police station were insufficient to cope with the demands of the court service.

On 29th January 1861, the *Kentish Gazette* reported:

> *'Frederick Hall alias Sidney Miller was charged with stealing a waistcoat from Henry Mann, the pot man at the Wheatsheaf Inn, Sittingbourne. Hall, a prisoner, was lodging in the Wheatsheaf at the time.'*

On 10th December 1861, another report in the *Kentish Gazette,* stated:

> *'Daniel Goodman, an ironmonger's assistant...from Mile End Road, London, was brought up in custody, charged with having attempted to commit suicide, by cutting his throat. It appeared that the rash act was committed on the road between Faversham and Sittingbourne; and that the prisoner came into the Wheatsheaf Inn, Sittingbourne, early that morning.......'*

It appears that being a lodging house holding prisoners, the Wheatsheaf was a meeting place where criminals met to plan their villainous pursuits. On one occasion in 1863, prisoners from the Wheatsheaf, planned and executed a robbery, cash being stolen, at the Fox & Goose public house, just down the road.

Perhaps one of the most notorious incidents in the history of the Wheatsheaf was reported in the *Tamworth Herald* on 2nd October 1880:

> *'CHARGE OF MURDER – William Hadlum, 58 described as a labourer, was charged at the petty sessions, Sittingbourne, with feloniously killing and slaying Thomas Holden, aged 45, at Eastchurch, Isle of Sheppy. It appeared that prisoner and Holden were both at the Wheatsheaf Inn, when a dispute arose and Hadlum struck the deceased a blow over the left eye with his fist, knocking him backwards off the form upon which he was sitting. He struck the ground with his head and expired almost immediately. The body was allowed to remain lying on the floor for two hours until the police arrived. Hadlum was remanded.'*

But horses were not the only inhabitants of the stables. On the 7th September 1867, *the Whitstable Times & Herne Bay Herald* reported:

> *'POLICE COURT – FRIDAY*
>
> (Before Rev G B Moore (chairman); and Lieut.-Colonel Dyke)
>
> *INDECENT ASSAULT – Thomas Hall, a labourer, brought up on remand, charged with having indecently assaulted Charles Kemsley, also a labourer, who was sleeping last Sunday night in company with the prisoners in a stable at the Wheatsheaf Inn, East-End, Sittingbourne, was convicted of a common assault, and was sentenced to two months imprisonment with hard labour.'*

On the 27th September 1864, the *South Eastern Gazette* reported, 'Thomas Chapman of the Wheatsheaf Inn, East End, Sittingbourne, was charged with keeping his house open on Sunday morning. He was fined £1, including costs.'

In 1870, the equine enterprise was taken on by the new occupier, Charles John Chapman, born in 1848, who was Thomas's son. The same year an advertisement appeared in the East Kent Gazette: 'Wheatsheaf Inn to be let with large yard, stabling and coach house. Would suit general dealer. Apply Sittingbourne brewery.'

Clearly, the brewery was still in control of the premises. In 1871, the Wheatsheaf acquired a new landlord, George Wilson. The Wheatsheaf Yard was now closed and along with it the various businesses. The inn was once more a functioning public house.

Among the various landlords were two almost dynastic families. Edward Allen took on the license around 1899 and his wife, Mary, continued the business until 1933. The baton was then handed to Alfred and Blanche Bartlett with Blanche continuing into the early 1960s.

George and Margaret Calver took charge of the pub in the 1970s. Derek Lee moved into the premises with his family and was the landlord from around 1990. In February 2010, Derek Lee was declared bankrupt at Medway County Court. The reason given to the Court for the business failure was the change in peoples' social lives being responsible for less frequent visits to licensed premises.

The pub was the last of those in East Street to close – seemingly having just closed for business in 2019.

92-98 East Street

These four red bricked, two storey cottages next to the Wheatsheaf Inn, were entirely unremarkable in appearance. The most significant event in their history, together with Norris Yard cottages 1 to 3, was their role as a Lodging House. On 3rd November 1910, an advertisement appeared in the *East Kent Gazette*, '*Lodging House consisting of seven cottages to be let'*.

The 1908 Sittingbourne Directory shows, Frank Jury as the Lodging House proprietor,

In 1921 the block, which was a freehold property, including the goodwill and furniture of a registered Lodging House, together with numbers 1 to 7 Norris's Yard, were put up for sale as a going concern. Auction bidding started at £200 with the lot eventually being sold for £460 to Leonard Keel from Bexon, near Bredgar. Mr Keel applied to be the Registered Keeper of the Lodging House which had previously been held by Mr Thomas. Following an inspection of the premises he continued the business until at least 1933.

At this time, Hope Cottages, also in Norris Yard were sold and thereafter the East Street cottages last inhabitant was Edward Swift at 96 East Street. Three years later in October 1936, the lodging house comprising of the four houses, numbers 92 to 98 together with 1 to 3 Norris Yard were sold to brewers Style & Winch for £900. The 1938 Ordnance Survey map of Sittingbourne shows Norris Yard and its' buildings intact, but by 1939 there is no record of these properties, which must be assumed to have been demolished.

An aerial view taken in 1946 appears to confirm this contention. In place of the seven cottages, Norris Yard contains a large circular structure. This may have been an emergency concrete tank used for storing water in case of fire during the war.

	92 East Street	94 East Street	96 East Street	98 East Street
1871	Richard Jenner general labourer	George Mainwaring labourer	William Ash general labourer	John Wildish blacksmith
1881	George Hills general labourer	uninhabited	Robert Howard general labourer	Elizabeth Dolman
1891	uninhabited	uninhabited	uninhabited	Arthur Bottle cement labourer
1901	George Hills brickfield labourer	Thomas Bassant, Family and lodgers	Joseph Richards, Family and lodgers	lodging house
1908	Frank Jury lodging house proprietor	Frank Jury lodging house proprietor	Frank Jury lodging house proprietor	Frank Jury lodging house proprietor
1922	No record	No record	Charles Butler, George Jarvis, Edith and Leonard Keel	No record
1926	Leonard Keel lodging house proprietor	Leonard Keel lodging house proprietor	Leonard Keel lodging house proprietor	No entry
1933	Owner: Leonard Keel form Bexon, Bredgar.	Owner: Leonard Keel form Bexon, Bredgar.	Owner: Leonard Keel form Bexon, Bredgar.	Owner: Leonard Keel form Bexon, Bredgar.

Norris Yard, East Street

The area immediately behind the Wheatsheaf public house and the adjacent cottages in East Street was divided into the Wheatsheaf Yard and what later became known as Norris' Yard. The 1840 tithe Map of Sittingbourne shows that at the rear of the Yard were eight cottages all owned by George Smeed, He was very much an up and coming business man, who was the tenant of the Ship Inn. The cottages were occupied by tenants with the one attributed as being occupied by George Smeed possibly being let out to a relative. By 1866 Norris' Yard had been re-developed and this row of eight cottages had been demolished and new buildings introduced. These structures remained largely in place until 1938 with a few minor changes. Further changes took place after the war and when Chilton Avenue was extended to intersect with South Avenue. In the early 1960s about half of the now former Norris' Yard was completely cleared of buildings. It has not been established how the Yard came to be named, although the 1881 census records a Thomas Norris, a carpenter, who may have used the yard as a carpenter's shop; it was first recorded as being designated Norris' Yard in the 1897 Ordnance Survey map of Sittingbourne. In the 1861 census, 'East Street' was referred to as 'High Street'. There is no separate description for Norris' Yard but the area was enumerated as the 'Wheatsheaf and the cottages at the back.' Later records show that there were at least nine cottages in the Yard. The first three were described as Norris Yard Cottages 1, 2, and 3. These properties were at the rear of 92, 94 and 96 East Street respectively.

In the early 1900s, numbers 1-3 Norris' Yard formed part of a '*lodging house*' run by Frank Jury. This enterprise also included numbers 92-98 East Street. Were these buildings in a state of disrepair? The 1902 council minutes reported:

> '*Notice is served on the owners of the lodging house near the Wheatsheaf Inn within 14 days to repair defective paving on the premises reported by the medical officer as injurious to health*'.

They were uninhabited in 1871 as it is possible they had just been purchased the previous year. In 1870, the East Kent Gazette announced '*Wheatsheaf Inn to be let with large yard, stabling and coach house.*' Between 1871 and 1891, more cottages in Norris' Yard were made habitable and these became known as '*Hope Cottages*', confirmed in the 1901 census. The numbering of these cottages was contiguous with the first three cottages, commencing at number 4 through to number 9.

Hope Cottages and Chilton Flats, East Street

The Sittingbourne tithe map of 1840 does not show the buildings that were later to become known as Hope Cottages. They are present in the 1865/6 map of Sittingbourne. Between this date and 1886 at least, there is evidence that one of the cottages was a hostelry known as the '*Hope Beer House'*. The Canterbury Journal, Kentish Times and Farmer's Gazette of the 27th February 1886 reports the case of a '*PRECOCIOUS YOUNG THIEF'*. The miscreant in question was William Payne, a 15 year old boy from Shakespeare Road, not too far from Hope Cottages. He was accused of stealing a rabbit. The paper reports, '*George West of New Brompton, a dealer, said while he was in the Hope beerhouse, East Street, on Wednesday afternoon, the prisoner, accompanied by another boy, offered him a rabbit for sale, which he purchased for 1s 3d'*.

The inhabitants of Hope Cottages were workers, many of whom were labourers. Some people like Kate Digby and Albert Byfleet were long term tenants. They were neighbours living at numbers 8 and 9 respectively. Rather unpleasantly, a report from the *East Kent Gazette* in 1921, states that Herbert Byfleet, the 14 year old son of Albert Byfleet who lived next door, assaulted Lilly May Digby, aged 10, the daughter of Mrs Kate Digby. The little girl could not corroborate the incident and the case was dismissed.

Hope Cottages were sold in 1933. The sale was held before a large audience gathered at the Bull sales room in Sittingbourne. Hedley Peters and Son ran the auction of properties in Sittingbourne and surrounding villages. Commenting at the time, Mr Peter's senior said, '*there would always be a demand for cottage property*'. They were sold for £310.

Following the sale there is the high probability that the cottages were refurbished and renamed '*Chilton Flats*', carrying on the same numbering sequence. The properties continued to be occupied by tenants up to the early 1960s, when they were demolished to allow the further development of South Avenue.

	4 Hope Cottages	5 Hope Cottages	6 Hope Cottages	7 Hope Cottages	8 Hope Cottages	9 Hope Cottages
1891	William Kelsey general labourer	Thomas Costin general labourer	John Thomas Living on own means	Harry Thompson general labourer	uninhabited	uninhabited
1901	Fanny Friday	Rose Cherrison	Thomas Yates farm labourer	William Brotherwood farm labourer	Rob Farmer wire worker	William Mead butcher
1911		Not listed	John Packman horse driver	Not listed	Not listed	Minnie Southgate
1915		William Daniel Harris and Harriet Anne Baker				
1922	Alfred Simmons	Edward Baker, Arthur and Mary Reed	Hannah and William Price	Mary and Matilda Simmonds	Kate Digby; Lilly May Digby	Albert and Herbert Byfleet
1926	Alfred Simmons	Arthur Read	John Jackson	Harry Simmons	Kate Digby	Albert Byfleet
1933	Alfred Simmons and Sarah Standen	Dorothy Cooper, George and Florence Reed	John and Mary Smith	William Page	Kate Digby	Albert and Herbert Byfleet
1933	Hope Cottages sold for £310					
	4 Chilton Flats	**5 Chilton Flats**	**6 Chilton Flats**	**7 Chilton Flats**	**8 Chilton Flats**	**9 Chilton Flats**
1939	William and Alice Gregg brickwork labourer	William and Caroline Deakins brickwork labourer	Ada Martin, Alfred and Beatrice Smith	Arthur, Eileen and Ronald Reed labourer, public walls construction	No record	Isabel and Elsie Gregory domestic servant
1951	Sarah Seeker	Mary and Maurice Stafford	Nickoleta and Sydney West	Kathleen and Robert Fitzgerald	Aubrey and Sarah Crayford	Charlie and Lottie Shilling
1960	Sarah Secker	Horace and Vera Stevens	Roy and Barbara Batchelor	Edward and Maud Simmons	No record	Jane and Wilfred Kemp

Residents of Hope Cottages and Chilton Flats

Chapman's Cottages

The buildings, which later became known as 'Chapman's Cottages' are mentioned in the 1840 Sittingbourne tithe schedule. At this time and for the best part of the next 50 years, they were probably known as *Chilton Orchard Cottages*. There were four two up and two down cottages numbered 1-4 and in 1840 were occupied by tenants Robert Parker, William Cheeseman, Benjamin Mitchell and George Sidders. All the cottages were owned by William Smeed.

Twenty years later, ownership of these cottages passed to Thomas Chapman who ran or rented several businesses from the Wheatsheaf public house. Around

1871 they were designated as 'Chapman's Cottages, East Street', close by to Mr Chapman's Orchard.

Apple orchards near Sittingbourne, 19th Century. (JM)

South Avenue c. early 1960s (JC)

This picture shows the junction of South Avenue with East Street before development was complete around the late 1950s or early 1960s. The recreation ground can be seen to the left with the pathway to Chilton Farm running parallel to South Avenue alongside the partitioning fence. The trackway led from just outside Chapman's Cottages across fields and orchards to Chilton Farm, similar to the apple orchards from the 1950s, shown in the photograph, whose appearance will have changed little down the decades.

The houses to the north side of East Street are still in place. To the right of centre is the end elevation of a building which are Chapman's Cottages. They were very small two up and two down terraced properties each accessed by a small set of steps with hand railings leading on to a common slightly raised footway from which opened the front doors to each of the cottages.

The cottages were occupied by working class families who were mostly labourers either in the brickfields or on nearby farms such as Chilton Farm. But in the late 1950s, number 3 was occupied by Les Court, a postman and his wife Florence.

East Street to Chilton trackway

East Street, was formerly known as Watling Street, a road built by the Romans from an existing ancient trackway. The Roman Road ran East-West across Great Britain from Canterbury to St Albans and beyond.

The junction today between East Street and South Avenue was also formed from an ancient trackway or lane. In her book, *'An Archaeological Mystery',* *Lesley Feakes* describes the pre-Roman system of the parallel 'streets' of North Kent, running up to half a mile apart in a North West, (NW) and South East, (SE) direction, off a main Roman Road. In the Sittingbourne area, East Street is the former Roman Road. The map shows an indication of possible ancient 'streets' in the East Street area. Some are now well established local roads and others are still pathways which were dominant routes of transport in the 19th century and before.

1940 Aerial photograph of East Street showing possible parallel 'streets'

The lane, it was probably lined by hedgerows, ran from its entry bounded by a picket fence on East Street, passed Chapman's Cottages and on to Chilton Farm and Chilton Manor, where local people worked as labourers and servants. The path probably formed part of an ancient route between the two parishes of Iwade and Milstead.

Chilton Manor

Chapman was a common surname in and around Sittingbourne in the 19th century and many were no doubt related to one another. Their stations in life covered the whole social spectrum from publican, businessman and gaoler to even Lord of the Manor.

Robert Chapman was indeed the incumbent of Chilton Manor with its sprawling farm acreage, for most of the 19th century. He was born in 1823 and by the time of his marriage to Hannah Matson in 1862, he was an accomplished farmer employing eight men and three boys. The 1911 census reveals Chilton Manor to be a building of considerable size having 12 rooms.

But of all the Chapman's, Robert Chapman was always known as 'Mr Chapman'. No likenesses of 'Mr Chapman' are known to exist. However, Harry Grenstead writing under the pen name of 'Urban Rus' in his 1882 narrative called 'Old Faces in Odd Places', does offer a description of 'Mr Chapmans' appearance. Of course, this name does not appear itself in the book, but reliable sources identify the books' characters, David and Elizabeth Doman, as Robert and Hannah Chapman. The supposedly fictional account of the inhabitants of Highstilts, in real life, Sittingbourne, actually portrayed important townsfolk of the time and how they went about their lives.

So, with this in mind, Mr Doman, a.k.a. Mr Chapman, is clearly a man with little hair. *'On Sunday mornings the top of Mr Doman's bald head was just visible above the red velvet cushions of the pew...'* In demeanour he was *'...a mild and inoffensive gentleman of no marauding tendencies...'* But some less kind people said that, *'...old David Doman was not blessed with all the brains God had given him...'* and that *'...he might have mislaid or parted with some of that mental power with which he had been blessed at birth; moreover he was not a learned nor even... a clever man. But he was a cheery, good-hearted and minded old man.'*

According to Urban Rus, Mr Doman was the last of his line having no heirs. On the other hand, Mr Chapman may have been the last of his line having no sons but he was blessed with a daughter, Mary Ellen. Were Mr Doman and Mr Chapman one in the same, possibly, but Mr Chapman was no fool. On his death in December 1920 at the age of 97, his effects amounted to £15,786 7s 6d which in todays' money (2017), would be the equivalent of £712, 000.

Further evidence of the paths antiquity lies in the discovery of Roman earthenware in 'cemeteries' near the gate leading into Chilton farmyard. *'Collectanea Cantiana'* which catalogues archaeological finds in *'the neighbourhood of Sittingbourne'* describes a cinerary urn of thick blue glass, in the style of Upchurchware, containing bones and small iron nails. The author, George Payne Jr, features in HSI in our section dealing with the brewery and bank run by Messr's Vallance and Payne.

From 'Collectanea Cantiana', George Payne, 1893

In more recent times, late 19th century maps show such a pathway running from East Street through the orchards to Chilton Farm. It is perfectly straight and runs in a NW to SE direction, which is further evidence for it originating as one of the ancient parallel *'streets'*.

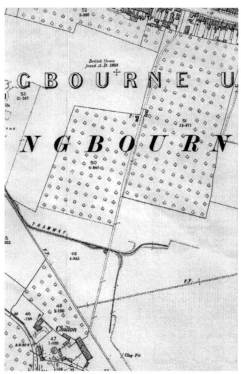

1897 Ordnance Survey map of Sittingbourne showing trackway from East Street to Chilton

In the late 1930s, the eastern side of what became South Avenue was developed alongside the existing pathway which continued to run along the boundaries of the remaining orchards to Chilton, up to the early 1960s. Further development of the Stanhope Avenue area, obliterated all traces of this direct route from East Street to Chilton.

However, a similar almost parallel pathway does still exist and in 2016 follows a route from the A2 via Commonwealth Close, skirting Fallowfield towards the Swanstree Avenue housing development exiting on to Swanstree Avenue. The view along this pathway provides an insight to the view along the original Chilton pathway a few hundred yards to the West, might have looked like. It could have run through open fields or may have been bounded by hedgerows on one or both sides.

Pathway on Swanstree Avenue looking NE towards the A2 (JM)

Pathway exiting Swanstree Avenue looking SW across Chilton Manor Farm (JM)

Perhaps a typical tenant of a Chapman's Cottage was Joseph Brenchley, an agricultural labourer, like as father before him. He married his wife Catherine, who was from Dover, in the early 1890s and moved into Chapman's Cottage at this time. Their first born was Ruth, followed by five other children, one of whom, Albert, died at the age of two years. Interestingly, in the 1855 census, Catherine, then aged 46 years old, was described as *'working at home'*. This is interesting terminology as the conventional term 'housewife', in the 19th and early 20th centuries, was reserved for women who did the majority of their chores within a farms' compound. Catherine did not actually live on a farm, so perhaps she earned extra income by taking in other people's washing or sewing. Wages were further supplemented by her son Amos, who in his mid-teens took on a *'provision round'*, possibly delivering groceries from Mr Chapman's business.

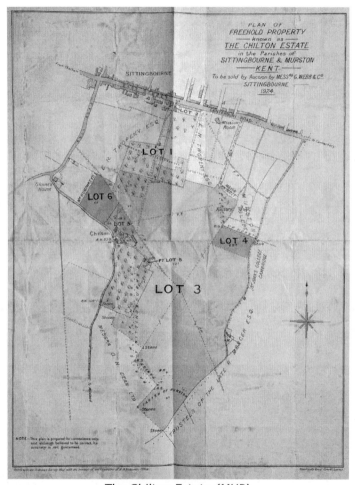

The Chilton Estate (MHP)

The map shows The Chilton Estate in the parishes of Sittingbourne & Murston. It was produced by George Webb & Co for their auction in 1924. Lot 2 was Chapman's Cottages which are situated on the corner of the footpath, which ran up to Chilton and was later to become South Avenue. The map, very nicely, confirms earlier investigations on the position of the Cottages and the route of the footpath.

Just before the Second World War in 1939, cottage number 1 was occupied by Thomas Baching, a builder's labourer. The other three cottages were all occupied by widows, Eliza Harris, Amy Lilley and Anne Hammond, who moved into number 4 with her husband, James, in the early 1920s.

After the war, the cottages showed patchy occupancy with only two of the cottages being tenanted in the 1950s and 1960s. During this period all the cottages were occupied at different times meaning they were still in good repair and habitable after some hundred and 30 years.

The cottages were finally demolished in the early 1960s when South Avenue's development was completed. Interestingly, aerial photography shows that the semi-detached houses, numbers (1 and 1a), South Avenue, occupy the land where Chapman's Cottages once stood. Both the new and the old buildings have approximately the same foot print, which means the original Chapman's Cottages each occupied half the space of their 1960s replacements.

	Chilton Orch. 1	Chilton Orch. 2	Chilton Orch. 3	Chilton Orch. 4
1840	Robert Parker (Owner: William Smeed)	William Cheeseman, (Owner: William Smeed)	Benjamin Mitchell (Owner: William Smeed)	George Sidders (Owner: William Smeed)
1861	James Daisy, basket maker	Thomas Sivyer, labourer	Thomas Crayden, labourer	John Barnes, labourer
1871	Mary Hughes farm labourer	George Reader, Brickmaker George Hills gen. labourer	George Smith gen. labourer	
	Chapman's Cott.1	Chapman's Cott.2	Chapman's Cott.3	Chapman's Cott. 4
1891	Joseph Brenchley ag. lab.	Thomas Bennet ag. lab.	Henry Anderson ag. lab.	Emma Cooper widow
1901	Joseph Brenchley, farm labourer	No record	George Baines, ag. lab.	
1908-09	Joseph Brenchley	Elize Hilliard	William Mannouch	
1911	Joseph Brenchley	No record	James Goodwin, horses keeper	
1922	Amos and Catherine Brenchley	Alfred Mead	Alfred Wraight (? Wright)	Anne and James Hammond
1926	Joseph Edward Brenchley	Alfred Mead	Alfred Wright	
1933	Catherine and Joseph (or ? James) Brenchley	Eliza Harris	Amy and Walter Lilley	Anne and James Hammond
1939	Thomas Baching	Eliza Harris widow	Amy Lilley widow	Anne Hammond widow
1951	Elizabeth Hawes	No entry	Richard and Rosina Chambers	No entry
1960	No entry	Leslie and Maud Calder	Florence Carr and Les Court	Sydney and Sylvia Harris

Residents of Chilton Orchard and Chapman's Cottages

Chapman's Cottages before their demolition.
Sketch by John Mount

The semi-detached houses that replaced Chapman's Cottages.

'PROPOSALS FOR SHOPS REJECTED'

This headline appeared in the East Kent Gazette in the mid-1960s. The article reported:

> *'A plan for the demolition of numbers 1, 2, 3 and 4 Chapman's Cottages, South Avenue, Sittingbourne and for the re-building of two shops with living accommodation above was rejected by Sittingbourne Council's Plans Committee on Thursday.*
>
> *The application was made by Mr E. Sandy of Prince Charles Avenue, Sittingbourne.*

The Surveyor, Mr A. W. Lloyd, reported that outline permission was granted in June 1964, to use the site for the erection of lock-up garages. The land, he said, was shown on the Town Map as residential.
"It is considered that the use of this site for shopping purposes would be likely to attract traffic, which would constitute an additional hazard to the conditions already prevailing at this important junction", he said.
The Surveyor recommended refusal of the plan, stating that adequate shopping facilities were available in the neighbourhood.'

Not long after this, the site was developed with a couple of houses occupied by Mr Sandy and his brother – partners in an electricians' business.

The White House

The White House, which was built several years after Chapman's cottages and located nearby had five rooms. It was known by several names including Plantation House or Cottage, Chapman's Orchard Cottage and Chilton. In 1871, Chilton as it was then known, was occupied by George Sweffer, a farm labourer. Between 1881 and 1933, the property was occupied by the Foster family. Charles Foster, who was born in Halstow, was a gardener and later a grocer and fruiterer. He had moved into the cottage by 1881 with his wife Sarah, originally from Bredgar and their children. They had previously lived in Bapchild.

Approaching retirement at the age of 70 years, Charles handed over his business to his son Albert, who was still living with his parents at this time. In fact, Albert never moved out of the cottage and was still there with his own family, Alice and Amy at least until 1933. Charles Foster died in November 1921 aged 80, after a long illness.

Numbers 100, 102, 104, 106 and 108 East Street

The South side of East Street from 100a to 120

The two dilapidated cottages on the near right of the photograph are represented on the 1840 tithe map on parcels of land designated as 203 and 204. When the houses were numbered in 1871, these buildings became numbers 100, 102. Next door, just visible, is one bay window of a double fronted house on parcel 211, which became number 108. Numbers 104 and 106 are set back out of sight.

As reference, the double-fronted white building at the far end of the row became number 120 East Street. The buildings in the picture designated as 100, 102 are thought to date from the early 18th century, but in the photograph, seem to have been remodelled to some extent since then. We have noted the windows on 102 – horizontal sliding-sashes to the first floor and the simple shutter to the ground floor. These buildings were demolished in the late 20th century and replaced by the buildings that now house Doves the Funeral Directors.

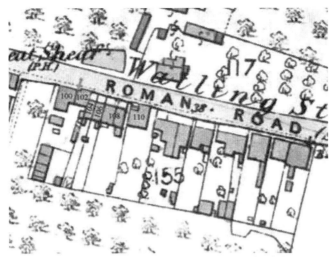

1865/6 Ordnance Survey map detail showing today's house numbers

104, 106 and 108 East Street from right to left. The two small terrace houses were built probably about two hundred years ago. (JM)

These were set back further from the road than their neighbours at 102 and 100, setting a building line that has been followed all along this stretch of the street.

In the previous photograph we can see one of the pair of single-storey bay windows on number 108. These bays were removed about 50 years ago and replaced with the rather bland front elevation, painted to hide the scars of the changed brickwork.

Numbers 100-102 East Street

Number 100 East Street

That part of the South Avenue-East Street junction which was bordered on its eastern side by plots 203 and 204 on the 1840 tithe map of Sittingbourne was owned by William Smeed – perhaps a relation of George Smeed, the aspiring man of business, who owned the row of cottages nearby, behind the Wheatsheaf Inn. Plot 203 was occupied by Richard Smeed, perhaps another member of that same family. Charles Wiles was the tenant in the cottage on plot 204. There were other cottages on this plot, also owned by William Smeed, which later became known as Chapman's Cottages – being part of Chilton Farm, they bore the name of the farmer.

View east at the shop at 100 East Street   *View west c.1935*

The photograph on the left was probably taken near the end of the 19th century. It shows 100 East Street when it was a shop. A 'Lyons' tea sign is just discernible on the wall near the doorway. This may have been the last commercial property on this side of the street at this time. The picket fence is the beginning of the pathway going to Chilton Farm. There is an indistinct notice on the wall of number 100, which may point to *Chapman's Cottages.*

The second photograph, circa 1935, views a similar scene but from the opposite direction. The advertisement is on the end elevation of 102.

This property may not have been used for business premises until around 1870, when William Taylor, who was in his 30th year, opened a bakers' shop.

He came from Eastchurch with his wife Sarah and son Albert. The house must have been quite crowded as the 1871 census reports that his mother-in-law and brother-in-law plus a servant were also in residence. William ran the business until 1876, when this house together with four cottages behind it were put up for sale. The property was sold to William Vincent Bradley, who continued the bakery running it alongside a similar business in West Street.

Three years later in 1881, Charles Dungey, with his family, had taken over the bakery, which must have been successful as now a bakery lad was employed. It is not clear how long the bakery continued because in 1890, Adolphe McCullen, who was a painter and glazier now occupied the premises. In

1898, Horace Savage, who lived at 157 East Street had a business here but due to family circumstances was forced into bankruptcy.(EKG) In 1899, William Sargent, a shoemaker moved in, followed by James Goodwin, his wife and nephew, who was a *carter* around 1901. At this time, Joseph Brown, a baker, was also in residence but occupied a separate part of the house. This rapid turnover of occupants continued until at least 1908 with the occupancy of Charles Ballard, a confectioner. During this time, it is likely that this address still functioned as a shop albeit in many guises.

Around 1911, Alfred Smith, another baker from Rainham, took up residency with his wife Beatrice. This census identifies the house as having only three rooms; perhaps because one of the original rooms became the shop. Alfred was born in 1871 and in 1901 married Beatrice Bradshaw at St Michael's church, Sittingbourne. At the time, Alfred was living at 49 East Street with his parents. His father was a wheelwright. Beatrice lived with her parents, John and Olive Higgins at the Rendezvous public house, 104 High Street, Sittingbourne. Her first marriage in 1899, was to Frederick Bradshaw but she was widowed shortly afterwards and two years later in 1901, married her second husband, Alfred Smith.

Alfred and Beatrice continued to run the shop as a confectioners and tobacconist for many years. Beatrice ran the shop mostly on her own as Alfred, a Journeyman Baker, plied his trade elsewhere retiring just before the outbreak of the Second World War. This puts the date of the rebuild just after the war, when the new houses became residential. In the 1950s up to 1960, the house was occupied by Brian, Gladys and Leslie Austin, although Brian must have died in the late 1950s – the name above the shop was G M Austin. They remained there until the 1960s when the incumbent house was demolished to make way for the continuing South Avenue development.

The houses behind 'Doves', on the site of 'Chapman's Cottages', were built in the 1960s for their own occupation by the Sandy brothers. They ran their own business as electricians.

Number 100a East Street

The directory for 1908 and the census for 1911, coupled with indications on the Ordnance Survey plans, tell us that, in the early years of the 20th century, numbers 100 and 102 had been restructured to form a third dwelling. The 1911 census records 100a as having four rooms. In 1908, the occupants were Henry Hinkley, a retired carman, and his wife; 1922, Alfred and Jane Cox; 1926, William John Hollands; 1933 Dorothy and Edwin Jury; 1939, Frederick Bassant, a brickfields labourer and his wife Nellie.

The next occupancy that we have traced was in 1951 – Betty and Eric Akhurst. They stayed there until the 1960s when the property was pulled down.

Number 102 East Street

This property was originally owned by the Smeed family in the 19th century; it is not known when that ownership ceased but it is likely that many of the occupants were tenants given the working-class nature of their occupations. By 1861, Soloman Wood, age 45, a general labourer and local preacher previously from Rodmersham, was living here with his wife, Hannah, age 47, nee Brooker and their four children, Sarah age 15; George, 19; Emily, 12 and Ellen, aged eight. Two other children, Mary Anne, 24 and Elizabeth, 21, are no longer living with the family. The family was still there in 1871 but by 1881 had moved on.

In that year, William Cackett, from Charing now age 33, a local tradesman, provided plumbing, painting and glazing services, was in residence with his wife Harriett, age 31, from Borden, together with their young daughter Rose Mabel, age three. By 1890, Mrs Elizabeth Johnson, a shopkeeper, had moved in but remained only for a short time, as in 1891, the house was occupied by Edwin Read. He was 32 years old and was a general labourer from Rainham. His wife, Cecilia, age 27, was born in Bobbing. Four years later they had their first child, a daughter named Hilda, followed by a son, William and a further baby daughter. Clearly, larger accommodation was now required, so they moved to 3 Shakespeare Road.

The 1901 census shows the house to be uninhabited, but by 1908, the occupants were Charles Ballard, a shoemaker; Emily & Henry Knight were there in 1922 and William Venner in 1926.

The next occupant was William Attaway, whose life was tinged with sadness. He was born in Faversham in 1874, but at the age of six, was living in the workhouse with his mother, Emma, age 30, a laundress. There was no husband and father, so it is not known what happened to him. Fortunately, they were only in this position for about a year as the 1881 census records them living in Water Lane, Ospringe. At the age of 27, William married Emma Bashford in 1901. Perhaps his fortunes were on the way upwards. But this was not to be. In 1906, just five years later, Emma died; she was only 32 years old. The unfortunate manner of her early death was reported in the *Whitstable Times and Herne Bay Herald* on Saturday 7th April 1906 as follows:

'CHATHAM

FATAL YAWN. A young married woman, the wife of a labourer named
William Attaway of Bassett Road, Sittingbourne, died at Chatham
Hospital on Wednesday from shock and weakness, after having a
dislocated jaw replaced. The jaw had slipped out of place whilst she was
yawning.'

There is no record of William remarrying. But before or around 1933, he moved into 102 East Street. He was there during the Second World War and remained there until at least 1951 and probably until 1960. Interestingly, throughout all this time, he shared his home with a widowed lady called Alice Rockliffe born in 1916. In the 1939 Register William was described as a retired widower and Alice, a widow who provided 'unpaid domestic duties'. Perhaps Alice was Williams's live-in housekeeper or companion but in his last few years, William achieved stability and companionship in his life, which had thus far eluded him. William died in Sittingbourne in 1958.

C P Studio

Around 1957, Paul Cook and Beryl Pritchard, both 21 year olds, opened C P Studio, the name being derived from the initials of their respective surnames. Paul and Beryl met at Art School where they had studied photography. Beryl's uncle Vic offered to rent them premises for 15 shillings a week, in East Street. Paul described the property as "*an old dilapidated one-bedroom cottage that had been converted into a shop in the unfashionable east end of Sittingbourne.*" The tiny upstairs room about the size of an attic, previously the bedroom, was covered in an accumulation of dust and cobwebs. Accessible via a narrow winding staircase, it had not been occupied for a number of years and the gap of four inches between the front wall and the floor, meant it was not habitable and certainly not suitable for a photographic studio.

C P Studio at number 102 and G. M. Austin's shop at number 100 c.1957
100a is squeezed between the two shops

The business was confined to downstairs, which comprised of a small front room for the reception area and shop and a rear ten foot by six-foot room for use as a studio.

After a week of trading, their first customer, turned out to be, what we would today call a scammer. They had fallen prey to a woman whose family was notorious in the district. Having made a booking for the following week to have her child's portrait taken, she left, but returned soon afterwards, claiming to have lost her purse and being unable to do her food shopping. Out of kindness Paul and Beryl offered the distraught lady their 15 shillings float from the till, to be paid back the following day; and that was the last they saw of her.

Their second customer was a young man, who wanted a passport photo; this proved to be a more profitable transaction.

Despite a small fire caused by the unguarded element of an electric fire setting light to a flimsy curtain, business soon picked up with bookings for weddings and studio portraits. Space in the shop was found to stock a small range of films and cameras.

As business increased, Paul and Beryl took on an employee, Carol. She was a cheerful and bright school leaver, who assisted in the darkroom.

After a few years and the growing need for more space an opportunity to buy the 'Old Wheel' café at the other end of town arose. Originally, a large rambling block of four buildings, number 25 West Street offered plenty of space for a studio, extensive darkroom and a finishing room. The café was an added bonus.

C P Studio relocated to West Street around 1962, (see Sittingbourne High Street West book).

As the premises had been rented from Beryl's uncle Vic Berry, when C P Studio relocated, Vic set up a betting shop, as he was a bookmaker by trade. Paul Cook recalls, "*As off-course betting was illegal in those days, the front of his premises purported to be a junk shop. It was an open secret that a thriving bookie's business existed behind the façade of rubbish and useless items and he prospered enormously having a surprising number of regulars willing to fill up his coffers with their hard earned cash.*"

The 1963 directory also records L. C. Meadmore living at this address. As Vic Berry did not live on the premises, spare rooms were probably let out to maximise his income.

New building at 100-102 East Street

In the early 1970s, in succession to the ancient cottages 100/102 East Street, a new property was erected and later redeveloped into business premises with flats above. Number 100 was occupied by a ladies hairdresser run by Alan Tidy.(HSI)

The living accommodation above the shop Number 102 was occupied by Lawrence Meadmore in 1970 and by John Parkhouse in 1990. The flat at Number 100a was occupied by Neil Redmond in 1990.

From 1985 until the present day, Doves Funeral Service combined these two addresses. Doves is a family business originally established in Bromley in 1985 by Mr Sean Costello. The business now occupies several locations throughout Kent.

Number 104 East Street

The 1840 tithe map shows that what is today 104 East Street was occupied by John Cooper, the freeholder being Robert Divers. In 1841 James Fry lived there with his wife and family.

The 1861 census reveals that 29 year old Thomas Luck, a labourer, was at home with his sister.

James Backhouse

By 1871, 47 year old James Backhouse was living at this address. He was a Suffolk man born in the old town of Saxmundham. On moving to Kent, he met a Newington girl, Sarah Chambers and they were married in June 1851. In the 1871 census, James is described as a 'Greenwich Pensioner'.

This designation identifies James as a former Royal Navy man, for the term 'Greenwich Pensioner' is the naval equivalent of a 'Chelsea Pensioner'. Their home was the Royal Hospital for Seamen at Greenwich. Designed by Sir Christopher Wren it was opened between 1696 and 1712. The hospital housed elderly and injured seamen and James must have fallen into the second category. Pensioners were allowed to leave the Hospital during their leisure hours. They were forbidden to marry but those who already had wives and families could visit them. At its peak in 1814, the Hospital accommodated 2,700 naval veterans whose average age was 56 years. When it closed in 1869, it transformed into the Royal Naval College until it too was decommissioned in 1998.

James may have lived in the Hospital for a short time but left to get married. Sadly, Sarah died at the fairly young age of 58 in 1879. This may have been the time that James left East Street for the 1881 census places James at 27 Bayford Road and confirmed he was a widower. James died in 1894.

'A Greenwich Pensioner with a wooden leg, standing in a landscape' (WI)

Henry Darby

The next occupant was 32 year old Henry Darby who had moved from Newington but was originally from Alton in Hampshire, who was there by 1881. He was living with his widowed mother Jane Darby as his father, John, had died a few years earlier. Other members of the household were his sister, Jane Jackson also a widow, who earned a living as a shirt needlewoman and four nephews and nieces. He found work as a traction engine driver and according to an amendment in the 1891 census used his skills in agriculture most likely travelling between different farms. He never married but was content to live with his widowed sister Jane even when they left number 104 by 1901 and moved to 133 East Street.

Hornsby's Portable Steam Engine and Threshing Machine. From 'The Illustrated London News' 1851. This is most likely to be the type of traction engine operated by Henry Darby. (JM)

William Thomas

William Thomas, who made a living as a butcher and slaughterman, lived at 104 in 1901 with his wife Emily née Feaver and three month old son, Leonard. William was born in 1868 in Upottery, Devon. They were married at St Michael's Church in Sittingbourne on the 23rd June 1900. Perhaps it was common practice but just before their marriage both bride and groom gave their residences as that of the bride's parents. The house is not listed in the 1911 census, so was probably empty. The whereabouts of the Thomas family is not known but they must have left this address.

Other Occupants

As with most private occupancy, information on the occupants is rather scant as very few were recorded in trade directories, except the more wealthy residents who would have paid a fee.

James Finn may have been the next occupier of 104 as his name is listed in the 1908 directory. After that, there was a Mrs Agnes Thomson, whose death at the age of 41 years following a serious illness, was noted in the *East Kent Gazette* of the 1st July 1916, She was followed by Bertha and Thomas Mannouch who were there by 1922 and, still there by at least 1926, the year of the General Strike. On the 23rd February 1935, a 'Thanks for Sympathy' notice appeared in the *East Kent Gazette*, from the family of Mr H. J. Baker which suggests that he lived there prior to his death. The next resident was probably a Mr & Mrs Elizabeth Milnes whose names are listed in the 1939 Register. He was a Council Labourer. Income towards the rent was provided by George Swinyard, a 74 year old widowed brickfield labourer. Immediately after the war, Elizabeth and Verney Hudson lived there at least until 1947 according to the electoral register. There is then a substantial gap in the records. Later residents included

Albert and Evelyn Fox from 1975; Ernest and Elizabeth Fuller at least between 1980 and 1985 and then in 1998, N. Clare, K . Jarvis and Michael Kidd.

106 and 108 East Street
The Coleman and the Watts Families

This is the brief story of two families, the Colemans and the Watts whose fortunes were inextricably linked. Eliza's birth name was Rutland and her father's name was John; they were a good Sheppey family. Eliza was born in 1813 in Harty, Kent. At the age of 26 she married George Coleman in Murston Parish Church. Over the next few years they lived at the Elmley Ferry House and had three children, Louisa born in 1840, of which, more later, Esther and Ephraim. Sadly, George's death came early after only ten years of marriage in 1849.

The Watts family hailed from Erith which was then in Kent but today is a part of south-east London. The 1840 census depicts the familiar large early Victorian family. Thomas, a brickmaker of which there were many in Erith and Elizabeth Watts had at least eight children including Robert born in 1826 and John Alfred born ten years later.

John was the first to migrate southwards to the Sittingbourne area perhaps initially to find work in the brickfields like his father, although he must have joined the Royal Navy at some point as in later life he was described as a naval pensioner. Robert, John's younger brother soon followed perhaps for the same reason initially, as he soon met a girl from Murston, home to several local brick fields. Her name was Eliza Coleman, who we have met before. She was a young widow whose husband George had recently passed away. They were married on the 28th May 1851.

But here there is a twist in the story because Eliza's daughter Louisa no doubt influenced by the proximity of the two families, then married Robert's brother John Alfred in 1863. Was this a case of a brother marrying his niece, a prohibited liaison? The answer is a firm no, because Louisa Coleman was in fact Robert's step daughter from a previous marriage. Although at first sight this may seem unlikely, there was not much of an age difference despite the status of their relationships in each family. John Alfred, Robert's brother was 26 years old and Louisa was 22 years old.

The final coincidence is that John and Robert lived in adjacent houses in East Street although not at the same time. John Watts lived at number 106 and Robert Watts occupied 108.

106 East Street

In 1840 Edmund Cruttenden was in residence, the freeholder again being Robert Divers. The 1841 census shows that Charles Hughes with his wife and son were there.

Alfred Swinyard

Alfred was a local village lad, born in Tunstall in 1835 and still living with his parents, Edward, a journeyman and his mother Sarah when they relocated to Chalkwell by 1851. On his coming of age, he married Sarah Anne Brenchley just before Christmas in 1856. He must have served an apprenticeship because in the 1861 census he is a blacksmith living in the High Street with his wife and son Henry. At this time, houses were not numbered but Alfred's 'High Street' address was in reality 'High Street East' as evidenced by the 'Wheatsheaf Inn being a little further along the same road. To make ends meet, Arthur had taken in a young coach builder from Maidstone whose name was Thomas. Alfred's address was firmly confirmed in the 1871 census as 106 East Street, the new name for High Street East. Alfred had put his blacksmiths' skills to good use and was now described as a Carriage Smith. Most likely he had teamed up with Thomas his coach builder lodger. But Thomas had moved out of 106, probably to make room for Alfred's ever growing family of at least five children. Alfred too had moved on by 1881 to Terrace Road.

In the grand scheme of things, this house move was almost literally a drop in the ocean, because four years later on the 20th June 1885, Albert and his family set sail from Liverpool on the steamship 'Wisconsin', for New York.

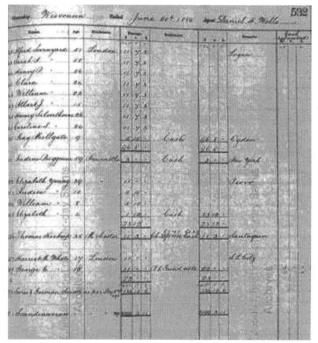

Passenger List for SS Wisconsin, 20th June 1885 showing the Swinyard family

Albert continued his work as a blacksmith and carriage builder and no doubt he and his family had a good life. But, this phase came to an abrupt end in 1896, when his wife, Sarah, passed away. Albert was to find happiness again and remarried; his new wife was Elizabeth Pollow Warn and they set up home in Ogden, Utah. Albert died in the United States on the 29th June 1913.

An obituary appeared in the local newspaper, *'The Herald – Republican'* with a rather blunt headline:

TOOK ILL EN-ROUTE TO CELEBRATION; NOW DEAD

Ogden, June 29. – Alfred Swinyard, 80 years of age, died this morning from acute indigestion at the home of his daughter Mrs H. J. Silverthorn. He had been ill four days. Mr Swinyard was born in England February 3, 1835 and came to Utah in 1885. locating in Logan, where he conducted a blacksmith and carriage building shop. Last Wednesday he left Logan with the old folks of Cache county to go to Wandamere in Salt Lake, but he became sick on the train and, when he reached Ogden, was removed to the home of his daughter. He is survived by a widow, four sons and a daughter………one sister, 17 grandchildren and five great grandchildren……

He was buried in Logan cemetery.

Arthur Bond, Ernest Thomas, George Henry Wood and Charles Robert Kidder

The next resident was Arthur Bond about which very little is known. Born in 1849 he lived in London, where he married a London girl, Marion and together they had at least four children. According to the 1881 census, the youngest was Ada, just two years old and born in Bethnal Green. They must have moved to Sittingbourne soon after Ada's birth. He found work as a Yard Foreman.

Ernest Thomas, a cement labourer, was 36 years of age by the time he moved to 106 according to the 1891 census. He previously lived in Westbourne Street and most likely moved there following his marriage to Priscilla Roberts in June 1878.

George Wood, from Whitstable and his wife Caroline née Hall, were at 106 by 1901. They had moved from Minster, where George was a shipwright at Sheerness dockyard. Their daughter, Lily was born six years earlier in Sheerness.

Charles Robert Kidder may have been the next resident for he was mentioned in the 1908 directory. A carpenter, he had married Fanny in 1895 but by 1911 he with his wife had left East Street and moved to 41 Cooper Road.

In 1911 the next resident was John Alfred Watts, he was then 74 years old and a naval pensioner still living with his wife Louisa who was then 70 years of age. His story has already been told.

Frederick Castle

Fred was born on the 22nd April 1906 and made a living as a house decorator. The electoral register for 1922 places him at 106 East Street together with Ada Castle. She may well have been Fred's mother having been born a generation before Fred in 1870.

The 1939 Register records Fred still living at this address, he is single and continues to share the house with Ada Castle. They continued to live there throughout the Second World War up to at least 1947.

Other residents

In 1975, 106 was home to Richard and Marion Stanley. By 1980, David and Jaqueline Atkins had moved in to 106 and were still there in 1998.

108 East Street 'Kimberley'

The land in the 1840 tithe map where number 108 East Street now stands was parcel 211. This land together with adjacent parcels was owned by Robert Divers. In 1840 the occupier was William Dadds. Between 1851 and 1861 the occupant was the curate of Murston the Reverend William John Brewer, a widower in his forties who lived there with his aged mother and a servant. He remarried on the 8th May 1866, to Sarah Panton and later took up a new post as Vicar of Farningham in Kent. It was here that he died on the 26th October 1890, leaving a personal estate of £2,775 11s 4d to his widow Sarah.

Robert Watts

Robert Watts was born in 1828 in Mile End, London. His parents were Thomas, a brickmaker, in whose footsteps Robert would later follow and Elizabeth; he was one of seven siblings. He was still at home with his parents in 1841, living in the Parish of Erith. But by 1851 he had made his way to Kent and was lodging at Elmley Ferry near Murston, no doubt having found work as a labourer in the nearby brickfields.

He must have travelled regularly back to London for it was there that he met his future wife, Eliza Coleman, a shepherd's daughter from Harty and now since widowed following a previous marriage. They were married on the 28th May 1851 in the Parish of St George, Middlesex.

By 1861, they had moved permanently to the Sittingbourne area with Robert having made good in the Murston brickfields as he now employed several men and boys. They were living as an extended family with Eliza's two children from her previous marriage, Esther and Ephraim and Robert's two younger brothers Samuel and Charles at Briar Cottage in the Parish of Borden.

The 1871 census records Robert and Eliza living at 108 East Street, not far from the Murston brickfields. In 1881 they were still there together with Robert's widowed mother Elizabeth who was in her eighties.

Eliza died in June 1885 in Maidstone which suggests that they may have left East Street following the last directory entry in 1882. Following his wife's death, Robert together with his aged mother, moved back to the parish of his parents, Erith, where his mother Elizabeth died in 1897 and her son, Robert a year later on the 2nd February 1898.

Frances Binder

Frances Binder, née Willson Divers, was one of twins born in 1820 in Luddenham, a small village north west of Faversham. On the 19th December 1850, she married Joseph Binder, a builder, in Sittingbourne. He was from St Marylebone in Middlesex, which was where they initially lived. There they had three children. Between 1881 and 1887 they had moved to Sittingbourne and according to Kelly's Directory they were certainly at this address in 1887. Frances at the age of 71, was by then a widow.

The 1890 Kelly's Directory, interestingly records that there was a Mrs Hartridge living at number 108a East Street and Albert Hunt a grocer's manager at number 108b. As Francis was also there in 1891, these entries suggests that the property had been sub-divided at this time. The census of that year confirmed this arrangement showing an additional household, Albert and Caroline Hart occupying part of the building.

France's married daughter Sophie Melville and grandson Audley Melville were staying with her on census night in 1891. By 1895 she had left East Street and was living with Sophie at 59 Park Road, where she died in April 1898. The death certificate recorded the causes of death as cardiac disease and dropsy and was certified by Dr Francis Grayling LRCP.

Philip Bishop and Frank Usherwood

According to the 1895 directory, the next occupant was Philip Bishop. He was the deputy registrar for births and deaths; but by 1899 he had moved his office to West Street, where we have more to say about him and his family, (see also HSI – number 119).

In February 1894 and again on the 14th April that year, the *East Kent Gazette* ran an advertisement: *'House to let, containing seven rooms, wash house and cellars, large garden with side entrance. For particulars apply to Mr F. Usherwood, County Court Office, Sittingbourne.'* With no applicants, the advertisement was repeated in July.

These advertisements make no mention of a separate 108a East Street, so perhaps the house had been re-established as a single entity once more, which it was according to the 1901 census.

Frank Usherwood was from Tunbridge Wells, where he was born in 1848 and where he met his wife Matilda née Clout. They were married on the 16th October 1867 and soon afterwards moved to Sittingbourne. By 1871 they were living at 165 East Street. Frank worked in the legal profession and was initially a Solicitors Managing Clerk.

He moved with his wife and family to the new County Court Office at 59 High Street where he was a Solicitors Clerk later becoming the County Court Registrar by 1901. At this time he lived at 108 East Street and was still there at the time of the 1911 census. Interestingly, the 1908 directory was the first one to refer to this house by name, 'Kimberley'.

Inspiration for the name most likely came from the Boer War as events unfolded. At this time, newspapers reported the progress of the war in great detail; so almost everyone would have heard about the various battles. During the South African War, the town of Kimberley was besieged by the Boers for 126 days until relieved by General John French on the 15th February 1900.

Consistent with Frank's occupancy of 108 East Street were the regular appearance in Kent's local newspapers, including the *East Kent Gazette* for various servants: *'Frank Usherwood, daily servant wanted'*.

Another advertisement, this time from the *Sussex Agricultural Express Friday 2nd April 1909,* read as follows:
*'HOUSEKEEPER or USEFUL HELP, where servant kept. Miss Usherwood
108 East-street, Sittingbourne.'*

On the 28th February 1913 a notice was published in the *Bedfordshire Times & Independent* on 23rd December 1912:
'To the DIRECTORS OF NATIONAL GYMNASIA AND ENTERTAINMENTS, LTD. DEAR Sirs – In accordance with your instructions. I have considered the best method of construction of the various Buildings giving the desired accommodation, and am the opinion that the cost of

the larger Halls will be about £15,250 and the smaller Halls at about
£4,500. May add that I have acted as Architect for a large number of
similar buildings in London and the Provinces.
(Signed) G. W. BOOTH.
It is computed that the time occupying and completing and equipping
the larger Theatres will be about six months, and in the case the smaller
Halls about three months only after the Company goes to allotment.
SITES – Options for the purchase of the following properties and sites
have been secured in the following towns:-'

A number of towns were then listed across the country including several in Kent. The Listing for Sittingbourne read as follows:

'SITTINGBOURNE - Dec 31st 1912. - Same and Frank Usherwood (as
Vendor), of 108 East Street, Sittingbourne Lease for 46 years at a
ground rent of £11 17s. and premium of £1500.'

The date given was the date of the contract and Frank Usherwood was the Party to the Contract.

Clearly, Frank was planning to let out his home on a long term lease for use as a small theatre or music hall and live somewhere else. However, there is no evidence that this ever happened. He remained at 'Kimberley' at least until 1913 before moving to Hastings where he died three years later. Probate was granted to his widow Matilda Usherwood, his effects amounting to £894 13s 1d.

Alexander Alfred Hollingsworth

Perhaps remembering the War of the Roses in the 15th century, Alexander Hollingsworth one of five siblings, was born in Yorkshire in 1875. He married Margaret Byron, a Lancastrian born in 1873, on Boxing Day 1896. He was an electrical engineer and just before his retirement worked for the Post Office in Essex.

En-route to Essex, the family passed through Richmond in Surrey, back to Stalybridge in Lancashire and then to Walthamstow when it was in Essex. While the family were in Richmond, their daughter Cicely Mafekin Hollingworth was born in 1900. Cicely's middle name appears today to be somewhat unusual. But The Boer War was in progress at this time and it was popular practice to give some battle names as middle names to newly born babies.(112) So, poor Cicely became Cicely Mafekin.

Exactly when the Hollingsworths came to Sittingbourne is unknown but it was after Cicely was born and close on the heels of the Usherwoods moving out between 1914 and early 1916. By 1919, however, a newspaper report and electoral rolls show that they had moved back to Dovercourt in Essex. On the 12th July 1919, the *East Kent Gazette* proclaimed: *'Marriage on July 5th James Henry Harris son of Mr and Mrs J Harris of Pleasant View, Cove, Hants to Cicely Mafekin only daughter of Mr and Mrs Hollingsworth of Kimberley East Street. Wedding by special licence. At St Augustine's Church, Dovercourt.'* The church, built in 1893, was demolished in 1997.

James Henry Harris was born on the 24th August 1896 and lived with his father, also James and mother, Rosina in Cove, Farnborough in Hampshire. James was also an electrician. Cicely and James went on to have two children, Cicely Joan and Lilian Jean. At the outbreak of the Second World War, they were living in Benfleet, Essex close to Cicely's parents. She died some 20 years after her husband James in 1986 and with her the practice of naming newly born babies after notable battles.

We believe that neither this family nor the Weavers, who occupied 'Kimberley' in later years, were related to the Harrises and the Weavers who, at about this time, were occupying other premises in East Street – see numbers 73, 75, 77 and 79.

Frederick Weaver, Edward Thomas and Charlotte Weaver

'Kimberley' was once again vacant around 1920. In keeping with common practice, trade directories while diligent about recording the details of commercial premises for which they were paid, were not so inclined to record the details of private residents. So it was that there are no details of the occupants of this address until 1926 when Frederick Weaver was in residence and in 1927 when a relative Edward Thomas Weaver was the occupier.

Edward Weaver, born in 1866 was from a Sheppey family. On the 30th December 1899 he married Charlotte Francis Maud Gibbon who was from Holloway in London. She was ten year his elder. Edward found work as a Chargeman Engine fitter, which may indicate that he worked in the dockyard at Chatham. Shortly after their marriage they had a son, Herbert. The 1911 census shows them living at 3 Windsor Terrace, Royal Road, Sheerness, which was a two up and two down house. So, it must have meant an upward change in circumstances that led them to move to a much larger seven room house in East Street, although it was entirely possible that they only occupied a small part of it, in a self-contained flat. They had moved there by 1922. How long they were there is not known.

Harold and Dorothy Maylum, Amelia Luckhurst, Elizabeth Newman and Muriel Webb

Harold Maylum was born on the 5th February 1904 to parents Thomas, a brickfield labourer and Rose and was the youngest of seven siblings. They lived in Goodnestone Road. Harold married twice, first to Ellen Harley in 1924 and then to Dorothy Evelyn Brunt in 1945. They must have been divorced because Ellen lived to a good age and died in Swale in 1985. Interestingly, the 1939 Register shows Harold living with Dorothy Maylum although they were not married until after the war in 1945. Perhaps this was simply for appearances as living together unmarried was frowned on in those days. Their address was 108 East Street but they must have occupied a flat in the house as also present were two elderly ladies a widow Amelia Luckhurst and a single lady Elizabeth Newman.

The Maylums occupied the flat until at least 1947 and possibly much longer as Dorothy died in Sittingbourne in 1975 and Harold moved to Canterbury where he died ten years later. Muriel G. Webb occupied another flat immediately after the war.

Harold Maylum

Other Occupants:

1963	G. Foster
1975	No entry
1980	Malcolm and Susan Fowler
1985	Malcolm and Susan Fowler
1990	Malcolm and Susan Fowler
1998	Stephen Fowler and Guy Goldfinch

Numbers 110, 112, 114, 116, 118 East Street

'Eastleigh House' 'Kimberley'

122 120 118 116 114 112-110 108 106-104 102 100

Numbers 110 and 112
Elizabeth Divers, Sarah Ann Hogwood and Henry Pell

The houses in the street were not numbered before 1871 and so, as we have pointed out many times throughout this series of volumes on our town-centre, we have had to construe who was living where during the years before the numbers were applied.

Numbers 110 and 112 are named Pelham Villas and form a semi-detached pair of Victorian houses. Henry Pell, of whom more below, owned these and, we believe, had them built. It seems that he made up the name Pelham Villas, which is inscribed in a plaque on the front wall, to incorporate his surname. As recounted below, Mr Pell acquired this site in 1878 by marrying Sarah Ann Hogwood, whose family had owned the freehold for some time.

In 1840, the owner/landlord/freeholder recorded here, at parcel 212, is Edward Hogwood. He features often in our various volumes about the history of our town-centre – notably in our account of the family home at 13 High Street (HSI) A butler with *"a position"* in London, Edward was blessed with several properties in his home town, including the properties under observation here and others along East Street – numbers 62, 64, 66, 97 and 99.

Here, as next door at 108, we confront some uncertainty about exact locations of the respective residents in the years before 1870.

In 1840, this site, within parcel 212, is scheduled simply as a stable and garden. Though the schedule mentions no house here, the accompanying map makes clear that this parcel also includes the house that in later years was numbered as 114. As mentioned below, we believe that numbers 114 and 116 were originally one double-fronted house – of the same proportions as the neighbouring houses now numbered 108, 118, 120 and 124.

In 1841, the census tells us that Edward Hogwood, the freeholder, was living here with his wife Elizabeth, another Elizabeth Hogwood aged eight – presumably a daughter – and a servant.

In 1840 we are told that the tenant of Mr Hogwood's stable and garden was one Thomas Tarpe. Tarpe was one of the two relieving officers of the Milton Union appointed when the workhouse opened in 1835. His was a very responsible position for which he was paid the considerable salary of £100 a year. The two men were required ride round to visit each parish in their half of the union area weekly, placing a list of those receiving out-relief that week on the church door, and giving out the bread or flour and money. They had to decide which applicants for relief were genuine and which were not and report their decisions to the Guardians. Thomas lived in High Street Milton where presumably he had no room for a stable.(5)

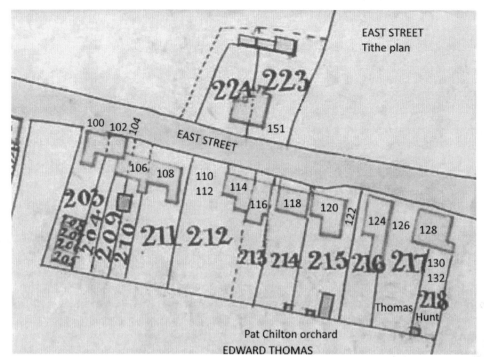

Parcel 212 can be seen where Sarah Hogwood lived with her grandmother. Parcel 213 was later numbered 116 and parcel 214 on the tithe was later numbered 118 East Street (Suggested street numbers added by us)

A study of the tithe schedule and map of 1840 indicates that the house where Mrs Divers and Sarah Hogwood lived was number 114 in parcel 214.

Sarah's father Edward Hogwood was then the owner. Edward Hogwood's will reveals that he served as a butler in the very select Upper Grosvenor Street, acquiring enough savings to purchase four houses in Sittingbourne and two in Milton.

Whatever the uncertainty in the 1840 schedule, it does seem that, by 1851, there was definitely an extra building on tithe parcel 212 between street number 108 and what became 114. This is probably the structure which appears on the 1865/6 Ordnance Survey Plan – see below. It is, of course, possible that this was the stable tenanted in 1840 by Mr Tarpe, but which, for some reason, does not appear on the map accompanying the schedule, produced at that time.

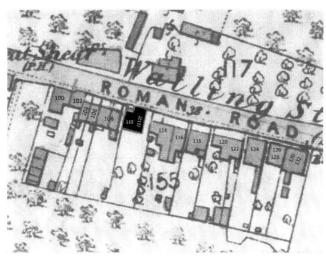

Ordnance Survey plan dated 1865/6 showing the 'extra' building between 108 and 114 (solid-shaded) and a partition on 108 indicating that it was divided at that time – the Eastern section was identified in later years as Laburnum Cottage

Edward Hogwood died in 1843 and is buried in St Michael's Churchyard. In 1847, his widow Elizabeth Hogwood re-married. Her husband John Robert Divers, from East Sutton, was aged 60 at this date and described himself as a 'house proprietor' He was, very likely, related to the Robert Divers who, in 1840, had owned the properties next door (parcels 211, 210 and 209 – street numbers 108, 106 and 104) However, John was not particularly well-off; dying in 1858, he left effects of under £200. Fortunately, his widow Elizabeth had retained at least some of the Hogwood family properties in her own right and in 1871 she was still living here with her granddaughter Sarah Ann and a servant. Mrs Divers then described herself for the census return as a 'house proprietor'.

She died in 1877 leaving the goodly sum of £3,000. Sarah Ann Hogwood was her executrix along with William Hinde of Milton. Sarah, unmarried and in her late thirties, had stayed at home, but she 'tied the knot' soon after her grandmother's death, though, being 39, she was an elderly bride for those days. Her lucky groom, Henry Pell, was a man of similar age. He hailed from Boughton -under-Blean and had been a farmer.(9) He too had never been married before. Given the bride's place of residence and her family connexions with St Michael's in Sittingbourne High Street it is perhaps surprising that they married in the parish church at Gillingham, but perhaps, at that time, Henry was living in that district.(HSI)

Maybe it was on the advice of Sarah's canny solicitor, Mr Hinde, that Sarah and Henry entered into a formal indenture recording:

- the date (18th June 1878)

- the location of their marriage ceremony at Gillingham listing various Hogwood/Divers properties which Sarah possessed including some that we can identify as numbers 60, 62, 64, 97 and 99 East Street and premises in Mackie's Yard in the vicinity of Crown Quay Lane & St Michaels' church.(HSII)

This marital schedule records that, in 1878 (when we have street numbers) occupancy of the property at number 110 was shared between Sarah Ann Hogwood (the new Mrs Pell) and William John Parrett the proprietor of the East Kent Gazette.(HSI) The same sharing arrangement had applied for at least four years – the street directory for 1874 records that Mr Parrett and old Mrs Divers were both residing at number 110. Why neither of them adopted the street number 112 is not known. We have traced no record of that number being in use at that time.

Soon after that, Mr Parrett having left the site – to live elsewhere, Mr and Mrs Pell set about maximising the value of the site by replacing the old building with the pair of houses now known as numbers 110 and 112.

The first recorded occupier of the new 110 was Robert Lake Denne (very likely a member of the Lake family of Rodmersham and Bapchild) After a couple of years Mr Denne moved away and in 1884 the house was offered to let as apartments.(N01,34)

In the early 1880s, Sarah and Henry had moved away to Hollingbourne and then later to Maidstone, where Henry died in 1916 and Sarah in 1919.

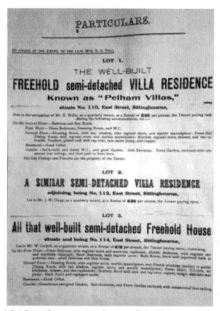

1919 sale particulars of Pelham Villas

George Geering, grazier, farmer and miller at 110

George Geering was born in Sussex in 1838. He had moved into number 110 by 1890 with his wife Emily and family at a stage in his life when he was ready to be less active although he still described himself in the 1891 census return as a grazier, miller and farmer. Ten years earlier he had been farming 600 acres at Pheasants Farm on the Iwade Road, employing three men and three boys there. Whilst living in East Street he still advertised good grazing on the Sheppey Marshes for cows and sheep.(N01)

Matters did not go well with Mr Geering, for during 1895:

  '*In the County Court of Kent, held at Rochester. In Bankruptcy - re George Geering of 110 East Street carrying on business at Eastchurch and Elmley in the Isle of Sheppey, Kent, and at Bexhill-on-Sea, Sussex. Grazier and miller. Receiving Order made 3rd July 1895.'*

Soon afterwards the Gazette reported:

'Failure of a local farmer. At the Rochester Bankruptcy Court, George Geering, farmer, grazier, miller etc., now residing at East Street, and formerly a landowner and in business at Eastchurch and Elmley.'

So it came about that in 1896, 110 East Street was advertised as to let:

'the convenient Family Residence, containing five bedrooms, drawing and dining rooms, kitchen, wash house etc., and cellar. Good garden at rear. Now in occupation of Mr. G. Geering. Low rental. Apply to John Peters and Sons of 15 High Street'.(HSI)

Mrs Geering might well have felt this to be a public humiliation and it could have hastened her death. She died in 1897 aged 58. When he was widowed George Geering moved back to his native Sussex, where, still calling himself a farmer, he rented two rooms in Dallington.(11) In old age he returned to Sittingbourne to live with his son, George junior, a cabinet maker in Station Street.(12) He died in 1917 aged 79.

Henry Willis, tailor and outfitter at 110

Henry Willis the tailor and outfitter of 14 High Street followed the Geerings as tenant of 110 and had moved in with his family by 1901.(HSII) Henry died aged 90 in 1920 which was when the ownership of the house had changed although the Willis family continued to be tenants of number 110 well into the 1930s. In 1920 they had been paying £23 a year in rent plus rates on top. Henry and his wife Mary who lived on until 1928 were stalwarts of the Baptist Church.

It was when Sarah (Hogwood) Pell died in 1919 that numbers 110, 112 and 114 were put up for sale by her executors. The auction particulars for 110, 112 and 114 have been shown to us by the present owners of number 110. They reveal that the ground floor of number 110 consisted of a drawing room at the front with a bay window and at the back a dining room. Both rooms had 'tiled register stove and marble mantelpiece'. A register stove (often called a register-grate) was a standard fitting in houses of this class during the Victorian period. In essence it was a cast-iron fireplace with bars across the front, forming a basket to contain the fuel. The tiles would have been in vertical strips, either side of the fireplace. A refinement was a casement register-grate – this had a lid which could be shut in summer, blocking off the chimney-flue to keep the grate free of soot when the fire was not lit. The particulars of sale also mention a kitchen and scullery; out at the back was a brick built toilet and a good sized garden. On the first floor were three bedrooms, a dressing room and a toilet. The second floor was made up of a further bedroom and a box room. The small front garden had iron railings and a tiled path. The house was completed by a good cellar. The lay-out of number 112 was identical – a mirror-image.

Charles Howland, builder at 110

Charles and Margaret Howland were the next residents of number 110. Charles was a builder with a yard in Borden Lane and in 1937 he placed this advertisement in the paper: *'Look. Value for Money!. Semi-detached Bungalows at Chestnut Street & Hearts Delight Borden. From £420. Small deposit secures. Also semi-detached Villas from £500. Garage room for all. Apply Chas Howland, 110 East Street. Works in Borden Lane'.*

The Howlands lived at 110 for many years and celebrated their 60th wedding anniversary there in 1962.(N01) Other members of the family continued to live in the house into the 1970s. Later occupants included Doris Carey and Terence and Valerie Tyler.

The Jay Siblings at 112

Soon after the construction of 'Pelham Villas' during the 1880s, retired butcher Frederick Jay moved from number 8 East Street into the new house numbered 112. He was probably its first householder. With Fred were his three sisters, Mary, Susanna and Maggie, who were all older than he and, like him, never married. The siblings had grown up at the family bakery at number 8 and had enough money to live comfortably together in this house.(see number 8) After a decade or so here, the Jays moved out – perhaps at the instigation of their landlord Mrs Pell. Frederick went to Mrs Pell's house next door – number 114 (where he died within a year or so) His three sisters went to number 116, where they stayed for the rest of their lives. We say more about this, when we reach that house.

In 1912 number 112 was for sale described as 'a double fronted house seven rooms, four bedrooms, cellars. Apply E. J. Thomas, Chalkwell.' This was Edward Jeffrey Thomas of Chalkwell House.(12) Born in Stockbury he was a nephew of Edward Thomas senior of 116/8 East Street. Like most of the Thomas clan, in our vicinity, the younger Edward was a fruit grower, but perhaps, in this advertisement, Mr Thomas was acting as the agent for the owner of the house, old Sarah Pell, who still owned it at the time of her death seven years later.

In 1919 Mr and Mrs J. W. Clap lived at 112 but we have not been able to discover anything about them. However, given their unusual surname, it is more than possible that this was the fruit-grower and poultry farmer of that name, who, in the 1930s and 1940s, occupied the orchard, located where our town's library car park is now. Michael Peters, one of our contributors, treasures memories of that orchard from his infancy – notably the sound of the flock of geese kept there. The orchard adjoined the garden of the Peters family home at 93 High Street, but in the late 1940s, Central Avenue sliced across the site and a car park was laid out on the remainder – on part of which, later on, our town library was built. The sounds of ducks and geese are no longer heard in that vicinity.

William George Reeve at 112

By 1922 this was the home of William Reeve, one of the sons of George Reeve the painter and decorator of number 131. Born in 1877 he had started his working life by being trained by his father. Old George had died in 1915 and William continued the business along with his brother Harry. William was a painter, guilder, grainer and sign-writer as we see from his advertisement. He and his wife Lilian were still at 112 in 1956.

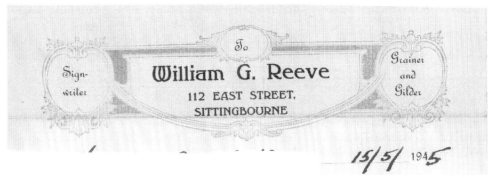

William Reeve's letterhead of the 1940s

The Reeve family were highly regarded in the district for the quality of their workmanship.

Later residents of number 112 included Gordon and Mary Taylor and Arthur and Lily Brockwell.

Numbers 112 and 110 in 2018 (CB)

Numbers 114 and 116 East Street

This structure which has been altered and divided into two is thought, judging by its external appearance, to be about 200 years old. Probably, at first, the front door was below the central window.

Some account of this house and its occupiers has been set out already on the site adjoining, but it is probably more convenient to our readers if we repeat ourselves here.

By 1851 this was the home of John Robert Divers a 'house proprietor' aged 60 from East Sutton and his wife Elizabeth whom we have encountered already at 110. Their 13 year old granddaughter Sarah Ann Hogwood was visiting and would soon become a permanent resident here. We recounted previously that John Divers died in 1858 leaving effects of under £200 and we understand that widowed Elizabeth Divers (formerly – Hogwood) owned houses in her own right, and on her death in 1877 bequeathed this and other property to her granddaughter Sarah.

The map accompanying the 1840 tithe schedule makes clear that the building, by then, had been divided. The part now known as 114, was in parcel 212, described as stable and garden and number 116 was the "house and garden" in parcel 213.

In 1851 the Divers neighbours were Charles Sivyer, his wife Mary Ann and their daughter, who may have been at 116 or sub-tenants of Mr Parker in part of 118

In 1861 we find here the Bones family, gardener and laundresses, and the Thomas sisters – dressmakers.

In 1873 Mrs Divers sold the eastern portion (now 116) to Edward Thomas (115). The late-Victorian style of the bay-windows on the front now suggest that the building was remodelled about that time when Mr Thomas took possession of 116 and Sarah's new husband, Henry Pell came on the scene (see above). The two owners must have co-operated in the transformation.

In 1874 and perhaps for some years earlier, Edward Bigg, officer to the sheriff of Kent inspector of weights and measure and constable to the Hundred of Milton and Sherriff's Officer, was living at number 114. He had moved from 73 High Street with his family.(HSI) Mr Bigg lived up to his name for he was of importance in the town. It was not long before he moved on to 74 East Street.

Mr Bigg was followed at 114 by Lewis Sillis of number 3 East Street who died in 1878 just after he and his wife had moved here. His widow Sarah stayed on with her niece and a servant. In 1882 a Mrs Brett made her home at 114.

John Whibley, draper

In 1890 John Whibley, the High Street draper, lived at 114 with his wife, two children and a servant until the death of his old father in 1898 when John moved back to number 10/12 High Street to be on hand to run the long-standing family business.(HSI)

Fred Jarrett, another manure merchant

Fred Jarrett grew up at Little Glovers Farm, where, with his siblings, he helped his widowed mother Emily who had a dairy herd. But by the age of 20 Fred was a printer's compositor.(9,10) It turned out that Fred liked printing as little as dairy farming for by 1901, married and in his thirties, he had become a manure merchant. This was not manure from his mother's farm for by then she had retired to the comfort of her married daughter's home above 66 High Street where her son in law ran a stationer's shop. By 1904 Fred had added the selling of mowers, rakes and reapers to manure; a sensible decision for it must have been hard to make much profit from manure. Fred remained in this trade but moved along with his wife and daughter to Canterbury Road. (12) A notable descendant of this family, living in our time, was Denis Jarrett MBE (1922-2017) – a highly respected and successful Head Teacher at Sittingbourne's Westlands School.

By 1908 Frank Woolley lived here – in case you are wondering, this was not the famous Kent and England cricketer of that name – he was still living in Tonbridge. This Mr Woolley's stay was brief and in the autumn of that year the house was to let: *'Four bedrooms dining room drawing room, bathroom, kitchen good garden and conservatory'.*

A tenant proved hard to find and so 114 continued to be advertised for letting in 1909 and again in 1910 when it was available with number 116 at £18 a year for 114 and £16 a year for 116, although both had the same number of rooms. (N01) The 1910 advertisement mentioned the scullery and cellar too.

Arthur Wakelin, an engine driver from Sheppey with a wife and two daughters moved in but needed four boarders in order to afford the rent. Soon the house was to let again. The 1912 advertisement described it as a 'convenient Villa Residence, contains four bedrooms, two reception, bath, kitchen, scullery etc. pleasant garden overlooking cherry orchard.'

By the time Sarah Pell died in 1919 she still owned number 114 but had sold number 116.

Here are the later tenants of whom we know:

1920-1922	Lilian and Walter Cockell
1933-1953	Daisy and Harry Knowles
1956	Edna and Frank Fleming
1960	Arthur and Ethel Feaver, Edna and Frank Fleming
1970	Ethel Feaver, Edna and Frank Fleming
1980	Ethel Feaver, Edna and Frank Fleming, Bernard and Lynee Back

By 1985 the house had been divided into four rooms to let and three flats.

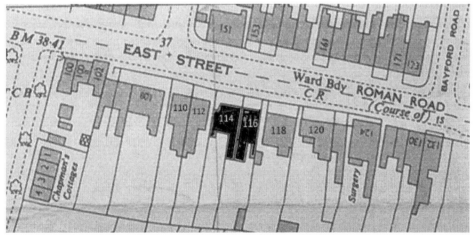

Ordnance Survey map 1960 (114 and 116 shaded)

The Thomas Family

We mentioned previously the dressmaking Thomas sisters who were living nearby, but by 1861 three other households of the Thomas family were living here side-by-side. Though their houses were not numbered, they can be identified by reference to neighbouring houses on the tithe map and schedule in 1840. In those days, parcel 214 (later numbered 118) was known as Parker's house – it was, in 1841 and 1851, still occupied by the Parker family – tenants of the wealthy brewer, William Vallance. Parcel 216 (later numbered 124) was occupied by Elizabeth Gouge for at least 20 years until the 1860s. We say more about Mrs Gouge and the Parkers in due course.

So, in 1861, whilst Mrs Gouge was still at 124, we find, at 118, John Thomas who described himself as a 'proprietor of homes' and was then in his fifties, living with his son John Augustus Thomas an unemployed printer.

John Thomas must surely have been related to Edward Thomas senior next door at what was known later as 120. Edward had been born at Rodmersham in 1793 where generations of his ancestors had lived before him. He was a fruiterer and nurseryman. By 1841, he and his wife Jane, in their forties, were living, as tenants of John Cowland, in the old house a few doors away – on the site where, later on, stood numbers 126 and 128. They were blessed with five sons; Edward junior, William, Henry, Jeffrey and Lewis. By 1861 Edward and Jane's sons had all left the family home although Edward junior had hardly gone a step as he was next door at number 116 which was convenient as he worked with his father.

In the 1874 directory Edward junior was still at 116 – perhaps living upstairs – because, for a short while, Henry Terrey was running a bakery there. Mr Terrey had moved here from the other end of town – the vicinity known as Water Lane Head, the junction of what is now West Street, Ufton Lane and the London Road, where he had been in the bakery business since the early 1850s. In the early years of the century, a John Terrey appears in that same location so perhaps Henry was second generation in that profession. After 1874 he seems to have left no trace hereabouts.

Edward Thomas senior died in 1865 aged 73. He was worth over £4,000 and described in the probate listing as a gentleman. His will was proved by his sons Edward junior the fruiterer, Lewis also a fruiterer, of Rodmersham and Henry of Newington a painter. Old Jane Thomas then moved from 120 to 118, to be next to her son, where she lived until her death in 1882 aged 85.

Edward junior continued his father's fruiterer's business from number 116. The two census returns of 1881 and 1891 give the useful information that Edward farmed 53 acres employing 12 labourers and five boys. He had also set up Harold Nursery (which took its name from Harold Road) by 1887 and employed one of the Goodhew family as manager.(N01) In the 1874 directory is this listing: *'Jesse Thomas & Son the nurseries Rodmersham Green and opposite the Plough Inn, East St, suppliers of fruit trees etc.'* The reference to the Plough is confusing; it might hark back to an earlier holding on Plough Orchard – see our account of numbers 51-57 East Street. Harold Nursery was across the road on land behind East Street and beside Harold Road. This Jesse Thomas was the brother of Edward senior.

Edward junior died in November 1893 and his wife Ann followed him to the grave a month later. By the following summer, their furniture had been auctioned. It included iron fenders, mahogany dining chairs, sofa, couch, easy chair, a four foot walnut chiffonier (a low cupboard with shelves above) with marble top and plate glass panel, Brussels carpets, pictures, engravings, a bookcase, mahogany chest of drawers, eight-day clock in mahogany case, and a four foot wide wardrobe.(N01)

In the autumn of the following year the local paper reported that there was to be an auction of the late Edward Thomas's properties: *'The remaining portion of the Freehold Estate of Mr. Edward Thomas, deceased, comprising his late residence, 116 East Street, with the adjoining cottage (118), the house, shop and grounds known as "Harold Nursery" which will be offered in plots, with cottages, to Canterbury Road and Harold Road, and two pieces of orchard and garden ground, with stable and stores, situate on either side of Bayford Road. The above, with lots to be offered for sale by auction, at the Bull Hotel.'*

Harold Nursery was bought by the exotically named Christian Poggensee who began to advertise his plants in the Gazette. *Poggen* is a North German dialect word for frog or, more commonly, a small fish that lives in the estuaries along the Baltic and North Seas. '*See'* is the German word for sea. Herr Poggensee was German and had married a Kentish woman.(12) They lived at the nursery at 25 Canterbury Road; he made a new entrance to the nursery in East Street across the road from the Thomas home.

In 1901 number 116 was occupied by old Mary Jay (who was by then in her eighties) and her sister Susanna, having moved along from number 112. Mary died in 1893 and the younger Susanna in 1911.

In 1912 a Miss E. Cheeseman announced via the local paper that she had commenced business at number 116 as a 'costumier & dress maker'.

Later residents of 116 that we know of:

1922-1933	Edgar and Eva Butler
1939	Diana Bedelle
1947-1953	Elsie and Leslie Bridgland
1956	James and Muriel Barry
1960	Kathleen and Frank Fleming
1970	William and Cynthia Daw

Numbers 116 and 114 in 2018 (CB)

Number 118, 'Eastleigh House'

We have included the double-fronted detached number 118 in this group, because, as we have seen above, members of the Thomas family lived in both 116 and 118 for a number of years.

The house is thought to be about 300 years old; it appears on parcel 214 on the 1840 tithe schedule, owned by William Vallance the brewer who possessed a number of other properties in the town.(HSII) The house was known as Parker's then because the Parker family lived there – probably they had done for more than one generation – in 1841 old Mrs Parker, was living there aged 85. Her son Robert was a brewer's servant born in Luddenham as was his younger son, Robert junior. Doubtless their landlord Mr Vallance was also their employer and this would have been a service tenancy. In 1851 Robert Parker and his wife Thomasine were still there but, with only one of their four children still at home, part of the house seems to have been sublet to Susannah Jarrett a dressmaker and maybe also an agricultural labourer, Charles Sivyer whose wife Mary Ann took in laundry. The Sivyers may have been at number 116 – see above – we cannot be sure.

After the death of old Jane Thomas in 1882, some of the later residents of number 118 were George William Swinierd, a lay reader of the Church of England who had moved from Minster with his wife Martha and daughter Mabel. (10) They later moved the short distance along to Canterbury Road.(11) Widowed Margaret Matt was the next tenant with her daughter and grandson.

 By 1911 this was the home of Frederick Worsfold from Woodnesborough who worked as a coal merchant's clerk and who, although only 40, was a widower with a child and two servants.

From an advertisement in the local paper we know that a Mrs Clairman lived here in 1919. She placed a notice in the paper: 'Wanted. Cook General at once. Two in family.'

Oscar Baker
Two years later Mrs Clairman had left and a musician named Oscar Baker had moved in. This advertisement appeared throughout the year in the local paper in 1921: 'Mr Oscar Baker. L.R.A.M. A.R.C.M. L.T.C.L. A.R.C.O Organist and Choirmaster at the parish church of St Michaels Sittingbourne. Lessons given also engagements for Organ & Pianoforte Recitals & Concerts etc accepted.'

The impressive array of letters after Mr Baker's name meant Licentiate of the Royal Academy of Music, Associate of the Royal College of Music, Licentiate of Trinity College London, and Associate of the Royal College of Organists. What a list of qualifications! The museum have a concert programme for January 1925 a 'pianoforte recital' by Mr Baker's students at the town hall. St Michael's choir boys were included in the programme. Research has revealed that Oscar Baker's first name was Hedley. When he arrived in Sittingbourne he was 30 years old. He had lived in Luton with his widowed mother who had a millinery shop there.

H. Oscar Baker moved away from East Street during 1925 and the next tenant was listed in the 1926 directory as Grenville Herbert Tempany. Mr Tempany was a teacher who had begun his career as an assistant house master at a Yorkshire boarding school. He soon moved from East Street to Park Road and was followed at 118 by Mabel and Percy Cheeseman, then Leonard Payn in the 1930s.

In 1937 the house came up to let: '118 East Street Detached dwelling house four beds, two sitting rooms, kitchen etc. Rent 17/6 per week and rates.'

Beatrice and Reuben Baker became the tenants and remained into the 1950s. Then by 1956 Ernest and Barbara Boorman née Clarke had bought the house and moved in. Barbara ran it as a bed and breakfast/boarding house business which she was still doing into the 1970s. This was later taken on by her nephew the late Martin Clarke, the martial arts expert and president of the British Sombo Federation whom we have met across the road in the Martial Arts Centre.

118 in 2018 (CB)

Numbers 120, 122, 124, 126, 128, 130 and 132 East Street

132-130 128-126 124 122 120   118   116   114   112-110

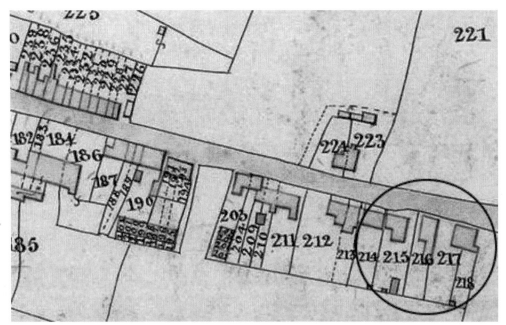

Number 120 stood on parcel 215 which can be seen on the bottom right of this section of the 1840 tithe map. Beside it, to the right, on parcel 216 stood number 124 – number 122 came later. Next door on parcel 217 stood a semi-detached building which occupied half the width of the site. This plot now bears numbers 126 and 128 East Street
The final house in the row was tithe number 218 later occupied by 130/2 East Street.

Numbers 122 and 120 in 2018 (CB)

When this group of houses were built their situation was a good one. Endowed with generous back gardens they lay just a short walk from the attractions of the town centre – though far enough away to be clear of the smells and clatter.

The London to Dover Road though busy was neither noisy nor filled with fumes. Nowadays the traffic is relentless and the lack of a large front garden has become a drawback for it leaves them close to the road.

Number 120 is a detached house, about 300 years old whilst number 122 is Victorian, smaller, tall and narrow and built right up against 120.

Number 124 in 2018 (CB)

Number 124 is a detached, listed building which, like 120, may be about 300 years old.

Numbers 128 and 126 (CB)

Numbers 126 and 128 are a pair of early Victorian cottages which were the last buildings in the street until 1900.(39) Then in 1901 a pair of more substantial red-brick houses were erected beyond them. Both had six rooms and a bay window upstairs and down. These were numbers 130 and 132 and are the final houses before we come to the modern block of flats which complete this side of East Street.

Numbers 132 and 130 in 2018 (CB)

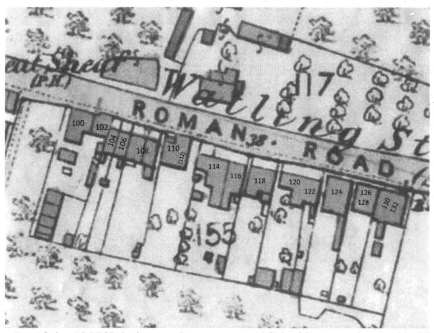

A section of the 1865/6 Ordnance Survey map with building numbers added by us

Number 120 East Street

In 1840 and 1841 the Piles were here – William, a mariner, and his wife Elizabeth. By 1851 and on into the 1860s, the occupiers were the Thomas family, the fruiterers whom we have met already.

By 1871, Alexander Gouge (pronounced Googe) had moved here from number 124 where he and his mother had lived since 1840 if not before. His widowed sister Eliza Lang, two Lang nieces and a young great-niece came to live with him. Alexander remained here until 1880 when he had his furniture auctioned and moved to Sheerness and then on to Rochester Cathedral precincts. He died in 1894.(N01)

He had not sold the house in 1880 but had let it out. As a former land agent (viz. census 1841) Alex obviously had a feel for property. The house was described in the East Kent Gazette as having six bedrooms, a drawing room, dining room and breakfast room. One of those who rented this house over these years was William Jarrett who had an intriguing combination of occupations according to the 1891 census return: land steward, manure merchant and insurance agent.

The inhabitants of the house in 1901 came from a lower social class. Edwin Saxby was a tailor's cutter from Milton with a wife and five children and the Saxbys took in a boarder to help with the rent. Saxby worked for the Co-op a fact which we learn from the 1911 census by which time Saxby and his wife lived round the corner in Harold Road. William Reeve lived here for a time by 1908 before moving on to number 112. (see 112)

We do not know when Edward Jeffrey Thomas of Chalkwell purchased the house, perhaps it was on the death of Alexander Gouge, but at any rate he owned it by 1910 when once more it was available to let.(N01) Frederick Saunders an engineer took the house for a year or so.(12) Fred, his wife Amelia, and their three daughters, all of them natives of Buckinghamshire, had come to Sittingbourne around 1900. After some years at 6 Rock Road, Edith, the eldest daughter, married Arthur Walker from Ilfracombe, who moved in with his in-laws. The birth of a daughter, Brenda triggered the move to this larger house in East Street. There the middle daughter, Kate, met Henry Harris, son of Ted Harris. living at number 77/79 (q.v.) But in 1912 it was again to let: 'Double fronted house, seven rooms, four beds, cellars – Apply to E. J. Thomas, Chalkwell.'

By 1922 Charles and Jessie Hales lived here with their family. Charles was employed as an assistant to a cornfactor.(12) Electoral registers show that one of their daughters, Jessie junior, was the tenant well into the 1930s.

Later inhabitants of number 120 that we know of:

1939	Hilda and Eva James
1947-1953	Hilda and Willie James
1956	Queenie and Walter French
1960-1963	Alfred and Brenda Gambell
1967-1971	Mr and Mrs Winzenburg
1970	Erica Smith who, perhaps, was the same person as:
1980-1985	Erica Miller-Smith

Number 122 East Street

This narrow six roomed house was built much later than the houses on each side of it. The tithe plan of 1840 shows its site as vacant – within the curtilage of number 120. The appearance of the house-front suggests to us that it was built around 1860 – it appears on the Ordnance Survey plan of 1866.

In the absence of more evidence, we can only speculate about the circumstances:

- The census returns suggest that it may have been built as early as 1851 – when, between Edward Thomas at 120 and Elizabeth Gouge at 124, we find the Spice family – William a tailor, his wife Frances and a daughter of the same name. If number 122 were not built as early as that, then the Spices must have been sharing number 120 with the Thomas family or number 124 with Mrs Gouge and Alex, her son.

- In 1861, we have two Thomas households living side-by-side – maybe they were sharing number 120 or maybe, by then, 122 had been built, providing a separate house for the younger Edward Thomas and his wife.

In 1915 the two houses (120 and 122) were still in joint ownership and belonged to Jeffrey Thomas.(115)

In 1871, armed with street numbers, we can be definite: William Cramp a young labourer from Ramsgate lived here at 122 with his wife, daughter and a boarder.(8) William Kirby, another labourer, was the tenant in 1881.

Alfred Goldup was a butcher who before his marriage had lived with his parents in Goodnestone Road. He had no shop of his own but worked for one of the East Street butchers. By 1901 he lived at 122 with his wife Elizabeth and family. The Goldup family grew to six children by 1911 and Alfred gave up butchery to work at the paper mill. Alfred and Elizabeth were still here in 1939 and members of the family remained at 122 into the 1950s.

Later residents that we know of include Daphne and Arthur Francis who followed the Goldups and had moved in by 1956. Arthur Francis worked at the council offices and prior to that for Hedley Peters & Son at 93 High Street. At that time, the freehold of 122 was owned by Jessie Hales – see above, number 120.

The Fosbraey family followed the Francis family at 122.

124 is in the centre of this 1966 image, the narrow 122 is squeezed in between it and number 120 which is the white house in the distance. (NMR)

Number 124 East Street – Abbey House

This is a listed building which is thought to be about 300 years old. It is two-storeyed, stuccoed, with slate roof and a parapet with moulded cornice. There are two sash-windows with glazing-bars intact and one blank window space. It has a central door-case with flat weather-hood, pilasters and a six panelled door.

It was already old in 1840 when widowed Elizabeth Gouge owned and lived in it.(4,5) She had been born in Devon and lived here with a servant and her 21 year old son Alexander who pursued the gentlemanly occupation of land agent. (5) Alexander had been born in Sittingbourne, but the Gouges were non-conformist and favoured Sheerness Bethel Chapel for his baptism. Gouge ancestors had been yeomen in Borden for centuries. Descendants of the family are still living locally today – see also HSI – 93 High Street and Mr Gordelier's Public Rooms in the former George Inn.

The Gouges were 'well-off'. By 1851 Alexander was described in the census as a gentleman (having no need to work, being possessed of sufficient money). His mother, Elizabeth, described as a fund-holder, lived to a great age and died aged 90 in 1867. Her will was proved by her surgeon, Edward Ray, and George Gouge the elder of Sittingbourne (resident at 93 High Street – viz HSI). Elizabeth's effects were worth over £5,000.

By 1881 a shipwright from Dover, Charles Webster, lived here and in 1891 it was Alfred Daniels a brickfield labourer who was the tenant.

The house must then have been renovated and reverted to being the home of people who could afford a resident domestic servant to keep the nine rooms clean. Thomas William Jarrett had lived next door but two at number 120 for a while with his parents when he was in his early twenties and now he moved in to number 124 with his own wife and family. He had worked as a land surveyor but in 1911 described himself as 'clerk to an estate agent.'(11,12) He and his wife Gertrude had three children and lived here for over 20 years from the turn of the century.

The Barnard family

Albert and Sarah Barnard lived at 124 in the 1930s. Various members of the Barnard family followed – in 1939 it was Charles Barnard who worked as an electrical fitter at H. M. Dockyard as well as John Abbott Barnard; and young Harry W. F. Barnard a Probationary Sorting Clerk Post Office. Later Fitzherbert Barnard and his wife Minnie moved in and remained into the 1950s.

Dr McKenzie

From 1956 and into the 1960s the building was in use as the home and surgery of a sole general medical practitioner, Dr James McKenzie and his wife Joyce. We have not been able to confirm whether the practice continued.

In the mid-sixties the house was occupied by Joachim Jurgen Winzenburg and his wife. Joe (as he was known in the local Round Table club) ran a German company on the Trinity Trading Estate at Milton. In their time here, the Winzenburgs made this one of the more stylish and best-maintained houses in this stretch of the street.

During the 1970s Anthony and Christine McLean were the residents.

In the early to mid-1980s, the property was converted back to residential use by a housing charity; the Carr-Gomm Society. Major Richard Carr Gomm (1922-2008) was the founder of the charity. He gave up a career in the Army to found a series of societies providing care and accommodation for vulnerable people, of which the largest and best known is the Abbeyfield Society.

Number 126 East Street

In 1840 this site (where 126 and 128 now stand) was owned by John Cowland and depicted as parcel 217 on the tithe schedule. The tenant was the fruiterer Edward Thomas whom we have met at number 120, to which he soon moved.

By 1851 John Moss from Essex lived here with his wife Ann, five children and a servant. His occupation on the census return was given as 'independent minister of Latimer Chapel.' The Latimer Chapel in the Butts was where the members of Sittingbourne Congregational church worshipped before their church was built in the 1860s.(HSI) Moss's ministry had involved moving far and wide with some of the children born in Hertfordshire and others in Cheshire. Mr Moss was obviously fervent in his free-church religion: we wonder how, in adult life, his eldest son enjoyed bearing the names Martin Luther Moss.

By 1861 the house had become home to a plumber from Lynsted – John Parham and his wife – yet another Mary Ann (we have met several of that name along this stretch of the street) They had a daughter and three sons, one of who was perhaps a forebear of the builder of the same name, who built a row of houses beside the driveway in Gore Court Park soon after that fine mansion was demolished.(82)

Perhaps this Mr Parham was involved in the redevelopment of this site – demolishing the old house here and replacing it with a pair – one of which was occupied by John Thomas who had moved here from number 118 in the late 1860s. Perhaps Mr Thomas carried out the redevelopment – or maybe he simply followed on, according to the ancient saying, which was doubtless coined by someone who had experienced the troubles always associated with building projects – *fools build, wise men move in after them*. John Thomas, who had been born in Milton in 1803, was still there with Louisa ten years later. His modest income came from the rents of houses he owned.(8,9) He died in 1890 aged 86, his wife had predeceased him and his will was proved by his daughter Louisa who was unmarried. His effects were worth somewhat over £200. Louisa then moved out of the house. Thomas is a common surname and this Thomas family do not appear to have been related to the others in East Street.

Widowed Jane Sedge from Doddington lived at 126 in 1901 with her two sons. In 1911 Jane was still here and her son Percy who worked as a painter lived with her as did her daughter Beatrice. Beatrice was a dressmaker who worked from home and continued to do so well into the 1920s. As historians, we subscribe to the rule against drawing attention to unusual surnames (though sometimes the temptation is quite strong) but perhaps we may be permitted to note that predecessors of the Sedge family on this site were called Moss.

In 1915 we know from the electoral register that the owner of 126 and 128 was Sidney Leigh who lived in Dover. We believe it was Sid's daughter-in-law Ivy (also of Dover) who still owned them in the mid-20th century.

By 1933 the property had been allowed to fall into disrepair and the council served notice that it must be made fit for habitation.

Later residents that we know of:

1933-39	Doris and Edward Coombes
1947-53	Ellen and George Jones
1956	George Jones
1963	G. A. Ralph
1970	John and Patricia Savage
1980	Christine Byrne

Number 128 East Street

Like 126 this is a small house with four rooms and must have bulged at the seams when we come across it for the first time in 1871 when labourer Thomas Hunt lived here with his wife and three young children. In order to pay the rent the Hunts managed to squeeze in two boarders and sublet a room to a young labourer from Dover, with a wife and baby. Perhaps their landlord was John Thomas who lived next door – if so, tensions between neighbours might have been quite high from time to time. Such uncomfortable overcrowding could not last and soon all these residents departed. A little hairdressing shop was opened in the front room by 1874 run by John Goddard. Taxidermist and hairdresser John James Couch from far away Falmouth had moved in by 1881. John and his wife who was also Cornish were in their fifties and before coming to Sittingbourne with their four children had lived in the Channel Islands. What a contrast they must have found in their new home.

The shop was closed by 1891 and Milton man George Batchelor a general labourer was the tenant. His wife Elizabeth took in laundry and with them lived George's old mother and a little granddaughter. The Batchelors were still there 1899 but by 1901 had moved next door but one to the new and larger number 132. They were followed as tenants by Jethro Miles from Oxfordshire who laboured in the brickfields to support a wife and five children. By 1908 William

Brunger a local labourer at the cement works was the tenant with his wife Florence and their daughter.(12)

Later residents that we know of:

1922	Lily and Caroline Gee
1926	Henry George Smith
1933-1939	Jack Wells
1947	Frederick Lumby and Edna Wells
1953-1970	Fred and Gladys Lumby
1980	Beryl and Phyllis Morley
1985	Beryl Morley

Number 130 East Street

This six roomed house was new when Milton man Henry Wickens lived there in 1901. He was a rigger in a shipyard and he and his wife Ada were looking after their little niece. The house was always residential.

Later inhabitants that we know of:

1908	Charles Pamplin
1911	Amelia Norris+7
1922	Elizabeth and Ernest Avis
1926	Ernest Avis
1933	David Avis
1936	S. L. Heathfield
1939	Albert and Lily Lasteer
1963	A. H. Lusted

In Mr Lusted's time, the freeholder was George Dutnall, a property owner whom we have met more than once in this account of a street where he owned several premises.

Mr Dutnall bought the building in the 1950s from the Executors of W. A. Mattinson, whose agents were Hedley Peters & Son of 93 High Street.

Number 132 East Street

George Batchelor and his wife Elizabeth were the first tenants of number 132 when it was new in 1901. They had made the short hop to this larger house from number 128. Elizabeth was still taking in laundry in 1908 but by 1911 when she was in her seventies the couple had moved round the corner to Shakespeare Road and Elizabeth no longer scrubbed and boiled other people's clothes.

Harry Price, chimney sweep

Another business was run from number 132 by the following tenant and just as with that of Mrs Batchelor it required no shop window. Harry Price was a chimney sweep so instead of steam and suds the house smelt of soot. Harriet Price, Harry's wife had Harry's brother and her own brother to cater for in the house too.(12)

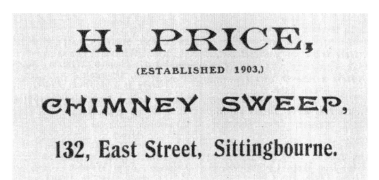

Advertisement from the 1927 directory stating that the business began in 1903

By the 1920s the Prices took in lodgers which continued for many years. Harriet died in 1937 in her seventies and Harry continued at the house until his death aged 80 in 1955.

Later tenants that we know of include the Bakers, the Goldspinks and the Coombers.

Sources and References

HSI	Sittingbourne High Street
HSII	Sittingbourne High Street
NA	National Archives
KHLC	Kent History & Library Centre, Maidstone
WS	West Street

Local Newspapers advertisements and articles

N01	East Kent Gazette 1856-2011
N02	North East Kent Times, various dates
N03	Sheerness Times Guardian, various dates
N04	South Eastern Gazette
N05	Kentish Gazette
N06	Maidstone Journal & Kentish Advertiser
N07	Dover Express
N08	Whitstable Times
N09	Canterbury Gazette
N10	Kentish Chronicle
N11	Tamworth Herald
N12	Dundee Courier

<u>Tithe award</u>

4	Sittingbourne Tithe Award schedule and plan

Census Returns

5	1841
6	1851
7	1861
8	1871
9	1881
10	1891
11	1901
12	1911

Directories

13	W. Finch, Kent, 1803
14	Pigot, Kent, 1823
15	Pigot, Kent, 1826-7
16	Pigot, Kent, 1828-9
17	Pigot, Kent, 1832-4
18	Stapleton & Co, Canterbury, Sittingbourne, Milton etc 1838
19	Pigot, Kent, 1839
20	Pigot, Kent, 1840
21	Post Office, Kent, 1845
22	Samuel Bagshaw, Kent, 1847
23	Post Office, Kent, 1852
24	Kelly, Kent, 1855
25	Melville, Kent, 1858
26	Post Office, Kent, 1859
27	Kelly, Kent, 1862
28	Post Office, Kent, 1866
29	Harrods, Kent, 1867
30	Kelly, Kent, 1867
31	Post Office, Kent, 1870
32	Post Office, Kent, 1874
33	Post Office, Kent, 1878
34	Kelly, Kent, 1882
35	Kelly, Kent, 1887
36	Kelly, Kent, 1890
37	Kelly, Kent, 1891
38	Kelly, Kent, 1895
39	Kelly, Kent, 1899
40	Kelly, Kent, 1903
41	Kelly, Kent, 1905
42	Kelly, Kent, 1907
43	W. J. Parrett Ltd, Sittingbourne & Milton, 1908
44	Kelly, Kent, 1909
45	Kelly, Kent, 1911
46	Kelly, Kent, 1913
47	Kelly, Kent, 1915
48	Kelly, Kent, 1918
49	Bennett's Business, Kent, 1921
50	Kelly, Kent, 1922
51	Kelly, Kent, 1924
52	W. J. Parrett Ltd, Sittingbourne & Milton, 1926
53	Kelly, Kent, 1927
54	Kelly, Kent, 1930
55	Town & Country, Kent, 1934
56	Kelly, Kent, 1934
57	Kelly, Kent, 1938
58	Borough Directories, 1963
59	Borough Directories, 1965-6

Publications

60   Parish Magazine, Holy Trinity Milton Regis, 1930
61   Sittingbourne & Milton Book Trade, 1770-1900 R Goulden, 1999
62   Historical Notes Relating to the Town & District of Sittingbourne, Scott Robinson, 1879
63   Sittingbourne, K. & A. Fosbraey, 1995
64   Official Guide Sittingbourne & Milton, Chamber of Commerce, 1937
65   Official Guide, Sittingbourne & Milton Urban District Council, 1963
66   Sittingbourne Town Centre Guide, Town Centre Manager, 1997
67   Wartime heroes of BGS remembered, Sally Jenkins, SHM, 2015
68   North East and East Kent, Buildings of England Series, John Newman, 2nd Ed, 1976
69   Sittingbourne in My Schooldays, W. G. Matthews, 1921
70   A Walk Through Sittingbourne in Days Gone By, Percy Hubbard, 1961, SHM
71   Statutory List of Buildings of Special Architectural or Historic Interest
72   Sittingbourne and Milton, P. Bellingham, 1996
73   Sittingbourne & Milton Regis, J. Clancy, 2002
74   Long Gone Cinemas of Swale, J. Clancy, 2003
75   A History of the Sittingbourne Co-operative Society, Helen Allinson, SHM, 2014
76   Sittingbourne Family Businesses, ed. Helen Allinson, SHM, 2010
77   The Inns, Taverns & Public Houses of Sittingbourne & District, SHM, 2015
78   History & Topographical Survey of Kent, Edward Hasted, 2nd Edition, 1798
79   Historic Buildings & Grand Houses of Sittingbourne, Clancy, Abbey & Allinson, SHM, 2013
80   More family businesses of Sittingbourne, Helen Allinson, SHM, 2013
81   Government & Politics in Kent 1640-1914 F. Lansberry
82   The Story of Gore Court House and Estate, Tunstall, Helen Allinson, SHM, 2006
83   The Diary of a Victorian Lady: Louisa Thomas of Hollingbourne, ed. Helen Allinson, 2011
84   Sittingbourne & Milton Regis Conservation Study, KCC, 1974

Other Sources

86   Sittingbourne & Milton Urban District Council Plans for buildings 1870s to 1930s
87   Recollections of the Nokes family of East Street
88   A Dictionary of English Surnames by Reaney & Wilson
89   Dictionary of Old Trades, Titles and Occupations
90   George Bargebrick esquire: George Smeed, Richard Hugh Perks, 1975
91   The Angelus chime – a history of the catholic church & parish of Sittingbourne – Father Edgar Dunn (1982)
92   information from Swale Borough Council Rating Officer
93   England & Wales National Probate Calendar, (Index of Wills and Administrations), 1858-1966, 1973-1995
94   British Army WWI Medal Rolls Index Cards, 1914-1920
95   East Street Wesleyan School Log Book C/Es338/7/1 at KHLC
96   The Wood family of Wormshill, Mary Connaughton
97   Deeds of the Barrow Charity
105   Council minutes
110   www.freebmd.org.uk
111   www.ancestry.co.uk
112   www.britishbabynames.com
115   Electoral registers
120   Ordnance Survey, various plans
121   Charles E. Goad, Sittingbourne town centre plan 1969 onwards
122   Plan of the Parish of Sittingbourne in the County of Kent, Thomas Yeakell, 1791

Index

This index does not refer to page numbers of the book but to property street numbers. Heads of businesses are here together with the name of the business or shop but many more members of the families are mentioned in the text. Private residents are not indexed.

Car Shop, The	30/32	Eke, Amelia	71
Carter, Herbert	29	Eley, George	60
Cassell, Eileen	10	Elfick, Henry	149
Cavern, The	35,71	Elli's	75
Central Pie Shop	6,30/32	Empire Cinema	72
Chadwick, George	101	Empress of India	24
Chadwick, Lilian	101	England, Leonard	151
Chambers, Oliver	42	Epps, Ted	61
Character Costumes	26/28	Etc Etc	48
Chocolate Box, The	67	Evans, Richard	34
Chapman, William	15,34,66	Eydin, Ismail	10
Charles, James	12/14	Fairbeard, Charles	19
'Chestnuts', The	70	Fairbrass, Mary	47
Cigar Box, The	11	Farrimond, Raymond	48
Clark, Dr John	70	Fermor, Phoebe	43/45
Clarke, Martin	127	Fermor Malcolm	69/71
Clinch, Charles	4	Fiasco	101
Clinch, Emma	4	Fisher, William	6
Coe, Mary	169	Flowers by Beatrice	8
Cohen, Samuel	17	Flowerworld	59,75
Colonial meat Store	29	Foresters Hall	93/95
Colwell, Harry	3	'Forge House'	26/28
Co-op Funeral Care	77	Forster, Stanley	17/19
Co-op Laundry	75	Fossey, Alec	4
Co-op Sheds	85	Foster, Edward	151
Copper & Brass	48	Fowle, Annie	30/32
Cook, George	139	Freegard Press	35
Cooper, A.	25,27	'French Houses'	78-82
Cooper, Jesse	151	Friday Car Sales	13
Cooper, John	49,129,131	Fuller, Thomas	61
Costcutter Convenience	21	Furner, John	17
Couch, John	128	Gallagher, Brian	167
Couchman, Charles	8	Gallagher, Delia	167
Cox, Henry	61	Gallaon, Oscar	8
Crane, George	77	Gallone, Amcot	25
Creating Cakes	63	Gallone, Emilio	25
Creative Cakes	65	Gambell, James	42
Crerar, Dr James	70	Gandon, Charlotte	62
Crowder, Florence	36,38,40	Gandon, William	62
Croxford, Ann	5	'Garden Place'	53-67
D & A Fashions	61	Gardener, William Cook	4,5
Davenport	69/71	Gaskin, Arthur	71
Dawes, James	84	Geering, Andrew	42
Dean, James	43	George, Grace	6
Dean, Jasper	82	George, Rhoda	6
Deans Ltd	20	Gibbon, Charles	24
Dennett, E. C.	67	Gibbon, Esther	18
Dill's Express store	75	Gibbs, William	50
Disco Carpets	43/45	Giraud, George	12
D 'n' J Smith	44/46	Glandfield, Robert	44
Donald, J.	23	Goddard, John	107,128
Dorrell, John	12/14	Godden, Emily	11
Dorrell, Ann	12/14	Godden, William	11
Doves Funerals	100/102	Golden House	29
Drill Hall	93/95	Goldfinch, Edward	59
Dungey, Charles	100	Goldsmith, Geoffrey	24,30/32
Dunham, William	71	Goodhew, Ashton	43/45
East End Delicatessen	8	Goodhew, Lawrence	8
East Street Bazaar	47	Goodhew, William	8
East Street Drapery & Millinery Company		Goodsell, Alice	17/19
	77/79	Goodsell, George	17/19
East Street News	44/46	Good Taste Restaurant	10
'Eastleigh House'	118	Gordelier, William	84
Eileen's	10	Gordon's	16

Gorman, Lily	24	Ian's	34
Grant, John	52	Inchcomb, James	6
Gray, Allen	77	Inchcomb, William	151
Greensted, Percy	81/83	Ingram, Frederick	63
Greensted, Walter	171/173	Ingram, Harriet	91
Gregory, Joseph	23	Ingram, J.	11
Grimsby Fisheries	163	Irwin, Sheila	33
Grimsdale, Albert	65	Irwin, William	35
Grimsdale, Ethel	65	Jacobs, Stephen	35
Grosvenor Photography	65	Jarrett, Frederick	114
Gulvin, Henry	77	Jay, Frederick	8
Hackshaw, Benjamin	6,30/32	Jay, William	8
Hadaway, Charles	17,19	Jarvis, Emma	60
Hair Zone	16	Jarvis, George	60
Hales, G. & Son	13,26/28	Jarvis, Sarah	60
Hall, A&E	147	Jaycrest	99
Hall, Alfred	149	Jessie's	71
Hall, Henry	18,31	Johnson, Elizabeth	102
Hammon, James	15	Johnson, Ernest	161
Hammond, Matilda	42	Johnson, Jim	11
Hammond, William	42	Johnson, Joyce	11
Hancock, Ellen	24	Johnson, William	149
Hancock, John	24	Jones, Edwin	79
Handcock, Edward	84a	Jones, Herbert G.	4, 6
Hanley, William	73/75	Jury, Edward	18
Hann, George	37	Jury, Frank	92/98
Harmer, Charles	16	K7 Barber	66
Harnden, George	16	Keel, Leonard	92/98
Harnden, Sarah	16	Keeler, Harriet	60/62
Harnden, William	10,14,16	Kemp, Fanny	65
Harris, Albert	59	Kemp, Stephen	65
Harris, Bernard	23,25,27	Kemsley, William	78,78a
Harris, Charlotte	45	Kennard, Lilian	13
Harris, Charles	45	Kenwood, Albert	60
Harris, James	73/75	Kent Aerials	35
Harris, Mary	23,25,27	Kent 7 Barbers	66a
Hart, Frederick	30/32	Kentish Carvery	6
Hatton & Tucker	101	Kentucky Fried Chicken	173
Hayden, Topsy	11	Kent Charcoal Grill	61
Hedgecock, Henry	42	'Kimberley'	108
Hedgecock, John	80,121	King, Mary	52
Henham, Jane	64	Kingfish	20
Henham, Thomas	64	Kite, Bryan	16,30/32
Hidden Gems	99	Kit, William	82
Higgins, John	50	Knowles, Edward	107
Higgins, Olive	33,35	La Pizzeria	20
Hills, Henry	43/45	'Laburnum House'	99
Hinge, Edward	149	Laid, Elizabeth	42
Hobbs, Maria	52	Laid, Ruth	42
Hoile, Henry	61	Lake, George	5
Hollands, James	17	Lamb, The	7
'Holly House'	5	Lambert, James	46
Home Bargains	50	Landen, Edward	163
Homecrafts	23,25,27	Lee, John	4
Homewood, Jabez	71	Lee, Lydia	20
Howe, A.	173	Lee, Mary Ann	4
Howland, Emily	12/14	Lee's Takeaway	29
Hubbard, Charlotte	25	Lime Kiln Joinery	133
Hucksted, William	60	Lockeyears	6
Hughes, George	167	Louch, Ernest	3
Hughes, Phyllis	65	Luscombe, Geoffrey	26/28
Hughes, Tommy	65	Mace, Robert	82
Hunt, Thomas	173	Mace, Sarah	82
Hurst, Edward	4	Magic Wok	173

Maharini Restaurant	24	Parr, Edward	107
Maidstone & District Bus	39,41	Particular Baptists	48
Maison Leslie	71	Parton, William	73/75
Mantle, Ian	34	Pattenden, Violet	8
Manuell, David	9	Patterson, George	42
Manuell, Victor	9	Payne, John	163
Maplesden, John	66	Payne, Winifred	163
Mario's Café	10	Pearcy, John	9,11
Marshdown	54/56	Pearcy, Rosetta	9,11
Masala Magic	163	Pearcy, William	9,11
Masters, Charles	71	Pepper & Ratcliffe	31
Masters, Charlotte	65	Periwinkle Press	23,25,27
Masters, John	9,65,103	Peters, Hedley	77/79
Masters, Stephen	11, 77	Peters, John	4,6,15,50/52
May, A.	46	Pharos Recruitment	99
McCartney, John	44	Pin House, the	71
McCartney, Albert	61	Pinnace Windows	73
McCartney, Thomas	61	Pittock, Harry	151
McKenzie, Dr James	124	Pittock, Henry	29,151
Mead, Corrie	16	Plaza Café	66
Mercer, Wallace	44	Plaza Cinema	72
Michael Andrew hair	131/133	Plough, The	58
Middleton, E.	67	Popperwell, Ann	109
Millen, Alfred	9	Popperwell, Hanry	109
Millen. John	81/83	Porter, Anita	11
Mills, Ethel	12/14	Porter, Laurence	11
Mills, Ivy	67	Premier Express Conv. Store	79
Mills, Jack	67	Price, Harry	132
Milner, Alfred	11	R & A Chinese takeaway	73
Milway, Denham	12	Ralph, R & S	61,135,161
Mitchell, Joyce	23	Ranson, George	61
Mitchell, Ray	23	Rate, John	46
Moonbeam	34	Ray's hair salon	161
Moore, Fred	20,41	Red Goa	163
Morris, Thomas	18	Redhead, Thomas	59
Mount, Edward	61	Read, Harriet	71
Mount, Norman	37	Read, Henry	13/15,71,171
Mount, Pam	37	Read, William	13
Mount, Stephen	35	Reed, Charles	34
Mungeam, George	9,17	Reeve, George	61, 131
Mungham, James	42	Reeve, William	112
Net Church	95	Ribbans & King	149
Newby & Sons	147	Reynolds, William	157
Newby, L. C.	135, 149	Roberts, Alice	10
Nichols, Frederick	84	Roberts, Ellen	12
Norris, Percy	66	Roberts, Herbert	10
Norris, William	11	Robinson, Edward Ledger	13/15
North Kent Kebabs	61	Robinson, Stephen	91
Old Oak Inn	68	Rogers, Robert	61
Ockenden, Joshua	84	Roland Car Sales	13
Ockenden, S.	69	Royale Furniture	35,37
Offen, George	3	Rugg, Charles	76
One forty	3	Rugg, George	76
Osbourne, Evelyn	157	Rumble, Frederick	48
Osbourne, John	157	Rutter, William	18
Ost, Ada	71	Sage, Thomas	42
Otterway, Thomas	36	Salisbury, D & J	44
Packer, Fanny	10	Sampson, Joan	131,133
Packer, John	10	Sandhu, Harpal	163
Packer, Margaret	101	Sandhu, Jasbarsingh	163
Panteny, George	17,19,21,23	Sandhu, Ranjitkur	163
Panteny, Herbert	21	Sargent, Robert	12/14
Parkerhire	63,73	Savage, Horace	100,157
Parker, William	37,39	Sawyer, William	3

Saxby, John	35	Stone, Eliza	20
Scott, Frederick	34	Streeton, William	169
Scott, L & M	35	Stroud, Thomas	4
Sellen, George	151	Swale Martial Arts	127
Sellen, James	82	Swift, Albert	38/40
Sharp, Emma	64	Swift, William	38/40
Sheerness Dist. Steam Laundry		Tan & Tone	67
	81/83	Taylor, Dr Roy	70
Sheila's fashion	43/45	Taylor, William	100
Shepherd, Charles	50	Technic Microwave service	35,37
Shilling, Edward	105	TemPer	99
Ship, The	22	Terry, Sarah	62
Shipp, Charles	30/32	Teynham Engineering Co.	20
Shipp, Emma	30/32	Thanet Driving School	29
Shipp, George	30/32	Thatch	37
Shooter's fish café	49	Thomas, Clara	173
Shrubsall, Edward	67	Thomas, Doreen	5
Shrubsall, Susannah	67	Thomas, Edward	116,118
Shufflebotham, Christina	71	Thomas, Eliza	71
Shufflebotham, Robert	71	Thomas, Emma	173
Sidders, Moses	6	Thomas, George	135
Sillis, Lewis	3	Thomas, Hilda	173
Simmonds, Francis	50	Thomas, William	79
Simons, Willis	41	Thomasson, J.	79
Silhouette	24	Thomsett, Alfred J.	69
Singer Sewing Machines	30/32	Thomsett, Harry	69
Sittingbourne Café	10	Thorner, William	15,25
Sittingbourne Co-op		Three Kings	2
69,78,78a,84,,88,119,121,123,125		Tidy, Alan	100
Sittingbourne Co-op chemist	81/83	Tommy's	5
Sittingbourne Fish Bar	20	Tong, John	44, 151
Sittingbourne Heritage Museum	67	Tong, Mary Ann	50
Sittingbourne Kebab & Pizza	66	Tucker, Bernard	101
Sittingbourne Pottery	73	Tucker, Mary	30/32
Skin Illustrations	161,167	Tumber, David	44,46
Sittingbourne Plumbing	88	Tumber, Elizabeth	44,46
Skinner, Frank	67	Turvy, Valentine	42
Smart, Ann	11	Tyler, James	26,28,151,157
Smart, Walter	11	Tyler, Thomas	88
Smeed, Esther	46	Tyler, Valentine	5
Smith, Alfred	49,100	United Methodist Church	127
Smith, Beatrice	100	Vasellina, Betty	10
Smith, Dr George L.	70	Vasellina, Johnny	10
Smith, Edward	21	Videomat	25,27
Smith, Sidney N.	44	Vino Vino	8
Smith, Stephen	69/71	Wade, H.M.	151
Snelling, Alfred	54/56	Wall, Annie	33,35
Snelling, Benjamin	62	Ward, Ernest	54/56
Snelling, Frederick	30/32	Waterman, J.	161
Snelling, Harry	54/56	Watts, Arthur	105
Snelling, Stephen	54/56	Webb, Eric	21
Snelling, Thomas	24	Webb, Ron	21
Snelling, William F.	44	Webb, William	21
Sombo Centre	127	Well pharmacy	85/87/89
Southern Domestic	42	Wesleyan School	72
Spice, Daisy	69	Westgate, John	21
Spicer, Ray	67	Wetherill, John	4
Spicer, Sheila	67	Wetherall, E. T.	157
Spillett, Sarah	47	Wheatsheaf, The	90
Starz Tailors	66a	White, Arthur	6
Star, The	13	White, Caleb	11
Stedman, Henry	71	White, George	82
Stedolph, Thomas	3	White, R. & Sons	44,46
Stems & Petals	46	Whitehead, Albert	139

Whittle, Monty	11
Wickenden, Harry	45
Wilcock, Ann	20
Wiles, Charles	107
Wiles, Horace	9
Williams, Amy	66
Williams, David	43
Williams, Doreen	17/19
Williams, Fred	17/19
Williams, Harry	66
Williams, Thomas	13/15
Willis, William	30/32
Wilson, James	5
Wilson, John	20
Windsor Kitchens	65
Winn, Victor	43/45
Wise, Sidney	38,40
Wise, William	38/40,44
Witten, Ernest	73
Wittwer, Ann	151
Wood, Ann	61
Woodhurst, William	52
Workbox, The	5,67

Illustration source or with kind permission of:

AP	Arthur Page
BA	Barry Allinson
CA	Charles Abbott
CB	Colin Benson
CC	Carole Corbett
DJ	David Jackson
DW	Dik Whibley
EKG	East Kent Gazette
FC	Flo Court
JC	John Crunden
JM	John Mount
JSH	John and Sheila Hepburn
MHP	Michael H. Peters
NMR	National Monuments Record
PN	Peter Nokes
SHM and unless otherwise stated, Museum Collection (original source unknown)	
TG	Tony Graham
WI	Wellcome Images. Licenced under the 'Creative Common Attribution 4.0 International License'

Acknowledgements

As with the two High Street volumes this has been very much a team effort. Michael Peters has made an enormous contribution by adding material to the account of most of the properties using his local knowledge and expertise. John Mount researched and wrote up the large section from numbers 90 to 108 bringing much new information to light.

During the first year of the project in 2015 Shirley Mannouch transcribed directories and made them easy to use by changing them from alphabetical to numerical. She also carried out extra research on a number of the families who lived in the street. As with all our museum publications Allen Whitnell has used his experience and artistry to format the book and in addition has enhanced it with his drawings.

The museum history group spent several evenings adding to our knowledge of the street by searching for information in old copies of the East Kent Gazette. John and Sheila Hepburn checked many facts for us, read through drafts for errors, gave us a number of illustrations from their collection and added extra details on a large number of families.

We are grateful to Barry Allinson and Colin Benson who took many of the photographs of properties as they are now. Peter Nokes was able to furnish us with much information on the links his family had with the street and to remember a good deal about the rest of the street too.

We are indebted to Dr Paul Staker of The Chestnuts Surgery for much of the history of number 70 and all of the illustrations which accompany it. The information about the early years of that building comes from the deeds which are still held by the practice. Thanks also to William Webb's grandson Graham who supplied information on the family and the family photographs.

Others who gave us help were John Couchman on number 8, David Jackson on Ivy Bartlett, Peter and David Hollins on the Burley family and Graham Webb on the Webbs. June Goodhew and her daughter Dilys gave information on the cycle shop at 77. Vivian Rich and her mother helped with the Fermor's business and Mary Breeds with the Forsters. Jessie Stevens gave valuable information about number 20, Jack Brett about numbers 26 to 32 and Shelley Tatler about number 33. We thank them all.

We would like to thank Nick Prior who has generously answered our many questions, and Nicholas Mayatt who has proof read and advised on the text.

Helen Allinson